W9-AEJ-837

COSMOPOLITANS AND HERETICS

CAROOL KERSTEN

Cosmopolitans and Heretics

New Muslim Intellectuals and the Study of Islam

Columbia University Press
New York

Columbia University Press
Publishers Since 1893
New York
cup.columbia.edu
© Carool Kersten, 2011

Kersten, Carool.
  Cosmopolitans and heretics : new Muslim intellectuals and the study
  of Islam / Carool Kersten.
      p. cm.
  Includes bibliographical references and index.
  ISBN 978-0-231-70239-3 (paper: alk. paper)
  ISBN 978-0-231-80004-4 (e-book)
  1. Islam—Study and teaching—History—20th century. 2. Islam—Study
  and teaching—History—21st century. 3. Islam—Historiography. I. Title.

  BP42.K43 2011
  297.092'2—dc22

                            2011001835

∞

Columbia University Press books are printed on permanent and durable acid-free
paper. This book is printed on paper with recycled content.
Printed in India

p 10 9 8 7 6 5 4 3 2 1

References to Internet Web sites (URLs) were accurate at the time of writing. Neither
the author nor Columbia University Press is responsible for URLs that may have
expired or changed since the manuscript was prepared.

CONTENTS

ACKNOWLEDGEMENTS

This book is based on earlier research conducted at the incomparable School of Oriental and African Studies (SOAS), University of London. Here I had the good fortune and privilege of working under Professor Christopher Shackle, a truly impressive scholar who appears to straddle with ease the venerable tradition of Oriental studies and exciting new approaches to the study of non-Western cultures, some of which are explored in this book. I am also grateful for the help I have received from Brian Bocking and Oliver Scharbrodt, formerly of the Department for the Study of Religions at SOAS, now both at University College Cork.

I gratefully acknowledge the financial support received from the Central Research Fund of the University of London, the Overseas Research Students Award Scheme (ORSAS), the Faculty of Arts and Humanities and the Department for the Study of Religions at SOAS.

I am also very appreciative of the encouragement I have received from my colleagues in the Department of Theology and Religious Studies at King's College London, in particular the former head of department, Oliver Davies, for his confidence and for giving me the opportunity to complete this work alongside my other duties.

Michael Dwyer of Hurst deserves credit for his vision and willingness to give space to new ways of exploring developments in the Muslim world. What he brings to the metier is everything an author can wish for in a publisher. I am also grateful to the editorial support I have received from Leilla Talebali and Jonathan de Peyer.

Early incarnations of this book have greatly benefitted from the advice, comments, and suggestions provided by Peter Clarke, R. Michael Feener, Hugh Goddard, Paul Janz, Ulrich Kratz, Michael Laffan, Johan

ACKNOWLEDGEMENTS

Meuleman, Peter Riddell, Raymond Scupin, Karel Steenbrink, and Imtiyaz Yusuf. I am indebted to Professor Bryan Turner for generously hosting me as a research affiliate at the Asia Research Institute (ARI) at the National University of Singapore, where I have also learned a lot from Syed Farid Alatas. My research in Indonesia was greatly facilitated by the hospitality, support and assistance provided by Azyumardi Azra, then rector of IAIN Syarif Hidyatullah in Jakarta, Paramadina staff member Ahmad Gaus, William Tuchrello of the Library of Congress Office in Jakarta. Greg Barton, Marien van den Boom, Ann Kull, Susanne Olsson, Rumadi (with the help of Dick van der Meij), and Yudian Wahyudi have been very generous in sharing their own research material. I am also grateful to Martin van Bruinessen, Howard Federspiel, Hasan Hanafi and Anthony Johns for responding to queries. John Maher has tirelessly commented on and corrected various versions of earlier drafts. A special word of thanks is due to Ana Jelnikar, for the continuous intellectual stimulation sprouting from her subtle mind, and—even more importantly—her sustained friendship.

One debt I cannot possibly repay is to my wife and children. In the early years of this research they have had to suffer lengthy absences, while in the later stages, even when he was there, they still had to cope with an often preoccupied and absent-minded husband and father.

Carool Kersten
London, September 2010

NOTE ON TRANSLATION, TRANSLITERATION
AND SPELLING

In writing this book I have drawn on material published in a variety of languages. Where published translations in English were available and accessible for consultation I have used and credited these accordingly. All remaining translations from Arabic, Dutch, French, German, and Indonesian are by the author.

For the transliteration of words, terms and phrases in Arabic, I have adapted and simplified the style used in the *International Journal of Middle Eastern Studies*, which is itself a modification of the *Encyclopaedia of Islam* system, whereby *jīm* is written as *j*, and *qaf* is *q*. There is no underlining of Roman double-letter equivalents; *l* of the definite article *al-*, is not assimilated to the following consonant; *ta marbuta* is rendered as *a*, not *ah*; *nisba* endings are rendered as *-iyya*. I have dispensed with macrons and other diacritical marks, unless they appear in direct quotes.

For Indonesian terminology I have followed the official spelling introduced in 1972, except for personal names where I have respected the choice of the bearer of that name or the way they appear in pertaining publications, i.e. 'Soekarno,' 'Soeharto,' 'Rasjidi,' etc., instead of 'Sukarno,' 'Suharto,' 'Rasyidi.' For Arabic loanwords used in Indonesian, I have adhered to the Indonesian conventions of transliteration.

'If I were able to go back in time, I would follow my previous method, i.e., pénétration pacifique, the "smuggling method" of introducing new ideas.'

Nurcholish Madjid, 'The Issue of Modernisation among Muslims in Indonesia: From a Participant's Point of View'

'I do not know if I am a follower of Husserl and Ricoeur or a phenomenologist by birth, analyzing living religions, philosophical and political experience. Or an old Muslim brother who suffered from Nasser's early persecution in 1954. May be I am a mystic describing his psychological states.'

Hasan Hanafi, personal communication

'For those of us who attend conferences, colloquia, national and international seminars in this transition from a century characterized by the scandalous defeat of humanist thought to a rather threatening one, the vital question then becomes as follows. How can we move beyond disposable thought, beyond a discourse that systematically misrepresents the violence that derives from the political strategies of all actors, beyond an economy condemned to produce to avoid the collapse of the workforce and yet excluding millions of potential consumers, beyond an education system that is so subordinated to the managerial requirements of the "human resources" necessary to production and bureaucracy that what we used to call "the humanities" has been reduced to the production of consumable knowledge.'

Mohammad Arkoun, 'The Answers of Applied Islamology'

PREFACE

In late 2006, Egyptian philosopher Hasan Hanafi became the centre of a scandal after giving a lecture in which he had likened the Qur'an to a 'supermarket, where one takes what one wants and leaves what one doesn't want.'[1] The religious establishment was swift in its condemnation, with one religious scholar accusing Hanafi of being a Marxist, while another suggested he seek treatment for what was evidently a psychiatric disorder. Hanafi was no stranger to controversy. As an upcoming scholar in the late sixties and early seventies, his writings on a new future role for religion in Muslim society had drawn the attention of the Egyptian security apparatus, forcing him for prolonged periods of time into voluntary exile in places like the United States, Morocco and Japan. In 1997, his bold reinterpretations of Islam caught the ire of both Islamists and their sympathisers at al-Azhar Islamic University, leading to demands for his removal from his post at Cairo University. In view of the earlier assassination of the writer Faraj Fuda in 1992 and the near fatal stabbing of Nobel Prize winner Naguib Mahfouz two years later—both motivated by the victims' alleged hostility to Islam—the same security authorities who ironically had earlier monitored Hanafi's activities now considered it prudent to put Hanafi under police protection.

Meanwhile, at the eastern end of the Muslim world, Indonesia's Council of Ulama (MUI) had issued a *fatwa* against the country's leading Muslim intellectual, Nurcholish Madjid, barely a month before he succumbed to a protracted liver condition in the summer of 2005. The condemnation of his liberal views on the role of Islam in public life also extended to his intellectual heirs, who advocated comparable progressive and pluralist religious principles.[2] In his younger years, Madjid had made a name for himself as chairman of Indonesia's Muslim student association from 1967 to 1971. In that capacity he had initially been regarded as the anointed successor of Muhammad Natsir, the country's leading Islamist politician. However, soon Madjid caused furore with the launch of the provocative slogan 'Islam, Yes; Islamic Party, No!' He was not only disowned by the modernist Islamic establishment, but his 'accommodationist' attitude towards the newly installed military government even led to accusations of being a stooge of General Soeharto's 'New Order' regime. Thirty years later, however, Madjid made again political headlines with his instrumental role in persuading the aging Soeharto to stand down as president and thus help inaugurate the so-called *Reformasi* era. With the military losing much of its political influence, a tense stand-off quickly developed between proponents of substantialist, contextualised and indigenised liberal interpretations of a 'cultural Islam' on the one hand, and advocates of overtly Islamist agendas, envisaging the formation of an Islamic state founded on the application of the *Shari'a* and based on narrow literal readings of the Qur'an and other legal sources. The breakdown in law and order in the wake of the fall of the New Order regime soon culminated in violent clashes between Muslims and Christians in eastern Indonesia, followed by the atrocities of the Bali and Jakarta bombings of 2002.

Such acrimonious relations between Muslims of differing dispositions are not limited to the Islamic world itself. Two days before 9/11, Mohammed Arkoun, an acclaimed Islamicist of Algerian descent and Emeritus Professor of Islamic history at the Sorbonne was challenged by fellow historian Mohamed Talbi, a Tunisian also resident in France. Although generally regarded as a moderate Muslim thinker in his own right, Talbi launched a sharp personal attack on Arkoun, criticising him for his alleged unwillingness to identify himself unequivocally as a pious Muslim and voicing objections to his deconstructive readings of the Qur'an.[3]

Arkoun, Hanafi and Madjid belong to the first generation of Muslim thinkers reaching intellectual maturity in the postcolonial age and are representative of a new type of Muslim intellectual emerging in the 1960s. Considering Islam not merely as a religious doctrine or a political ideology but taking account of its broader civilisational heritage—*turath* in Arabic—they are interested in its significance for a Muslim *Weltanschauung* which is in tune with the contemporary world. In this regard they attach great importance to re-engaging with Islam's philo-sophical legacy and tradition of critical thinking. As academic special-ists in the study of Islam, their approaches are also influenced by Western scholarship in Islamic Studies and inspired by developments in other fields of the humanities and social sciences. The bold cosmo-politanism that underlies such an alternative outlook and its associated methodological innovations is still very controversial in the Islamic world, and even considered heretical in the eyes of many Muslims.

These differences are not limited to obvious opponents, such as the traditionalist Islamic scholars, who are jealously protective of their turf and highly suspicious of any return to speculative philosophical thought, or revivalist reformers who advocate a narrow literalist inter-pretation of Islam as the solution to all political wrongs and moral shortcomings in the Muslim world, but also extend to the 'classical' Islamic modernists. In their efforts to reform or modernise, both reviv-alists and modernists tend to pay scant attention to Islam's legacy of traditional learning and its broader cultural heritage.

These new Muslim intellectuals are more familiar with the complexi-ties surrounding the notion of modernity and acutely aware that 'an element of cultural imperialism permeates Western attitudes and poli-cies where Muslim societies are concerned.'[4] Therefore they are very critical of superficial efforts to modernise Muslim societies, as well as the uncritical acceptance of ideas from the West. However, although they have a reduced confidence in the modernisation project along Western lines, they refuse to subscribe to the radical and militant Islamists' categorical rejection of the West and are highly sceptical of their habit to reject out of hand the rich Islamic tradition accumulated over a millennium and a half in favour of an unquestioned embrace of what is perceived as 'the authentic Islam' practised by *al-salaf al-salih* or 'the Pious Ancestors' of the first century of the Islamic era (seventh and eighth century CE).

The objective of this book is to trace the intellectual origins of these new advocates of Islam's wider civilisational heritage. It will show that even though they only began to gain wider recognition from the 1980s onwards, their exciting agendas and proposals for new ways of engag-ing in the study of Islam and the Muslim world are grounded in a worldwide intellectual fermentation that had actually already started in the 1950s and 1960s, evincing deeper roots that belie the tendency to associate their emergence with the allegedly sudden appearance of a resurgent Islam from the late 1970s onwards. The pioneering efforts of these intellectual trailblazers are instrumental for the alternative and often provocative discourses formulated by a new generation of cosmopolitan and progressive Muslim thinkers who are now beginning to make their own influence felt.

'*Muslims need to seek their modernity through tradition, for if we imagine modernity as a rupture with our past, the most arduous efforts will come to naught.*'

Anouar Majid, *A Call for Heresy*

'*The heretic denied this authority, refused to accept the tradition* in toto. *Instead, he picked and chose from the contents of the tradition.*'

Peter L. Berger, *The Heretical Imperative*

'*The test of a first-rate intelligence is the ability to hold two opposed ideas in mind at the same time and still retain the ability to function.*'

F. Scott Fitzgerald, 'The Crack-Up'

1

INTRODUCTION

WRITING AN INTELLECTUAL HISTORY
OF THE CONTEMPORARY MUSLIM WORLD

In the final decade of the twentieth century there was increasing mention of a new type of Muslim intellectual who appears to defy easy categorisation and classification.[1] Distinguished by an intimate familiarity with the Islamic heritage and an equally solid knowledge of recent achievements by the Western academe in the humanities and social sciences, these intellectuals generally operate from the margins, working in the interstices between and betwixt cultures and academic traditions, or what Homi Bhabha has called the 'Third Space.'[2] Their liminal cultural hybridity does not seem to fit in any of the conventional categories applied to Muslim practice and thought: such as Islamic traditionalism, reformism, modernism or revivalism. Most of the existing writings about these intellectuals deal primarily with their views on the role of Islam in public life, leaving the methodological, epistemological and broader philosophical underpinnings of their ideas and thoughts largely unexplored. Whereas the emergence of these new Muslim intellectuals can be detected throughout the Muslim world, few studies have treated this phenomenon from a truly global perspective. This book intends to redress these imbalances.

A Return to Islam?

Making their appearance at about the same time as the rise of Islam to new political prominence in the late 1970s and early 1980s, there is tendency to link these new Muslim intellectuals to this alleged Islamic resurgence. However, a more detailed examination of their intellectual roots challenges the suggestion of such a close association. It also calls into question the positing of an immediate causal connection between specific political crises affecting the Muslim world and the alleged 'return' of religion in the public sphere of the Muslim world and elsewhere. With regard to the Middle East, the impact of the Arab-Israeli wars of 1967 and 1973 is often given as an explanation for the Arab rediscovery of Islamic political identity. In spite of Ibrahim Abu-Rabi''s acknowledgement that this intellectual engagement with the Islamic heritage vis-à-vis modernity extends back to the nineteenth century and that some Arab thinkers even reject a 'thesis of a crisis in modern Arab and Muslim thought,' the title of one of his books, *Contemporary Arab Thought: Studies in Post-1967 Arab Intellectual History*, nevertheless suggests such a causality.[3]

Although admitting that iconic Arab writers such as Taha Husayn (1889–1973), Abbas Mahmud al-Aqqad (1889–1964), and Naguib Mahfouz (1911–2006) had begun addressing Islamic themes as early as the 1930s, in *Trends and Issues in Contemporary Arab Thought* the literary historian Issa Boullata makes the same contention. From what he calls the painful post-1967 introspections three trends of thought emerge, which have continued to engage with each other in the ensuing decades. While one group of intellectuals retains its confidence in a cultural revolution that will jettison the religious outlook in favour of a transformation towards a secular one, they are opposed by a vocal group committed to the religious aspects of Arab culture and restoring conformity to what they consider as its authentic Islamic origins, by insisting on the elimination of all external influences. Finally, there is a third cluster of thinkers who believe that Arab-Islamic culture requires a renewal rather than a radical change to accommodate modernity. This group has made 'the issue of heritage (*turath*) [...] the hub of much intellectual activity' and includes the new Muslim intellectuals examined in the present book.[4] Diametrically opposed to the narrow literalist interpretations of the Salafi ideologues, they are—at one and the same time—also critical of the 'blind imitation' or *taqlid* hampering traditionalist Islamic scholarship, the unquestioned embrace of the Western secularisation thesis, as well as the essentialist outlook of many 'classical' Islamic modernists. Among them are unabashed advocates of a return to the lost philosophical traditions of the rationalist theology school known as the Mu'tazila, and the ideas of philosophers such as Ibn Sina (Avicenna) and—in particular—Ibn Rushd (Averroes).[5]

Although he projected the Muslim Brotherhood ideologue Sayyid Qutb (1906–1966) as the emblematic figure filling the intellectual void from the 1920s to the 1960s, the resulting asymmetry in this temporal gap left the Italian scholar of Islam Armando Salvatore apparently so uneasy that he proposes the oil crisis emerging in the aftermath of the 1973 war as a crucial juncture. At the same time, however, he also points to the 'Islam and Social Change' project directed by Leonard Binder and Fazlur Rahman of the University of Chicago as the earliest scholarly initiative identifying an increase rather than decrease in religious commitment in the Muslim world.[6]

When contextualising new Muslim intellectualism it is therefore important not to conflate this phenomenon with the admittedly cataclysmic political events of the late 1960s and early 1970s. In fact, tracing the interest of these intellectuals in their religious heritage to influences and writings predating these events will demonstrate that their explorations of Islam's civilisational legacy fit into a continuous narrative and must not be regarded as merely the outcome of forces of change set in motion by specific incidents. This suggests that these events functioned as catalysts rather than immediate causes, let alone unavoidable teleological factors.[7] The evidence also points to the need for rethinking the validity of the currently prevailing conceptualisation of the secularisation process.

The amplification of political Islam is not just due to the predominance of political scientists and historians in the study of the present-day Muslim world—other specialists too tend to focus on political ideas at the expense of concerted efforts to trace in detail the intellectual genealogies of contemporary Muslim thinkers and the epistemological and methodological underpinnings of their work.[8]

Whereas a political scientist like Armando Salvatore recognises intellectuals as 'modern producers of publicly relevant meaning, who invoke scholarly traditions often constructed for the task of the moment,'[9] it is important to bear in mind the observation made by Mohammed Arkoun. As one of the new Muslim thinkers featuring in this study, he asserts that an intellectual is not the same as a scholar or an expert, while a scholar is not necessarily an intellectual, because the latter's role is regarded more expansive because he or she is expected to engage in debates on issues beyond the confines of a particular area of expertise.[10] However, some intellectuals also happen to be good scholars, and the individuals examined in this book fit that description.

An examination of the selected new Muslim intellectuals as Islamicists and scholars of religion will not only contribute to a deeper penetrating and more accurate assessment of the substance of their ideas, but also help gauge how their work contributes to the refashioning of Islamic studies as a field of academic investigation and its position vis-à-vis both the study of religions as a generic field and area studies programmes. In that sense their work is not just valuable in the context of recent intellectual developments in the Muslim world, but can actually contribute to redefining a field of scholarly inquiry where the rules of engagement are still predominantly determined by the Western academe.

Towards a Global Islam: Learning from the Peripheries

The other shortcoming, the scarcity of intellectual histories of the contemporary Muslim world with a global scope, can to a large extent be attributed to the compartmentalisation of the study of Islam into area studies programmes. There is still a widespread tendency to associate Islam closely or even exclusively with the Middle East, so that the study of Islam is often relegated to Near and Middle East studies departments or programmes.[11] Although certainly very useful when dealing with detailed examinations of local or regional particularities, the area studies approach is less suitable for accessing global processes, including intellectual developments currently unfolding across the world of Islam and in the Muslim 'diasporas' in Europe and North America.[12] That it is possible to study Islamic civilisation from a world-historical perspective while simultaneously accommodating the specificities of its inherent cultural cosmopolitanism has been demonstrated by the late Marshall Hodgson in *The Venture of Islam* (1974). Unfortunately, an untimely death prevented him from fleshing-out the final sections on the contemporary history of the Muslim world. Acceptance of the suggested model was also hampered by what critics considered the idiosyncratic jargon of what is otherwise generally recognised as a magisterial piece of scholarship. Regrettably it has left Hodgson with 'few followers and no school to carry on his work.'[13]

An example of the undesirable consequences of this lack of truly global accounts is the stepmotherly treatment of Islam in Southeast

Asia, reflecting a 'lack of due recognition by international scholars, both Western and Middle Eastern.'[14] Notwithstanding the fact that the region is home to one in every five Muslims, Islamicists have largely ignored this part of the Muslim world, whereas Southeast Asianists for their part tend to regard Islam as a peripheral cultural phenomenon in the area of their geographical specialisation—a thin veneer covering an allegedly more pervasive and venerable Indic heritage. Consequently, the study of one of the most populous parts of the Muslim world has long suffered from what can be called a 'dual marginalisation.'[15] A partial explanation for this lies in the region's relatively late Islamisation, a development for which—as Anthony Johns called it—'there is no single big bang-theory.' Instead it was a process that waxed and waned over centuries, taking 'strength from an irregular series of pulses.'[16]

Aside from the pioneering work of Johns himself, the contributions to the mapping of Indian Ocean networks linking maritime Southeast Asia with centres of Islamic learning in the Middle East by such specialists as Azyumardi Azra, Martin van Bruinessen, Michael Feener, Ulrike Freitag and William Clarence-Smith, Michael Laffan, and Denys Lombard have established the Malay-Indonesian archipelago as an integral part of the Muslim world. It has also led to calling into question the persisting viewpoint that somehow its 'conditions are 'different' and subject to other rules of interpretation than prevail in the 'central Muslim world.'[17] Furthermore, studies of the translation of Islamic source material from Arabic into Malay and research on the resulting indigenous religious literature in Arabised Malay or *Jawi* by, for example, Syed Naguib al-Attas and Peter Riddell, and the investigations of Taufik Abdullah, Zamakhshari Dhofier and Karel Steenbrink into the role of the typical Southeast Asian Islamic education institution called *pondok* or *pesantren*—the 'Islamic boarding schools' led by often highly revered religious scholars and spiritual guides, called *guru* or *kyai*—have been instrumental to our understanding of the sustenance and transmission of the hybrid Muslim culture of these *Jawi* Muslims.[18]

Apart from the above mentioned polyglot historians and linguists, social scientists too have not entirely neglected the study of Southeast Asian Muslims. However, until the 1980s, their preoccupation with classification and categorisation led to questionable extrapolations from the now classical 'ur-typology' of *abangan*, *priyayi* and *santri* introduced by Clifford Geertz in his influential book *The Religion of*

Java (1960), as well as a tendency to downplay the role of Islam in the formation of the cultures of insular Southeast Asia.[19] Even though by 1964 the Indonesian social scientist Harsja W. Bachtiar had written an extensive and critical review of *The Religion of Java*, it was not published until 1973 in a relatively obscure Indonesian periodical and it would only be until the 1980s that a younger generation of American anthropologists began using their own fieldwork experiences to challenge the essentialist nature of these categories and introduce alternative representations which also sought to correct Geertz's reluctance—somewhat surprising given his admitted literary interests—to engage with textual material.[20]

Set on tracing the assumed Indic origins of Javanese court and popular religion, Mark Woodward has vividly illustrated how he eventually ended up arguing that 'Islam is the predominant force in the religious beliefs and rites of central Javanese, and that it shapes the character of social interaction and daily life in all segments of Javanese society.'[21] Drawing on his experiences in East-Java's Tengger highlands, Robert Hefner turned his gaze on the classical Orientalists with their tendency to concentrate on high culture and has pointed to their lack of appreciation for the everyday meaning that Islam may have for ordinary Muslims.[22] Although he credits Geertz for his interest in 'everyday' Islam, he remains critical of the latter's narrow standard for distinguishing what constitutes and what does not constitute Islam, which has resulted in an unwelcome divide between ethnography and the study of texts.[23] In regard to the latter, John Bowen, an anthropologist of religion with extensive experience in studying Muslim communities on Sumatra, has observed that anthropologists are seldom equipped to study Islamic topics *per se* because their comparative frameworks operate from the presumption that the most interesting parts of cultures are exhibited in their most localised features, which are more often than not the least 'Islamic.'[24] Moreover, Western scholarship on Indonesian Islam is fashioned in accordance with the 'rule observance model' which tends to leave out 'the creative interpretive work done by Islamic intermediaries: the scholars, judges, teachers, and village intellectuals,' resulting in a lack of appreciation for the interrelations between authoritative texts, exegesis, and everyday behaviour.[25]

The decision to specifically include an Indonesian intellectual like Nurcholish Madjid in this study is therefore motivated by a desire to help redress these particular imbalances in the study of the present-day

Muslim world. First, to fill the gap resulting from the relative neglect of the most populous nation-state; secondly, because of the still felt need for correcting the stereotypical understanding of Southeast Asian Islam itself; and finally, as a response to Anthony Milner's observation that there is a particular lack of intellectual histories of insular Southeast Asia.[26] Perhaps even more important in the context of exploring new directions in contemporary Muslim thought is the indication that Indonesia's intellectual milieu actually appears to provide a particularly fertile environment for developing new ways of engaging with the Islamic heritage and its very real potential for refashioning existing scholarship in Islamic studies by Muslims and non-Muslims.

In this regard the words expressed by Wilfred Cantwell Smith more than half a century ago seem nowadays almost prophetic. As a renowned historian of religion and founder of the Institute of Islamic Studies (IIS) at Canada's McGill University, he observed that 'the role of Islam in contemporary Indonesia, and of Indonesia in contemporary Islam [...] makes clear that there is Islamically something distinctive and fascinating and potentially very rich,' adding in a footnote that 'altogether there could be an argument, over against the widespread view of Indonesians as "poor Muslims," that on the contrary the rest of the Muslim world may well have something vital to learn from them, even religiously.'[27] Twenty-five years later, the US-based Pakistani Islamicist Fazlur Rahman noted that 'in recent times there has been a high degree of Islamic intellectual activity in Indonesia.'[28] Comparing it with developments in his home country and in the Arab world, he envisaged that 'future progress of Islam will occur in Indonesia [...] not in the Middle East.'[29] A telling and at the same time deplorable indication of how ingrained the marginalisation of Muslim Southeast Asia has remained even in current scholarship is that as recently as 2001, Peter Mandaville, author of a book on transnational Islam could only express regret of his late discovery of Indonesia as a 'particularly fertile setting in which to study the interface of Islam and globalising modernities.'[30] On the other hand, Dale Eickelman and Jon Anderson, two leading anthropologists working on the Muslim world with a particular interest in the role of religious discourse, identify Indonesia as the country to watch when it comes to finding ways to accommodate Islamic ethical norms and 'civil pluralism.'[31]

Paying attention to intellectual developments in Indonesia can thus be regarded as a 'dispatch from the provinces' challenging the 'pomposity of the center.'[32] It points to one of the central questions that this book seeks to answer. What makes Indonesia's intellectual milieu so conducive both to generating indigenous contributions to alternative ways of dealing with the Islamic heritage and to acting as a generous host to ideas for formulating new agendas for the study of Islam introduced from the outside?

New Muslim Intellectuals: Context and Profile

The intellectuals who are the subject of the present investigation deserve 'to be taken seriously not merely as interlocutors between Muslims and Westerners,' but also as representatives of a current within Islamic intellectualism envisaging an objectified and critical engagement by Muslims with their own heritage.[33] Their elaborations evince a blending of insider and outsider perspectives on Islam, in which the assumed binary opposition of tradition versus modernity collapses too.[34] The significance of these intellectuals lies therefore in their function as scholars of religion who can help break down such 'boundaries and assumed dichotomies.'[35] Identifying them as members of an emerging group of Muslim scholars, who 'lacked nothing of the historical, linguistic, and philological qualifications of their teachers and predecessors, but [who] had grafted onto this powerful heritage the systematic and phenomenological concerns which they have absorbed at the feet of their mentors in the history of religions,' Charles Adams anticipated their prominent role in the 'partial but growing conquest of the gap between the history of religions and Islamic studies.'[36] A lack of attention for their academic formation and the merit of their scholarship has left this potential still largely untapped.

The present book is the first study to focus on Mohammed Arkoun, Hasan Hanafi and Nurcholish Madjid in their role as academic scholars of Islam. Having earned their academic qualifications at institutions of higher learning both at home and abroad, they pursued university careers using their grounding in the Islamic heritage and familiarity with relevant developments in the Western human sciences to engage in a double critique of both Muslim and Western discourses on Islam, and develop alternative epistemologies and methodologies. However, so far there has been no detailed investigation of the provenance of the research agendas and programmes they have proposed for rethinking, reconstructing and reactualising Islam. In concentrating on the new approaches to the academic study of Islam developed by these three contemporary Muslim Islamicists I also try to foreground the wide variety of intellectual influences informing these suggestions and propositions.

As postgraduate students at the Sorbonne during the 1950s and 1960s, Mohammed Arkoun and Hasan Hanafi were exposed to the tumultuous developments in the Parisian intellectual scene, where existentialist thinkers like Sartre and Camus were at the high of their fame. Inspiring and supporting a cohort of assertive intellectuals from the colonies and former colonies, such as Aimé Césaire, Franz Fanon, Albert Memmi, and Léopold Senghor, this intelligentsia challenged not only the West's political but also its cultural hegemony. Others, such as Maurice Merleau-Ponty, Paul Ricoeur, and the latter's student Jacques Derrida retained a connection with German philosophy, but began taking the phenomenology and hermeneutics of Edmund Husserl, Martin Heidegger and Hans-George Gadamer into new directions.

Perhaps a bit more secluded but no less influential developments were taking place in the social sciences and history. Advances made in structural linguistics were taken up by Claude Lévi-Strauss and applied to anthropology, while historiography was revolutionised by the *Annales* School, seeking to develop a comprehensive approach to the study of history which would accommodate the structural influences of the *longue durée* effects of geographical and economic condition on world history, with attention to micro-level developments through an anthropological history of everyday life on regional and local levels. Within the study of Islam and the Muslim world, the Sufi specialist Louis Massignon and the social scientist Jacques Berque were renowned for both their academic expertise and engagement with contemporary political developments.

The Indonesian Islamicist Nurcholish Madjid was more influenced by Anglo-Saxon social and theological thought, which played a prominent role in the secularisation debate in the 1960s. Originally conceived in medieval Christendom as a way of constructing and understanding the world, it came to be regarded as such a defining element of modernity that it resulted in the positing of a modernisation-secularisation thesis and can be said to denote 'any kind of emancipation of inner-worldly actions, motives and institutions from the dominance and influence of the church,' as well as 'the transference of Christian values to the "secular" world'—giving it a positive connotation in the view of many Protestant theologians.[37] In theological thinking the figure of Schleiermacher has cast an 'immense shadow' over this field, setting 'the agenda for an entire era.'[38] The voluminous sociological literature on the subject can be traced back to the writings of continental thinkers such as Marx, Weber and Durkheim. In the wake of this double impact by the 'father of modern theology' and the 'blessed sociological trinity' Protestant theologians like Emil Brunner, Rudolf Bultmann, and Paul Tillich, as well as Catholic thinkers such as Maurice Blondel, Alfred Loisy, and Jean Guitton, caused a further sea change in Christian theological thinking, with Karl Barth and Jacques Maritain stirring up the counter currents.[39] Elements of these debates also influenced Hanafi's anthropocentric approach to the study of religious phenomena.

The theological debate on secularisation was reignited by John Robinson's *Honest to God* (1963) and across the Atlantic principally by Harvey Cox's seminal *The Secular City* (1965). Their apparent embrace of a Nietzschean 'Death of God' thesis generated heated discussions. Not long after that the sociological studies of Peter Berger, Robert Bellah, David Martin, and Bryan Wilson began appearing, which were predominantly conceived in the vein of Weber-inspired 'value-free' investigations seemingly corroborating that 'Judaism, Christianity, and Protestantism inadvertently and ironically incubated and nurtured the seeds of their own decline.'[40] Simultaneously secularisation proves to be a rather elusive concept, leading one prominent theorist to observe that 'historians and social scientists find it hard to agree on what secularisation has been in the past and on what it is today—let alone what its future course will be.'[41]

Notwithstanding the differences in their formation, outlook and programmatic focus, the common denominator shared by Arkoun, Hanafi, and Madjid is a propensity to creatively apply this acquaintance with recent achievements of Western scholarship in the human sciences in their engagement with Islam's civilisational heritage. Reflective of a cosmopolitan attitude grounded in postcolonial cultural hybridity, it is suggested that this commonality is a feature shared by other like-minded intellectuals of their own and successive generations. At the same time, the inherent fluidity of notions like cosmopolitanism and cultural hybridity make such intellectuals resistant to being pigeonholed in accordance with existing typologies of modern Islamic thought.[42] Defining this cultural hybridity poses a challenge not only because—as Peter Burke has explained in his eponymous book—all cultural groupings are in the end part of a 'cultural continuum,' but also usage of the term has been 'maddeningly elastic.'[43] At best it can be said cultural hybridity is the outcome of imitations and appropriations, accommodations and negotiations, and a degree of eclectic mixing through which a variety of influences are reworked into new cultural expressions fitting with local circumstances.[44]

The reserved reaction or even complete lack of response to these kinds of Muslim scholars as 'standard-bearers of the new *ijtihad*' (independent reasoning) on the part of fellow Muslims can to a certain degree be ascribed to their often 'rather obscure vocabulary and complex forms of reasoning.'[45] Indeed, because of the cerebral nature of their work, the scholars in question find their audience mainly among the highest educated segments of the population. At the same time it must be admitted that, at present, they 'exercise little influence on any institutionalised organisations.'[46] When and where their suggestions have elicited a response from fellow Muslims, in today's polarised political climate the ideas of these *turathiyyun*—or 'heritage advocates' as Salvatore calls them—have become the targets of sharp criticism, outright rejection and even open attacks originating in both *'ulama* and Islamist circles.[47] And yet, this strand of Muslim intellectualism can be expected to grow in importance because of future demographics throughout the Muslim world. In the decades to come, the middle classes will increase not only in absolute numbers but also proportionally as a cohort of the total population. This, in turn, will lead to an expansion of the student body in higher education, which is the constituency producing and consuming these particular discourses.

An assessment of the significance of these Muslim intellectuals must also take into account the introspective and self-critical discussions on the study of Islam triggered by Edward Said's *Orientalism* (1978). Although polemical and cavalier in its treatment of facts and half-facts, it can't be denied that Said's critique invited some very fundamental soul-searching among specialists in the study of non-Western cultures. The book's huge success also encouraged others to jump on the bandwagon, thus obscuring more subdued reflections and self-reflections.[48] Although he made much of the importance of eighteenth-century French Orientalist scholarship, historically more penetrating accounts by writers such as Maxime Rodinson and Thierry Hentsch, or—more recently—Robert Irwin and Daniel Varisco, challenge Said's arbitrary decision to situate the beginnings of Orientalism in Enlightenment

France. In *Europe and the Mystique of Islam*, Rodinson has posited the Renaissance scholar Guilleaume Postel and his student Joseph Scaliger as more appropriate starting points for Orientalist scholarship, while Hentsch's *Imagining the Middle East* juxtaposes Postel with Bodin and Machiavelli, two figures who were no longer informed by medieval Christian apologetics. These examples illustrate the emergence of much earlier material and intellectual duality between East and West, positing a deep socio-cultural breach between the southeast and northwest shores of the early modern Mediterranean.[49] As my research will show, this particular geo-historical caesura has also influenced the scholarly preoccupations of the historian Arkoun and the philosopher Hanafi.

Where Said saw the first germinations of Orientalism emerge in the Enlightenment, Rodinson interprets that discourse very differently. Although admitting that Orientalists lagged behind other intellectuals and even the general Enlightenment public in accepting ideological relativism, the atmosphere at the time had a liberating effect on scholarly research. Instead of being a hostile 'province of the Antichrist,' the Muslim world came to be regarded as a place of pure enchantment and by the beginning of the nineteenth century three major trends can be discerned in European attitudes towards the East.[50] Alongside a 'romantic exoticism mesmerised by the magical East,' there emerged a contemptuous Western sense of superiority marked by pragmatism and imperialist aspirations, and 'a specialised erudition focused on the great ages of the past'[51]—attitudes more recently characterised by Nobel laureate Amartya Sen as exotic, curatorial and magisterial Orientalism.[52]

Around the same time, the American political scientist Leonard Binder too developed his own deconstructive triad of Orientalism. Distinguishing between good, bad and pragmatic Orientalism, he cites Geertz's *Islam Observed* (not 'because of its inductive empiricism,' but as 'an interesting combination of French structuralism and Parsonian functionalism'), Crone and Cook's revisionist *Hagarism*, and Hodgson's earlier-mentioned *The Venture of Islam* as respective examples.[53]

The latter can indeed be considered as another 'insider' critique of sorts of Western Orientalist scholarship, albeit an implicit one, because Hodgson's comments must be teased out from the extensive footnotes.[54] Drawing underexposed areas such as Indonesia into the scope of analysis, even sceptics of the notion of global-historical processes

14

have had to acknowledge the value of Hodgson's work as a rejection of Eurocentric historiography, while its sociological orientation has helped correct the 'neglect of more local or lower-class social conditions.'[55] Ranking it 'with the best in religious historical scholarship,' Earle Waugh lauded *The Venture of Islam* for the methodological challenges it poses to the study of *sui generis* religion.[56] Even though Hodgson's Quaker convictions effectively neutralised his attempt to avoid essentialising religious traditions, they were at the same time responsible for his appreciation of the role of individual human creativity in shaping religious traditions.[57] This led Albert Hourani to qualify Hodgson as a 'humanistic historian' who amplified the importance of creative individuals producing new alternatives in 'the interstices of history when "habitual, routine thinking will no longer work" [...].'[58] One admirer even suggested that, had it not been for Hodgson's premature death, *The Venture of Islam* might have achieved a canonical status similar to *Orientalism*.[59]

Evidently inspired by Derrida's deconstructionism, Binder's incisive *Orientalism* critique proceeds along *via negativa* and provides an illuminating contrast to the Foucauldian 'discursive formations' dominating Said's argument. The inherent nihilism of Foucault's demonstration of the limitations of knowledge on the basis of the 'contingent particularity of a given human being' and overriding influence of the political in any discourse, led ultimately to a 'dispersal of man.'[60] Displaying a similar negation of individual agency, Binder claims that Said's amplification of the political backfires, because if Orientalist scholarship indeed represents merely an ideological discourse, then how could Said's critique of it be any different? Moreover, interpreting Orientalism as a purely fantastic Western discourse, without any interest in themes that are the results of actual events in the Middle East, also implies a depreciation of Muslim discourses on Islam.[61] In fact, Said was so preoccupied with demonstrating the West's hostility towards Islam that the 'negation of orientalism' left no space for an 'affirmation of Islam.'[62] This led Binder to his rather devastating judgment that, by refusing 'Islam as the point of reference for the learned discourse on the peoples of the Middle East,' Said effectively claimed that 'spiritual entities have no cognitive standing,' thus denying 'the reality of Islam itself in a more extreme manner than the orientalists themselves.'[63]

Even if Binder's dismissal of Said is too radical, the latter's lack of appreciation for subaltern agency is still reflected in the inconsistency of his 'ambivalent oscillation between a radical and Foucauldian critique of representation and a humanistic stance that appears profoundly incompatible with Foucault's own work,' as pointed out by Richard King by way of explanation for Said's failure to formulate an alternative conception of the Orient.[64] For more constructive engagements with this phenomenon we must turn to adjacent Orientalist fields, such as King's own *Orientalism and Religion*, an intellectual history of the field of Indology, or J.J. Clarke's examination of the Western fascination with Chinese thought in *Oriental Enlightenment*. Both authors regret that the all-pervading influence of *Orientalism* has distracted the attention from what they call respectively 'enlightened' and 'affirmative Orientalism.'[65] King's criticism of Said's lack of appreciation for the ability of colonised people to take charge of their own destiny and his desire to show how indigenous people have 'used, manipulated and constructed their own positive responses to colonialism using Orientalist conceptions' drove him to Homi Bhabha's notion of hybridity.[66]

The notion of subaltern agency also expressed through what Anouar Abdel Malek (b. 1924) and Syed Hussein Alatas (1928–2007) refer to as 'endogenous intellectual creativity.'[67] Sociologists by training, their work can be traced back to the *Tiers Mondisme* or the Third Worldist discourse emanating from what is more poetically referred to as the 'Spirit of Bandung,' which took hold in many newly independent countries after the 1955 Asia-Africa conference held in that Indonesian city and led to the formation of the Non-Aligned Movement (NAM).[68] An Egyptian Copt, Abdel Malek had in fact established his name by publishing a critique of Orientalism a full fifteen years before Edward Said.[69] Following an intellectual trajectory from Marxist-inspired criticisms of liberal Developmentalism and structuralist theorising towards an exploration of the significance of 'cultural specificity' and examinations of authenticity as an expression of social emancipation and cultural recognition, he eventually moved to developing alternative epistemes.[70] This interest was shared by Syed Hussein Alatas, a scion of a prominent family of descendant from Southern Arabia's Hadramaut region now settled in Southeast Asia. Before embarking on a career as a scholar and university administrator in Singapore and Malaysia, during his student years in Amsterdam he edited a short-lived journal—*Progressive Islam* (1954–5)—modelled after Rashid Rida's *Al-Manar* and emblematic of the Islamic internationalism fashionable among Muslims during the decolonisation period.

16

The 'Spirit of Bandung' is not just relevant for the present account because Arkoun, Hanafi and Madjid come from prominent NAM member states, but because it suffused the political and cultural climate in which the three reached their intellectual maturity. It is this author's contention that Third Worldist discourse constitutes a suitable vehicle for connecting their work to postcolonial studies. Aside from criticising and challenging the West's continuing cultural imperialism through its assertion of subaltern agency, Third Worldism also calls into question the assumed 'naturalness' of the nation by examining non-national spatial configurations and positioning the third world in an 'interstitial location between the superpowers.'[71]

Although Third Worldism tends to be dominated by secular subdiscourses, the particular strand represented by Abdel Malek and Alatas retained or regained a quiet appreciation for the religious aspects of non-Western cultural heritages. Supportive of Dependency Theory, it promotes multidisciplinary approaches which account for 'the historical experience of peripheral countries' and 'the necessity of identifying the specific political-economic, social-institutional and cultural linkages of centres and peripheries.'[72] Thus it reflects the cultural hybridity found in the interstices and margins of cultures and academic disciplines, where creative and pioneering contributions to the rethinking of the Islamic tradition can take place, including those produced by Arkoun, Hanafi and Madjid.

Three Exponents

Aside from reflecting the global span of new Muslim intellectualism, the selected thinkers also cover a spectrum that is both representative of the diversity in intellectual formation and capable of accommodating a variety of ways of engaging with religion. In this regard, I find merit in Russell McCutcheon's rethinking of religious studies. With publications such as *The Manufacturing of Religion* and *The Discipline of Religion*, he follows in the footsteps of figures like Jonathan Z. Smith and has become one of the most radical and influential new voices in both theorising the study of religion and the historiography of this academic specialisation. Whereas Smith primarily concerned himself with the challenge of the comparative study of widely varying phenomena classified as 'religious' and with the understanding of 'religion' as an object of academic imagination, McCutcheon's objective is to subject the ways religions are studied to an even more rigorous interrogation, choosing as his main target the Chicago school of the *sui generis* study of religion associated with Mircea Eliade, which posits that there is such a readily identifiable phenomenon as 'the religious' or 'religion' requiring its own unique methods and institutional settings.[73]

McCutcheon rejects this Eliadean ontology and its concomitant phenomenological methodology, opting instead for a nominalistic conceptualisation and suggesting the redefinition of religious studies as a part of cultural studies, 'so as to include the history of the academic study of religion itself.'[74] For this purpose he has developed a taxonomy of his own, categorising scholars of religion by distinguishing between: (1) theologians, (2) phenomenologists and other liberal humanists,[75] and (3) those who act as 'critics not caretakers,'[76] with the ambition to become 'anthropologists of credibility.'[77] Although I immediately add the caveat that, based on the findings of the present study, I tend to agree with Mark Taylor and Tylor Roberts that it is not possible to establish an as straightforward dichotomy between examinations of religion or religiosity, on the one hand, and the study of religion, on the other, as McCutcheon and his intellectual mentor Smith seem to imply. However, I do believe that the dispositions, output and influence of the three selected Muslim intellectuals nevertheless generally reflect the respective classifications introduced by McCutcheon.[78]

On the meta-level on which McCutcheon conceived his taxonomy, theologians function in a similar way as the native informants of ethnographers. They are 'elite ritual and textual practitioners' producing a particular and detailed vision of the world.[79] While these discourses provide guidance to adherents of respective religious traditions, the same material also forms the data for other types of scholars of religion. McCutcheon refers to these theological procedures as 'mythmaking'—in the sense that in this meaning-giving process the discourses in question are dehistoricised and decontextualised.[80] Although Nurcholish Madjid's scholarship can certainly be characterised as an insider reflection on the deeper truth and meaning of Islam, we shall see that he actually encouraged his fellow 'theologians' to account for the historicity and cultural contextualisation of the ways in which religious truth and meaning have found expression. I will also argue that the significance of the 'theologian' Nurcholish Madjid lies in his contributions to creating an intellectual climate and academic environment for

Indonesia's Muslim believers and their 'mythmakers' that is open to what Anouar Majid refers to as 'new forms of inquiry and protocols of discussion.'[81]

Hasan Hanafi's search for an Islamic philosophical method is indeed conceived as an investigation of what McCutcheon called 'the descriptive where, when, what, who, and how of religious traditions.' What makes Hanafi a phenomenologist or liberal humanist rather than a critically detached investigator is his concern for 'what religion means, either to the participant or for humanity in general.'[82]

The ways in which, during a career spanning more than five decades, Arkoun has consistently advocated the introduction of a comprehensive and multidisciplinary research agenda comes therefore closest to the critic—not the caretaker—of religious discourses, operating on the meta-theoretical level envisaged by McCutchoen. This type of scholar 'presumes all meaning and value (including the social practice named theology) to be a thoroughly human, historical, even ad hoc concoction,' a 'presumption makes the latter approach thoroughly anthropological.'[83] Avoiding metaphysical speculations even more rigorously than Hanafi, Arkoun's approach to the study of Islam corresponds to the 'methodological reduction' advocated by McCutcheon through which scholars of religion can properly account for 'the historically grounded nature of all human attempts to know the world around us, making them instances of mythmaking and thus candidates for theoretisation.'[84]

Before discussing how the identification of these various types of religious scholars has impacted on the theoretical framing and scope of my own examination of Madjid, Hanafi and Arkoun, a very brief biographical introduction and tentative evaluation of the existing secondary literature on each of these three Muslim intellectuals are detailed in the subsequent sections, which will be elaborated further and examined more critically throughout the book.

Nurcholish Madjid

After a combined secular and Islamic education, the Java-born Nurcholish Madjid (1939–2005) rose to prominence as a Muslim student leader in the early years of Soeharto's *Orde Baru* or 'New Order' regime. This position gave him the platform to help launch the 'Renewal of Islamic Thought' movement, which caused a transformation in Indonesia's intellectual milieu. After having established his credentials as a scholar with a PhD in Islamic studies from the University of Chicago, his work at the crossroads of academia, civil society, and politics turned him into both an innovator and facilitator of public religious discourse in Indonesia. An enterprising individual with a knack for developing new outlets for his ideas, he became one of the country's most prominent Muslim intellectuals. Through his 'think tank' the *Yayasan Paramadina* or Paramadina Foundation he was very success-ful in reaching the growing and increasingly affluent urban Muslim middle class.

Because of his high public profile he has been the subject of numer-ous studies in Indonesian.[85] However, the literature in English is again limited. Aside from an unpublished MA dissertation by Siti Fathimah and the PhD theses of Greg Barton and Yudian Wahyudi, in which Madjid is presented in comparative perspectives, the only published monograph-size study I am aware of is Ann Kull's *Piety and Politics*.[86] Barton and Fathimah focus primarily on Madjid's thought during the early 'New Order' years, while Yudian Wahyudi's earlier-mentioned comparative study of Hasan Hanafi, the Moroccan philosopher Muhammad Abid al-Jabiri, and Nurcholish Madjid is organised around the 'renewalist-salafi' slogan 'Back to the Qur'an and the Sunna.' Wahyudi uses Hanafi as the benchmark because of the geo-strategic importance of Egypt and because he considers him the most articulate of the three. Suitably framed by a thematic approach, Wahy-udi's treatment lapses into a rather fragmented narrative, which—al-though comprehensive enough—suffers from a degree of superficiality. Relying on Barton and Fathimah's studies for biographical data and using her own interviews with Madjid himself, his associates and his critics, Kull provides the most up-to-date account of the development and dissemination of Madjid's ideas during the later part of his career, as well as a valuable analysis of their reception and influence.

Hasan Hanafi

Hasan Hanafi Hasanayn is one of Egypt's leading philosophers. He was born in 1935 into a Cairene family of musicians of mixed Moroc-can-Berber and Bedouin ancestry. After studying in Cairo and Paris, he returned to his homeland and spent most of his academic career at Cairo University, but he has also worked as a guest professor at universities in Belgium, the United States, Sudan, Morocco and Japan, which increased his international visibility. As an academic philosopher and student of Islam, Hanafi is primarily known for his 'Heritage and Renewal Project.'[87] Presented in more bellicose terms as a campaign fought on 'three fronts'—a critical examination of Muslim attitudes towards their own tradition, the challenge of the West, and the current reality of the Muslim World—this project of intellectual emancipation searching for an Islamic method of philosophical investigation is at the same time inspired by the philosophical phenomenologies developed in continental Europe with which Hanafi had become acquainted during his postgraduate studies in France.

Although implicitly acknowledged by some commentators, the philosophical underpinnings of Hanafi's project have never been the subject of an in-depth investigation.[88] In fact, while Hanafi features in various intellectual histories of the contemporary Muslim world and has been the subject of journal articles and book chapters, so far there has appeared no book-length study in English. Aside from PhD theses by Susanne Olsson on Hanafi's Islamic ideology and a comparative study by Yudian Wahyudi, there is another, now rather dated, PhD thesis in Dutch, written in the early 1980s by the theologian Marien van den Boom, which juxtaposes Hanafi with the French-trained Moroccan philosopher Mohammed Lahbabi (1922–1993).[89]

Both van den Boom and Olsson's studies provide valuable and comprehensive overviews of Hanafi's oeuvre, but have had only very limited circulation. Van den Boom is only interested in epistemological questions insofar as they are informed by the thinker's worldview. Although addressing the phenomenological and hermeneutical aspects of Hanafi's thought, his treatment is primarily guided by Hanafi's existentialism and the revolutionary élan underlying his humanist ideology. Olsson's 'Renewal and Authenticity: The Quest for Authenticity in Hasan Hanafi's Islamic Ideology' forms a very welcome update of van den Boom's work. She considers Hanafi from the perspective of the history of ideas and acknowledges the importance of both Islamic and Western influences for his work. However, as she discusses mainly Hanafi's political ideas, socialist reading of Islam and the relation between his liberation theology and universal ethics, Olsson's attention focuses mainly on the ideological dimensions of Hanafi's thought.

Mohammed Arkoun

Mohammed Arkoun (1928–2010) was an ethnic Berber from Kabylia in Algeria. He received a Francophone education at state schools and instruction in Arabic and Islam from an uncle who was a practising Sufi, before moving on to the University of Algiers and—eventually—to the Sorbonne for postgraduate studies in Arabic and Islam. While lecturing in Strasbourg, he became interested in the innovative historiography of the *Annales* School. Given this biographical background and intellectual profile, Arkoun finds himself in a 'position on ethnic, geographical, and methodological frontiers.'[90] For this reason he has been called a cultural and intellectual *Grenzgänger* or 'border crosser.'[91] Unlike Madjid and Hanafi, Arkoun did not return to his home country after completing his postgraduate studies. Instead he spent his working life as a professor of Islamic thought at the Sorbonne, tasking himself with a mission to uncover 'the unthought' in Islam, by which he meant an alternative research programme designed to quarry elements of the Islamic heritage which had hitherto been ignored, as well as retrieving elusive dimensions of critical reason found in the margins and interstices of ideological polarisation between the Muslim world and the West. Since the 1980s he has presented this new and comprehensive agenda for Islamic studies as 'Applied Islamology,' which was eventually expanded into a general critique of reason and methodology for the cross-cultural study of religious phenomena.[92]

The secondary literature on Arkoun in both English and French is limited to book chapters, journal articles, and a few theses. The only book-length publication in a major European language is written in German.[93] Ursula Günther's biography, *Mohammed Arkoun: Ein moderner Kritiker der islamischen Vernunft*, provides a useful overview of the various theoretical concepts which Arkoun developed during his forty-year career as an intellectual historian of Islam, further augmented with a glossary containing explanatory notes on key terms from the often idiosyncratic Arkounian jargon. These form the basis for Günther's examination of the impulses for Arkoun's 'Applied Islamology' agenda and a discussion of his main publications, as well as a survey of the secondary literature. However in Günther's book the intellectual influences informing his work are generally confined to footnotes. Finally, the extensive appendix containing a bibliography of his publications and unpublished manuscripts is an important resource for Arkoun students.

Remarkably, three monograph-size publications on Arkoun have appeared in Indonesian and they are indicative of that country's earlier noted relative openness to alternative Islamic discourses. Johan Meuleman, a Dutch convert to Islam and former university lecturer in Algeria and Indonesia, edited *Tradisi, Kemodernan dan Metamodernisme: Memperbincangkan Pemikiran Mohammed Arkoun*,[94] and was also involved in the publication of two Indonesian translations of writings by Arkoun.[95] Aside from the editor's own input explaining the relevance of developments in semiotics and the literature on postmodern philosophy for studying Arkoun, contributions by a number of Indonesian Muslim scholars evince not just their intensive engagement with the writings of Arkoun himself, but also with other contemporary Muslim intellectuals, such as Fazlur Rahman and Seyyed Hossein Nasr, Western hermeneuticians such as Bauman, Crapanzano, Gadamer, and Ricoeur, as well as postmodernist thinkers like Barthes, Derrida, and Foucault, and the work of Western scholars of Islam.

A few years later, one of these contributors to this edited volume—Suadi Putro—published his own study of Arkoun. Acknowledging that any discussion of modernity in relation to the Muslim World can ill afford to ignore Arkoun and noting that this is also recognised in Indonesian academia, the discussion in *Mohammed Arkoun tentang Islam Modernitas*[96] revolves around the challenges posed by modernity and how Islam is to meet them. Ruslani's *Masyarakat Kitab dan Dialog Antaragama: Studi atas Pemikiran Mohammed Arkoun*[97] uses one of Arkoun's concepts to discuss his significance in interfaith dialogue, but its substance is less germane for the topic of the present study.

Scope and Organisation of the Book

The challenge of defining a workable scope for the present undertaking lies in balancing a treatment that is sufficiently comprehensive and diverse to be considered representative of the different intellectual milieus in which these three scholars worked with a detailed enough discussion of the actual substance of their epistemological and methodological contributions to both the interpretation of Islam and academic specialism of Islamic studies. An assessment of the significance of the three selected thinker-scholars for the way the study of Islam and the Muslim world can be refashioned also needs a proper theoretical and methodological framing, and must be embedded in the wider intellectual context of the postcolonial world. The discussion in Chapter 2 serves these purposes.

In what is still an explorative investigation of contemporary Muslim contributions to the study of religion in general and the Islamic heritage in particular, it is appropriate to observe a degree of modesty and humility in theorising such an effort. Therefore I prefer to only speak of heuristic considerations, which can be profitably employed to capture the epistemological underpinnings of these new Muslim intellectuals. Going light on theory in my own approach, my heuristic selections are instead prejudiced by what, through my readings of Madjid, Hanafi and Arkoun, I have identified as the focal points of their epistemological and methodological conceptualisations. The next chapter has therefore been subdivided in three sections, respectively discussing the continuing importance of phenomenology and hermeneutics, the significance of the secularisation debate, and the viability of employing a postcolonial vocabulary.

My discussion will be guided by the post-phenomenological hermeneutics of Gavin Flood. The fact that its development is heavily dependent on Ricoeur's rereading of phenomenology and hermeneutics enables me to make a connection with the writings of both Hanafi and Arkoun. A self-confessed phenomenologist Hanafi engaged intensively with the writings of Husserl, Gadamer, and phenomenologists of religion such as van der Leeuw and Waardenburg during his postgraduate studies, when he was partly supervised by Ricoeur. Heavily influenced by the *Annales* School, structuralism and postmodernism, Arkoun is much firmer embedded in the world of French academe. However, corroborated by frequent references, his oeuvre too is suffused with a Ricoeurian spirit that seeks to reconcile various strands of continental philosophy. Ricoeur's work thus offers an opportunity to juxtapose the Teutonic influences informing Hanafi's work and the Gallic *habitus* of Arkoun. The catholicity of Ricoeur's philosophy also makes it possible to draw out the commonalities and distinctions between the two.

Although the beginning and heyday of the scholarly careers of all three selected thinkers coincided respectively with the secularisation debate emerging in the mid-1960s and the questioning of its validity from the 1990s onwards, the underlying modernisation-secularisation thesis is particularly prominent in the early reformist thought of Nurcholish Madjid. Based on some remarkable similarities in their writings, I believe to have discovered an affinity between Madjid's views and those of the leading secularisation and desecularisation theorist Peter Berger; a resemblance that has so far remained undetected.

As my borrowing of terms like cultural hybridity, liminality, interstitiality and Third Space already indicates, I believe that the perhaps somewhat amorphous field of postcolonial studies provides a useful vocabulary when dealing with exponents of the first generation of post-independence intellectuals. The connections between important strands of contemporary thought and intellectual movements emerging in an increasingly globalised post-war world and the ideas developed by Madjid, Hanafi and Arkoun will be picked up again and further elaborated in the respective parts of the book dedicated to each one of them. The synergies arising from their ambitious research agendas fertilised by an eclectic mix of endogenous Islamic ideas and appropriations from Western thought reflect the multilayered identity of the postcolonial Muslim intelligentsia to which they belong.

I then proceed with providing rounded depictions of Madjid, Hanafi and Arkoun in (sometimes virtual) conversation with a variety of Muslim and Western thinkers, thus complementing the existing secondary literature on these individuals and the intellectual history of the contemporary Muslim world in general. There are practical difficulties associated with having to deal with three prolific writers from different cultures and the voluminous output of their intellectual interlocutors. Aside from the sheer quantity of writings, the range of languages required, another complication is finding a suitable format for presenting the work of three scholars who have tapped into very different sources of Islamic learning and the Western human sciences in order to fuel their widely varying agendas for resetting the beacons of Muslim thinking about the Islamic heritage.

The particular sequence I have chosen is motivated by the significance of Madjid as the creator and facilitator of an intellectual setting in which ideas of other controversial thinkers, such as Hanafi and Arkoun, could flourish. Moreover, the ways in which this trio has reactualised, reconstructed or rethought Islam as a field of intellectual engagement also traces the theological, phenomenological and critical-anthropological approaches to religious studies identified by McCutcheon. The chapters in each part are organised around the various phases that can be discerned in their development as scholars and thinkers, with the last chapter of each part containing a tentative characterisation and assessment of the intellectual in question by way of preliminary conclusion. Finally, the discussion is wrapped up in a more general conclusion establishing the significance of Madjid, Hanafi and Arkoun as new Muslim intellectuals.

2

REFASHIONING THE STUDY OF ISLAM
AND THE MUSLIM WORLD

As a first examination of contributions by new Muslim intellectuals to the refashioning of the academic study of Islam, the present research operates on a more tentative level than the more intensely debated issues related to the theory and method in the general field of religious studies. Although appreciative of McCutcheon's critique of the Chicago School's *sui generis* approach to religion, I do not subscribe to the qualification of the academic study of religion as just another 'public technique of social formation.'[1] Despite such reservations against what McCutcheon himself refers to as his 'methodological agnosticism' or 'pluralistic methodological reductionism,' the identification of rhetoric, contestation, and social formation as important factors in the shaping of academic disciplines cannot be denied.[2] In the present case they are not just immediately relevant when looking for new ways of embedding the study of Islam in the wider field of religious studies, these notions also bear a close affinity with the postmodernist and postcolonial strands of thought informing the intellectual milieus in which Arkoun, Hanafi, and Madjid matured and operated.

Although I have already acknowledged in the previous chapter that McCutcheon has provided a useful categorisation for different ways of engaging in the study of religions, I believe it is important to remain aware of the significance of self-references and self-identifications employed by scholars of religion. I also recognise the value of questioning the secularist outlook, which tends to dominate this approach by one reviewer of McCutcheon's *The Discipline of Religion*.[3] Moreover, and here I again invoke Taylor and Roberts' criticism of McCutcheon's confidence in being able to clearly distinguish between examining religion or religiosity and the study of religion as a field of scholarly inquiry, an explorative investigation of the pioneering efforts by Muslim scholars of Islam to refashion the study of Islam should remain open to the assumption that these three scholars intended to say something substantial about religion.

In order to avoid the reductionist explanations and interpretations, which will result from an uncritical acceptance of McCutcheon's approach or locking up Madjid, Hanafi and Arkoun in a postmodern or postcolonial framework, I suggest a more cautious and substantive treatment inspired by Gavin Flood's assertion not to underestimate the force and importance of phenomenology. It offered not just—as Flood himself formulates it—'a welcome antidote to theological dogmatism, opening 'the way for the West to encounter other horizons of possibility' as when engaging in the study of religions.[4] In *Beyond Phenomenology* he has also shown how religious studies has carved out a space for itself amidst traditional theology, comparative studies, and postmodern theorising and can thus be used for repositioning Islamic studies vis-à-vis this generic academic specialisation and areas studies programmes. Equally congenial is the way he avoids working from a singular theoretical position, while retaining a meta-theoretical concern for the 'debates within the social sciences and humanities and develop a more acute awareness of its procedures and contexts of occurrence,' so as to employ these in the study of what we conveniently refer to as religious traditions.[5]

As noted at the end of the introduction where the plan of this book is laid out, my own meta-theoretical considerations remain tentative. They begin with a survey of what I regard as relevant aspects of late twentieth-century developments in religious and philosophical phenomenology, hermeneutics and structuralism held together by the figure of Paul Ricoeur and his ability to synthesise apparently disparate strands of thought into a coherent whole. After that, I will venture into postmodern discourse analysis and postcolonial studies in order to assess the usefulness of employing concepts such as cultural hybridity and cosmopolitanism in analysing the work of the new Muslim intellectuals who are the subject of this study. This section will also illustrate the problematic nature of the notion of modernity and I will end this chapter with a brief discussion of the secularisation debate to provide an appropriate historical and discursive background for the alternative ways explored by Madjid, Hanafi and Arkoun to engage with religious traditions in the contemporary world.

Towards a Post-Phenomenological Hermeneutics

Phenomenology is a gloss applied to a range of approaches in the human sciences, which are not necessarily in agreement with each other. It encompasses the phenomenology of religion[6] which has its starting point in the historical-philological approach of Schleiermacher; the multifarious offspring of Husserl's philosophical phenomenology, including existentialism and the hermeneutics of Gadamer and Ricoeur; and its synthesis with Weberian sociology in the work of Alfred Schütz and his disciples.[7]

The question of the relationship between Islamic Studies and the phenomenology of religion was first raised explicitly in the early 1960s by Jacques Waardenburg in an essay entitled 'Une Approche Compréhensive de l'Islam' which relied heavily on the work of an early predecessor and fellow Dutchman, Gerardus van der Leeuw.[8] Thus Waardenburg's suggestions appear to affirm Flood's observation that 'there has been no development of the phenomenological approach since its adaptation by van der Leeuw in his seminal *Religion in Essence and Manifestation.*'[9] This had already been noticed by Hartford Seminary Islamicist Willem Bijlefeld in 1972, when he lamented the 'intolerable superficiality' of the phenomenology of religion because it remained stuck on the level of 'cursory comparative study.'[10] Distinguishing between phenomenology of religion as a discipline and Husserl's philosophical phenomenology as a method, Bijlefeld privileged the latter and advocated a consistent and deliberate investigation of the meaning, experience and transmission of religious traditions in relation to individual believers and their communities. At a conference on the place of Islam in religious studies held in 1980, Richard Martin also seemed to subscribe to Eliade's insistence 'that religion as such constitutes a coherent field of data that is susceptible to explanation and interpretation.'[11] In contrast to Bijlefeld, he regarded the phenomenology of religion as directly inspired by the continental philosophical movement of the same name and its willingness 'to posit human religious experiences as responses to deeper realities.'[12]

Another issue, identified by Charles Adams, is that the exchange between historians of religions and Islamicists also seems to be hampered by their interests in different levels and types of religiosity. Briefly the divide comes down to the Islamicist's preoccupation with texts versus the focus on religious practices and rituals in often non-writing cultures on the part of the religionist. Consequently the tools of the trade of these respective approaches appear to have little relevance for each other.[13] Although, important for theorising religion in general, it is the minimal contribution of phenomenology to concrete and relevant methodologies which, according to Adams, Bijlefeld and Martin, go a long way towards explaining why philologically-trained Islamicists retain their Orientalist *modus operandi* while holding the 'parvenu' religionists at arm's length. More problematic is Waardenburg's later claim that the need for high levels of language competency and a shortage of scholars possessing such skills prevent Islamicists from taking an interest in other domains of religious studies. The fact that specialists in Orientalist fields with similar demands for linguistic aptitude— like the Indologists Max Müller and Mircea Eliade, and more recently Gavin Flood and Richard King—have made important pioneering contributions to both the theory and methodology of the study of religions clearly undermine that argument.[14] However, Waardenburg's subsequent shift towards a concern for more precise structural analyses of data gels with Bijlefeld and Martin's stance on the potential of continental philosophical phenomenology, while the suggestion that Islamic studies should become attuned to the achievements made in such fields as semiotics have actually been taken up and applied to the study of Islam by Arkoun and to some extent Hanafi as well.[15]

In summary, the key issues therefore seem to be the relevance of the methodological contributions by the phenomenology of religion for the study of Islam, and the tendency to look at its philosophical counterpart for more rigorous alternatives. Such concerns parallel the debates among academic philosophers whether phenomenology and its hermeneutical offspring should be regarded as a method or not. After all, it was Husserl's lifelong preoccupation to find a method for the human sciences which would turn them into a *strenge Wissenschaft* or 'rigorous science,' whereas Gadamer tried to show in his somewhat misleadingly entitled *Truth and Method* that hermeneutics is not a method for interpretation.

To Gadamer, the recovery of a fundamental hermeneutics was closely intertwined with the problem of application, which actually obscures true understanding. Although he conceded that procedures such as the

ones applied in legal hermeneutics were useful for 'restoring the hermeneutical problem to its full breadth and so re-establishing the former
unity of hermeneutics, in which jurist and theologian meet philologist,'[16]
he nevertheless challenged the *General Theory of Interpretation* of the
Italian legal historian Emilio Betti, because his own rigorously philosophical interrogation had established that such procedural hermeneutics were actually an 'integral part of the process of interpretation,
locking it into the hermeneutical circle.'[17] Extending his examination of
what it means to understand the question of truth, in unpacking this
problematic Gadamer introduced notions like 'fore-structure,' 'prejudice,' and 'historically effected consciousness,'[18] which are in turn
closely linked to the case he made for a 'rehabilitation of authority and
tradition.'[19] This took him away from Husserl's inherently optimistic
search for a rigorous science that would explain everything and back to
the more subdued *Verstehen* of Dilthey, leading him to concede that
eventually we are locked into a hermeneutical circle and that the best
we can hope to achieve is a fusion of horizons.

Recognising it neither as a methodology nor an epistemology, but
'an ontological starting point of all human action and thought,' Richard King's argument for turning to Gadamerian hermeneutics is the
way it has exploded 'the myth of objectivity.' Accordingly, the realisation that the Enlightenment project's display of 'prejudice against
prejudice' in favour of an assumedly neutral and objective approach is
itself a result of a particular set of socio-cultural factors or the 'historically effected consciousness' expressed in the Enlightenment.[20] Gavin
Flood too has taken these notions onboard 'because we are embedded
within history and within narratives of our traditions,' and there can
therefore 'be no closure of the process of understanding.' In such a
hermeneutics 'understanding [...] is not an act of individual subjectivity, but is rather the result of tradition in which the individual is
bound.'[21] It is against this background that he projects his definition of
religion as: 'value-laden narratives and behaviours that bind people to
their objectives, to each other, and to non-empirical claims and
beings.'[22]

In *Beyond Phenomenology* Flood traces yet another important
strand of contemporary philosophy to Saussure's structural linguistics
and its sequel of poststructuralist deconstructions of language and discourse, and those forms of postmodernist thought at the basis of reductionist interpretations of (the study of) religion—such as McCutcheon's—

which conceive of it as a social formation grounded in the political rather than the *sui generis* taxon.[23] To fend off this kind of cynical emptying of religious phenomena, Flood proposes a hermeneutics 'at the confluence of the phenomenological tradition, on the one hand, and the narrativist and dialogical on the other.'[24] Identifying Husserl, Ricoeur and Bakhtin as 'enormous figures always in the background of this study,' his alternative to both the foundational epistemologies challenged by Gadamer and to the skepsis of poststructuralist deconstruction and postmodern social sciences, is developed out of the triad influences of hermeneutics, the narrativist tradition, and dialogism.[25] Flood's critique of Husserl's phenomenology of consciousness from the perspective of the philosophy of the sign reflects a 'Copernican revolution' from transcendental subjectivity to intersubjectivity. Advocating a more interactive dialogical form of research accounting for the contexts, values and power structures which govern epistemologies, it simultaneously rejects reductionist explanations of religious phenomena, because even if all discourse on religion is ensnared in one or another cultural setting, that does not invalidate a substantive discussion. Finally, notwithstanding his privileging of hermeneutics over epistemology, Flood does not argue for a complete cleavage between explanation (knowledge) and interpretation (understanding).

King seems to agree as he too is of the opinion that even if there exists 'no possibility of a universally applicable meta-narrative or birds-eye view of reality,' this does not need to result in a pessimistic epistemological outlook.[26] Instead they both appear to embrace a 'fallibilist view' of knowledge.[27] Characterised by what he refers to as 'soft relativism,' Flood's fallibilism accepts that 'knowledge about religion cannot be grounded on certainty, and that this indeterminacy allows for a dialogical process in which the research programme, through focusing on language, is constantly open to the further possibilities of its dialogical object.'[28] King, on his part, while drawing on the 'methodological agnosticism' characterising McCutcheon's refashioning of religious studies as cultural studies, tones down its more extreme consequences by introducing Robert Bellah's notion of 'secondary naïvité' which is in turn inspired by Paul Ricoeur.[29]

Flood's emphatic demand for 'critical distance' is indicative of the influence of Ricoeur.[30] Rejecting the implied dichotomy of the fusion of horizons characterising Gadamer's hermeneutical circles whereby 'we either adopt the methodological attitude and lose the ontological density of the reality we study, or we adopt the attitude of truth, and must then renounce the objectivity of the human sciences,' Ricoeur insists it is possible to retain some association between explanation and interpretation.[31] In this respect, his phrase 'to explain more is to understand better' prefigures Flood's assertion 'that explanation cannot so easily be distinguished from interpretation.'[32]

Ricoeur's position on the relation between knowledge and understanding was the outcome of a hermeneutical turn open to contributions from various intellectual traditions, always with the objective of placing them in conversation with each other. This marvellous ability to mediate between conflicting philosophical positions has been referred to as Ricoeur's 'generous' or 'charitable' interpretations.[33] Informed by a sympathetic and careful reading of counter-positions it is a disposition based on a self-declared 'primacy of conciliation over paradox.'[34]

Through his engagement with linguists, such as Saussure, Benveniste and Hjelmslev, and anthropologists like Lévi-Strauss, Ricoeur demonstrated that, as an intermediate stage between naïve superficial and deeply critical interpretation, structuralism can help integrate explanation and interpretation along a 'hermeneutical arc.'[35] Evidently comfortable with employing postmodernist jargon, Ricoeur used seemingly opposed terms like 'distanciation' and 'appropriation' to accomplish an 'Aufhebung' of the antithetical opposition between explanation and interpretation in order to 'bring out the articulation which would render structural analysis and hermeneutics complementary.'[36] To close the cultural distance and resolve the estrangement from meaning inherent to communications through texts because author and reader are not in immediate contact, interpretation as appropriation is central to Ricoeur's hermeneutics as the 'final brace of the bridge, the anchorage of the arch in the ground of lived experience.'[37] Thus resolving the 'polarity between familiarity and strangeness,' Ricoeur's mediation resonates not only with Gadamer's observation that the 'true locus of hermeneutics is this in-between,' but also with comparable notions developed by postcolonial theorists and students of the postmodern condition.[38]

Cultural Hybridity, New Cosmopolitanism and Second Modernity in the Postcolonial Age

The anti-foundationalist discourses of post-modernity extend also to social theory and relatively new interdisciplinary fields such as postcolonial studies. Although they have only been tentatively formulated, developing idioms rather than grammars for articulating social and discursive formations, they provide vocabularies that can be fruitfully employed in reconnoitering the 'cultural continuum' constituting the hybridity of new Muslim intellectualism.[39]

The relationship between postcolonialism and postmodernism is complicated by their distinct political agendas, whereby the latter operates from within 'the luxury of the dominant order' controlled by the West, potentially even displaying a hegemonic tendency in trying to even dominate postcolonial discourse.[40] Distinguishing sharply between 'oppositional' and 'complicit postcolonialism,' Mishra and Hodge have argued that, because the latter has borrowed from every conceivable postmodern theory it has become the most pervasive form, making common cause with the postmodern on both the theoretical and political levels.[41]

Also Stuart Hall recognised the ways postcolonialism 'collapses different histories, temporalities and racial formations' as a feature shared with the poststructuralist anti-foundationalism of postmodernist discourses.[42] In his examination of what some critics have called the 'dizzying multiplicity of positionalities' and the wild proliferation of anti-essentialist discourses on the subject and identity, Hall unpacks what he calls the temporal and critical dimensions of the postcolonial.[43] Just as in post-modernism and post-structuralism, also the 'post' in post-colonial refers to both an after and a going beyond. Thus postcolonialism is not just a descriptive term, but carries 'in its slipstream a powerful epistemological, conceptual and indeed political baggage.'[44]

Hall's critical dimension of postcolonialism as going beyond is located in an 'in-between framework' of privileging and distanciation not dissimilar to what is already foreshadowed by Gadamer's hermeneutics. But the uncertainties associated with such an approach need not be disabling. Rather than an epistemological break in the Althusserian or structuralist sense, postcolonial discourses are shifts of paradigms, reconfiguring fields of academic investigation by a Gramscian deconstruction or—in the terms of Derrida—through 'double inscriptions' and operations of 'erasure.' These forms of what Hall calls 'thinking at the limit' show how the interstitial position of the postcolonial cultural hybrid becomes a precondition for new modes of understanding.[45]

The pluralism and multiplicity inherent to postcolonial ways of narrating history move away from 'here/there cultural binaries' and the 'clearly demarcated inside/outside' towards transculturation and cultural translation.[46] Postcolonial texts evince a slippage of language in which meaning is deferred and only grows 'out of a dialectical process of a relationship between the margins and the centre.'[47] This leads to the kind of un-decidability and indeterminancy which is so irritating to its critics.[48]

Also Michaela Wolf's exploration of the connection between postcolonialism and translation moves away from 'the Manichean divide of self and other.'[49] Taking leave from the same binary oppositions dismissed by Hall, Wolf turns to a key concept of cultural studies, which is also extensively discussed in postcolonial theory, namely hybridity. Tracing linguistic rupture, syncreticism, hybridity to the work of Bakhtin, she shares Hall's appreciation for Homi Bhabha's examination of the subversion of authority and—I add—the assertion of subaltern agency through hybridisation:[50]

Hybridity, syncretism, multidimensional temporalities, the double inscriptions of colonial and metropolitan times, the two-way cultural traffic characteristic of the contact zones of the cities of the 'colonised,' the forms of translation and transculturation which have characterised the 'colonial relation' from its earliest stages, the disavowals and in-betweenness, the here-and-theres, mark the *aporias* and re-doublings whose interstices colonial discourses have always negotiated and about which Homi Bhabha has written with such profound insight.[51]

Wolf links the double vision with which Bhabha endows 'migrants or social minorities, positioned at the merging of cultures' to Nobert Elias' metaphor of the man on the threshold of a new age—holding a position from which to gaze forward and backward.[52] This in-between space which 'can neither be reduced to the *self* nor the *other*, neither to the First nor to the Third World, neither to the master nor to the slave' forms the place where new meanings can be produced: 'It is in this Third Space between former fixed territories that the whole body of resistant hybridisation comes into being in the form of fragile syncreticism, contrapuntal recombinations and acculturation.'[53] An example of such resistant hybridisation is Richard King's intercultural mimesis—through which indigenous people have 'used, manipulated and constructed their own positive responses to colonialism using Orientalist conceptions.'[54] The outcome of such cultural interchange between Asians and Western Orientalists in the construction of Western knowledge about non-Western cultures is that it showed how the agency of those who are subjected to the disciplinary powers of the more powerful can also be applied inversely.[55]

Peter Mandaville has developed a more concrete and conventional understanding of Third Space as an actual locale for the production of meaning by Muslims.[56] His suggestion of Third Space as coterminous with what is defined as the translocal space can also be used to 'read difference and disjuncture *within* Islam.'[57] Unpacking the concept of translocality, he weaves his account around the notions of travelling theory and diaspora. Indicating a phenomenon wherein not only people, but also ideas are on the move, I believe it possible to give these notions a wider currency than the political sciences and employ them in the intellectual history of the contemporary Muslim world.

Edward Said, who otherwise left little room for autonomous human agency, in *The World, the Text, and the Critic* developed the notion of travelling theory. Most significant in the present context is his conclusion that an accommodated or incorporated idea is transformed 'by its new uses, its new position, in a new time and place'—the outcome of what of an approach refers to as contrapuntal readings.[58] Mandaville extrapolates from this that 'reformulated interpretations of religion are sometimes enabled through translocality to *travel back* to their points of origin.'[59] Said's account, however, betrays a similar blind spot as *Orientalism*; namely a tendency to ignore the circulation of ideas within the so-called Third World. Adjusted versions of Said's travelling theory and contrapuntal readings accounting for King's affirmative Orientalism or the endogenous intellectual creativity of Abdel Malek and Alatas can therefore illustrate how intellectuals like Arkoun, Hanafi and Madjid refract the Islamic heritage through the appropriation of insights from Western scholarship in the human sciences.

Cultural hybridity too can thus become a device in the hands of 'other' Muslims seeking to speak for Islam in order to challenge 'privileged readers of traditions and the bearers of "true" Islam,'[60] in other words, functioning as 'a convergence of differing interpretations within a single discursive space'—in this case the Muslim world.[61] For this Mandeville seeks support with students of cultural hybridity in the context of globalisation, such as Appadurai and Nederveen Pieterse. Rejecting the interpretation of globalisation as 'a story of cultural homogenisation' they take issue with facile associations between globalisation and modernity and the assumption that this 'ready-made package' originates in the West.[62] The failure to take into account the multiple paths to modernisation leads not only to the simplistic assumption of a move 'in the direction of cultural uniformity and standardisation,' but also to the neglect of the 'influence of non-Western civilisations [...] on one another.'[63] By adopting a world-historical instead of a Eurocentric point of view it becomes possible to recognise cultural particularity as a global value, a phenomenon which Nederveen Pieterse refers to as 'global mélange' and for which Robertson coined the somewhat awkward neologism 'glocalisation.'[64]

These suggestions also point towards Ulrich Beck's concept of 'second modernity.'[65] Unlike the drive of 'first modernity' towards a universalism of global equality, the 'realistic cosmopolitanism' underlying second modernity tries to synthesise universalism, relativism, nationalism and ethnicism, as well as—I would add—religious diversity.[66] The author of a 'ringing cosmopolitan manifesto,'[67] Beck has joined a growing number of political scientists, legal scholars, anthropologists, historians, theorists of postcolonial studies, philosophers, and literary critics who have begun using the notion of cosmopolitanism with increasing frequency during the last decade or so.[68] This new cosmopolitanism must be clearly distinguished from the Enlightenment cosmopolitanism first developed by Kant which drew its inspiration from the Hellenic legacy. Claiming universal validity, it was much less responsive to diversity and particularity.[69] Aside from the fact that this notion of new cosmopolitanism is—to borrow Lévi-Strauss' canonical formulation—'good to think with,' another reason for using it here is that this term, as well as the adjective 'cosmopolitan,' have entered contemporary Muslim discourses, most notably in Indonesia, but also in Iranian and Turkish settings.[70]

In applying the concept to the current investigation, I take my cue from two perspectives identified by Vertovec and Cohen, presenting cosmopolitanism as an 'attitude or disposition' and as 'a practice or competence,' which are in turn informed by Ulf Hannerz's seminal text 'Cosmopolitans and Locals in World Culture.'[71] Aside from underscoring the individual agency underlying this particular understanding of the concept, reflecting both a 'state of readiness' and 'built-up skill,' Hannerz's essay has the additional attraction of singling out intellectuals as an apt illustration of what it means to be cosmopolitan.[72] The stress on the role of the individual in conceiving this more open attitude and versatile competence is also reflected in Chan Kwok-Bun's dialectics of cultural contact. He argues that cosmopolitanism's hybridising and innovating aspects enable people to be less tenaciously attached to their 'cultures of origin' and explore instead the new possibilities cosmopolitanism opens up.[73]

These aspects connect the new thinking about cosmopolitanism not only with the recent theorising of cultural hybridity but also with its role in managing or producing meaning.[74] It can be regarded as a further sophistication of the 'processual theory of hybridity,' which moves beyond the inadequacy of modernist insights associating cultural hybridity with liminality, marginality, and the interstitial—allocations of space that render such modernist understanding of hybridity static.[75] Instead, this theory provides broader postmodernist and postcolonial contours along the lines of Stuart Hall's process of differentiation and exchange between the centre and the periphery and between different peripheries, as suggested by Papstergiadis, rather than Homi Bhabha's 'third space,' while at the same time avoiding throwing away the baby of modernity with the bathwater.[76]

Although more distrustful of modernity and bearing the postcolonial signature of 'real, if incomplete, ruptures with past structures of domination' anthropologist James Clifford's *Routes* used references to Amitav Ghosh's *In an Antique Land* and Marshall Hodgson's world-historical approach in support of a 'diaspora discourse and history currently in the air' which also seeks to recover 'non-Western, or not-only-Western models for cosmopolitan life.'[77]

Inspired by Bakhtin's distinction between the historicity of unconscious or organic hybridity and the subversive agency implied by intentional conscious hybridity, and Hannerz's parallel differentiation of transnational (unconscious) hybridity from cosmopolitan (conscious) hybridity, Werbner resists the nihilism that has marred many postmodernist discourses, the focus of which on power or text can be considered essentialist.[78] Instead, she wants to preserve the heuristic gains of select modernist social scientists such as Durkheim, Lévi-Strauss, and Douglas. The intentional hybridity of the new cosmopolitans, argues Werbner, 'creates an ironic double consciousness' operating dialogically in its search for an openness to new meanings.[79]

The Secularisation Thesis: Between Theology and Sociology

This new cosmopolitanism and the concomitant second modernity, also invite another caveat regarding McCutcheon's methodological reductionism and agnosticism, and that is the question of 'the secularism with which this study is intimately associated.'[80] The pervasive influence of the secularisation-modernisation thesis in the 1950s and 1960s has already been noted. Social scientists also began applying the notion in their analyses of the role of religion in non-Christian societies. Using Karl Mannheim's work on cultural analysis, Matthes argues, however, that socio-cultural formations as unique as religion and secularisation 'cannot be defined in an abstract manner,' because that would 'conceal the wealth of cultural notions associated with [them].' Although an inherent part of the global spread of Western culture, also Matthes insists that secularisation 'does not force the rest of the world onto the same path of development that the West has taken.'[81]

In the final decades of the twentieth century the debate received new currency, when the presumed pervasiveness of secularity was called into question because of a growing realisation that this 'premature requiem for the death of religion' was clearly erroneous.[82] Reacting to what seemed a worldwide resurgence of religion in the public sphere, affecting places as culturally diverse as the Middle East, India, the United States, and Latin America, scholars—including some of the earlier advocates of the modernisation-secularisation thesis—began to rethink the extent to which secularisation permeates the contemporary world.

Regarding his own sociological work as a 'theoretical marriage' between the sociologies of Schütz and Durkheim,[83] Peter Berger had used his earlier work on the sociology of knowledge, to support his argument in *The Sacred Canopy* that 'the *same* human activity that produces society also produces religion, with the relation between the two products always being a dialectical one,' exemplified in 'plausibility structures' through which humans make sense of that world and give meaning to it.[84] Although generally addressing them in separate books, Berger has persistently pursued this interest in religion on the crossroads of sociology and theology, claiming that he has remained relatively intellectually 'homeless' between the two disciplines, never quite managing to find the 'heresy' that befitted his theological views.[85] Whereas Bryan Wilson was uneasy about making such connections between theology and social science, David Martin thought it perfectly legitimate, as 'we all employ rhetorical genres with their varied resonances.'[86]

While *The Precarious Vision* (1961) was still suffused with the spirit of Karl Barth, in *A Rumour of Angels* (1970) Berger began unpacking an anthropological theology.[87] Affirming that a search for 'signals of transcendence' in the face of secularisation is not futile, as a sociologist he forced theologians to cross 'the fiery brook' and take man as the new starting point, whereas as a theologian he continued to entertain the subversive position of standing Feuerbach's reduction of theology to anthropology on its head.[88] Pointing to the parallel between modernity as a situation in which humankind is confronted with a plurality of worldviews forcing a shift from fate towards choice and the 'sharply illuminating' etymology of heresy as being rooted in the 'Greek verb *hairein* to choose,' Berger continued his theological reflections in *The Heretical Imperative* (1980).[89]

Navigating between conservative theology's deductive reliance on tradition and the excessive reductionism of Feuerbach's anthropology or Bultmann's demythologising, Berger opts for an 'inductive Schleiermacherian approach' to chart an alternative route towards the theological possibilities of Protestant liberal theology openness to human experience.[90] He also recognises that Schleiermacher's historical-philological examination of the breaking-in of the infinite into the finite stands 'at the methodological roots of what came to be known in the twentieth century as the phenomenology of religion.'[91] His own 'solely methodological' endorsement of liberal theology constituted not just a 'fruitful third option between the neo-Orthodox reconstructions on the "right" and the capitulation to secularism on the "left,"' it also prepared the ground for the radically changed perspective of his later sociological works.[92]

A Far Glory (1992) and *The Desecularisation of the World* (1999) challenge the significance of 'European exceptionalism' and the 'international knowledge class [...] composed of people with Western-type higher education, especially in the humanities and social sciences,' as the respective venue and advocates of the secularisation theory as an explanatory model.[93] His argument that it is not strongly-felt religion that needs explanation, but rather its absence in Western Europe and among a globalised *elite* is a concern shared by Hanafi, Arkoun, and Madjid.[94]

Even though David Martin's *A General Theory of Secularisation* (1978) and *On Secularisation* (2005) concentrate on Christianity, the differentiations identified in a plurality of national and regional trajectories can also be applied to other religious traditions. Martin's emphasis on gaining a 'rich understanding of particular situations, not only in the West, but on the global scene,' helped instil a realisation that 'the trajectory of history moves forward in an erratic course' and that 'we tidy up history in [an] intolerable manner.'[95]

Berger and Martin's later works have influenced a younger generation of scholars of religion. Two studies from the 1990s no longer speak of secularisation, but suggest the alternative term 'detraditionalisation,' providing the following working definition:

> [D]etraditionalisation involves a shift of authority from 'without' to 'within.' It entails the decline of the belief in pre-given or natural orders of things. Individual subjects are themselves called upon to exercise control in the face of the disorder and contingency which is thereby generated. 'Voice' is displaced from established sources, coming to rest with the self.[96]

Admitting that even in its radical form this process is not one of individualisation *per se*, Paul Heelas posits a more toned-down 'co-existence thesis,' whereby detraditionalisation takes places alongside 'tradition maintenance.'[97] Evidence shows that 'traditionalists' are not exclusively tradition-informed, neither are 'post-traditionalists' completely autonomous; 'the fact remains that we are socio-cultural beings.'[98] Not only are traditions open to human agency, with those participating in traditional societies not being unreflective about their own convictions, anthropologists also emphasise that even supposedly closed societies are pluralistic, both internally and in their capacity to absorb external influences.

In a later essay collection, *Religion, Modernity and Postmodernity* (1998), Heelas asserts that there is not only a functionalist differentiation between religion and politics, but also within religion itself. However, modernity evinces also countervailing tendencies of 'dedifferentiation,' exemplified by Kantian categorical imperatives and the Romantic quest for a unifying soul. Therefore 'differentiation can never be total [and] dedifferentiation can never be comprehensive.'[99] From these notions of differentiation and dedifferentiation Heelas extrapolates a postmodern condition, which is primarily characterised by dedifferentiation. Because of its 'shift from the muffled majesty of the grand narratives to the splintering autonomy of micronarratives,' postmodernity underscores the freedom of the self to draw on all that is available.[100] But at the other extremity one finds a postmodern differentiation that is expressed in the freedom of the self to live itself instead of being dominated by others.

Although Heelas concerns himself mainly with the unfolding of these processes in the cultural context of the West, both 'differentiation-dedifferentiation' and the co-existence thesis of tradition and detraditionalisation can also be applied to other religious traditions. In an essay referencing Berger's *A Far Glory* and Cox's *Secular City* and pointing to the work of Nurcholish Madjid, the earlier-mentioned anthropologist and Indonesianist Robert Hefner uses the Durkheimian model of differentiation and specialisation to present a 'soft version' of the secularisation theory which retains a potential for spirituality, challenging the disenchanted and depersonalised worldviews of Nietzsche and Weber.[101]

Together with the phenomenological and post-phenomenological approaches developed by Ricoeur and Flood, selected notions from the postmodern and postcolonial nomenclature, this fine-tuning of the secularisation thesis provides a suitable heuristic apparatus for examining the ways in which three new Muslim intellectuals have engaged in the refashioning of Islamic Studies both as a subfield of the generic study of religion and within the context of contemporary Muslim intellectual discourses.

'One may suppose that this possibility of heresy has always existed in human communities, as one may suppose there have always been rebels and innovators. And, surely, those who represented the authority of the tradition must always have been troubled by the possibility.'

Peter L. Berger, *The Heretical Imperative*

'wetenschap we lachen er wel om
maar het is natuurlijk
om ten hemel te schreien
nooit klikte het tussen ons
en de dichter'

Ramsey Nasr, 'Het Complot'

3

FROM *WUNDERKIND* TO *ENFANT TERRIBLE*

THE EARLY CAREER OF NURCHOLISH MADJID

Even though various scholars anticipated an increasingly important role for Indonesia in shaping the intellectual scene in the contemporary Muslim world, it has as yet received relatively little attention within the field of Islamic Studies. With his bold proposals and high public profile, Nurcholish Madjid was one of the key contributors to the creation of a progressive and liberal Islamic-intellectual climate in Indonesia reflecting inspirations from Islamic reformism and modernism as well as Western thinking and scholarship on religion.

As his significance is not limited to the academic formulation of alternative ways for engaging with the Islamic heritage, but—perhaps even more importantly—also extends to that of a public intellectual actively disseminating and communicating such innovative ideas to wider audiences, Madjid's influence must be properly contextualised. Therefore, this chapter will not only pay attention to his personal intellectual formation, but also address relevant aspects of Indonesia's political- and cultural-historical setting, including the development of a Muslim intellectual milieu and sketches of several prominent interlocutors who had an impact on his career.

Navigating between Communal Identity and Cultural Specificity

To appreciate the cultural, religious, and political surroundings in which Nurcholish Madjid was raised, it makes sense to take a closer

45

look at the historical formation of the Indonesian Muslim milieu until the mid-twentieth century. As noted in an earlier chapter, the scholarly networks connecting the insular Southeast Asia to centres of Islamic learning in West Asia from the seventeenth century onwards helped establish the region as an integral part of the Muslim world. These relations were even sustained when European imperialist expansion ended the Malay-Indonesian archipelago's political independence in the nineteenth century. As nodal points in the transmission of traditional Islamic learning in the Dutch colony of the East Indies, the *pesantren* or *pondok* tended to remain physically apart from the rest of society. Functioning as 'enclaves of high Islamic culture in the interstices of the village world,' they consciously distanced themselves from both colonial authorities and the collaborating *priyayi* ruling class in order to safeguard the integrity of their religious teachings.[1]

Ironically, technological advances introduced by the Europeans such as the steamship eased travel and increased the significance of the pilgrimage or *Hajj* in sustaining the contacts with the Holy Cities of Makkah and Madinah. These opportunities to meet co-religionists while simultaneously merging into local communities of expatriate Jawi Muslims 'fostered seemingly contradictory ideas of both local and Islamic identities.'[2] Improved communications further enhanced the hybrid character of the societies in maritime Southeast Asia by a parallel explosive growth in migration from the Hadhramaut region in South Arabia. In spite of Dutch attempts to restrict pilgrimage participation and keeping so-called *Vreemde Oosterlingen* ('Foreign Orientals') under close surveillance, both traffic flows remained remarkably resilient.[3] As a result, Malay-Indonesian Muslims found themselves negotiating between what Laffan, with a nod to Hodgson, refers to as 'Islamic *communitas* and Jawi ecumenism.'[4] This oscillation between Islam's universal values and the regional cultural specificities has not just remained a recurring theme in Indonesian Muslim intellectualism until today, it also forces Islamicists to recognise the historicity of globalisation and its concomitant cosmopolitanism, and realise the need for rethinking the context of their field of inquiry.

Moreover, new ideas began percolating through from another centre of Islamic learning: Cairo.[5] The reputation of its almost thousand-year-old al-Azhar university aside, Cairo grew further in importance when Islamic reformists, such as Jamal al-Din al-Afghani (1838–1897), Muhammad Abduh (1849–1905) and Rashid Rida (1865–1935), used it as a base for the dissemination of their ideas for an Islamic revival and renewal. The vibrant alternative of this 'Cairene reformism' was first pioneered by itinerant Hadhramis, soon followed by reform-minded indigenous Southeast Asian Muslims. By the late 1890s the Jawi Muslims were not merely consumers but active participants in formulating this new Islamic discourse.[6] Aided by another technologi-cal innovation—the printing press—journalism became the prime vehicle through which reformist and modernist Islamic ideas were spread. Publishing houses in Istanbul, Cairo, Makkah as well as South-east Asia itself were no longer just printing seminal texts in Jawi and increasingly in Rumi or Latin script as well, but soon expanding into the production of newspapers and other periodicals. By the 1920s, the legacies of al-Afghani and Abduh spread through Rida's journal *Al-Manar* were echoed in Southeast Asian counterparts like *Seruan Azhar, Al-Iman* and *Al-Munir*.[7]

By now a split began to occur among Southeast Asia's Muslims, pit-ting the supporters of Cairene reformism, known as the *kaum muda* or 'New Group,' against the *kaum tua*, or 'Old Group' who continued to adhere to traditionalist interpretations.[8] The former cohort received a boost as political overtures initiated by the Dutch Indies colonial administration at the instigation of its chief adviser on Islamic affairs, Christiaan Snouck Hurgronje (1857–1935), singled them out as the acknowledged representatives of the Muslim community. Thanks to this political support the *kaum muda* soon 'enjoyed almost exclusive rights to the linkage between the lands on either side of the winds.'[9] However, as the government did not tolerate any Pan-Islamist tenden-cies and only allowed space for activities with no overt political agen-das, the first reformist Islamic organisations to emerge in 1912 proclaimed apolitical emancipation missions.

Presenting itself as a kind of trade union for urban Muslim mer-chants, the *Sarekat Islam*'s ideological foundations were somewhat ambiguous as its leader Tjokroaminoto (1882–1934) had a brief flirta-tion with socialism, while his Western-educated co-founder Agus Salim (1884–1954) took a hybrid approach to Islam, using 'Western cultural constructs' in his writings to explain its basic principles.[10] In the same year, the Yogyakarta-based religious scholar Ahmad Dahlan (1868–1923) established the Muhammadiyah, stressing practical reforms befitting its Javanese environment as a counterbalance to more aggres-sive Islamic initiatives issuing from other parts of the archipelago,

47

especially the Minangkabau region on Sumatra.[11] The Muhammadiyah set out to establish a wide network of alternative Islamic schools enabling its graduates to navigate between the colonial and traditionalist education systems.[12] For this they also received support from abroad; benefactors from the Ottoman Empire and the Hadhrami community sponsored a Sudanese scholar, Ahmad Surkati (1875/6–1943), to provide academic and organisational assistance.[13] In response to these incursions by Muslim reformists into what the *kyai* and *gurus* running the *pesantrens* and *pondoks* considered their domain, the traditionalist *'ulama* led by K.H. Hasjim Asj'ari (1875–1947) countered with the formation of their own mass organisation, founding the *Nahdlatul Ulama* (NU) in 1926.[14]

This concentration on education was a result of the rising concern among Muslims over the introduction of a secular state schooling system by the Dutch colonial administration. The focus on the educational implications of different interpretations of Islamic learning reflects what Steenbrink considers as the key determining feature of Indonesian Muslim intellectualism since the late nineteenth century. What is important is not so much the divide running 'between *kaum tua* and the reformists, between "traditional Mecca" and "modern Cairo," but between those who received a secular Western education and those who devoted their youth to religious studies, either in Indonesia or in Mecca, Cairo, or elsewhere.'[15]

This alternative dichotomy is exemplified by the iconic figure of Mohammad Natsir (1908–1993)—to whom the young Nurcholish Madjid would later be compared. In spite of being a product of the Dutch colonial education system and not having received any formal Islamic training, he became a prominent Muslim educator, publicist and activist, eventually developing into Indonesia's leading post-war Muslim politician.[16] As early as the 1930s, Natsir began expounding the view that 'state and religion were indivisible,' deploring 'the Turkish model of the secular state which another leading nationalist, Soekarno (1901–1970), very much admired.'[17] Muslim politics in the final decades of Dutch domination and the formative years of the Indonesian republic has been competently covered by historians and political scientists, less well explored are the intellectual responses to the political and social conditions of this period, even though they reflect a 'considerable array of perceptions, notions and justifications put forward by committed Muslims.'[18] Just as in the Arab world and in

British India, such views were expressed by activists such as the Muhammadiyah's Mas Mansoer (1896–1946), Islamic legal scholar Muhammad Hasbi Ash-Shiddiqy (1904–1975) and engaged modernist writers like Hamka (1908–1981).[19] However, as they kept doctrinal and textual arguments to a minimum, their positions have since been challenged by younger generations of Muslim intellectuals as 'gross oversimplifications.'[20]

The roots of the first Islamic political party in independent Indonesia can be traced to the Second World War, when Muslim activists and Japanese courted each other. In 1943, both the Muhammadiyah and NU joined the *Madjelis Sjuro Muslimin Indonesia*, the 'Consultative Council of Muslim Indonesians,' or *Masjumi* for short.[21] A year later, the Japanese administration also created an Indonesian Office of Religious Affairs (*Shumubu*), appointing NU leader Hasjim Asj'ari as its first head.[22] Consequently, 'at the end of the occupation the Muslims had arrived at a position of strength which they had not enjoyed in colonial times.'[23] But this was not to last.

Even though Natsir managed to turn Masjumi into the main vehicle of political Islam, he was quickly outmanoeuvred by the secular nationalists. At the eleventh hour, Soekarno negated on an alleged deal known as the 'Jakarta Charter' or *Piagam Jakarta*, which contained a crucial stipulation declaring 'the obligation for the adherents of Islam to practice Islamic Law' (*dengan kewajiban menjalankan Syari'at Islam bagi pemuluk-pemulukny*—henceforth referred to as 'the seven words').[24] Concerned about the potential divisiveness of such a phrase in the constitution of a multi-ethnic and multi-religious budding nation-state like Indonesia, the nationalist leaders dropped it at the last minute from the constitution's preamble. Instead Soekarno introduced the *Panca Sila* or 'Five-Principles Doctrine,' one of which reiterated the belief in one God (*Ke-Tuhanan Yang Maha Esa*).

Internal bickering between the various factions within Masjumi, which eventually led to the departure of NU, prevented the party from realising the implementation of the Jakarta Charter. This led one commentator to conclude that by 1955, 'free Indonesia had turned out to be not yet a truly Muslim country—let alone an Islamic state!'[25] The country's government deliberately left the position of Islam vague so that the country could neither be regarded as 'an Islamic state according to orthodox Islamic conceptions,' nor 'a secular state which would consider religion merely a private matter.'[26] In contrast with the politics of the time, the 1950s have also been described as a 'period of positive development within the Muslim community.'[27] An important factor in this was the introduction of a government-supported Islamic education system.

Just as their colonial predecessors, the young republic too used education to placate Islamic activists. As early as the summer of 1945, Vice President-designate Hatta (1902–1980), Masyumi leader Natsir, and Wahid Hasyim (1914–1953), the son of the NU chairman, launched the initiative for a 'Higher Islam School' (*Sekolah Islam Tinggi*, SIT), which was renamed *Universitas Islam Indonesia* (UII) three years later. Following the elevation of Yogyakarta's *Universitas Gadjah Mada* (UGM) to state university level under the pressure of the secular nationalists, the Islamic bloc was again appeased with the establishment of a 'State Islamic Higher Learning Institute' (*Perguruan Tinggi Agama Islam Negeri*, PTAIN). In 1960, PTAIN merged with the Ministry of Religious Affairs' own 'State Academy for Religious Officials' (*Akademi Dinas Ilmu* Agama, ADIA) into the first two State Institutes for Islamic Studies (*Institut Agama Islam Negeri*, IAIN), located in Jakarta and Yogyakarta.[28] The internal organisation and curricula of three of their five faculties were initially modelled after those of al-Azhar.[29] Eventually, IAIN campuses proliferated in other major Indonesian cities and were destined to become the battlegrounds for competing interpretations of Islamic thought, instigated not least by the radically innovative ideas launched by one of its own alumni, Nurcholish Madjid.

A Hybrid Upbringing

Biographers and commentators agree that, aside from this cultural-political environment, also the family from which Madjid came was an important ingredient for the development of his future outlook and ideas. However there are considerable differences in the assessment of Madjid's background—a first indication how difficult it is to fit new Muslim intellectuals into clear-cut categories. Whereas Siti Fathimah presents Nurcholish Madjid as a 'blue-blooded *kiai*' with solid orthodox credentials, Greg Barton amplifies his common origins in the enchanted world of Java's *pesantren* culture, where currents of Javanese spiritualism (*kebatinan*), Islamic mysticism or Sufism, and traditionalist Islamic learning ran alongside each other and sometimes intermingled.[30]

Nurcholish Madjid, also known by the nickname 'Cak Nur,' was indeed born into a pious Muslim family in the East Javanese district of Jombang, a NU stronghold and home to the famous Pesantren Tebuireng of the organisation's founder Hasjim Asj'ari. Madjid's father, Abu Thahir Abdul Madjid, maintained close connections with the kyai and his son, the later Minister of Religious Affairs, Wahid Hasjim. Future relations between the two families would be further cemented when later Nurcholish Madjid struck up a friendship with Wahid Hasjim's son Abdurrahman Wahid (1940–2009), who was not only destined to continue the family tradition of holding senior leadership positions in NU, but would eventually become Indonesia's president.

In spite of his intimate relationship with these prominent NU leaders, Abu Thahir married into a Sarekat Islam family and founded his own reformist Islamic school or *madrasa*.[31] His activism in Masyumi further widened the family's horizons, because the party was not as exclusively Java-oriented as the NU. But his decision to remain loyal to Masyumi after the NU breakaway of 1952 had serious consequences. As a member of a political party now dominated by modernists, while simultaneously working as a teacher in NU territory, Abu Thahir and his family were ostracised by both camps, finding themselves inhabiting a no-man's land between two opposing segments of Indonesian Muslim society, located in the interstices of recognisable social groups without fully belonging to either.

Following the untimely death of Wahid Hasjim in a car accident, Madjid's father felt obliged to remain loyal to the former minister's vision of uniting traditional and modern Islam and was keen on providing his son with an education that merged the best of both.[32] Having completed a secular and religious primary education and in order to escape from the growing social isolation at home, Madjid moved to the renowned Pesantren Pondok Modern Gontor in Ponogoro.[33] Founded in 1936 and inspired by institutions like the reformed al-Azhar, Aligarh Muslim University, Tagore's Santiniketan and Ki Hadjar Dewantara's Taman Siswa, Pondok Gontor has been alternatively characterised as truly cosmopolitan in outlook and a cultural hybridity.[34] Not connected to either Muhammadiyah or NU, its political inclination tilted nevertheless towards Masyumi.[35] However, founder K.H. Imam Zarkasji's (1910–1985) insistence that his graduates stay away from state institutions and not seek government employment seem to affirm Robinson's observation regarding the peripheral social positioning of *pesantrens*.[36]

Their transfer to this innovative Islamic school was another step in Madjid's 'cultural and intellectual migration process.'[37] Emphasising 'the intellectual aspect of religion, in contrast with most other *pesantrens* which usually placed emphasis merely on the spiritual aspects of religion,' the school featured a progressive, and professionally run modern and liberal curriculum synthesising classical Islamic learning with a modern Western education. It also enforced a strict language policy requiring students to converse only in Arabic or English, not Indonesian or Javanese.[38]

As one of the first batch of Santris who were exposed to a partly Western education, the 'Enlightenment' (*Pencerahan*) associated with that experience, enabled Nurcholish Madjid to escape from his family's traditional geographic and cultural confines and strictures of other forms of Islamic education.[39] The hybrid intellectual baggage he had thus acquired, qualified Madjid to enter a secular university, but instead he opted for the Islamic State Institute Syarif Hidayatullah in Ciputat, South Jakarta—even though this institution was not regarded as being of the same academic standard as one of the state universities.[40] Moreover, rather than pursuing one of the disciplines taught in the traditional Islamic faculties, Madjid enrolled in the Department of Arabic Literature and Islamic Culture at the Faculty of Cultural Studies (*Adab*)—the IAIN's most 'university-like' section. Here he distinguished himself by an exceptional linguistic aptitude, adding French and Persian to his repertoire of languages in order to widen the scope of his readings.[41] From 1963 onwards Madjid also became a student activist, launching himself into the vortex of an already turbulent political period.

Political Heretic and Religious Innovator

By this time, Indonesia's political situation had become increasingly complicated and confusing, further aggravating Islam's already precarious position in the state structure and turning frustrated Muslims against the central government, with armed rebellions erupting in West Java (1948–62), South Sulawesi (1950–65), and Aceh (1953–9).[42] As Masyumi withdrew from the cabinet, Muslim activists and intellectuals like Hamka continued to argue in vain for the re-instatement of the 'seven words.' In an attempt to break the political impasse in 1959, Soekarno introduced a 'Guided Democracy' and reinstated the 1945 constitution. Muslim politicians used this to once again advocate the inclusion of the Jakarta Charter's status. Although he acknowledged that it had 'not only influenced the preamble of the constitution, but the whole constitution,' Soekarno nevertheless refused to reintroduce the 'seven words' claiming that the charter was now only a historical document without political validity.[43] To further tighten his grip, the president dissolved Masyumi and had Hamka and soon also Natsir arrested, when the latter joined the renegade anti-Soekarno 'Revolutionary Government of the Republic Indonesia' (*Pemerintah Revolusioner Republik Indonesia* or PRRI), based in Sumatra.[44] Three years later, in 1965, the military used rumours of a communist conspiracy against its top brass to stage a coup and effectively take over the government.

When Nurcholish Madid became the first IAIN student ever to be elected president of the 'Islamic Students Association' (*Himpunan Mahasiswa Islam*, HMI), he was by his own admission still very much an *anak Masyumi* or 'scion of Masyumi.'[45] Dawam Rahardjo, himself a participant in student politics at the time, stresses that this refers to the less rigid Masyumi of the 1940s and early 1950s.[46] A similar qualification must be made in regard to the other appellation by which Madjid was then known: *Natsir Muda* or 'Young Natsir'—referring to the widespread anticipation that he would follow in the footsteps of Indonesia's internationally most renowned Muslim activist.[47] While acknowledging his admiration for Natsir, Madjid explained that this applied to the 'early'—pre-independence—cultural thinker and general man of letters with interests in Western and Islamic philosophy, rather than the discredited leader of the now defunct political party.[48]

Taking office shortly after the coup against Soekarno and the ensuing massacre of (alleged) communists, Madjid was confronted with a very precarious political situation. After General Soeharto (1921–2008) formally succeeded Soekarno to the presidency, his *Orde Baru* or 'New Order' regime's policy towards Islam became an intricate game of give-and-take.[49] He too refused to incorporate the Jakarta Charter and emphatically refused to consider lifting the ban on Masyumi. Prevented from returning to active politics, Natsir shifted his activities towards proselytisation, using the 'Indonesian Council on Islamic Propagation' (*Dewan Dakwah Islamiyah Indonesia*, DDII) as his main vehicle.[50] On the other hand, when in later years conservative Muslims felt further rebuked by parliamentary proposals to elevate mystical belief (*kepercayaan*) to the same status as 'religion' (*agama*) and the introduction of a civil marriage law that was regarded as an affront to Muslim practices, the government stepped in to tone down the proposals tabled by secular-minded politicians.[51]

The new government's first priority was to improve Indonesia's economic situation which had steadily deteriorated under Soekarno's 'Guided Democracy.' As part of this the New Order Regime envisaged the involvement of a 'new type of intellectual, who could be expected to participate in government-directed development efforts.'[52] Since this policy appeared to allow a certain space for the emergence of a 'Civil' or 'Cultural Islam' (*Islam sipil, Islam cultural*), a number of progressive-minded young Muslim intellectuals were inclined towards a degree of cooperation with the New Order regime.[53] Among them was also Madjid, who was becoming frustrated by the political intransigence of Natsir's generation. Aside from their advocacy of conflating religion and state, the former Masyumi leadership was also hesitant to join the new government-endorsed Islamic Party, *Partai Muslim Indonesia* (*Parmusi*). Whereas the HMI supported such a merger, the old party establishment was opposed to what they regarded as an undesirable accommodation with the new regime.[54]

The HMI presidency enabled Madjid also to raise his international stature; becoming the head of the Union of Southeast Asian Islamic Students (1967–69) and co-founding the International Islamic Federation of Student Organisations (IIFSO), while his intellectual maturing was further enhanced through visits to America and the Middle East.[55] The literature collected during this first major overseas journey introduced Madjid to the ideas of scholars like Bellah and Cox.[56] Students of this part of Madjid's career have debated the impact of these experiences. Greg Barton disagrees with Kamal Hassan's conclusion that these travels and readings were responsible for change of heart, leading to Madjid's uncritical embrace of Western secularism and his subsequent controversial proposals for the renewal of Islamic thinking. Barton argues that an analysis of Madjid's writings from before and after his voyage evinces a maturing of thought rather than the adoption of radically different ideas.[57] Moreover, Madjid himself wrote that his experiences in the Middle East, followed by a second visit later in 1969, left a more indelible impression than America and the introduction to secularisation theories. Curious about different Islamic ideologies, he met 'numerous interesting people' who engaged him in 'interesting conversations,' while he also managed to obtain 'some very important reading materials, including the outlawed books of Hasan al-Banna,' the founder of Egypt's Muslim Brotherhood.[58] It was during one of these visits to the Middle East that Madjid first met Abdurrahman Wahid, who was then studying Arabic literature in Baghdad. This encounter heralded the beginning of a friendship and cooperation lasting for almost forty years, during which both men rose to great public prominence.[59]

Given the rigidity of former Masyumi establishment and the radically different development agenda of the New Order regime, Madjid concluded that change in Islamic thought would have to come from a new generation of Muslim intellectuals. He therefore decided to write a booklet containing his own version of an Islamic ideology. Dissatisfied with the inadequacies of Sarekat Islam founder Tjokroaminoto's *Islam and Socialism* and envious of the young communists' succinct manifesto, Madjid used a text by the German SDP politician Willi Eichler to compose his *Nilai-Nilai Dasar Perjuangan* or 'Basic Values for Struggle.'[60]

Madjid further unfolded his views of the place of religion in contemporary Muslim society in a collection of texts released between 1968 and 1972. In an essay entitled 'Modernisation is Rationalisation not Westernisation,' written just before his first visit to America, he advocates embracing a rational methodology in order to modernise Indonesian society. At the same time, however, he warns against the dangers of falling victim to any of the Western secularist ideologies: humanism, rationalism, liberalism or communism.[61] In spite of the latter and Islam's similar positions regarding justice and equality, Madjid invoked the Indo-Pakistani poet and philosopher Muhammad Iqbal's characterisation of Islam as 'Bolshevism plus God,' to underscore the crucial contrast between Marxism's absolutised dialectical materialist worldview and Islam's acceptance of a transcendent God as the basis of all being.[62]

In this article Madjid argues that modernisation does not necessarily mean traversing the European or North American routes towards modernity. This position is very much in line with revisionist interpretations of the secularisation thesis and the critique of reductionist Development Theory, whereas the suggestion that Islam's earliest sources already exhort Muslims to pursue learning on their own accord, supported with a reference to the *hadith* in which the Prophet calls upon Muslims to 'seek knowledge even if it be in China,' is no different from that of classical modernists.[63]

But his use of controversial concepts like liberalisation, secularisation and desacralisation, on the other hand, provoked a storm of criticism from fellow Muslims, creating a watershed in Indonesian Islamic thinking.[64] Through his intervention Madjid effectively dictated the tone of Muslim intellectual discourse for years to come triggering a protracted polemics with his detractors. In one of the most detailed and decidedly partisan accounts in English, the Malaysian scholar Muhammad Kamal Hassan joins Madjid's critics at home not just in questioning his scholarly credentials, but appears to share their irritation over the new generation's 'irreverent attitudes,' 'inept religious formulations, pretentiousness and defiant adolescent temper,' dismissing Nurcholish Madjid's ideas as an 'accommodationist response' to the political situation created by the New Order Regime.[65] Later commentators on the newly evolving concept of 'cultural Islam' prefer to speak of a 'curious synergy between "renewal" leaders and moderate Muslim officials at the Ministry of Religion' or a 'mutual symbiosis between the new generation of Muslim intellectuals and the New Order.'[66]

At the centre of this controversy is what Kull calls Madjid's two 'paradigmatic' speeches.[67] The first, 'The Necessity of Renewing Islamic Thought and the Problem of the Integration of the Ummat,' given on 3 January 1970 in what Madjid had assumed to be a closed seminar, caused a furore when the text was leaked.[68] Aside from contentious terms like secularisation and desacralisation, it was here that Madjid launched also his provocative slogan 'Islam, Yes; Islamic Party, No!'[69] Such words from an HMI chairman and—in the eyes of some—anointed heir of Natsir shocked the Masyumi establishment. Evidently no longer sharing their ambition to establish an Islamic state in Indonesia and exchanging their excessively nostalgic orientation towards the past for a forward looking attitude, Madjid effectively parted ways with the classical modernists and their conflation of state and religion. Convinced that organisations associated with the old Masyumi leadership, such as the Muhammadiyah, could not be relied upon to throw their weight behind this renewal process, while the NU had reluctantly embraced it, there was a need for a different 'liberal group of renovators' unhindered by traditionalist, sectarian or ideological constraints.[70] When, later that year, the text was officially published together with some of the critical responses as *Pembaharuan*[71] *Pemikiran Islam* or *Renewal of Islamic Thinking*, that title caught on as the name for a new movement of young intellectuals advocating a different way of engaging with Islam.

After contemplating the criticism, Madjid responded with an elabo-ration of his position in 'Reinvigorating Religious Understanding in the Indonesian Muslim Community.' The fact that this address was delivered only two years later at a public meeting in Jakarta's prestig-ious *Taman Ismail Marzuki* (TIM) Arts Centre is an indication that, notwithstanding the hostile reactions to the first speech, Madjid's ideas were rapidly finding acceptance.[72]

For his distinction between secularisation, as the separation of tran-scendental from temporal values, and secularism, as 'the name for an ideology, a new closed world view which functions very much like a new religion,' Madjid took his cue from Cox.[73] Even though his critics dismiss this differentiation as 'sophistry,'[74] Madjid maintained that secularisation is a process temporalising (*menduniawikan*) the values pertaining to humankind's this-worldly life, thereby effecting the full consummation of its role as God's Vicegerent on Earth (*Khalifa Allah fi-l-'ard*). In a clever inversion of the argument used by his opponents to condemn secularisation, Madjid retorted that their sacralisation of the Islamic state is in itself a 'distortion of the proportional relation-ship between state and religion.'[75] Safeguarding the integrity of Islam's core tenet of *tawhid*, the belief in the One God, or monotheism, as absolutely transcendent, imposes an inescapable need for desacralising this-worldly existence, divesting it from all divine connotations, because failing to do so would constitute a violation of *tawhid*. Another conse-quence of the preoccupation with the political is a propensity towards 'fiqhism,' or the portrayal of 'Islam as a structure and collection of laws.'[76]

Madjid's conception of secularisation has not just theological conse-quences but also epistemological implications. Distinguishing between a human's 'transcendental life' (*kehidupan uchrawi*), represented by the vertical axis of an individual connection with God, and the hori-zontal relations maintained with nature and fellow human beings in his or her this-worldly existence (*kehidupan duniawi*), even though these two aspects of human existence merge in individual lives, they require different epistemological approaches.[77] The horizontal domain of temporal matters or the realm of the secular (*duniawi*) is inaccessi-ble to the spiritual methods drawing on revealed knowledge, while eschatological law (*hukum uchrawi*) governing the vertical spiritual dimension of humankind's relation with God cannot be comprehended in a rational manner.[78]

In contrast with the spiritual dimension, which is inward and personal, dealing with the horizontal dimension of life demands a certain openness to the world, because the limitations of their mental faculties force humans to rely on and cooperate with each other:

With their rational faculty humans developed themselves and their lives on this earth. So there is consistency between secularisation and rationalisation. Because the essence of secularisation is to solve and understand the problems of this world by marshalling intelligence or reason.[79]

If the absolutely transcendent were not beyond this-worldly (rational) human comprehension, but could be brought into the realm of human understanding, which as Madjid had already argued in 1968 is always relative knowledge, that would imply that God can be relativised, which contradicts *tawhid*.[80] This epistemological theory is not only reflective of what Rahardjo has called Madjid's 'radical monotheism,' but also places Madjid in conversation with Peter Berger.[81] After all, in his Barthian phase Berger had argued that by 'denuding the cosmos of its divinity and placing God totally beyond its confines, the biblical tradition prepared the way for the process we now call secularisation.'[82] This response to revelation is bound up with Madjid's view of humankind's relation with God, in which he attached central importance to the concept of *taqwa* or 'God-consciousness'[83] or the sense of what Otto called 'the numinous' in which faith or belief in God (*iman*) is grounded.[84] Within the Islamic context this is considered to be the outcome of *fitra*, a disposition intrinsic to the human inclination towards Truth, with which God endowed the 'primordial monotheist' or *hanif*.[85] While this vertical dimension is characterised by spiritual congruence based on faith, the coherence of human life in its horizontal aspects is brought into material congruence through knowledge (*'ilm*), which humans can acquire by using their faculty of reason.[86] Madjid's consistent retention of the conviction that knowledge achieved through the use of human reason is always relative and that ultimate truth is only accessible through revelation shows that he had not made a 'complete *volte de face*' from the standpoints expressed in his 1968 article as Hassan has alleged.[87] The speeches did not present a marked change in his thinking *per se*, but rather 'the choice for a new *modus operandi*.'[88]

Later Madjid also produced two codas which are especially valuable for assessing the further heuristic underpinnings of the case he argues for the compatibility of the secularisation process with Islam. Emulating Cox's search for Biblical sources of secularisation, in 'A Few notes on the Issue of the Renewal of Thought in Islam,' Madjid appealed to the same Qur'anic verse as his opponents but now to back up his claim that although 'secularism does not match with religion, especially with Islam,' the latter is compatible with secularisation.[89] The other afterthought, 'Secularisation Reconsidered,' was not written until after Madjid's return from a long study period in Chicago. It evinces not only a greater sophistication of thought but contains also an apology. Admitting to having underestimated the difficulty of making the distinction between secularisation and secularism understandable, Madjid regretted having caused so much confusion by using these terms, instead of opting for a 'technically more correct and neutral terminology,' although he does not provide any alternatives.[90] On another occasion he had stated that: 'If I were able to go back in time, I would follow my previous method, i.e., *pénétration pacifique*, the "smuggling method" of introducing new ideas.'[91]

The latest essay's main concern was however to underscore the greater significance of a sociological understanding of secularisation rather than its political-philosophical meaning based on Bellah's essay 'Islamic Tradition and the Problems of Modernisation,' in which the latter engages with secularisation in the Islamic setting as an example of the contrast between two heuristic ideal types: an enchanted cosmic continuum, resulting from a 'dreaming innocence,' and its opposite, 'perhaps closely approximated in Harvey Cox's *Secular City*,' where myth, magic and ritual have disappeared.[92] Bellah argues that the social infrastructure of pre-Islamic Arabia could not sustain the structural elements of Islam. That is to say, its absolute transcendence of God, the appeal to individual responsibility, and the 'radical devaluation, one might legitimately say secularisation, of all existing social structures in the face of this central man-God relationship,' which were all 'too modern' for the early Muslims to cope with.[93]

In view of the fuller appreciation of Islam's historicity he later acquired in Chicago, Madjid's apparently uncritical agreement with such an essentialist account of Islamic history is surprising, even more so as Bellah's anachronistic interpretation suffers from the same oversimplifications for which Madjid had criticised the classical Islamic modernists.

Bellah's essay is actually more interesting in other places. For example, his sketch of the growing disparity between the envisaged ideal

Muslim community and the political realities of Islamic history highlights the failure to develop a sense of citizenship. Moreover, in regard to the application of Islamic law Bellah argued that its formulation was defined more by post-Qur'anic practice than Qur'anic injunctions, which had particularly dire consequences for family law, where the return of 'patriarchal arbitrariness' undermined the envisaged improvement of the position of women.[94] These sections provide stronger support for Madjid's case against the foundation of an Islamic state than the ones he invoked himself. Correcting his initial reductionist account, Bellah also notes towards the end that a 'perfectly reasonable religion and a perfectly rational man would conform to the ideal type of the secular city.' Echoing Madjid's exposition on the respective rational and spiritual dimensions of human existence, he recognises that 'man is not only a secular-critical being, but also a mythical, non-rational being,' even to the extent that, in order to make sense of the whole, humankind has given 'a certain psychological priority' to mythical thought.[95]

Since Cox and Bellah's understanding of secularisation is very much informed by the functionalism of Weber, Durkheim and Parsons, some commentators have also characterised Madjid as a functionalist.[96] However, I suggest that his approach should rather be regarded as an attempt to negotiate between his participation in New Order's development policy, the anti-reductionism motivating his distinction between modernisation and Westernisation, and the global perspectives of Dependency Paradigm theorists and world historians like Prebisch, Frank and Wallerstein.[97]

Qualifying Madjid as a 'mere' functionalist falls also short in accounting for his theological concerns. In that respect Madjid's attitude towards modernisation and secularisation was actually closer to Peter Berger's position than that of either Bellah or Cox.[98] For example, Berger's social engineering by means of new 'plausibility structures,' which take into account the advances in human knowledge, has its counterpart in Madjid's advocacy of the temporalisation of this-worldly values. This shows that their theorising on secularisation arises from very similar epistemological assumptions. Both share a progressive or evolutionary understanding of knowledge, in the sense that 'the apprehension of the socio-cultural world as an *opus alienum* everywhere precedes its apprehension as man's *opus proprium*.'[99] In Madjid's case this becomes clear when reading his pleas for secularisation in conjunction with the 1968 essay on the inescapable connection of Islam to progressive rationalisation. His distinction between the collective-horizontal and individual-vertical dimensions of human life has its parallel in Berger's explication of a 'duplication of consciousness,' resulting from the confrontation in human experience between the socialised and non-socialised components of self. As long as these components continue to engage in conversation with each other, the social world will remain 'an open area in which the individual expands his being in meaningful activity.' However, when this dialectic is lost to human consciousness, the ensuing process of alienation will turn the social world into a 'closed aggregate of reifications.'[100]

A comparison between Berger's theological writings and Madjid's caution against embracing Western '-isms' such as humanism and secularism shows that the similarities run even deeper.[101] As discussed in the previous chapter, Berger initially advocated a Barthian separation of the transcendent from this-worldly existence, calling on Americans to face up to modernity and its 'desacralising logic.'[102] In *The Precarious Vision* he challenges the 'bad faith'[103] inherent in the ways churches tried to carve out social roles for themselves in Western society, inviting people instead to 'face honestly the immense precariousness of our existence.'[104] He argues that using religion to sanction the imposition of law and order on this worldly existence was nothing short of blasphemy, and that it would be preferable to heed Bonhoeffer's advice and 'welcome secularisation as an expression of the maturity and liberty of modern man.'[105] Madjid replicated that stance in condemning the stubborn advocacy of an Islamic state by classical Muslim modernists as exhibiting the same 'bad faith' of which Berger accused Christian churches, while the Islamist refusal to desacralise politics and relegate it to its proper place in the realm of the secular is an equally sacrilegious violation of the doctrine of *tawhid*.

Obviously Berger's historical description of the secularisation process is predominantly based on data from Western societies, but Madjid's examination of the phenomenon in Islamic settings echoes the same key points: shrinking the scope of the sacred; emphasising the radical transcendence of the Divine; and the vertical 'polarisation between God and man, with a thoroughly "demythologised" universe between them,' which as a historicised world becomes the realm of 'activity of highly individuated man.'[106] When Berger dropped his Barthian guise in *The Heretical Imperative*, he developed a position comparable to Madjid's attitude towards *iman* and *fitra*. Presenting Schleiermacher's inductive investigation of religious experience as a third possibility beside Barth's deductionism, which denied the experience of God as an 'anthropologically given quality' and affirmed tradition instead, or Bultman's reductionist modernisation of that tradition reflects the way Madjid's renewal or *pembaruan* thinking navigated away from Masyumi's conflation of state and religion while at the same time steering clear of naked secularism.[107]

Responses

The most incisive critique of Madjid's project came from Mohammad Rasjidi (1915–2001) who, together with Hamka and Natsir, was one of the most assertive Muslim modernists of that generation. Despite his acrimonious reaction to Madjid's ideas, they were not just part of the same intellectual milieu, but Rasjidi's biography prefigures some aspects of Madjid's career.

Born as Saridi in what he called himself an 'abangan family,' he received his first education from the Muhammadiyah and attended a Hadhrami-sponsored school run by Surkati who also gave him the name Mohammad Rasjidi. Between 1931 and 1938, he studied philosophy at Cairo University under Mustafa Abd al-Raziq (1885–1946), brother of the notorious Ali Abd al-Raziq (1888–1966) who had denied the need for an Islamic state, and was introduced to Sayyid Qutb (1906–1966). After independence he served two terms as Minister of Religious Affairs before embarking on a diplomatic career in the Middle East, which he interrupted to pursue a doctorate at the Sorbonne under the Sufi specialist Louis Massignon.[108] Following a brief stint as ambassador to Pakistan, Rasjidi avoided being caught up in the power struggle between Soekarno and Natsir by joining Cantwell Smith's Institute of Islamic Studies (IIS) at McGill in 1958. There his fierce attacks on Joseph Schacht's writings on the origins of Islamic law led to calls for Rasjidi's expulsion. Leaving Montreal in 1963 for the directorship of the Islamic Centre in Washington, Rasjidi continued his polemics by challenging Madjid Khadduri's writings on Islamic international law. After taking up a professorship in Islamic law at Jakarta's University of Indonesia in 1966, Rasjidi went on defending not only 'the purity of Islamic doctrines but also the faith of the Muslim ummah' against the liberal reform attempts of the Pembaruan Movement.[109]

Rasjidi led the charge by questioning Madjid's scholarly credentials, leading some other critics to blame the educational system at Pondok Gontor for Madjid's perceived heresy and demanding that Natsir address the issue with the school's administrators.[110] Invoking names like Cantwell Smith, Barth, and Louis Gardet (Papal advisor on Islamic affairs), Rasjidi contrasted Madjid's 'newfangled Islam which conformed to the Christian missionaries' conception of true religion' with the allegedly more genuine purification attempts of Muslim *mujaddidun* or 'renewers' of earlier generations.[111] Even if the association with Christian theology may not have been entirely off the mark, the deliberate use of the Arabic term for renewal instead of the Indonesian *pembaruan* was clearly intended to insinuate *bid'a* or 'unlawful innovation,' on the part of the 'ummat's *enfant terrible*,' Nurcholish Madjid.[112]

More than anything else, however, it was his reliance on Cox and Bellah, with the shadows of Weber and Durkheim in the background, which provoked the sharp reactions of Madjid's critics, notwithstanding the fact that despite the influence of these functionalists Madjid managed to retain his piety. Never disavowing the significance of human life's 'vertical dimension,' he foreshadowed the reversal in the initial positions of some of these very proponents of the secularisation-modernisation thesis who had inspired him and their renewed appreciation for the religion factor and reconsideration of secularisation along 'softer' lines noted in the preceding chapter.

Having obtained his MA degree in 1968 with a thesis written in Arabic entitled, 'The Qur'an, Arabic in Language, Universal in Meaning,' Nurcholish Madjid joined the faculty of IAIN Jakarta after completing a second term as HMI chairman.[113] Here he was soon involved in revamping the Islamic higher education system initiated by the new Minister of Religious Affairs, Abdul Mukti Ali (1923–2004), and implemented by the IAIN rector, Harun Nasution (1919–1998).[114] With figures like Natsir and Rasjidi increasingly sidelined, the stars of Mukti Ali and Nasution were on the rise under the New Order Regime and education became once again the battleground. The new duo had markedly different views on Islamic education, already foreshadowing the new Muslim intellectuals who would prove not only capable of transcending the traditionalist-modernist schism but also of making Islamic thought palatable to secular-inclined thinkers.

Originally named Boedjono, Mukti Ali had received a secular education at a Dutch state school and Islamic formation at East-Java's

Pesantren Termas, one of first to be modelled on the Western schooling system, but equally highly respected as Hasjim Asj'ari's Pesantren Tebuireng.[115] Here he was also given his new Muslim name and advised to give up his Sufi allegiances. After further studies at Sekolah Tinggi Islam in Yogyakarta and performing Hajj in 1950, Mukti Ali first went to Pakistan to study Islamic history at the University of Karachi, and then moved on to McGill's IIS.[116] Here he became very appreciative of the 'holistic' approach to Islamic studies and the fact that the programme was not associated with Middle Eastern Studies.[117] The programme was specifically designed to acquaint Muslim students with modern discourses on such issues as intellectual freedom, the concept of the state, women's rights and interfaith dialogue. Particularly captivated by this last subject Mukti Ali decided to major in comparative religion, becoming 'the first Muslim scholar in Indonesia to be an expert in the field.'[118] His personal friendship with Cantwell Smith meanwhile would become instrumental in establishing a longstanding programme of cooperation between the IAINs and McGill.

Upon returning to Indonesia, Mukti Ali introduced the first comparative religion programmes at the recently established IAINs, which were not merely envisaged as the comparative study of religions from an academic perspective, but also to instil a greater tolerance towards other religious traditions.[119] To counter the negative effects of the dualism caused by Dutch colonial educational policies, which had resulted in either a wholesale adoption or outright rejection of Western learning, Mukti Ali also advocated the development of a discipline called 'Occidentalism' or 'Western studies' to better prepare Indonesian Muslims for engaging in a dialogue (*berdialoog*) with the West.[120]

Aside from these official activities, Mukti Ali hosted a special study circle at his home in Yogyakarta, called *Lingkaran Diskusi*, usually translated as 'The Limited Group.' Running from 1967 to 1971, the core participants, Djohan Effendi (b. 1939), Ahmad Wahib (1942–1973) and Dawam Rahardjo (b. 1942) were all destined to become prominent Muslim intellectuals and their deliberations constituted an important 'stepping stone for the "Renewal Movement of Islamic Thought" (*Gerakan Pembaharuan Pemikiran Islam*).'[121] Effendy's inventory of the group's findings mirror Madjid's own articulations of *pembaruan pemikiran* or renewal thinking:

(1) Qur'an and Sunna do not provide any clear-cut evidence for the obligation to establish an Islamic state.

(2) Islam recognises certain socio-political principles without ideologising them.

(3) Islam is timeless and universal, and must therefore be understood in a dynamic way, and as subject to constant transformation.

(4) As only God possesses absolute truth, man's understanding of Islam is always relative, and so the resulting poly-interpretability prevents any authoritative truth claims, stimulating an attitude of tolerance instead.[122]

Its existence evinces not just the importance of cross-pollination between successive generations of liberal and cosmopolitan intellectuals in the emergence of a new Muslim 'ideoscape' envisaged to imbue the government's development policies with Islamic values, but, without taking anything away from his prominence, also shows that Madjid was not the sole architect of the Pembaruan Movement.

Once he was appointed Minister of Religion in 1971, Mukti Ali began defining a 'Weberian' religious policy in which all religions would become involved in socio-economic development.[123] In response to a spectacular growth in conversions to Christianity during the 1950s and 1960s, he initiated an interfaith dialogue by establishing a *Musyawarah Antar-Umat-Beragama* or 'Forum for Inter-Religious Consultation' in 1972.[124] It was against this background that Mukti Ali was able to facilitate the necessary preconditions for the emergence of a new Muslim intellectual capable of elaborating the earlier mentioned concept of 'cultural Islam.' This called for a major overhaul of the Islamic education system, including 'the rejuvenation of the *pesantren* value system and for the Islamic schools to act as change agents in Indonesian society in order to facilitate community development.'[125] These revamped *pesantrens* provided the seedbed for a new 'hybrid' Muslim intelligentsia and received the enthusiastic support of the future NU leader Abdurrahman Wahid.[126] The hands-on revision of the curriculum for the Islamic higher education system fell to Harun Nasution.

Nasution came from a Sumatran family of religious officials or *penghulus*. After completing a secular primary school and Dutch-run Modern Islamic Teachers' College, followed by a brief spell in Saudi Arabia, he transferred to Cairo where he attended the American University after al-Azhar rejected him because of his inadequate Arabic. Having spent the War in Egypt and marrying an Egyptian woman, Nasution acted as consul in Cairo for Indonesia's embryonic diplomatic service in the

Middle East, set up by Mohammad Rasjidi.[127] When his career collapsed in 1959 because of his vehemently anti-Communist convictions and Sumatran origins, which became a liability after the PRRI secession, Nasution briefly returned to Egypt. Subsequently he was admitted to McGill on the recommendation of Rasjidi, where he obtained an MA based on a study of 'The Islamic State in Indonesia: The Rise of the Ideology, the Movement for its Creation and the Theory of Masjumi.' Having developed an interest in the rational aspects of Islamic thinking, he went on to complete a PhD in 1968 with a thesis entitled, 'The Place of Reason in Abduh's Theology: Its Impact on his Theological System and Views,' in which he associated the Egyptian reformist with Mu'tazilite philosophy.[128] Upon his return to Indonesia Nasution joined the faculty of IAIN Jakarta, where he would find opportunity to introduce his version of *Islam Rasional* or 'rational Islam.'[129]

After his appointment as rector in 1973, he was made responsible for the development of a new national curriculum designed to equip students with a concept of Islam as an integral system of culture and civilisation. The underlying rationale was to raise awareness of the division between absolute and relative Islam, whereby the former remained firmly grounded in the Qur'an and Sunna, and the latter is found in interpretations as they developed historically.[130] The newly introduced programme comprised not only the study of the various legal and theological schools, but also philosophy and Sufism, including the 'deviant' works of the Mu'tazila and Ibn al-'Arabi.[131] One commentator qualified Nasution's historicist and ethical approach, along with his decision to single out the 'elite as a strategic target' for his programmatic innovations, as a *real politiker*'s accommodation to Indonesia's 'New Order.'[132]

The IAIN's Azhar-inspired education system was now augmented with aspects of a Western-style of education, affecting both its substance and teaching methods.[133] These included new reading lists encompassing Western philosophers, Orientalists and Muslim scholars of Islam drawing themselves on Western scholarship, such as Fazlur Rahman, Mohammed Arkoun, Hasan Hanafi, and Muhammad 'Abid al-Jabiri.[134] No direct contacts can be established between Nasution and Fazlur Rahman, but Martin and Woodward nevertheless concluded that:

Because of the more tolerant political and religious climate in Indonesia, and because he has not emphasised controversial doctrines such as that of the created Qur'an, Nasution's impact on Islamic education has been far greater than that of his more famous contemporary. Curiously, Rahman mentions the development of Islamic higher education in Indonesia as an example of promising developments in the Muslim world, but fails to note the pivotal role that Nasution played in the process.[135]

However, also in Indonesia such innovations did not go unchallenged and once again the opposition came from Rasjidi. His objections against the new curriculum introduced in 1973 focused in particular on his former protégé's allegedly unquestioned embrace of Western 'Orientalist' scholarship on Islam and his emphasis on the historicity of the Islamic legacy.[136] Although both had obtained advanced degrees from the West, contrary to Nasution, who advocated a multiplicity of views and emphasised a detached academic approach, Rasjidi was reluctant to address historical-critical aspects and remained doctrinal in his teachings.[137] In that sense he remained close to other early Muslim intellectuals, including Agus Salim and Mohammed Natsir, who even though they 'used Western materials explaining Islam, they were very selective and did not embrace Western methodologies as intellectual tools for analysing religion.'[138]

Aside from his involvement in Nasution's restructuring of the IAIN study programmes, Nurcholish Madjid also joined a number of research institutes. He served as associate director of the Institute for the Study of Social Sciences and joined the Samhudi Foundation, where he worked together with former 'Limited Group' members Djohan Effendi, Dawam Rahardjo and—occasionally—Abdurrahman Wahid.[139] In addition to these academic activities, Madjid began editing a provocative new magazine called *Mimbar Jakarta* through which he continued to expound his controversial views on religious renewal. Although many classical Islamic modernists continued to oppose Majdid's views, even a critic like Muhammad Kamal Hassan had to admit that 'one cannot but be impressed by his eloquent style, his encompassing knowledge and his magazine's attempt to cultivate the spirit of intellectual freedom, cosmopolitanism, cultural pluralism and modernism among educated Muslims.'[140]

4

ENGAGING WITH ISLAMIC TRADITION

Although he did not have the same high public profile as during his years as a student leader, throughout the 1970s Nurcholish Madjid remained an important contributor to the intellectual debates in Indonesian Muslim circles and continued to draw international intention. It was therefore not entirely surprising that when Fazlur Rahman and Leonard Binder visited Indonesia in 1974 in search of participants for their 'Islam and Social Change' project, they tapped Madjid to take part as an observer in the half year-long programme which they were co-directing at the University of Chicago. Ironically, Madjid was picked because the other candidate, his intellectual nemesis Mohammad Rasjidi, was considered too old. In more than one way, the 1976 'Islam and Social Change' seminar turned out to be a landmark academic undertaking. Its output included both Fazlur Rahman's *Islam and Modernity* (1982) and Leonard Binder's *Islamic Liberalism* (1988), while the opportunity to engage with established and promising scholars of Islam induced Madjid to return to Chicago for postgraduate studies in 1978.[1] Initially working with Binder on political science and the sociology of religion, he then switched to a subject of more intrinsic and greater pertinence to his interests, pursuing a doctorate in Islamic philosophy under Fazlur Rahman.[2]

The 'Chicago School' of the Study of Islam

Like himself, Nurcholish Madjid's supervisor was also the product of a traditional Islamic and Western educational formation. As the son of a respected scholar from the Deoband School, he went on to obtain a degree from Punjab University in Lahore and a doctorate from Oxford. After lecturing at Durham and McGill, in 1961 Fazlur Rahman returned to Pakistan to lead the Central Institute of Islamic Research in Karachi, founded to support the modernisation efforts of President Ayub Khan.[3] Finding himself often at odds with the *'ulama* establishment and the influential *Jamaat-e-Islami* leader Maududi, as Ayub Khan's hold on power became increasingly precarious, Fazlur Rahman's position became untenable, forcing him in 1968 to leave Pakistan for the United States.[4]

At the University of Chicago, he began developing a new research agenda and methodology, which he regarded as a 'prerequisite of Islamic renaissance.'[5] Initially dubbed Islamic neo-modernism, he soon preferred to call it contemporary or postcolonial modernism because it was the latest in a sequence of Islamic renewal efforts, beginning with eighteenth-century Islamic revivalist movements, followed by the classical modernists of the late nineteenth century and neo-revivalists of the twentieth century.[6] Fazlur Rahman's approach envisages increasing the profundity of earlier reform efforts through a combination of independently rethinking the core tenets of Islam, a fresh appreciation for classical Islamic learning, and selected borrowing from Western hermeneutics. He dismissed conservative and neo-revivalist objections to admitting such foreign influences but countering that 'in early Islam Muslims had absorbed so many ideas of non-Muslim provenance in all spheres of life without any strain.'[7] He regarded his proposal for integrating *ijtihad* and critical engagement with the Islamic heritage as a counterweight to the stripped-down neo-revivalism which founds it expression in socio-political movements rather than intellectual endeavours, as well as a suitable alternative to *ad hoc* approaches of classic Islamic modernism and bulwark against secularism resulting from Weber's this-worldly asceticism.[8]

Inspired by the writings of the Japanese scholar of religions Toshihiko Izutsu,[9] who in turn had drawn on the ethno-linguistics of Whorf and Sapir linking language to larger cultural patterns, Fazlur Rahman first experimented with this new methodology in *Major Themes in the Qur'an* (1980) and then elaborated it in *Islam and Modernity: Transformation of an Intellectual Tradition*.[10] Critical of the 'atomism' dominating conventional philological exegesis, Fazlur Rahman advocated a contextualised and substantivist treatment of the Qur'an which had already been explored by early Muslim philosophers and Sufis. Unfortunately, in the course of their intellectual history Muslims lost sight of the key issues of method and hermeneutics, leaving them with an imperfect and imprecise set of interpretative tools.[11] Moreover, as time progressed, scholarship consisted increasingly of writing commentaries and even supercommentaries on earlier studies rather than engaging with the original texts themselves.[12]

Fazlur Rahman's new research agenda was rooted in a differentiation 'between normative and historical Islam' that is reminiscent of Nasution's distinction between absolute and relative Islam.[13] Conceived as a systematic study of the historical development of the Islamic disciplines, including Sufism, philosophy, and the sciences, Fazlur Rahman's approach depended on a cooperative and interdisciplinary effort involving historians, social scientists and ethicists.[14] Admitting that much of the groundwork was already being done in the Western academe, Fazlur Rahman deemed Muslim participation necessary not only because of the sheer scope of work, but also because his project was not motivated by academic curiosity alone but geared towards meeting the future needs of Muslim societies.[15] In this respect he considered Muhammad Iqbal's *Reconstruction of Religious Thought in Islam* as an encouraging attempt in the right direction.[16]

A key element of this new methodology was what Fazlur Rahman called the 'double movement.' This hermeneutical *ijtihad* first contextualised the message of the Qur'an as a response to the historical setting of seventh-century Arabian society. Through a careful study of its contemporaneous circumstances it would be possible to deduce the underlying ethical guidelines, which must then be transposed to the conditions of present-day Muslim world. For similar reasons he also advocated the reconstitution of ethics and law as two separate disciplines—a distinction not made in traditional Islamic learning. Using the central moral concept of *taqwa* as the starting point for teasing out Islam's moral values, ethics acts as the crucial pivot for law and forms only the final stage in the long chain governing 'all the "religious," social, political, and economic institutions in society.'[17]

Although, except for Shi'a Persia, philosophy had been effectively banned from the Islamic curriculum since the twelfth century, Fazlur Rahman considered philosophy as a 'perennial intellectual need,' indispensable for instilling an analytical and critical attitude in future generations of Muslim intellectuals. In spite of possible tensions with the discipline of theology, through a critical interrogation of Mu'tazilite and Ash'arite doctrines, philosophy should not be regarded as a rivalling but a supportive of the field of religious studies.[18]

This is also an opportune point to introduce Fazlur Rahman's caveat on philosophical hermeneutics. In the introduction to *Islam and Modernity* he intervened in Gadamer's debate with the so-called objectivity school in hermeneutics represented by Betti.[19] Fazlur Rahman sided with the latter, because Gadamer's 'hopelessly subjective' reading of 'effective history' completely undermined Fazlur Rahman's own double-movement theory.[20] According to Fazlur Rahman, modifications of traditions are the outcome of a questioning of historical facts, followed by a response informed by the ethical evaluation of those facts. He therefore rejected Gadamer's position that 'these two moments are utterly inseparable and indistinguishable,' since there can be no such clear contrast between historical and dogmatic method. In this view, the effective history of any existing philosophical and religious tradition consists in the indefinite process of question and response, because there is no 'fixed or privileged point' immune to such questioning.[21]

In addition to the immediate influence of his mentor Fazlur Rahman, Nurcholish Madjid's studies in Chicago exposed him also to the work of Marshall Hodgson, the historian of Islam whose career was cut short by his premature death in 1968 and whose monumental three-volume *The Venture of Islam* was only just beginning to exercise its influence on the field after its delayed publication in 1974. Until then Madjid had not paid any serious scholarly attention to the classical heritage of Islam.[22] The encounter with Hodgson's historiography changed all that and Madjid began quarrying the classical sources for ideas expounded by earlier Muslim reformist thinkers and movements.[23]

Hodgson's revisionist and ecumenical approach in *The Venture of Islam* also offered a promising prospect of gaining recognition for Indonesia as an integral part of the Muslim World. Madjid's growing awareness of the importance of cultural traditions in asserting a religion's vitality dovetailed nicely with Hodgson's insistence that the East was not subject to 'millennial torpor' and that, just as in Europe, 'in other parts of the world there was a comparably active past.'[24] This challenge of an oversimplified single antithesis of traditional-modern extends to the overall understanding of the notions of modernisation and modernity. In Madjid's view, Hodgson's suggestion of interpreting terms like development, rationalisation, and industrialisation in a limited 'technicalistic' sense were compatible with his own circumscription of currents of rational knowledge to the horizontal, this-worldly aspects of human life, connecting the two also to Dependency theorists like Frank, Amin and Wallerstein.[25]

On a more personal level, Madjid and Hodgson shared a similar understanding of the interrelations between epistemology and religious conviction. I surmise that Madjid's horizontal and vertical epistemes paralleled Hodgson's distinction between personal piety and the ecological circumstances governing the social spaces that limit the inner creativity of individual conscience, and that these attitudes were grounded in Madjid's *taqwa* and Hodgson's Quaker persuasion. Also Bryan Turner and Albert Hourani noted that Hodgson's emphasis on 'religious virtuosity' assumes, at least implicitly, 'variations in the quality and quantity of personal devotional life,'[26] producing a system of religious stratification in which an elite functions as the vanguard for exploring new alternatives at crucial 'interstices of history,' not dissimilar to Madjid's Movement for the Renewal of Islamic Thought.[27] As what Turner calls a 'religiously musical' sociologist of religion, Peter Berger too can be considered as equally congenial to the ensuing openness towards a hermeneutical phenomenology of religion along the lines explored by Hodgson and Madjid.[28]

Tradition and Renewal: The World of Ibn Taymiyya

Hodgson's qualification of the medieval scholar Ibn Taymiyya's reformist activism as a 'positive programme' was an important factor in Madjid's decision to pursue this as the subject of his PhD dissertation.[29] Generally associated with the narrow literalist interpretations of the Hanbali School and infamous for his fierce attacks on intellectual opponents, it has become commonplace to emphasise Ibn Taymiyya's intolerance of those who held ideas that were different from his own. His inclusion in the intellectual genealogies, or *silsila*s, of Muhammad ibn Abd al-Wahhab and later-day radical Islamists have only amplified this notoriety. Also Fazlur Rahman's characterisation of 'the almost lonely figure of Ibn Taymiyya' as 'a top-brass scholar of theology' profoundly grounded in the speculative philosophy and theosophical mysticism of Ibn al-'Arabi inspired Madjid to explore this less well-known side of Ibn Taymiyya.[30] These joint influences directed Madjid towards uncovering Ibn Taymiyya as a *mujaddid* or reformer rather than a *mujahid* or prolific issuer of *fatwas*.[31]

The dissertation, entitled 'Ibn Taymiyya on *Kalām* and *Falsafa* (A Problem of Reason and Revelation in Islam),' is an ambitious and comprehensive attempt to tackle Ibn Taymiyya's response to the centuries-old debate on the clashing views held by such prominent figures as Ibn Sina, Ghazali, and Ibn Rushd. By 'systematically uncovering his methodology and exposing his critique of *kalām* and *falsafa*,' the thesis tries to present a more rounded view of Ibn Taymiyya.[32] As the only monograph-size text ever written by Madjid it is regrettable the thesis was never published. For that reason it never received much attention, even though it contains valuable information for understanding the further development of his epistemology.

In positioning Ibn Taymiyya's sweeping double critique of theology and philosophy, Madjid argued that in spite of 'important identifiable points that significantly distinguish *kalām* from *falsafa*,' the former's inception in Mu'tazilism had endowed it with such distinct Hellenic influences that the 'boundaries between the two disciplines often cannot be clearly drawn.'[33] Both in theology and in the philosophies of Farabi and Ibn Sina these influences were overridingly neo-Platonic. Inversely, the theologians shared also some of the philosopher's Aristotelian traits: even a firm proponent of Ash'arism such as Ghazali held the conviction that reliable knowledge and argumentation was grounded in the 'art of *al-mantiq*' or logic.[34] To shore up this argument Ibn Taymiyya took Aristotelian syllogistic logic as the target for a detailed refutation, demonstrating that with their shared sympathy for deductive reasoning there was more that united than divided the theologians and philosophers.[35] Ibn Taymiyya was also critical of their secondary use of revelation, blaming both groups for their preference of the 'foreign, non-Islamic element' of Hellenism to provide rational explanations and interpretations of revelation instead of unmediated reliance on the Sacred Scriptures.[36]

In his analysis, Madjid traced the starting points of this critique to both mainstream Sunnism and Ibn Taymiyya's Hanbali background. To make this alleged merger of Hanbalism and the general Sunni tradition plausible, Madjid invoked the challenge to conventional accounts of classical Islamic intellectual history by the Islamicist and Arabist George Makdisi, criticising them for overplaying the importance of Ash'arism and minimising or overlooking the importance of traditionalism.[37] And yet, apart from its contrasting temperament, Hanbalism is 'in many ways different in nature and spirit' from the other recognised *fiqh* schools. Because of its advocacy of continuous engagement in *ijtihad* by 'anyone who is competent to freely start afresh according to the needs of his place and time,' Madjid suggested that Hanbalism must not be understood as a mere school of law, but a comprehensive intellectual movement 'with its own distinctive Weltanschauung.'[38] He presented Ibn Taymiyya as the prime exponent of a radically critical school of thought that 'patiently took its time to be revitalised.' Describing his methodology as an attempt to 'escape from the rigidity of the scholastic methods,' Ibn Taymiyya stands nevertheless apart from the Wahhabi movement he is considered to have inspired and which led to his association with religious fanaticism and intolerance.[39]

Given his own epistemological preoccupations, Madjid concentrated on Ibn Taymiyya's theory of knowledge, identifying as its central notion the Qur'anic principle of *fitra*, which underlies the human faculties of reason (*nazar*) and volition (*irada*). Whereas the first deals with the epistemological function of accepting truth and rejecting falsehood, the second introduces a moral category. The crux of Ibn Taymiyya's epistemology, however, lies not in humankind's cognitive faculties, but the apodictic statement that all knowledge ultimately originates from God. Moreover, the human capacity of knowing God is limited as opposed to knowledge about the world. While the latter is accessible through the 'secondary' channels of sense perception (*hiss*) and rational reflection (*tafakkur*), the former depends on the 'primary' channel of 'religious instruction' (*khabar*). Thus 'true knowledge' is sent down or communicated vertically from God to the prophets in the form of 'revealed religion.'[40] Revelatory knowledge is further sustained through remembrance (*dhikr*), but in order to gain genuine consciousness of God remembrance must be augmented with contemplation (*tadabbur*). Rational reflection, remembrance, and contemplation are thus all regarded as expressions of a concept of reason that does not rely on the inference of Hellenic deduction, but an inductive method premised on the Qur'an.[41] This interpretation, in which there is 'no antagonism between intellect and faith,' shows a remarkable parallel with Madjid's earlier writings on the links between the rationalisation of this-worldly, or secular, knowledge and mankind's dependence on God consciousness and faith in its connection with the transcendent.[42]

Characterising Ibn Taymiyya's mission as a programme of 'purifica-tion and rejuvenation' intended to liberate Muslims from the uncritical acceptance of doctrines (*taqlid*) and preparing them for meeting the challenges of their times, Madjid sketched a world governed by an ever-expanding and inflexible body of jurisprudence controlled by increasingly intolerant legal scholars,[43] and a place where superstitions and fatalism prevailed as 'the corollaries of popular Sufism, justified by *'ulamā'* on the basis of *ijmā'*.'[44] I suggest that by presenting these depictions as extrapolations from Iqbal and Fazlur Rahman's reading of Ibn Taymiyya, Madjid established an alternative *silsila* of renewalist Muslim intellectualism connecting his own reformist ideas to this alter-native interpretation of Ibn Taymiyya.[45]

In his incisive and empathetic analysis of Ibn Taymiyya, addressing a wide range of themes and presenting him as a profound and original thinker, Madjid did not shy away from engaging in a revisionist or even contrarian interpretation of a thinker who by temperament and outlook appeared to be his polar opposite. He ended with the sugges-tion that 'it would be fairer to Ibn Taymiyya to remember how he insists that people should be judged only on the basis of their *taqwa* (God fearing) and the extent of their service to humankind, not their ascriptive qualities.'[46] Madjid's own reliance on *taqwa* or God con-sciousness as the only touchstone in matters of faith allowed him to identify with Ibn Taymiyya as a fellow Islamic reformer with an equal reputation for controversy.

'Retaining From the Old What is Good, Taking from the New What is Better'[47]

Madjid's postgraduate work in Chicago completed his transformation from 'Young Natsir' and firebrand reformer into a leading Muslim intellectual. While the early Natsir could indeed also be considered a Muslim renewer, the post-war Islamist politician turned preacher, Dutch-educated and self-taught in things Islamic, stood in marked contrast to the scholar of religion with a solid, albeit hybrid, Islamic upbringing and advanced degree from a prestigious American univer-sity. Earlier controversies notwithstanding, from now on Madjid's 'mastery of traditional Islamic sciences and his expertise in the secular or Western sciences were fully acknowledged.'[48] With these credentials he was able to reinvent himself as 'the most prominent intellectual leader of the urban, Western-educated Islamic community.'[49]

Charting the later development of Madjid's thought, particularly in regard to his methodology for Islamic studies, poses a few challenges. First of all, Madjid is less concerned with defining concrete research agendas or formulating explicit methodological questions than with addressing thematic issues affecting Muslims in contemporary society. Consequently his methods must be teased out from a voluminous body of essays on a broad range of topics written during the last two decades of his career.[50] In constructing a vision of Islam, he continued to freely borrow concepts from both the Islamic heritage and Western human sciences. Finally, Madjid's inductive epistemology oscillates between the local and global settings as he sought to accommodate both by extrapolating the general features of Islam's cultural cosmopolitanism from its concrete manifestations in Indonesia. The dialectics between Indonesia's cultural milieu and the Universalist pretensions of Islam as a religion would remain a persistent concern in Madjid's later work. Essay titles like 'Islam in Indonesia: A Move from the Periphery to the Center' underscore not just the central role of Islam in shaping Indonesian culture, but in suggesting Indonesia increased significance within the Muslim world, they are also indicative of the growing assertiveness on the part of Indonesian Muslims.[51]

Madjid also attributed the earlier noted lack of recognition for Indonesian Islam in international scholarship for an important part to the perception that 'culturally speaking, Indonesian Islam is the least Arabised [...]' and therefore not completely Islamised.[52] Earlier, Madjid had challenged this inclination to take Islam as co-extensive with Arabism in his MA thesis. He addressed it again in his essay 'Islamic Universalism and the Status of the Arabic Language,' noting that—aside from Arabic—the linguistic and literary influences of languages such as Persian and Malay were just as important for the formation of the Islamicate cultures.[53] The failure to appreciate Indonesia as an integral part of the Muslim world has resulted in a very limited interest in maritime Southeast Asian Islam on the part of Muslims from elsewhere, while among Western Indonesianists, social scientists underestimate the significance of Islam in shaping Indonesian culture and public life.[54] The lack of appreciation for Islam in Indonesia on these two fronts reflects the 'dual marginalisation' noted earlier by Hefner.[55]

The counter argument that 'Islam has thoroughly influenced the shaping of Indonesian culture' is grounded in Hodgson's world-historical approach.[56] It is therefore not surprising that Madjid sided with

Hodgson in putting the blame squarely at the feet of Clifford Geertz, whose interpretation of *The Religion of Java* as 'not the Islamic religion as it is perceived universally' had become the 'source of stimuli and point of reference for many Indonesianists.'[57] The tendency to characterise certain aspects of Javanese religion as un-Islamic, while they were actually local representations of features found throughout the Muslim world, was due to Geertz's failure to account for 'the acculturation of such a universal teaching as Islam to meet the requirements of local and regional imperative conditions.'[58]

Whereas Hodgson's global perspective was geared towards highlighting the Muslim world's cosmopolitanism with its inherent capacity to accommodate widely varying cultures, Geertz's perception was obscured by the limited scope of his research in a small community in Java and the influence of his 'modern "Shari'a-minded" informants,' who were dismissive of aspects of Indonesian Islam that did not match their views.[59] Ironically this also served the interests of Christian missionaries and scholars, who display a propensity towards a 'Geertzian' privileging of Javanism or *kejawen* as the 'main partner in dialogue' for Indonesia's sizeable Christian community.[60] Madjid's depiction of Christian-Muslim antagonism as occurring on three levels: religious understanding, socio-political confrontation, and cultural misapprehension are also based on Hodgson, mirroring the latter's distinction between Islam, Islamdom, and Islamicate civilisation.[61]

To correct Geertz's taxonomy, Madjid drew on Hefner and Woodward's anthropological investigations of the 1980s, mentioned in the introduction, and their identification of supposedly 'Indic' influences as Islamic acculturations that had hitherto gone unrecognised.[62]

To set the record straight on Indonesian Islam, Madjid also added his voice to the Orientalism debate making the Dutch Islamicist and former colonial adviser Snouck Hurgronje bear the brunt of his criticism. As the chief architect of government policy towards Muslims in the Dutch East Indies, the latter had put his ideologised scholarly output, on an earlier occasion termed 'Snouckisme' by Madjid, to the service of a strategy designed to stamp out any manifestation of political Islam.[63] Madjid alleged that the tremendous influence of Snouck's views contributed to the prevailing tendency among other Orientalists to deny the significance of Islam in Indonesian culture altogether.[64]

Although Madjid appreciated the plausibility of ascribing the widespread failure to judge Indonesian Islam on its proper merits to the religion's relatively late arrival in the region, coinciding with what is frequently regarded as the civilisational decline of the Muslim world from the thirteenth century onward, he nevertheless considered this as a misrepresentation.[65] Instead, he argued that it was 'post-Ghazālī Islam,' filtered through Persia and India, which had turned the Indonesians into faithful followers of this leading Ash'ari theologian, making them not only 'firm adherents of the Sunni (*Ahl al-Sunnah wa'l-Jama'ah*) school,' but also accommodative of Ghazali's 'marked inclination towards mysticism.' Along with the influence of other Sufis, such as Ibn al-'Arabi, 'Indonesian classical literati' were profoundly influenced by this multilayered heritage.[66]

Drawing both on experiential knowledge grounded in his personal immersion in Java's Islamic culture and recent advances in the academic study of the Islamisation of Southeast Asia, Madjid went on to argue that the resulting emergence of a distinct Southeast Asian Islamicate culture was helped by the use of Malay. Aside from being the language of learning in *Jawi* culture, its spread was further stimulated by its use as the regional language of politics, diplomacy, and commerce. More egalitarian than the linguistic intricacies of Javanese because of the Island's social stratifications, Madjid contends that Malay had a greater potential for cosmopolitan inclusiveness, 'more or less comparable to the position of Arabic in the Arab world, and of Persian in the Muslim world of continental Asia.'[67] The objective of the foregoing critique of received knowledge of Indonesian Islam and his re-examination of its heritage was:

To prove that Indonesian Islam is as truly Islamic as elsewhere in the world. There are features that are peculiarly Indonesian, but these never impede Indonesian Islam from being truly Islamic. To underestimate that fact would result in an aberrant assessment, leading to grievous incorrect conclusions on the situation, as Hodgson reminds us.[68]

However, Madjid made not only a point of highlighting the diversity, but also of acknowledging the tensions it could cause within Indonesian Muslim society. In modern times such internal plurality manifested itself in the Islamic state controversy and in the different opinions regarding Islamic education, which remained a defining aspect of Indonesian Islam in the modern period as well. Such diversity could easily lead to friction and fragmentation. For example, it had caused a split between the NU, which wanted to preserve the integrity of the *pesantren* world, and the Muhammadiyah and al-Irsyad, two organisations displaying greater willingness towards accommodating elements of the Dutch schooling system in their *madrasas*.

Whereas *pesantren* and *pondok* had continued to function 'as a bastion in safeguarding the Islamic faith from encroaching alien cultures through the colonial government,' it had also isolated many Muslims from the Dutch colonial system, turning them, after the introduction of modern education by the colonial administration, into 'the least educated colonial subjects.'[69] This deprivation was reflected in their limited influence on post-independence politics, a vicious circle that was only broken in the 1970s when the reformed Islamic education system began to produce its first graduates and which resulted in a 'genuine reawakening of Islam and Indonesian Muslims.'[70]

In the wake of the Iranian revolution of 1979, another component was added to what was becoming an intricate religious mix when Indonesian Muslims began developing an interest in Shi'a Islam.[71] An explanation for the appeal of Shi'ism can be found in the ideological underpinnings of Iran's Islamic revolutionary élan, which heavily relied on the ideas of the sociologist Ali Shari'ati.[72] The 'Third World nationalistic and anti-colonial attitudes and sentiments' imbuing his work were not unfamiliar to Indonesians, given their country's prominent role in the Non-Aligned Movement since the Bandung Conference.[73] Madjid had studied the Iranian revolution as one of the most important manifestations of a wider Islamic resurgence, a phenomenon he referred to in an earlier article with Fazlur Rahman's designation 'neo-fundamentalism.'[74] Apart from Shari'ati, he also mentioned Jalal Al-e Ahmad as the chief ideologue inspiring Iran's anti-government forces in the 1960s and 1970s.[75] The latter's *gharbzadegi* or 'westoxification' was a crucial element in the anti-Western ideology driving the Iranian uprising, and he managed 'to crystallise the issue as a subject for serious analysis in Iran.'[76]

According to Madjid, neo-fundamentalism only managed to establish a foothold 'because "modernists" have not yet succeeded in formulating a methodology for their understanding of Islam based on the sacred texts as a whole.'[77] However, he rejected neo-fundamentalism on grounds of the negative ways of thinking to which its proponents were prone, manifested not only in their anti-Western rhetoric but also in the tendency to declare Muslims who do not agree with them as infidels.[78] Even if it was obvious to Madjid 'that "neo-fundamentalism" was not the future of Islam anywhere,' he recognised that it was very much a modern phenomenon, in the sense that it emerged out of the Muslim world's frustrating experiences in its encounter with modernity.[79] While the heirs of Abduh's classical modernism may have squandered their legacy:

> This does not end the possibility that new sources of *élan vital* will emerge, possibly this time to learn much from the mistakes of 'modernists' in their attitude towards the traditional intellectual wealth. This would make possible the revival of a proper appreciation of the wealth of intellectual tradition, which could then be utilised to enrich a new Islamic intellectual outlook.[80]

To demonstrate that Islam can cope with the development issues affecting contemporary Indonesia, in the essay collection *Islamic Tradition: Its Role and function in the Development of Indonesia*, Madjid adopted Hodgson's notion of 'technicalisation' as a starting point.[81] Hodgson used that term as a generic reference to the 'condition of calculative (and hence innovative) technical specialisation,' which began dominating the *Oikoumene* ever since the industrialisation process associated with modernisation took off, effectively closing the preceding agrarian age.[82] Madjid read this particular functionalist interpretation of modernisation in terms of Thomas Kuhn's characterisation of scientific progress as 'problem-solving,' because this did not impinge on the realm of 'ultimate truths,' leaving intact the complementary correlation between the 'amelioration of the condition of this world' and 'world reform' on the basis of the moral imperatives derived from the Qur'an.[83] It also enabled Madjid to reiterate the assertion made in 1968, that 'modernisation does not mean Westernisation.'[84] Moreover, as one of Madjid's close associates at the time noted, Madjid's acceptance of the implicit criticism of the preponderance of technical knowledge by Hodgson connects them both also to the postmodernist discourse.[85]

Aside from Western historians, social scientists, and philosophers, Madjid continued to rely on modern and contemporary Muslim intellectuals, such as Muhammad Iqbal, his own mentor Fazlur Rahman, and writers like the Algerian Malik Bennabi. While the latter was primarily brought into the conversation because he shared Bellah's diagnosis of a growing disjunction between Islamic civilisation from Umayyad times onwards and the original Islamic outlook of the early *ummah*, Iqbal and Fazlur Rahman present examples of intellectuals who examined the influence of the Hellenist worldview on the formation of Islamic thinking.[86] Realising the contradiction between Hellenism's static concept of the universe and the Qur'an, Iqbal and Bennabi both claimed that medieval Muslim thinkers became increasingly critical of the Greek heritage, until 'this awareness reached a climax with Ibn Khaldun (1332–1406), who gave expression to an intellectual revolution in Islam.'[87] According to Iqbal and Fazlur Rahman, Ibn Khaldun must be credited for introducing the notion of social change into Islamic thinking. While Iqbal regarded history henceforth as 'a purely creative movement,' Fazlur Rahman began speaking of an Islamic positivism, that is, a concern for 'the conditions of the Islamic community *in this world*,' which could also be detected in the writings of Ibn Taymiyya.[88] Although this notion was adopted by the classical Muslim modernists, they have fallen short of fully appreciating it, because they remained 'too much bound up in transcendentalism, and thus their concepts of the laws of God are very literal.'[89]

Influenced by Hodgson's critique of the antithesis between modernism and traditionalism, Madjid too began questioning whether such a clear-cut dichotomy actually existed, arguing that 'modern' and 'tradition' are highly value-laden terms entangled in a complex problematic involving 'personal consideration and subjectivity.'[90] He attributed this erroneous distinction to the tendency of conflating tradition and traditionality, suggested by the sociologist Samuel Eisenstadt.[91] This misapprehension was only dispelled after the discovery of the great varieties among traditional societies and the recognition that tradition is 'seen not simply as an obstacle to change but an essential framework for creativity.'[92] In their study of Muslim intellectuals during the New Order period, Ali and Effendy also noted a blurring of the distinction between modernist and traditionalist thinking.[93] New ways of engaging with Islamic thought were systematised by a type of Muslim scholar working in the Western academe, 'personified by the famous Fazlur Rahman.'[94] This alternative approach, widely referred to as neomodernism or neo-modernism:

constitutes a new product transcending the two earlier main patterns of thought: modernism and traditionalism. The basic difference between neomodernism and the two above patterns of thought is its readiness to accommodate the most progressive modernist ideas and at the same time [take account of] traditionalist ideas.[95]

It is quite understandable for someone without any formal links to either the NU or the Muhammadiyah, and whose outlook was shaped by the progressive Pondok Gontor, IAIN scholars like Mukti Ali and

Nasution, and subsequent studies at the university of Chicago under Fazlur Rahman, to feel an affinity with this hybrid strand of Islamic intellectualism.[96] However, as will be discussed in the next chapter, 'neo-modernism' is a somewhat misleading term, which has created considerable confusion when trying to qualify and categorise the thought of new Muslim intellectuals like Nurcholish Madjid.

Aside from escaping from the reductionist interpretations of Islamic heritage associated with classical Islamic modernism, neo-modernism also offered Madjid an opportunity to re-introduce his earlier argumentation of the complementary domains of revelatory and rational knowledge in the context of his evolving hermeneutics. Together with a persistent advocacy for a culturally specific Indonesian Islam as an integral part of the Muslim *Oikoumene*, these two abiding aspects of his thought can be regarded as the propadeutics to an interpretation of Islam as a universal set of values applicable to every human being, while at the same time respecting the historicity and cultural particularities of how these values unfolded on a collective level in human societies.

Based on this understanding that modernity is not incompatible with 'tradition *an sich*,' Madjid's invitation to return to the 'storehouse' [*khazana*] of traditional Islamic learning resonates with Gadamer's restoration of tradition in *Truth and Method*.[97] It also echoes Daniel Brown's 'reversal of the Enlightenment metaphor.' In an attempt to show that modern Muslim thinking should not be viewed as diametrically opposed to its earlier heritage, Brown suggested that 'rather than viewing modernity as a source of light, dispelling the darkness of tradition, we should instead imagine tradition as a beam of light, refracted through the prism of modernity.'[98] Madjid reasoned along similar lines that:

The ever-increasing demands of the age can be met only if there is intellectual development of Islam in two branches: an Islamic intellectualism that takes its inspiration from the rich and flexible classical treasury of Islam, and an attempt to develop the ability to provide quick answers to the ever-increasing demands of the age. [....] or in the jargon of the *ulamā'* how to implement the guiding adage [...] Preserving what is good from the old and adopting what is better from the new.[99]

The Indonesian rendition, *mempertahankan yang lama baik, dan mengambil yang baru yang lebih baik,* and the original Arabic expression, *al-muhafaza 'ala al-qadim al-salih wa'l-akhdh bi'l-jadid al-aslah,* frequently reoccur in Madjid's writings from the mid-1980s onwards.[100] Ali and Effendy also cite the same saying when identifying neo-modernism as the predominant strand of postmodernist Islamic thinking.[101] Although this can be considered as a Gadamerian hermeneutical fusion of horizons, it is important to recognise that Madjid joined Fazlur Rahman on the side of Betti's objectivity school. Like Fazlur Rahman's double-movement theory, Madjid's point of departure in defining Islam's universal values differs from Gadamer's historically effected consciousness in the sense that it also seeks a normative method to distinguish a right from a wrong interpretation. He thus positioned himself in an interpretative tradition extending from Schleiermacher via Dilthey and Betti to Fazlur Rahman, which regards hermeneutics as 'a foundational discipline [looking] for what is practical and useful.'[102]

Towards a Humanist Hermeneutics of Islam

Madjid's own hermeneutical project is laid out in a lengthy introduction in what can be regarded as his *opus magnus*, published under the title *Islam: Doctrine and Civilisation: A Critical Analysis of the Problem of Faith, Humanity and Modernity*.[103] Written during the years as visiting professor at McGill University in 1992, it provides not only an inventory of Madjid's intellectual concerns during the latter part of his career, but also constitutes a veritable roll-call of thinkers and scholars who influenced his methodological approach. In this essay collection Madjid presented what commentators have called his substantialist understanding of Islam in which *kemanusiaan*, which can be translated as 'humanity,' 'humanism' and 'humanitarianism,' *peradaban* (civilisation) and *kemajemukan* (pluralism) replace the earlier preoccupations with rationalisation and secularisation as key notions in Madjid's thought.[104]

What has so far gone unnoticed is the comprehensive and fundamental philosophical outlook of the book's structure. Prefiguring the themes covered in the first three parts of the book, the discussion of the interconnections between faith, knowledge and action in the introduction relates the respective sections on 'Tawhid and the Emancipation of Human Dignity,' 'The Disciplines of Traditional Islamic Learning' and 'The Development of an Ethical Society' to the three Kantian questions of philosophy.[105] *Islam: Doctrine and Civilisation* also contains a number of essays which can be considered pivotal for the earlier mentioned propaedeutics to Madjid's more sophisticated understanding of the role of tradition during the latter part of his career. As such they form a hinge between the reformist agenda of his student years and the hermeneutical concerns of a mature intellectual.

'Faith and the Development of Science' connects the epistemes generated by 'faith' and 'reason' to Ibn Taymiyya's inductive methodology.[106] Assessing the originality of Islamic thought, Madjid joined Iqbal in privileging Ibn Taymiyya's appreciation of inductive knowledge resulting from observation and experiment, at the expense of speculative philosophical thinking and the deductive logic of the theologians. Like Ibn Taymiyya, Madjid advocated a return to the non-inferred premises of Qur'an and Sunna.[107] Madjid used the Qur'anic imagery of man's simultaneous connection with the Transcendent through the 'Rope of God' (*Habl Allah*) and the here-and-now through the 'Rope of Mankind' (*Habl al-Nas*) to illustrate the vertical and horizontal dimensions respectively governing the epistemological relationship between God and humans, and that between people.[108]

In 'Islamic Universalism and Islamic Cultural Cosmopolitanism' this inductive preference is temporarily suspended.[109] In what reads more like a meditation than methodological discourse, Madjid traced the origin of Islamic universalism in its generic sense to the notion of *fitra*, which refers not merely to the human inclination towards Truth, but is also associated with submission to God or *al-islam*. This fundamental concept of Islam finds its concrete manifestations in the history of prophethood that started with Abraham. Rejecting any immediate associations of this early prophetic activity with either Judaism and Christianity as anachronistic, Madjid insisted nevertheless that Abraham, and after him Moses and Jesus, had all taught self-surrender to God, until finally the religious tradition called 'Islam found its historical, sociological, and theological expression in the mission of Muhammad who introduced '*al-islām par excellence*.' He also mentioned Wilfred Cantwell Smith's observation that this is further articulated by the fact that Islam is the only world religion with a 'built-in name.'[110] Whereas Islam claims to be 'relevant to any time and any place,' the doctrine 'may vary in its external forms according to time and place' as evinced by the history of prophethood, which saw apostles sent to 'every nation and community [...] using different languages.'[111]

This move from the universal to the particular or—in epistemological terms—from general to specific, introduced an explicitly humanist way of thinking to define the relationship between religion and culture. This is further elaborated in another essay collection, entitled *Islam: A Religion for Mankind*, where Madjid used the phrase 'Religion and culture: Not separate but different.'[112] Whereas religion is universal and absolute in its dealings with the realm of the transcendent, culture as the province of human thinking will always be particular and relative. As a continuation of the universal teaching addressing all mankind the historical religious tradition introduced by Muhammad is expressed through a cultural cosmopolitanism with both inward and outward vectors. Madjid elaborated this further in his discussion of the 'problem of pluralism,' which affects both relations within Muslim communities and those between Jews, Christians, and Muslims.[113]

Advocating a substantive understanding of the complexities of plural societies which transcends the level of 'socio-political jargon,' Madjid presented an inclusivist pluralism encompassing the three Abrahamic religions which takes the core concept of *Tawhid* as its point of departure for a recapitulation of surrender to God as its 'most important consequence.'[114] To explain *al-Islam* as 'the essence of all true religions,' Madjid again turned to Ibn Taymiyya's conclusion that this implies the unity of all prophetic religions.[115] To shore up his case for religious pluralism as a concept vindicated by the Qur'an, he also referred to the writings of 'classical' Islamic modernists and contemporary Muslim scholars, such as Rashid Rida, the Sumatran reformist Abd al-Hamid Hakim, Muhammad Asad, and Yusuf Ali.[116] Shifting the focus to the diversity found within the Islamic community, he pointed not only to the wide range of opinions among Muslims in present-day Indonesia, but also to the 'historical milestones in the development of Islam' and variety of figures associated with these achievements, identifying no fewer than thirty-one significant contributors.[117]

This concern with substantiality, inclusiveness, and pluralism also informed Madjid's treatment of the epistemology of the various disciplines in traditional Islamic learning, such as theology (*kalam*), philosophy, jurisprudence (*fiqh*), and Sufism. In these discussions Madjid's interest in Islamic scripture at a practical rather than theoretical level shines through, because—unlike Arkoun and Hanafi—he never developed 'a systematic scheme for returning to the Qur'ān and the Sunna.'[118] In spite of his earlier work on Ibn Taymiyya's revivalism, which revolved around a strict reliance on the Qur'an and Sunna, and his continued advocacy of 'returning to the Holy Book and Traditions of the Prophet' there are no discussions of the disciplines of Qur'an exegesis (*tafsīr*) or Hadith studies.[119] Madjid's pragmatic approach was 'far removed from the cerebral concerns with literary theory of a scholar like Nasr Hamid Abu Zayd' and his principles for Qur'an interpretation 'need to be inferred from his writings on other topics.'[120]

This practical or pragmatic interest is evinced by an essay on anthropological concepts in the Qur'an. According to Majdid, this had 'evidently not received much attention,' not because earlier generations of Islamic scholars deemed human existence and behaviour unimportant, but due to the fact that 'in the world of classical Islamic thinking the issue was addressed in a dispersed way, such as in sciences associated with Sufism, without being made an explicit and separate subject of investigation.'[121] One anthropological concept that can be teased out from the Qur'an is humankind's stewardship of the earth (*kekhalifahan manusia*) and the ethical and epistemological implications associated with that task.[122] Aside from imposing a sense of responsibility as the starting point of morality, it also implies that human existence is situated in a spatio-temporal realm, imposing a need for acquiring an understanding of the physical environment, which can be historicised as a move from mythology towards scientific and technological knowledge.[123]

Although an inherent aspect of human nature as manifested in *fitra*, finding an ethical grounding confronts humans with their limitations and fallibility. The realisation that even when endowed with faculties to create not only a technological environment but also a cultural setting that give existence meaning and significance, these human abilities fall short of acquiring a complete understanding of absolute—as opposed to phenomenological—being or *wujud mutlak*.[124] In order to find this ultimate point of certainty in life the human agency of reason must recognise its limitations and concede to faith and submission to the Creator. Aside from affirming Madjid's persistence in maintaining these two distinct epistemological realms, it also connects the ethics developed in the third part of *Islam: Doctrine and Civilisation* with the metaphysics presented in part one. Thus Madjid has managed to create a closed philosophical system, which remained firmly grounded in a theological interpretation of Islam, as understood by McCutcheon, whereby the scholar of religion acts as a caretaker rather than a critic of a given religious tradition.[125]

The fact that the cultural specifics of Indonesian Islam were discussed in a fourth section appended to this coherent philosophical edifice shows that Madjid's pluralism was not informed by a conviction that these particularities matter for their own sake, but rather that they are rooted in his non-formalist understanding of Islam as a universal teaching addressing the whole of mankind.[126] This contextualisation of Islam as a living religious tradition in Indonesian culture was already discussed in detail in Madjid's first essay collection released in 1987.[127] This link between religion and culture also connects his ethics with his epistemology, and forms the basis for the conjecture that:

[t]he Indonesian experience may not be an example to be copied by other Muslim nations. And yet, being the most populous among Muslim nations, Indonesia could offer itself as the laboratory for developing modern religious tolerance and pluralism.[128]

5

REACTUALISING ISLAM

UNIVERSAL DOCTRINE AND
CULTURAL COSMOPOLITANISM

During Madjid's absence from Indonesia, significant changes had been set in motion. Hefner called these developments the 'fruits' of Madjid's own Renewal Thinking. In contrast with the political turmoil which began to affect the wider Muslim world between 1978 and 1988, Indonesia witnessed a further retreat of Islamic political parties combined with a 'great leap forward in the social and intellectual vitality of the community.'[1] Improved socio-economic conditions had enabled the Department of Religious Affairs, led between 1983 and 1993 by the energetic former diplomat Munawir Sjadzali (1925–2004)[2] to give a new drive to the government's religious policy, which must be regarded as a response to an important side-effect of the economic boom in the early 1980s: the emergence of a relatively prosperous urban Muslim middle class. Becoming increasingly uncomfortable with what they regarded as the narrowing or 'privatisation' (*pribadisasi*) of moral concerns in the 1970s, their search for a new moral anchor in religion brought about a broad Islamic resurgence in civil society. It was in these circles that Civil or Cultural Islam began to manifest itself most spectacularly.[3]

The new policy was incorporated into what Sjadzali called a 'reactualisation agenda.'[4] It envisaged giving the country's development policies a 'new theological underpinning' by emphasising 'the holistic nature of Islam' and the 'dynamism and vitality of Islamic law,' while at the same time taking account of 'Indonesia's own local and temporal particularities.'[5] Sjadzali even brought Fazlur Rahman to Indonesia to advise him on how to advance these policies. With the booming metropolitan regions of Indonesia at the centre of this advancing cultural Islam, and the universities acting as its vanguard, it is not surprising that a further expansion of the country's Islamic higher education system formed an important part of Sjadzali's programme. By the late 1980s the number of young scholars sent overseas to obtain advanced degrees in Islamic or Religious Studies was surging, creating a new Muslim intellectual elite mainly concentrated at the IAINs in Jakarta and Yogyakarta.[6] Thanks to the earlier ties forged by Mukti Ali and Nasution, McGill University played a pivotal role in grooming this intelligentsia.[7]

Guru Bangsa: Madjid as Indonesia's Leading Muslim Intellectual

Returning to this rapidly transforming Indonesia in 1984, Nurcholish Madjid rejoined the faculty of Jakarta's IAIN where he became a key participant in the ongoing educational reforms. Although most of his work gravitated around the postgraduate programme introduced by Nasution, in 1998 Madjid was also appointed Distinguished Professor of Philosophy and Kalam in the Faculty of Ushuluddin [usul al-din]. During his tenure at the university, he developed a following among a younger generation of scholars, who subscribed to his methodological approach and way of thinking. Many of them had also either returned with degrees from abroad or would pursue advanced studies at overseas universities in the future. This community came to be referred to as the Mazhab Ciputat, or 'Ciputat School,' named after the southern district of Jakarta where the IAIN is located.[8] The group consisted of fourteen 'members,' including two of the university's future rectors: the Columbia-educated historian Azyumardi Azra (b. 1955) and the philosopher Komarudin Hidayat (b. 1953), who had obtained his doctorate in Turkey.[9] Eventually Madjid inherited Nasution's mantle as the leading proponent of 'a version of Islam that was acceptable to the New Order Government.'[10]

In spite of the political homogenisation following the 1984 reaffirmation of Pancasila, the combined effect of the new openings made during Sjadzali's term in office, economic affluence, and a reawakened religious awareness led to the formation of a new political paradigm, under which approved political parties and the top brass of the military hierarchy began establishing their Islamic credentials.[11] President Soeharto joined in as well, demonstrating his own commitment to Islam by making the pilgrimage to Makkah in 1991, accompanied by an entourage including top army officials and select business leaders.[12] With green being the symbolic colour of Islam this phenomenon was called the 'greening' [penghijauan] of Indonesian society.[13]

Even the old Islamist establishment was able to make a comeback of sorts through the expanding activities of the DDII, which, after Natsir's death in 1993, was led by Rasjidi.[14] Hostile to the reform of the IAIN curriculum and the policy of sending Muslim students to universities in North America, Europe, and Australia for advanced studies, they also managed to turn Islamic education, once again, into a contentious issue. In 1996, they successfully lobbied the government, obtaining both a Memorandum of Understanding for student exchange with Saudi Arabia and securing approval for the opening of branches of al-Azhar University on IAIN campuses. However, given the decline of al-Azhar's reputation, the government also decided to explore alternative forms of Islamic education in India, Iran, and Malaysia.[15]

In this highly competitive environment, Madjid managed to remain 'at the forefront of this newly robust cultural Islam' replacing 1970s renewal thinking with another confidently assertive 'antihegemonic subculture' grounded in the Islamic tradition and intent on subverting the position of the dominant Javanese elites as heirs to the *priyahi* court culture. For this purpose, Madjid's activities outside academia began focusing on the increasingly affluent urban Muslim middle and upper classes.[16] As a vehicle for this 'urban proselytisation' he founded in 1986 the *Yayasan Paramadina* or Paramadina Foundation.[17] During Madjid's lifetime the daily management of this organisation was first in the hands of Mazhab Ciputat member Komarudin Hidayat and then Budhy Munawar-Rachman, a graduate of Jakarta's *Sekolah Tinggi Filsafat Driyarkara* and since 2005 effectively the executor of Madjid's intellectual estate.[18] To cultivate the urbanites dominating the state bureaucracy into what he called the 'new *santri*' Madjid also established a special unit within Paramadina, called the *Klub Kajian Agama* (KKA) or 'Religious Study Group.'[19] In 1998, Madjid extended the foundation's ambit by establishing a private university under the name *Universitas Paramadina Mulia* (UPM).

Madjid's focus on the elite follows not only the examples of Mukti Ali and Nasution but also invites a reference to Preston's observation in regard to the critics of Development Theory, who all stressed that their alternative Dependency Theory is 'oriented towards the political practices of elites committed to the pursuit of national strategies of development.'[20] Aside from teaching at IAIN Jakarta and lecturing at Paramadina, Madjid was also closely involved with the *Ikatan Cendekiawan Muslim Indonesia* (ICMI) or 'Association of Indonesian Muslim Intellectuals.'

When what had started out as a careful probing by a number of young Muslim intellectuals into the possibility of holding an academic seminar on Islam and society received the backing of figures like Nurcholish Madjid and Dawam Rahardjo, the government seized this initiative and steered it towards a more institutionalised approach, thus taking control of the manifestation of a resurging interest in Islam among intellectuals, bureaucrats and politicians. Indicative of this intervention was the launch of ICMI under the chairmanship of Soeharto's key political protégé, Minister of Research and Technology B.J. Habibie, who until then had never been associated with any religious discourse of sorts. With eight cabinet members serving on the Paramadina board Madjid had apparently acquired the necessary political clout to be invited to draft the organisation's first mission statement and then appointed vice-chairman of the ICMI advisory board.[21]

ICMI provided Madjid with another and internationally most visible platform to present himself as Indonesia's leading Muslim intellectual of the late twentieth century. Not only did he become 'part of a transnational conversation, engaged in, in the United States, by intellectuals like Robert Bellah,' he was also recognised as part of a worldwide network of Muslim thinkers, which included Arkoun and Hanafi.[22] Having raised his public profile through these forums, Madjid was now well-placed to capture a pole position in catering to the spiritual needs of the upcoming Muslim middle classes.

The release of *Islam: Doctrine and Civilisation* in 1992 can in fact be regarded as a prelude to an important lecture which Madjid delivered in the same year under the title 'Some Reflections on Religious Life for the Coming Generation,' at the same location as his notorious 1972 address. If the two speeches from the 1970s came to be considered paradigmatic then the 1992 event was not just 'a stocktaking of "20 years of renewal of Islamic thinking,"' but a paradigm shift towards a new way of reinvigorating religious understanding, directed not only at the Muslim populace but also at the Indonesian nation as a whole.[23] From then on Madjid was broadly recognised as a *guru bangsa* or 'national figure who leads the way for his/her people.'[24]

Although discussing religiosity in generic terms, 'more or less in tune with the famous prophecy of Wilfred Cantwell Smith,' Madjid refused to write off existing religious traditions.[25] Recalling his own bold slogan 'Islam, Yes; Islamic Party, No!,' he dismissed the motto introduced by the futurologists Naisbitt and Aburdene: 'Spirituality, Yes; Organised Religion, No,' as lacking any strong basis.[26] What their fellow-futurologist Alvin Toffler referred to as cults, were in Madjid's view manifestations of one and the same phenomenon: the disorientation and spiritual dislocation of modern-day humans as a result of what Fromm had diagnosed as a prevailing sense of alienation. In preparation for presenting his own panacea, Madjid added that with their emphasis on seclusion, their strict disciplinarianism and their promise of firm salvation, fundamentalist movements within established religious traditions are 'not much different from cults.'[27]

In contrast with the bleakness of fundamentalism, Madjid appealed to a more 'optimistic-positive view of humanity, which has become stronger under modern humanism' and which he traced to the influence of Arab-Islamic civilisation on its founding father, Pico della Mirandola.[28] This cleared the way for the introduction of an alternative and more open understanding of religion, consisting of an inclusive theology and commitment to pluralism.[29] Grounded in the premise that 'it is impossible for humans to live in serenity and happiness without realising the meaning and objective of life itself,' Madjid drew again on Fromm to argue that 'humans have always had an instinctive need for religion.'[30] Together with the Islamic notion of *tawhid* as what Weber called the most authentic example of 'strict monotheism,' and a shared historical experience of Prophethood, this allusion to the notion of *fitra* as a unifying feature of human nature are at the heart of Madjid's inclusivist and pluralist understanding of human religiosity. It constituted in his view a 'true "liberation theology," if we should (and may) use a popular term among the activists of Catholicism in Latin America.'[31]

At this point Madjid established an explicit connection between Islamic doctrine and its tradition, drawing his preferred readings of Ibn Taymiyya, Rida, and others together with Fromm's description of this-worldly idols, and the logic of radical monotheism in which God is conceived as 'the Absolute Being [who] transcends the completely relative perceptions of humankind.'[32] This variety of sources served also as a caution against the 'spirit of communalism and sectarianism' which prevents a 'sincere and pure search for the Truth,' exemplified by the *hanif*, who as a 'continuation of *fitrah* [...] will eventually bring about "self-surrender" (the meaning of *islām* in its generic sense).'[33] Thus his approach remained grounded in the strictly monotheist theological concept of the 'Oneness of God,' the historical and sociological implications of which translate into the unity of prophethood and unity of humanity respectively.[34]

In the final part of his 1992 address Madjid unfolded what Kull calls his 'turn to spirituality.'[35] Madjid himself used the expression *al-hanifiyyat al-samhah*: the inclusive and moderate search for the Truth, which does not lose sight of humankind's rootedness in this-worldly existence for which he again invoked the imagery of the Rope of God and Rope of man as 'two important values in life [that] will guarantee human salvation.'[36] Islam is presented as a kind of 'open humanism' drawing on Sufism to cater for the spiritual dimensions of human life and a reinvigorated *ijtihad* to dispel what Iqbal had called a 'reading of the Qur'an with the eyes of the dead':

In order to do all the things mentioned above, there is a need for intellectual enrichment regarding the past, the present as well as the future. Given Islam's rich legacy, one way to achieve this intellectual enrichment is to reread, to understand, and to properly appreciate the cultural heritage of the community. However, it would be incorrect if such an effort was to merely gain authority from the past, since the past is not always wholly valid or authentic. [...]

Thus, what we seriously need to do is to return to the meaning of the saying declared by classical religious leaders: to preserve what is good from the old and to adopt what is better from the new.[37]

According to Ann Kull, Madjid's reliance on Islamic mysticism is so significant that he should be characterised as 'first and foremost a Sufi.'[38] While a cursory look at some of his publications at the time seems to validate this description, on closer examination it becomes clear that Madjid's understanding of Sufism was multilayered. In some instances he showed a fascination with Ibn Arabi and the 'perennialist' writings of René Guénon, Martin Lings, Seyyed Hossein Nasr, and Fritjof Schuon.[39] Elsewhere his examination of the relationship between *tariqa* (the Sufi way) and *shari'a* (Islamic law), and its role as an opposition movement points towards an understanding of Sufism as a form of 'this-worldly' activism.[40] In other instances he supported this with a careful qualification of Ibn Taymiyya's condemnation of Sufism as extending only to 'excessive Sufism,' while fully acknowledging the usefulness of '*neo-sufism* or new Sufism (also referred to as "positive *tasawwuf*")' or by referring to the work of Hamka.[41] Given his interest in Miskawayh's *Javidan Khirad* or 'Sophia Perennis' Madjid's take on Sufism can also be related back to the earlier mentioned 'humanist streak' in his thought.[42]

'Nationally acknowledged as a *princeps modernistarum*, the most prominent spokesman of renewal in Islamic thinking,' Steenbrink opined that, qua stature, by the early 1990s 'Madjid surely may be compared with his teacher, Fazlur Rahman.'[43] Rahardjo and Feener, meanwhile, have suggested that—in spite of irreconcilable political differences—after his return from Chicago he had moved even closer to Natsir's pre-war profile as an intellectual defending the civilisational legacy of Islam, sharing the latter's holistic and totalising view of Islam.[44] Such different characterisations are again indicative of how difficult it is to fit Madjid and his ideas into neat boxes.

Defying Categorisation

This still leaves open the question of how Nurcholish Madjid should be characterised. Bakri and Mudhofir note that the ideas which Madjid began developing in the 1970s, and which helped shape contemporary Indonesian discourse on Islam, have since shifted from being considered deviant or heretical to becoming the dominant discourse in the country's Muslim circles.[45] Defining Madjid's position in recent Muslim intellectual history becomes thus a bit like the proverbial question of the chicken and the egg. Unfortunately, the issue is further complicated by the variety of designations that have been used to label Madjid: renewal thinker, contextualist, inclusivist, pluralist, substantialist, transformationist, Islamic liberal, and even a Sufi.

In the secondary literature on Nurcholish Madjid and on the intellectual history of independent Indonesia, he is most commonly referred to as a 'neo-modernist,' but that designation can be called into question too. Even Budhy Munawar-Rachman, one of Madjid's closest collaborators and the person probably most intimately familiar with the development of his thought, seems unsure whether the term is actually adequate. In an interview he commented that 'on a global level [...] Nurcholish would probably be classified as a neo-traditionalist,' only to add that probably the best fitting label would be 'neo-Sufi.'[46] Greg Barton's seminal articles, meanwhile, are generally accepted as the most detailed and authoritative accounts of the evolution of Madjid's thought into 'neo-modernism,' but on closer scrutiny they too can be considered problematic.

In 1991, Barton had argued that the term neo-modernism was coined by Fazlur Rahman, but at the same time insisting that he was not the originator of Indonesian neo-modernism, because Madjid's Renewal of Islamic Thinking or Indonesian Neo-modernism emerged as early as 1969, and it was not until 1973, when the latter visited Indonesia for the first time that Madjid and his peers came to know of Fazlur Rahman.[47] However, according to Barton, because their ideas were so similar the term neo-modernism was also used to describe Madjid's views. Then, in a later study Barton phrased it slightly differently: saying that once Fazlur Rahman's paradigmatic ideas became more renowned Indonesia's *Pembaruan* Thinking too was henceforth referred to as neo-modernism.[48] And yet, given the considerable differences between the early 'Young Natsir' and the later *Guru Bangsa*, equating the *Pembaruan* Movement with neo-modernism is, as also Barton had to admit earlier on, 'fraught with difficulty.'[49] While Fazlur Rahman may indeed have introduced the term, he subsequently referred to it only very sporadically, preferring the terms contemporary and postcolonial modernism instead.[50] Also Nurcholish Madjid did not use the term in his own publications. Even though the two key exponents of this strand of thought rarely used it, perhaps the term neo-modernism caught on because it was used when presenting Madjid's first essay collection and in Ali and Effendy's influential study of the reconstruction of Islamic thinking in Indonesia's New Order Period.

This obscure situation has consequences not only for the assessment of Madjid's intellectual development, but also for gauging the nature of Fazlur Rahman's influence on Madjid and on Indonesian Muslim intellectualism in general.

According to Kull, Fazlur Rahman was not just a 'source of inspiration,' but according to some it was difficult to exaggerate his impact on 'the continued formation of Nurcholish's methodology and ideas.[51] Not only had 'America opened up new intellectual horizons, [while] his encounter with Fazlur Rahman had given Nurcholish a broader perspective on the problems facing the Islamic world,' the experiences in Chicago also introduced him to 'the notion of "contextuality" as a heuristic device.'[52] Rahardjo says that under Fazlur Rahman's influence, 'Madjid became a scholar of religion par excellence.'[53] Munawar-Rachman meanwhile qualified neo-modernism as a hermeneutics, and also stated emphatically that 'this *"hermeneutics of neo-modernism"* [...] was initially developed by the American-Pakistani Muslim thinker Fazlur Rahman.'[54] Siti Fathimah presents a contradictory picture. On the one hand she agrees with Barton that Fazlur Rahman coined the term 'neo-modernism,' but also accepts the contention that 'The Limited Group' and Madjid had already developed their ideas independently from Fazlur Rahman in the 1960s. On the other hand she claims that it was Fazlur Rahman who introduced the principles of neo-modernism when he visited Indonesia at the beginning of the 1970s, as well as through Indonesians who studied with him in Chicago, only to note later a lack of recognition for Fazlur Rahman's influence among Indonesian Muslim intellectuals.[55]

One commentator on Fazlur Rahman's broader influence in Islamic Studies, himself a former student, argued that although his approach was part of a humanist agenda compatible with the work of other religious specialists at the University of Chicago like Eliade and Tillich, at the same time 'one cannot speak of a Fazlur Rahman school, or a Chicago school, or even of a Fazlur Rahman tradition in scholarship' on Islam.[56] Instead he saw him as part of a 'distinctive group of Islamic modernists, that is, those who call for a new hermeneutical stance to be taken to the whole Islamic corpus of knowledge,' in which Hanafi and Arkoun were also included.[57] Another commentator, Abdullah Saeed, notes that Fazlur Rahman has been particularly influential in Turkey and Indonesia.[58]

Such differences in opinion are indicative of how difficult it can be to establish the exact nature of intellectual influences and the way ideas travel. Instead of only looking at the impact of Fazlur Rahman on the Indonesian intellectual milieu, I propose therefore to consider a more dialectical process; a possibility that has not yet been entertained. Ideas may very well have travelled in the opposite direction, whereby Fazlur Rahman was also influenced by developments in Indonesia.

I have mentioned Fazlur Rahman's awareness of intellectual developments in Indonesia, but this does not mean that it only began with his first visit to the country in 1973; a recollection of his earlier experiences at McGill may also have had an impact. It will be recalled that, in *Islam in Modern History* (1957), the then director of McGill's Institute of Islamic Studies (1951–64), Wilfred Cantwell Smith, had written about Indonesia's potential for making interesting and enriching contributions to contemporary Islamic intellectualism. At that time, the future Minister of Religious Affairs, Mukti Ali was doing his graduate work in comparative religion under Smith's supervision. One year later Fazlur Rahman began his own stint at McGill (1958–61). Even if Mukti Ali was no longer there, this period coincides at least in part with Muhammad Rasjidi's tenure at the institute (1958–65). So there was ample opportunity for Fazlur Rahman to acquaint himself with ideas current among Indonesian Muslim intellectuals even before travelling to the country himself.

This is also supported by further coincidences in both timing and content between Mukti Ali, Nasution's IAIN reforms, Nurcholish Madjid's move to Chicago, and Fazlur Rahman's elaborations of his 'Islam and Social Change' project, which were not published until 1979, six years after his first visit to Indonesia and meeting with Madjid. To my mind, the fact Madjid was involved in both reforming the Indonesian Islamic education system and the 'Islam and Social Change' project makes it quite plausible that he acted as a conduit for this exchange. Moreover, although she does not develop it any further Kull has rightly noted that Fazlur Rahman dedicated a separate section in *Islam and Modernity* to Indonesia.[59] In 'Some Remarks on Indonesia,' he wrote approvingly of the emphasis on the intellectual quality in the country's Islamic education, through the introduction of a programme for the scientific study of Islam as well as the stress on the learning of Arabic.[60]

However, more problematic than resolving the mechanics of Fazlur Rahman's influence on Indonesia's Muslim intellectuals is Barton's equation of Madjid's earlier renewal thinking with neo-modernism. In view of Barton's own acknowledgement that the impetus for Madjid's provocative views in the early 1970s did not come from the Islamic tradition, and that Madjid's subsequent return to the Muslim heritage was due to the influence of Fazlur Rahman from the mid-1970s onwards necessarily calls that equation into question.[61]

Then there is the issue of Madjid's overall status and reputation as a Muslim intellectual. As was noted earlier, commentators agree that after his return from Chicago Madjid was indisputably regarded as an all-round scholar of Islam with a solid understanding of and appreciation for the classical heritage, a recognition that was definitely withheld by his critics in the 1970s who explicitly called his academic credentials into question.[62] On these grounds alone, I would argue that Madjid's early Renewal Thinking and neo-modernism constitute two distinct phases in his intellectual development. In spite of Giddens' misgivings about making such temporal distinctions in the development of a thinker's ideas (he was thinking of Marx), in the present case distinguishing between the 'young' and 'mature Madjid' can actually help correct certain inaccuracies in earlier assessments of his work and influence.[63]

The most convincing evidence for Madjid's shift from advocating a straightforward—'classical' modernisation agenda towards a more careful consideration of how the civilisational legacy of Islam and concrete local cultural circumstances may contribute to that process is provided by the analysis of Madjid's own writings. An examination of his first edited volume of articles written between 1968 and 1985 shows that, throughout the 1970s, there was a predominant interest in the issues of modernity and rationality. However, by the mid-1980s, the absolutised Islamic imperative to modernise, based on empirical and historicist-functionalist grounds, has given way to a more culturally sensitive and hermeneutically inclined approach. There is a stronger appreciation of the relevance of local cultural circumstances and the specific historical experience of Indonesia's Muslim society. Both his PhD thesis and the collection of translations from the classics released in 1984 are indicative of a growing concern with Indonesian Islam's embeddedness in the wider context of Islamic civilisation.

I suggest that, while I agree with Barton that there was no radical break in Madjid's thinking during the 1968–1972 period, there certainly occurred a significant shift in focus while he was in Chicago. His interest in the classical Islamic heritage at large, combined with a deeper appreciation of the specific circumstances of Indonesian Islam fused his earlier ideas on renewal into the broader horizon of a new hermeneutical circle.

My claim that there was a shift in Nurcholish Madjid's thinking after 1984, in both substance and strategy is corroborated by Azra's assertions to that point in an interview with Ann Kull. The mature Madjid no longer focused 'wholly on the issue of modernism and modernity,' and no longer used terms such as secularisation. Instead he had become engaged in a social engineering exercise 'towards the development of an Islamic civilisation (*peradaban Islam*) that would be both viable in a post-modern milieu and strongly rooted in classical

Islamic tradition.'[64] With respect to the substance of Madjid's thought, Azra noted a reliance on the Islamic tradition in its totality. Although critical of the Muslim modernists' propensity to 'fiqhism,' Madjid saw a contextualised *fiqh* as conducive to a reconstruction of Shari'a.[65] At the same time he developed a vivid interest in the esoteric (Sufi) dimensions of the Islamic heritage. However, Azra also added that with his interest in modern humanism, Madjid was too complex a thinker 'to pin down to a certain "absolute" typology.'[66]

Although a prominent participant in developing Muslim thought in Indonesia, the fact that Madjid was not only embedded in a complex social formation, but also took part in a cosmopolitan global academic and Muslim intellectual milieu poses a challenge to accurately gauging the nature and extent of his influence. His early career as an intellectual was shaped by the possibilities afforded by the newly emerging New Order regime, leading some to characterise him as an accommodationist. However, as Vatikiotis observed:

Today, contemporary Muslim intellectuals, like Nurcholis [sic] Madjid, are satisfied what looked like a sell-out to the government in fact allowed the incubation of a more far-reaching and meaningful Islamic movement: We have much greater freedom to interpret our religion and equate it to the demands of modernity without being apologetic.[67]

The *Keterbukaan* or 'Opening Up' in the later New Order period (1988–1994), coinciding with the latter part of Munawir Sjadzali's term in office as Minister of Religious Affairs, enabled Madjid to carve out a niche in the Indonesian equivalent of the 'divine supermarket,' developing new initiatives in tandem with Abdurrahman Wahid.[68] We should namely not lose sight of the fact that formulating this new Islamic discourse was not a project of Nurcholish Madjid alone. In an early mapping of Indonesian Muslim intellectualism in the post-Renewal Thinking Period, Ali and Effendy had already juxtaposed Madjid with Abdurrahman Wahid as key representatives of Islamic neo-modernism.[69] Barton, and Bakri and Mudhofir too, have made comparative studies of this duo.

There are indeed similarities: both were exposed to a 'double education' and drew inspiration from the Western human sciences, creating a certain conformity in methodological approach and ideas, which had been set in motion a generation earlier by Rasjidi, Nasution and Mukti Ali. Aside from sharing this universal humanist outlook, Gus Dur's empiricism bears an affinity to Madjid's inductive methodology. Moreover, both were also acutely concerned with the need for reviving the spiritual aspects of the religious life of Muslim modernists.

But there are also differences: Whereas Madjid's closely resembled the intellectualism of Fazlur Rahman's ideas, in Abdurrahman Wahid's case 'neo-modernism had been his way of thinking for quite a while, disseminated it through the Indonesian version of the *Ahlussunnah wal jama'ah* culture [as embodied by] the NU.'[70] Although a further analysis of his views is beyond the purview of this book, it is important to stress that, in contrast to Madjid's scholarly and historical interests, Gus Dur's concerns are more acutely pragmatic and contemporary. His interpretation of the *Ahlussunnah wal jama'ah* doctrine, in Indonesia often abbreviated to *Aswaja*,[71] has been described as an 'intellectual improvisation of traditional doctrine,' suffused by the 'universal spirit of humankind' and where Madjid had some hesitation in drawing parallels, Wahid's concern with issues of poverty and justice were directly influenced by Latin American liberation theology.[72]

Perhaps the clearest indication of the multifarious legacy of neo-modernism is the non-identical twin offspring of Madjid and Gus Dur's rethinking of Islam. On the one hand, there are the *Anak Muda NU* or 'Young NU Members,' sometimes also referred to as *Postra* or 'Post-Traditionalists.'[73] These are the exponents of a new hybrid culture prevailing among a younger generation of NU intellectuals; the outcome of a moving back and forth between their often rural NU roots in reformed *pesantren*, exposure to a more scholarly-inclined Islamic education at IAINs in the country's major cities, and their subsequent employment in NGOs and think tanks active in the interstices of urban and rural Indonesia.[74]

Originating from smaller towns in rural areas they are more readily identifiable with Abdurrahman Wahid's outlook than the intellectualised strand of 'urban Sufism' developed by Madjid, which caters predominantly to middle-class and upper-middle-class elites.[75] In the cities too groups of young intellectuals, not dissimilar to the slightly older *Mazhab Ciputat*, began organising themselves around initiatives such as *Jaringan Islam Liberal* (JIL) or 'Liberal Islam Network.' Whereas their intellectualism betrays a greater affinity with Nurcholish Madjid, such academic inclinations seem less well-equipped to penetrate into other segments of society.[76] These are relatively recent phenomena which only began springing up in the wake of the fall of the New Order regime. However, in the last decade or so, the first studies and analyses of these new exponents of contemporary Muslim thinking and action in Indonesia have started to appear.[77]

When it comes to the creative and innovative use of the tradition advocated by Madjid, it is now possible to re-appropriate from his critics the conventional term 'renewal' used in the Islamic intellectual tradition for the revival of both rigorous scholarship and vigorous piety. After all, Madjid 'did not relate innovation to *bid'a* but to *tajdī-'d*—to be achieved only through *ijtihād*.'[78] Moreover, invoking to the traditionalist Muslim view that in every Islamic century a scholar is recognised as that era's '*seorang tokoh pembaru*' (*mujaddid*, renewer),[79] Bakri and Mudhofir saw no reason why such a figure could not arise in Indonesia, claiming Cak Nur had all the characteristics. On the other hand, the term might again blur the distinction between the 'early' and 'later' Madjid.

Such challenges of existing categories are, as I argue throughout this book, the hallmark of the hybrid new Muslim intellectual operating in a Third Space where cultures and academic disciplines intersect. Nurcholish Madjid's prominent but exceptional position as a 'new Muslim intellectual' on the interstices of different intellectual milieus, is also reflected in Bakri and Mudhofir's observation that he 'stood virtually on his own in Indonesia's intellectual configuration.'[80] 'The particularity of Nurcholish Madjid, the influential proselytiser among Indonesia's Muslim intelligentsia,' noted by his close intellectual collaborator Dawam Rahardjo, is yet another affirmation of his dual role as an initiator of intellectual debate and a theologian, in the sense used by McCutcheon for those scholars of religion who see themselves also as custodians or 'caretakers' of existing traditions.[81]

'Our "heritage" is not a sealed package we pass from hand to hand, without ever opening, but rather a treasure from which we draw by the handful and which by this very act is replenished.'

Paul Ricoeur, *The Conflict of Interpretations*

'...in his work of reconstruction the interpreter must follow the signposts erected by Spinoza himself and, secondarily, the indications which Spinoza left accidentally in his writings.'

Leo Strauss, 'How to Study Spinoza's *Theologico-Political Treatise*' in: *Persecution and the Art of Writing*

'The Scientists are in terror and the European mind stops.'

Ezra Pound, Canto CXV

6

THE TRANSFORMATION OF
A MUSLIM MODERNIST

THE EARLY YEARS OF HASAN HANAFI

The Egyptian philosopher Hasan Hanafi is one of the thinkers from the Arabic-speaking world who has found an audience among Indonesians with an interest in innovative and progressive interpretations of Islam. Part of an explanation for this may lie in the fact that two features in his thought have an affinity with the ideas of Nurcholish Madjid. Hanafi too is convinced of the universal validity and applicability of the teachings of Islam, but that it also has to accommodate different historical and cultural circumstances. Where Madjid focussed on the particularities of Indonesia, Hanafi is primarily occupied with explaining how Islam can function in the contemporary Egyptian setting. This would also explain why these two Muslim intellectuals have primarily published in Indonesian and Arabic respectively. Another commonality is the distinction between the vertical (spiritual and individual) and horizontal (collective and social) dimensions of the Islamic message, although Hanafi concentrates almost exclusively on the horizontal dimension and does not elaborate on the vertical one.

Hanafi's scholarly work in the field of Islamic studies is driven by the search for a new mode of inquiry which uses the Islamic heritage to develop a comprehensive method of philosophical investigation applicable to both the individual and collective lives of Muslims. Both this scope and the volume of Hanafi's oeuvre pose a challenge to presenting a manageable overview of his work as a Muslim thinker. As

105

with Madjid, it is therefore helpful to distinguish between different phases in the development of Hanafi's thought, except that in this case, instead of 'young' and 'mature,' I suggest using the terms 'early' and 'later,' because in my view Hanafi's early methodological work is anything but immature and must be considered as defining for the increasingly ideologically informed writings of his later career. In fact, almost the opposite seems true, since various commentators are of the opinion that the political agenda underlying Hanafi's later work compromises its scholarly rigour.[1] However, in spite of the fact that his writings have also been characterised as heterogeneous and diffuse, I claim there is nevertheless a discernable, pervasive and sustained consistency to Hanafi's approach.[2] The following chapters will demonstrate that the ingredients for Hanafi's ideological motivations and his later politicised writings are already found in the earliest writings dating from his postgraduate years at the Sorbonne in the late 1950s and early 1960s.

Aside from this shift in focus, Hanafi's writings can also be broken down according to the different audiences they address: namely, his intellectual peers and the general educated public.[3] In a survey of contemporary Islamic philosophy, Hanafi makes his own distinction between 'professional philosophy' and other 'important research projects, gaining more and more popularity via philosophers.'[4] I suggest that the methodological writings published between 1965 and 1980 belong to that first category whereas the increasingly engaged elaborations from the 1980s onward fit under the second rubric.

Those students of Hanafi's work who have paid attention to the massive three-volume dissertation he wrote in French for the degree of *doctorat d'état* have primarily engaged with the substance rather than intellectual provenance of the methodology he has developed there.[5] This concern with method was instigated by the state of crisis affecting the study of Islam in both the Muslim world and the Western academe. It is also reminiscent of Edmund Husserl's *The Crisis of the European Sciences and Transcendental Phenomenology* with which Hanafi became acquainted during his studies at the Sorbonne. However, Hanafi has a more explicit openness to the world whereby Husserl's phenomenology is refracted through the lens of an existentialist approach advocated by Paul Ricoeur, who acted as his supervisor. This turned Hanafi's methodology into what his mentor called one of the 'heresies' issuing from the Freiburg disciplinarian's search for a *Strenge Wissenschaft* or 'rigorous science.'

In his principal thesis entitled, *The Methods of Exegesis*, Hanafi quarries the heritage of traditional Islamic learning for an academically rigorous philosophical methodology.[6] In *The Exegesis of Phenomenology* this is subsequently expanded into a method for examining the religious phenomenon in general, and finally applied in an existentialist-hermeneutical interrogation of The New Testament, entitled *The Phenomenology of Exegesis*.[7] A close reading of these earliest writings in the next chapter will demonstrate how the approaches developed in these theses interlock into a comprehensive method for philosophical investigation and function as the propadeutics from which Hanafi extrapolated his massive Heritage and Renewal Project, conceived as a tripartite multi-volume analysis of the Islamic and Western heritages and their proposed synthesis into a renewal or reconstruction of an allegedly authentic Islamic method. This project was launched in 1980 with a study entitled *Heritage and Renewal: Our Attitude towards the Old Heritage*.[8] As a general introduction to this undertaking it forms not only the methodological hinge between the scholarly writings of the academic philosopher for an erudite audience of peers and those of the 'prophetic' public intellectual addressing the educated segments of the Muslim *ummah*, but affirms also the sustained methodological consistency of Hanafi's approach, without invalidating the earlier-noted criticisms of the degree of redundancy and superficiality marring his later writings.[9]

This chapter contains a heuristic survey of the sources of Hanafi's reworking of Islamic thought, mapping the philosophical influences and identifying his principal interlocutors in an attempt to balance the insider view of Islamic modernism and the outsider perspective of Western human sciences in the envisaged general method of philosophical investigation.

The Early Formation of a Muslim Modernist

Hanafi's intellectual roots can be traced through an autobiographical sketch he published in 1989.[10] Structured as a multi-layered narrative rather than a strictly chronological account, Hanafi discusses his maturing as a scholar and thinker under three rubrics dealing with religious and philosophical awareness, and life experience respectively, roughly covering the years from 1952 to 1966.

During his undergraduate years a student of philosophy at the University of Cairo (1952–56) he became interested in religion and briefly joined the Muslim Brotherhood. Disillusioned by the way Islam was taught at university, he notes how he considered Ibn Sina's philosophy so off-putting that he dropped studying Islamic philosophy and *kalam* altogether on the grounds that these were merely 'hypothetic theories which did not teach [anything] about Muslims,' while clashes with his professors over the personal tone of his essays alienated him further from his intellectual heritage.[11] Consequently, in his private time he began reading the works of Muslim Brotherhood activists, Islamic reformists, and modernists, such as Hasan al-Ashmawi, Abd al-Qadir al-Awda, Muhammad al-Ghazali, Said Ramadan, Abul Hasan Nadwi, but especially Sayyid Qutb and the Indo-Pakistani poet and philosopher Muhammad Iqbal.[12] Summing up his years as an undergraduate in Cairo, Hanafi opined that he had 'learned nothing in university, except for reacting against the crisis in Islamic studies.'[13] These experiences, combined with the impact of the political repression of the Muslim Brothers under Nasser, resulted in 1956 in a personal crisis, developing into a pattern, he said, that has since repeated itself every ten years.[14]

This experience coincided with the significant change in the writings of Sayyid Qutb. Starting out in the 1930s as a man of letters influenced by Abbas Mahmud al-Aqqad and his *Diwan* group, Qutb joined the new literary trend which 'drew upon the Arab-linguistic and Islamic religious traditions of Egypt's collective heritage (*turāth*).'[15] During this phase of his career he was primarily concerned with asserting a spiritual East against a materialistic West, a preoccupation resonant with the ideas of Muhammad Iqbal, whose notion of 'the human soul as the source of poetic creativity' exercised a considerable influence on Qutb.[16]

With *Social Justice in Islam*, he produced his 'first significant Islamist work,' but Qutb's religious turn was not completed until he returned from a two-year stay in the United States (1948–50), an experience which had only confirmed his dissatisfaction with the West's perceived materialism and superficiality.[17] Deciding to join the Muslim Brotherhood, he later exclaimed dramatically that 'he was born in 1951.'[18] As the organisation's chief ideologue, Sayyid Qutb briefly joined the executive council of the Free Officers Movement, which staged the 1952 revolution and ousted King Faruq. However, after a failed attempt on President Nasser in 1954, Sayyid Qutb was singled out as one of the latter's personal targets in the ensuing persecution of the Muslim Brothers.[19] The lengthy incarceration that followed is generally regarded as the reason for his further radicalisation:

In prison, Qutb abstracted himself from all except the Qurānic text, which became his only intellectual framework and reference to life. Being absorbed in the text made him to structure a utopian political existence, as opposed to the wicked universal institutions webbed together under the umbrella of colonialism and Zionism, and permitted him to image the existence of an angelic Muslim vanguard opposed to the reality of a devilish hypocritical society.[20]

From then on Sayyid Qutb rejected all other philosophical, theological and spiritual thought, relying exclusively on the Qur'anic message itself for the formulation of an all-encompassing system of explanation and moral direction, which he called *fiqh al-waqi'i* or 'New Realist Science.'[21] In defiance of al-Afghani, Abduh, and Iqbal, who believed humankind was capable of attaining (some) knowledge on his own accord, Qutb sided now with the theocentric views of Maududi and 'considered the secrets of human knowledge as known to God alone.'[22] With increasing frequency the notion *hakimiyya Allah* or 'sovereignty of God' begins to occur in Qutb's vocabulary, regarding it as the only panacea against the prevailing human condition likened to the condition the Arabs found themselves in prior to the arrival of Islam: *jahiliyya* or 'Era of Ignorance.'[23]

The resulting 'icon text,' entitled *In the Shadow of the Qur'an*, combines a highly personal reading of the Qur'an with an indirectness and abstraction analogous to Gramsci's *Prison Diaries* that also affected later editions of *Social Justice in Islam*.[24] Sayyid Qutb's revolutionary vision culminated in what in hindsight can be considered his political testament: *Ma'alim fi'l-tariq*, which can be translated as 'Milestones' or 'Signposts on the Road.' Its publication shortly after his release from prison in 1964 led to new charges of treason, and his eventual execution in 1966. Although Salvatore claims that Sayyid Qutb was almost entirely banished from the public sphere during the early 1960s and that therefore his writings 'had no immediate impact on the corresponding, contemporary public arena,' does not mean his work did not affect a budding new generation of intellectuals.[25] Perhaps even more important, this generation was probably still acutely aware of the multifarious character of Qutb's legacy which is now often ignored.

His influence on Hanafi is a case in point. In his own monograph-length study of Sayyid Qutb, he notes that the latter's literary phase (1930–50) was actually the longest of his intellectual career. Identifying *Artistic Imagery in the Qur'an* (1945) and *Signs of the Resurrection in the Qur'an* (1947) as transitional works between Qutb's literary and religious phases, Hanafi regrets that the notion of 'concept,' 'idea,' or 'image' and the theory of aesthetics which Qutb developed during that stage have not found their way into the writings and ideologies of Islamic activists and organisations who claim to be inspired by him.[26]

Hanafi's assessment of Qutb's radicalisation as a direct result of his imprisonment and maltreatment during Nasser's persecution of the Muslim Brotherhood is in line with those of leading Western experts on Sayyid Qutb.[27] He even speculates that had his own association with the Muslim Brothers caused him to go underground then he might have ended up writing in the vein of Qutb's *Milestones*.[28]

However by that time Hanafi had already left for France, where, thanks to the close contacts between the philosophy departments of Cairo University and the Sorbonne, he had obtained a place at the Parisian university. Arriving on the eve of the Suez Crisis and the eruption of the Algerian war of independence, Hanafi found himself in a city fermenting with political and intellectual turmoil.[29] But where Arkoun remained wary of the revolutionary élan permeating both academic life and wider public discourse, amidst this heightened drive towards decolonisation and the rise of the Non-Aligned Movement, Hanafi readily identified his own philosophical preoccupations with the emancipation of the Third World. Moreover, the personal disillusionment over the demise of the Muslim Brotherhood after the arrest of Sayyid Qutb was alleviated by the exposure to the new intellectual influences he received in Paris.

In his autobiography Hanafi notes that his philosophical awareness was only really awakened when he began writing his PhD research plan for an investigation into the 'general Islamic method' of philosophy, which he envisaged taking two forms: 'a fixed form of concept and system, and a dynamic form of potentiality and movement.' Whereas in Hanafi's own view such a point of departure had an affinity with Sayyid Qutb's New Realist Science, his French mentors pointed to its close resemblance to Kant's philosophy. Aware that his project faced a similar challenge as the Kantian synthesis of *a priori* and *a posteriori* truths derived from rationalism and empiricist investigations respectively into a transcendental idealism, Hanafi nevertheless persisted in presenting his plan in Islamic terms. The outline included therefore a 'long introduction of the thought of the Muslim Brotherhood and the obstacles it faced,' as well as copious references to other Islamic modernists. And yet, the articulation of such a philosophical method would require a composite intellectual input. Apart from channelling the thought of a variety of Muslim thinkers, another tributary of Western thought began feeding into the envisaged methodology of philosophical inquiry as well, and Hanafi noted how these various strands actually 'came together in the philosophy of Iqbal.'[30] Thus Iqbal fulfilled not just a double role as a mediator of Islamic reformist thought and source for philosophical ideas of Western provenance, but he also replaced Sayyid Qutb as the main motivator for Hanafi's attempt to develop an Islamic method of philosophical investigation.[31]

Attending British-run schools in Lahore where Muhammad Iqbal was educated, among others, by the Arabist Sir Thomas Arnold (1864–1930), Iqbal graduated with a master's degree in philosophy. Initially opting for a career in teaching, he then decided to continue his studies in Europe. Arriving in Cambridge in 1905, he worked with the neo-Hegelian McTaggart while also obtaining a law degree. Moving on to Heidelberg and Munich, Iqbal completed his overseas studies with a PhD in philosophy on the basis of a thesis on Persian metaphysics.[32] Aside from demonstrating a 'remarkable knowledge of European theology from Thomas Aquinas to Adolf von Harnack, and of German philosophical thought,' the dissertation was an important 'contribution to the history of religions since it brought to light some Persian Sufis who had been hitherto unknown in Europe.'[33] As an exponent of the first generation from a Muslim community for whom Western education had become acceptable Iqbal can be considered as an early precursor of the new Muslim intellectuals discussed in this book.[34]

In the South Asian part of the Muslim world, however, Iqbal's stature as a Muslim thinker and spiritual father of Pakistan rests primarily on his reputation as a poet. Juxtaposing Iqbal with other Muslim modernists in *Overcoming Tradition and Modernity*, political scientist Robert Lee remains sceptical: 'Although [Iqbal] rescued the "true Islam" from the grasp of reason, it is less clear that he saved it from the ravages of autonomy and particularity, which are fundamental to his definition of authenticity.'[35] In long philosophical poems in Persian, such as *The Secrets of the Self*, *Mysteries of Selflessness*, or the poem 'East and West,' the tensions of such binary thinking as the 'brain-malady' of the West versus the East's 'heart-malady' were explored, denied, but ultimately not resolved.[36] In Lee's assessment:

To appreciate Iqbal's significance to modern writers, one must see him as a theorist of authenticity, seeking to liberate humanity from the clutches of both

111

tradition and modernity, from the mysticism of the East and the reason of the West, from the imperialism of the West and the submissiveness of the East.[37]

The central idea in Iqbal's thought was the notion of a strong, vigorous and creative self, leading to the claim that 'in great action alone the self of man becomes united with God without losing its own identity.'[38] Such assertions rested on a view that the world as we know it is a product of human enterprise. In the case of Sayyid Qutb too, inspiration for his literary studies had in part come from this emphasis on individual human creativity. This aspect of Iqbal's thought would become important for the reorientation of Hanafi's philosophical project from Qutb's theocentrism towards a more anthropocentric approach. The latter's dualism of the 1950s and 1960s was increasingly at odds with Iqbal's attempts to synthesise Western and Eastern thought. Consequently, in his later writings Qutb objected to the poet's exaggerated celebration of the ego and also criticised Iqbal's 'intellectual aimlessness.'[39]

Of crucial significance for the present account is Iqbal's seminal work, *The Reconstruction of Religious Thought in Islam* (1930).[40] Based on a series of lectures at the universities of Hyderabad, Madras and Aligarh, it is one of the very few scholarly philosophical discourses he has produced, receiving a mixed reception among scholars of Islam. While McDonough notes that it is only thanks to this publication that 'we know of his maturity and originality as a philosopher,' Hamilton Gibb insists that 'had it not been for Iqbāl's prestige as poet and leader in Indian Islam, it is doubtful whether so revolutionary and heretical a work would ever have been published.'[41] Gibb's student Fazlur Rahman, by contrast, hailed it as the only systematic attempt to devise a modern metaphysics of Islam. While he admitted that Iqbal's reconstruction was primarily structured around contemporary elements of thought rather than the Qur'an, he took issue with Gibb's assessment of Iqbal's philosophy being less faithful to 'the Qur'ānic matrix of ideas' than Ash'ari theology, which in Fazlur Rahman's view represents an 'almost total distortion of Islam.'[42] The significance of Iqbal's contribution to Islamic studies lies in the fact 'that the work of Islamic reconstruction does not mean a mere adjustment to modern conditions but a new interpretation of the inner meaning of Islam.'[43]

Iqbal's denial of 'dichotomies such as being and becoming, man and God, mind and matter, reason and intuition, science and religion, sacred and profane, subject and object, thinking and action' also seem to reflect the necessary liminality of the creative individual posited by Mikhail Bakhtin.[44] This is what Majeed calls the 'interrogative nature of Iqbal's work,' which suspends any final judgment on what Islam exactly means.[45] *The Reconstruction* aims 'to reconcile and validate earlier Islamic thought with and through modern European thought and science.' The 'cosmopolitan eclecticism' underlying Iqbal's hybrid identity composed of idealist Western philosophy and Indo-Persian poetic sensitivity, turned the author into an early postcolonial intellectual trying to subvert Western dominance.[46]

Initially Hanafi was primarily attracted to Iqbal's discourse on life, creativity, and innovation, but soon sympathised with his 'Islamic thinking, which united past and present, imagining a Muslim reality behind [Ibn Sina's] theory of the ten intellects [...]. This was the kind of philosophy [Hanafi] wanted to examine.' Although he was told that such ideas were associated with Western thinkers and philosophies, such as Bergson and existentialism, Hanafi stated that based on his own impression of Iqbal he thought something similar could be achieved in an Islamic context. By placing Iqbal in conversation with, for example, Kierkegaard, Sartre and Marcel, Hanafi envisaged a crystallisation of an 'enlightened Islamic position.'[47]

At the Sorbonne: Introduction to European Philosophy

It was at the Sorbonne that Hanafi seriously began exploring French and German philosophy on his own accord, gradually reaching an understanding of how the European schools of thought were connected to each other by a 'law of action and reaction.' He became convinced that it was therefore possible to construct an understanding of European consciousness as consisting of a deductive (*a priori*) line of thought based on rationalism and an inductive or empiricist (*a posteriori*) strand.[48] Indicative of Hanafi's awareness of Ricoeur's Philosophy of the Will, he distinguished a third: 'the school of life and volition' oscillating between the other two. It also reflects the view of a skeptic thinker like Isaiah Berlin who accepted the 'truism that European history is a kind of dialectic.'[49] Taken together they could thus be related to philosophy's three core concerns: soul, nature, and being. The European consciousness associated with these philosophies was also grounded in three primary sources. While the Sorbonne introduced him to its Graeco-Roman and Judeo-Christian origins, he explored the third one—the modern European intellectual milieu—by himself. Thus he became aware of the parochial setting of the European philosophical tradition, discovering that, in spite of its claims to universality and comprehensiveness, it was circumscribed by its own specific circumstances.[50] As will become clear later, this realisation foreshadows the critique of Western civilisation in Hanafi's Heritage and Renewal Project, which has as one of its objectives to 'confine Western thinking to within its proper boundaries.'[51]

Hanafi already had a particular interest in German idealism, phenomenology, the 'Hegelian left' and Marx's German Ideology, tracing them back to his wartime experiences in Egypt, which had kindled an admiration for all 'things German.'[52] He was especially fascinated by the 'philosopher of resistance' Johann Gottlieb Fichte.[53] Even though he presents him as a representative of German idealism it is important to bear in mind that, as 'the true father of romanticism,' Fichte also stands at the forefront of the opposition to French Enlightenment thinking.[54] A more intimate acquaintance with German romanticism and its aftermath was only acquired during Hanafi's studies in France, recounting in his autobiographical sketch the impressions left by Hegel, the German romantics, Schleiermacher, Dilthey, Gillot,[55] Nietzsche, and vitalists like Bergson and Driesch as foundational for contemporary hermeneutics.[56] This familiarisation with what Berlin has called German romanticism's challenge to 'the levelling rationalist pedantry of French thought' made Hanafi acutely aware of the complexities he faced in formulating an alternative Islamic method that could pose a counterweight to European philosophy and function as a 'grammar of resistance.'[57]

Apart from the romantics, Hanafi confessed an interest in other 'rebel-thinkers' like Spinoza and Kierkegaard. Although admitting that he never quite understood the latter, he considers Spinoza's Tractatus Theologico-Politicus as a seminal contribution to European philosophy, adding that in Bergson's view 'every person has two philosophies: his own and Spinoza's.'[58] In a later publication he also identifies his own approach of rationalism as a form of 'spinozism.'[59]

A compilation of Hasan Hanafi's intellectual genealogy is not complete without mentioning his most important mentor during these Parisian years: Jean Guitton (1901–1999). Although his name does not feature prominently in Hanafi's writings the influence exercised by this French theologian and philosopher on Hanafi's development as a scholar is corroborated by their respective autobiographies. When discussing his years at the Sorbonne, Guitton singles out Hanafi as a student who left an indelible impression.[60] Hanafi's own account is even more telling:

For my entire philosophical formation I am indebted to Jean Guitton, professor of philosophy, student of Bergson, and Catholic renewer. The first layperson in history to address the Vatican Council, friend of Popes John XXIII and Paul VI, member of the French Academy [...], he was my professor and teacher. I called him 'My Christ,' and he called me his 'Beloved Disciple.'[61]

Aside from guiding Hanafi through Western philosophy and introducing him to Christian theology:

[Guitton] had the most far-reaching influence on my awareness of life, on the move from idealism to realism, from thinking to being. [From him] I learned to give lectures and how to write for the masses [...] as a philosopher, he was capable of speaking to the initiated and the general public [alike]. My relationship with my professor was like that of Aristotle with Plato, Marx with Feuerbach, and Feuerbach with Hegel.[62]

Guitton's influence was also significant for Hanafi's approach to method, recording how the latter once told him: 'What interested you were methods. In other words, you were a professor of methods, as well as—as you sometimes used to say—of strategies.'[63] Apart from introducing him to the history of European philosophy through his lectures, Guitton's advanced research seminars were crucial in preparing Hanafi for 'how to reconcile opposite views,' an ability for which Hanafi described him as 'the philosopher of ecumene.'[64] Guitton's courses did not so much give a view of a subject as open up a way, 'revealing the principles and methods, which could clarify no matter what, placing us in the presence of the thing itself, as Husserl used to say.'[65] In spite of their adherence to different religious traditions, Hanafi observed:

You are Christian, I am Muslim. You follow Jesus and I Muhammad. But when I listen to you, I find your way of presenting Christianity different from [other] Christian professors. You seem to ignore all religion; you depart from ignorance, *disinformation*, and from what I call 'point *zero* [...] and what Kant called *pure reason*. [...] Like Muhammad, you are an iconoclast.[66]

I suggest that such avoidance of fixed positions by a Christian thinker encouraged Hanafi to try something similar under the rubric of his envisaged 'general Islamic method.' What Guitton had discovered through his search for the lowest common denominator of the schools of *Solvitur in Excelsis* [Salvation is in the Supreme] and *Le Christ ecartelé* [Christ torn apart], Hanafi 'found in the unity of the Islamic sciences,' the defining motif underlying both his first methodological investigations and later reconstruction of the disciplines of traditional Islamic learning.[67]

In the autobiographical section entitled 'life experience,' Hanafi stressed how his intellectual maturing was not only informed by academic study, but also contains a more personal dimension that made him realise that philosophical idealism cannot be equated with real life, which is an altogether more comprehensive experience.[68] As someone who for some time had tried to pursue a dual career as an academic and performing musician, Hanafi was torn between music as beauty without thought, and philosophy as thought without beauty, until he discovered that in the philosophies of Hegel, Fichte, Schelling, Kierkegaard and Bergson 'beauty and thought were united.'[69] During his sojourn in Europe, he also spent the summers travelling to visit places associated with the poets, literati, composers, and thinkers he was interested in—especially the German romantics whom he regarded as the combined embodiment of idealism and existentialism.

The defining event for the development of Hanafi's methodology was his encounter with Edmund Husserl's philosophical phenomenology, which was very much *en vogue* at the time.[70] The significance of that discovery can be gleaned from the autobiographical account in which it is not only recognised as instrumental to his philosophical awakening, but also for Hanafi's nascent consciousness of life, for which Husserl forms a nodal point of a variety of philosophical influences. When by 1960, he had read through Husserl's entire published oeuvre, it completed a transformation from religiously informed consciousness via German idealism into a *Lebensphilosophie* with discernable traces of Bergson's *vitalisme*.[71] Contemplating the sum of these experiences Hanafi noted:

Discovering the world of consciousness, and applying it in a spontaneous way to the natural world, transforming the reality confronting me into a living experience, [...] I rejected abstraction and superficiality. [...] When I was in high school, I had wandered from discipline to discipline, until I ended up in philosophy. I was dismayed that it was a discipline composed of the humanities without the sciences. It seemed to me that the humanities could be changed into an exact science.[72]

A word of caution is in place regarding the use of the word 'science' in the context of human sciences. No doubt under the influence of

Husserl's argument that the very 'mathematisation of nature' bears responsibility for the crisis in the European sciences, Hanafi notes that science has become synonymous with the natural sciences.[73] Even though in his own writings he is not consistent, Hanafi proposes that, when speaking of fields of scholarly investigation within the purview of the human sciences, 'the word "discipline" is a better translation than the word "science."'[74]

The important transformation caused by the reading of Husserl, whose plea for dealing with the things-in-themselves, enabled Hanafi to trade idealism for realism and then move on to the existentialist philosophies of Heidegger's *Sein und Zeit* and Sartre's *L'Être et le néant*.[75] In his autobiography Hanafi notes somewhat arrogantly that, within the timeframe of his own eight-year journey from his studies of rationalist idealism to an existentialist engagement with life, realism and being, he was able to complete a trajectory encompassing four centuries of modern European philosophy with its two moments of consciousness: the 'thinking self' or *cogito* of rationalism, and the 'existing self' or *ego* of existentialism.[76] Aside from the immediate impact of Husserl, I also think that the influence of Hanafi's mentor Paul Ricoeur must be taken into account. Ricoeur's intimate knowledge of Husserl's phenomenology,[77] combined with his ability for the charitable or generous interpretation of opposing philosophical positions, must be considered as instrumental in helping Hanafi find a way to synthesise the rationalist and existentialist aspects of modern Western thought.

However, as a Muslim thinker intent on developing an Islamic methodology, Hanafi's own teleological orientation remains also very much informed by the same drives and objectives as those of Muhammad Iqbal. To the latter teleology was not a preconceived goal, but 'a progressive formation of fresh starts, purposes, and ideal scales of value as the process of life grows and expands.'[78] Robinson interprets this 'sense of personal responsibility, and the centrality of action on Earth' suffusing Iqbal's work as a prime example of what he calls 'this-worldly Islam.'[79] Moreover, Robinson's reference to the final words of *The Reconstruction* also points up a parallel between Husserl and Iqbal's interest in the development of the self or ego in the context of Western philosophy which Hanafi took to heart:

It is in the ego's effort to *be* something that he discovers his final opportunity to sharpen his objectivity and acquire a more fundamental 'I am,' which finds

117

evidence of its reality not in the Cartesian 'I think' but in the Kantian 'I can.' The end of the ego's quest is not emancipation from the limitations of individuality; it is, on the other hand, a more precise definition of it. The final act is not an intellectual act, but a vital act which deepens the whole being of the ego, and sharpens his will with the creative assurance that the world is not something to be merely seen or known through concepts, but something to be made and re-made by continuous action.[80]

The Genesis of the Sorbonne Theses: Criticising Islamic Studies

Hanafi's familiarisation with Husserl coincided with drafting a first version of his principal thesis in 1960. Originally it had been the plan to work on rationalist and existentialist philosophies of religions through respective examinations of Kant and Kierkegaard, but after a reading of Husserl's *Ideas* he discovered that it was possible:

...to retain the optimism of idealism and leave the pessimism of existentialism behind. I held on to reason and its role in idealism, and said farewell to the irrational in existentialism. My objective remained idealist, and I dropped the nonsensical of existentialism. [...] To my mind, reason and reality are two sides of the same coin.[81]

On the plane of general philosophical outlook merging these two philosophies offered the prospect of reconciling rationalism with the challenges of romanticism and thus contribute to the *Aufhebung* of the propensity of Western philosophy to think in binary terms. On the methodological level, it appears Hanafi had also picked up on Ricoeur's observation that, as far as method and modes of analyses are concerned, existential phenomenologies remain indebted to Kant even if their inspiration comes from elsewhere and they have other concerns.[82]

Initially he had intended to make a comparative study of the way his French teachers had presented Kant's attempts to reconcile *a priori* and *a posteriori* methodologies for establishing scientific truths and the challenge confronting Muslim thinkers as they tried to accommodate the ideal order of revelation and the world as a natural system within the Doctrine of Unity or *tawhid*.[83] Now he was convinced that the envisaged general Islamic method could even meet the double challenge posed by the Enlightenment claim to universal but ahistorical validity and the romantic-existential slide into relativism. Having become conversant with Descartes and Husserl,[84] whose philosophies he regarded as the respective starting and end points of the uncovering of the thinking self or *cogito*, he began entertaining the idea of including a more precise critique of Western thinking 'from the perspective of a non-

European consciousness,' with the ambitious objective of 'announcing the end of European consciousness and the beginning of the Third World as representative of non-European civilisations.'[85] This evolution from his more modest original intentions to a comprehensive critique of existing systems of thought and subsequent introduction of an alternative philosophical methodology, resembles not only Arkoun's Emerging Reason, but is also reminiscent of Husserl's intellectual trajectory. According to Ricoeur:

> Three times—in the period of the *Ideas* (1911-*ca* 1925), of the *Cartesian Meditations* (1928–31), and of *The Crisis* (1931–36)—Husserl attempted to combine into one comprehensive work the philosophical interpretation of his method and phenomenological exercises that would be at once the application and justification of phenomenology.[86]

The 'rigorous science,' which Husserl had pursued in *Ideas*, was in danger of falling into solipsism and was therefore problematised anew with the introduction of the notion of 'the other' in *Cartesian Meditation V*. The resulting concept of individual inter-subjectivity was then taken to a collective level in *The Crisis of the European Sciences* with the positing of a *Lebenswelt* or 'Life-World' which Ricoeur described as 'the matrix of our existence.'[87] Reflecting a radical and definitive change of direction in Husserl's thinking during the final decade of his life, Ricoeur has characterised this deepening of the former's transcendental phenomenology as 'an "existential" turn.'[88]

Hanafi's oeuvre betrays a similar constant reworking of his abiding interest in designing an Islamic method for philosophical investigation, which he had first attempted in his doctoral theses.[89] The exposure to phenomenological philosophy had helped him to reformulate the work plan for his principal dissertation into an Islamic variant of Husserl's 'rigorous science.' Commencing with a study of revelation in the Islamic context, he intended to extrapolate from those findings a general contribution to religious studies which was then to be tested in a case study of the New Testament.[90] By stepping out of his own religious heritage (*turath dini*), he intended to show how revelation, reason, and reality in effect form a unity.[91]

This engagement with material from two religious traditions can be considered as the equivalent of Husserl's explorations of inter-subjectivity, just as expanding his research project into the comprehensive three-pronged critique of the intellectual histories of Islam, Europe, and the current cultural situation of the Muslim world in his later Heritage and Renewal Project mirrors Husserl's concerns with the crisis affecting Western thinking and scholarship. The 'radical life-crisis of European humanity' which Husserl had tried to resolve in *The Crisis* parallels Hanafi's constant preoccupation re-establishing the unity of the Islamic sciences.[92] It also points towards a progression along the lines anticipated by Iqbal who, having declared Europe dead in its soul and Asia in its will, found that salvation would need a 'radical transformation of the human condition.'[93] After all, behind Iqbal's reconstruction of Islamic thought there also lay 'the philosophy of life of Bergson and Nietzsche, and the practical idealism of Fichte.'[94]

Hanafi soon discovered that his proposal for a general philosophical method of investigating religious phenomena was falling through the cracks between established academic disciplines, pointing up the liminal or interstitial space in which new Muslim intellectuals often find themselves. Islamicists criticised as too general his plan to deal at one and the same time with issues of concept and order, as well as accounting for the dynamics involved in the practical realisation of revelation in the world. Instead they insisted on a study of a particular historical figure, or a specific legal or theological school. The historians of Western philosophy were on their part also expecting the examination of a concrete theme as elaborated by this or that philosopher (ME: vi-ix).[95]

Eventually Jean Guitton and Louis Massignon came to the rescue. The former brought about the 'necessary transmutation in the author's mind' to enable him to retain a subjectivist angle and at the same time select a determined point in history from which to start his research.[96] Meanwhile, Hanafi learned from Massignon that within the Islamic tradition, the discipline of *'ilm usul al-fiqh* or 'Foundations of Jurisprudence' actually approximates the general philosophical method he was looking for.[97] Applying a phenomenological analysis to this core discipline of Islamic learning could be considered as coming closest to an Islamic equivalent of the 'exact science for the humanities' which Hanafi wanted to establish.[98] After further consultation with the hermeneutician and specialist on Ismaili esotericism Henri Corbin, Hanafi resolved that:

[For] a general method dealing at one and the same time with consciousness and tradition; why not make the question of hermeneutics its point of application? A description of both the micro- and macrocosmos, starting with an existentialist analysis of the Sacred Text, would become the point of departure.[99]

This was also the time that Gadamer released his seminal *Truth and Method* and there are some noticeable commonalities between his views of the role of hermeneutics in other human sciences and the plan laid out by Hanafi. Despite the former's objection to equating philosophical hermeneutics with method, he acknowledged elsewhere that his hermeneutics is nevertheless 'phenomenological in its method.'[100] Hanafi's intention to link Husserl's concern with consciousness his rereading of Islamic tradition to Husserl's central concern with consciousness and capture what he called the micro- and macro-cosmos in one explanatory framework has a parallel in Gadamer's discussions of 'the rehabilitation of tradition,' 'historically affected consciousness,' and 'the fusion of horizons.'[101] In regard to the latter it is also relevant to recall that the whole concept of horizon featured prominently in Husserl's phenomenology.

Finally, notwithstanding Gadamer's differences of opinion with Betti on the implications of a rigorous philosophical interrogation of theories of interpretation, Gadamer acknowledged that philological, legal and theological hermeneutics originally belonged closely together. Consequently, from a procedural point of view, he regarded the hermeneutician's task as 'redefining the hermeneutics of the human sciences in terms of legal and theological hermeneutics.'[102] In the context of Hanafi's aim of turning a legal theory like *'ilm usul al-fiqh* into a method of philosophical investigation, the continued relevance of the procedural hermeneutics governing human sciences has also much more recently been reaffirmed by Thomas Seebohm's more recent research in which he revisits the relationship between philology, jurisprudence, and methods of interpretation.[103]

Whereas Husserl's *The Crisis* was the result of an attempt to absorb the concept of a 'Life-World' into a transcendental phenomenology, Hanafi's ambition to present an alternative, philosophically grounded, method for studying Islam was triggered by a comparable state of crisis he perceived in the field of Islamic Studies. The persistence of his concern and lack of response to his proposed alternative is evinced by the inclusion of a lengthy section entitled 'The methodological crisis in Islamic Studies' in his introductory study of 'Heritage and Renewal,' fifteen years later.[104] It appears Hanafi was combating the same kind of disinterest as Arkoun faced when introducing his Applied Islamology.

Hanafi's sense of crisis was not limited to the way Islam was taught and passed on by traditional Muslims, but also extended to Islamic

Studies as a field of modern academic investigation in both the Muslim world and the West. In analysing this situation he distinguished between two issues. The first concerns the primary material, that is to say: the body of traditional Islamic learning where the problem revolves around finding suitable ways of presenting the material to audiences living in different cultural settings and using languages other than Arabic. The other is the issue of the secondary literature produced by intellectuals and scholars examining the Islamic heritage.[105] This encompasses both reflections on the primary corpus by Muslim thinkers, the emic or insider accounts of what Hanafi calls *chercheurs à l'intérieur de la culture en question*, and the etic or outsider perspectives provided by non-Muslim academic specialists or *chercheurs appartenant aux cultures avoisinantes* in their contributions to the discipline of *Islamologie* or 'Islamology.'[106]

Hanafi acknowledged the value of this modern scholarship as it offers helpful hypotheses for further study, thus advancing the understanding of the primary texts, as well as opening new horizons of reflection on the material at hand. However useful these studies may be, both Muslim and non-Muslim approaches suffer from certain shortcomings which hamper the introduction of the newly envisaged hermeneutics. *The Methods of Exegesis* is therefore also designed to expose the principal errors and their origins in both the intellectual setting and scholarly formation of the researchers in question. He considers his proposed alternative methodology as a corrective for what he refers to as 'scienticism'—a term borrowed from Husserl—affecting the work of non-Muslim Islamicists, and the 'rhetoricism' obscuring the writings of modern Muslim scholars.[107] This double critique positions Hanafi as a new Muslim intellectual negotiating between acknowledging the achievements of Western human science and staying true to Islamic authenticity:

This new era in the history of Islamology is not in the least obliged to apply foreign methods, such as depth psychology or phenomenological methods, to its object of study. But if the researchers succeed in shedding themselves of all negative methodology and Islamology's principal error, [the discipline] will remain open to its object [of study] as it is in itself, which will—in accordance with its own nature—suggest a method that is proper to itself. In other words, neither depth psychology nor comparative mysticism, modern logic nor the philosophy of values, can—as independent systems—reveal the object under investigation. What matters is the unveiling of the object itself, using any possible means of linguistic expression that might be available.[108]

The most important shortcoming of Islamology is its apparently inescapable tendency to obscure the things in themselves as the primary material passes through scholarly disciplines and methods originating in other cultural settings. It is therefore 'necessary to establish a science dedicated to the verification of the secondary literature at the heart of Islamology' through a historical interrogation of the discipline itself and critical assessment of its objectives, because:

This genre of scholarship is a branch of European civilisation named 'Orientalism.' This science—if you can call it that—is a purely European creation. It was established to furnish information about a world called the Muslim World in the wake of colonisation process. This process had two objectives: one economic, [...] the other military. [...] Thus Islamology and colonialism are two complementary movements.[109]

Together with Anouar Abdel Malek's 'L'Orientalisme en Crise,' this assessment foreshadows Edward Said's eventually more influential study *Orientalism*. Deconstructing academic disciplines by making specialists and their scholarship objects of investigation can actually prove helpful in stimulating critical self-assessments by the scholars themselves. Hanafi singled out the article 'La Situation de l'Islamologie' (1961), written by his own professor Robert Brunschvig, and Jacques Waardenburg's *L'Islam dans le miroir d'occident*, as successful attempts towards such self-examination. Although he believes the latter's work is to a degree still encumbered by the very scientism it seeks to challenge, he lauds the earlier mentioned essay 'Une Approche Compréhensive de l'Islam'—which was included as an appendix to the book—as a rare example of an Islamicist's interest in a general religious methodology.[110]

Hanafi criticises Orientalist scientism for what he calls its four negative historical, analytical, projective, and 'ex-effective' methods.[111] The first and most important one treats religious phenomena as brute and mundane realities occurring in history, completely neglecting the psychological and eidetic dimensions and thus reducing the explanation of events, as well as the significance of important figures and notions, to their historical conditioning. The resulting historicism is subsequently extended beyond Orientalism's proper limitations and also imposed on scholars belonging to the culture under study, turning them into representatives of the scientist approach within that other culture itself.[112] This historicist focus is a consequence of both the Islamicists' academic formation and the specific cultural milieu in which they originate and operate, which are predominantly informed by historical and philological methods at the expense of philosophical investigation.[113]

The other three methods are also conditioned by the environment and education of the scholars who apply them. The projective method is undermined by its focus on the researcher's own consciousness rather than the schematic structure of the phenomenon under investigation, causing its findings to be reduced to mere value judgments.[114] At the same time, Hanafi accepts that a scholar's research is inevitably subject to the methodological prejudices of his milieu and that, in the absence of completely neutral research, uncompromisingly objective research can therefore never be realised. The method of 'suspension' or 'relegation,' for which Hanafi coined the neologism 'ex-effective method' is equally flawed. In this approach the origins of religious phenomena are attributed to external causes, emptying them of all content and effectively making them non-subsistent in themselves. As an object no longer mounted on its own 'axis' but rather like 'a satellite orbiting another object,' the religious phenomenon becomes 'centrifugal' instead of 'centripetal.'[115] This concern for restoring what Isaiah Berlin—with a reference to Herder—has called a society's 'own centre of gravity' forms an important aspect of Hanafi's search for authenticity, which underlies both *The Methods of Exegesis* and the Heritage and Renewal Project.[116] Finally, the analytical method tends to sacrifice the historical importance of tradition for the immediacy of human reason. However, in combination with the historical method this approach can actually be turned into a productive step towards knowing a thing under its various aspects.[117]

'The principal cause of the current crisis in Islamology' is therefore the lack of philosophical training on the part of scholars of Islam.[118] But Hanafi remains optimistic because, once the historical conditioning of Islamic Studies is recognised and provided that the study of Islam becomes as much a philosophical as a historical exercise, it should be able to reinvent itself. In his estimation, the exigency of a purely philosophical order that is replacing the specific circumstances under which Islamology had originally emerged is already opening a new chapter in its history. Moreover, according to Hanafi 'it is easier for an Orientalist to become a philosopher' than the other way around, because the former 'already knows the languages to engage directly with the primary sources of the culture.'[119]

Where non-Muslim scholarship in Islam is affected by scientism, the rhetoricism colouring the analyses and interpretations by Muslim intellectuals is also erroneous.[120] He refers to the exponents under this rubric as '*méthodes negatives exposantes*,' because they only expose religious phenomena as they manifest themselves in a culture from within that culture without attempting to analyse the things-in-themselves underlying these manifestations.[121] Hanafi puts it even more strongly, alleging that rhetoricism is not just endemic to religious studies—especially in (scriptural) exegesis—but actually affects any reflection on the religious. Of the four forms of rhetoricism, aside from tautology, apologetics, and rhetoric, for the present account the most relevant is the so-called intuitionist approach.[122] This refers to 'every immediate expression of intentions, visions, or grasping of immanent primary truths of the religious, without any regard for scientific demonstration, proof, or analysis.'[123]

Although, as the most advanced stage of rhetoricism, it avoids most of errors committed by the other methods, intuitionism is nevertheless found wanting, because—instead of relying on the evidence provided by 'lived experience'—it is grounded in the text which is regarded as giving sufficient ground for truth. In spite of using a rationalised language it still manifests the same apologetics and rhetorical devices as the other forms of rhetoricism. Consequently, even if an intuitionist interpreter may be regarded as either a religious intellectual or intellectual religious person, he can never be considered a pure scholar.[124]

7

THE SEARCH FOR METHOD

Hanafi's attempt to conceive of a comprehensive philosophical method grounded in the Islamic tradition and suitable for analysing the generic phenomenon of religion was one of trial and error.[1] Aside from being awkwardly positioned on the interstices of existing academic disciplines and other scholarly fields dealing with Islam and the Muslim world, Hanafi also struggled to find the right structure and language because he initially adopted the theocentric approach of Sayyid Qutb.[2] He accepted Paul Ricoeur's criticism that the first draft was hampered by a language which, although perhaps satisfactory to Islamicists, was not the independent and autonomous phenomenological language required of a pure philosophical examination.[3] Moreover, retaining the vocabulary and style of conventional renditions of the original Arabic carried the danger that non-Muslim readers would regard it as confined to Islamic culture and therefore consider the proposed methodology of limited value to them.

Thus Hanafi decided to trade Sayyid Qutb's New Realist Science for Muhammad Iqbal's *The Reconstruction of Religious Thought in Islam*, which he regarded as initiating the third phase of the Islamic modernisation project after al-Afghani's awakening of the Muslim world to its predicament vis-à-vis the West and the first tangible reform attempts by Abduh and Rida.[4] Hanafi saw it now as his task to complete the anthropocentric reconstruction proposed by Iqbal who, as early as 1909, had identified the liberation of man as 'the central proposition which regulates the structure of Islam.'[5] However, the regimented format of *The Method of Exegesis* was very different from the lecture-style of *The*

127

Reconstruction of Religious Thought, forcing Hanafi to precede the main work with a nearly three hundred-page introduction explaining the structure of the thesis and the alternative language it employed.[6]

In this chapter the introduction and concomitant structure of *The Methods of Exegesis* will be subjected to a detailed examination, because they are essential for understanding Hanafi's methodology. They not only form the blueprint for the Sorbonne theses but also for the Heritage and Renewal Project which would occupy him for the rest of his academic career. The subsequent discussion of his first auxiliary thesis, published as *The Exegesis of Phenomenology,* will show how Hanafi completed the argument in favour of his eventual decision to opt for a hermeneutics grounded in phenomenology as the most effective tool for the generic study of religions.[7] Together with his first test case—an analysis of the New Testament in *The Phenomenology of Exegesis*—these three theses actually prefigure the tripartite agenda for the Heritage and Renewal Project and its prospective three-front campaign examining the civilisational heritage of Islam and Christendom respectively, and the current reality faced by the Muslim world today.

A General Islamic Method as Endogenous Intellectual Creativity

The first decision Hanafi took was to radically rephrase the theocentric language of his first draft into a bold alternative idiom more in tune with the contemporary human condition. In regard to the title of the thesis, it meant switching to a generic term like 'exegesis' by which he anticipated expanding his potential readership.[8] Somewhat surprisingly for what is otherwise an exhaustive attempt to develop a new philosophical vocabulary, Hanafi's treatment is at times rather cavalier. Even though he has identified his own approach as hermeneutical, in other places he limits that designation to the 'esoteric interpretations' (*ta'wil / interprétisation*)[9] of the Sufis, which he emphatically excluded from his examination.[10] In another instance, exegesis is restricted to *tafsir* in the sense of a 'rational and objective interpretation of a text.'[11] A little further on this is then explicitly dissociated from the theological methodologies of radical rationalists such as the Mu'tazila and the Ash'arite determinists.[12] In the remainder of the thesis he frequently regresses to an interchangeable use of exegesis, hermeneutics and interpretation.

Hanafi's definition of exegesis as 'a method, not a doctrine' is almost literally the same as Ricoeur's characterisation of Husserl's phenomenology as 'less a doctrine than a method.'[13] While it helps to position Hanafi as an explicit phenomenologist, together with the linguistic deficiencies of the first draft, this decision to develop a phenomenological-hermeneutical methodology not limited by any theoretical straightjackets nevertheless invites a deeper meditation on the complex interplay between hermeneutics, exegesis, and interpretation.

Realising that any particular method of exegesis is 'neither a discovery of the tradition in question nor inherent to its primary sources, but rather an invention of the researcher,' and therefore a conceptualisation of method as a human construct, demonstrates an awareness of the problem of subjectivity.[14] Hanafi's attention for the error of confounding discovery and invention resonates not only with the solipsistic objection confronting Husserl's transcendental phenomenology, but also shows a degree of self-reflection that is evidently absent from, for example, Feuerbach's *The Essence of Christianity*, which—in contrast to Hanafi's acknowledged interventionism—seeks 'not to invent, but to discover, "to unveil existence."'[15]

The key term 'method' is made operational on three different levels. Apart from being the very theme of the book, it is not only used to describe an author's inwardly directed reflection on his own consciousness and how he is affected by things-in-themselves, it has also a more concrete reference as the road towards a goal; either in the sense of a tentative as yet unmapped route or a defined programme or particular procedure for achieving an objective.[16] In this context it is important to take note of Hanafi's qualification of exegesis in regard to the original subject matter of the 'Foundations of Jurisprudence.' He is adamant that it entails a moving beyond (*dépasser*) the differences between the four authoritative Islamic Schools of Law.[17] This means that exegesis must not be considered as the specific engagement with the minutiae of legal issues, but as a general philosophical method investigating principles rather than individual cases. As a researcher of foundational disciplines instead of auxiliary sciences, Hanafi is engaged in philosophical not historical study, examining the structure and not the development of religious phenomena.[18] Emphatic about excluding specific Islamic dogmatic positions, history, law, and theology, a religious phenomenon must be taken up as grounded in a *donné révélé*—a 'revealed given' or 'revealed datum':

It is called a 'given datum,' that is to say, something [coming from] beyond human acquisition, and consequently, something outside the limits of human knowledge. It is called 'revealed' in order to indicate the essential characteristic of this 'given datum,' distinguishing it from artistic, philosophical or scientific inspiration which are also 'given.'[19]

Thus his method appears to become ahistorical, deductive, and descriptive-analytical.[20] And yet, it was Hanafi's objective to reconstitute an inductive, bottom-up approach commencing with historically revealed data. I suggest that his approach in delineating what he understands by method and exegesis reflects the same kind of bracketing which Husserl deemed necessary for a viable phenomenology.[21] The remainder of the introduction is dedicated to detailed explanations of the three core themes of *The Methods of Exegesis*: (1) contemporalising the language of *usul al-fiqh* to bring it up to par with the philosophical requirements for what he calls (2) a reflective analysis of humankind's being-in-the-world on the levels of (3) historical, eidetic and active consciousness.

Transposition

Hanafi calls the radical rewriting of the first draft in a rigorously scientific format, which remains at the same time capable of rendering the historical data from one religious tradition into a language accessible to contemporary Muslims and non-Muslims alike, 'transposition.'[22] Contemplating the question of how to give expression to revealed data received in one cultural setting in their fullest possible sense in the language of another, Hanafi defined transposition as 'rephrasing the material in such a novel way that it simultaneously accounts for the terminology and the idea or thing described.'[23] Although essentially a linguistic tool, it takes transposition beyond techniques such as transliteration and transcription and conceives it in terms close to those employed in structural linguistics and translation studies.[24]

A phenomenological methodology cannot be satisfied with a mere translation of terms and expressions. On the contrary, it must encompass a radical or, in Roman Jakobson's words, 'creative transposition' of the contents of things-in-themselves.[25] Aside from remaining truthful to Husserl's dictum '*zurück zur Sache selbst*' (back to the thing-in-itself), as a Muslim modernist Hanafi also saw it as his task to complete the three-stage progression of the Islamic reformist project. As he considered *The Reconstruction of Religious Thought in Islam* 'the best contemporary work in which this transposition clearly comes through,'

Hanafi agreed with Iqbal that the transposed culture of Islam must be rendered into the language of the transposing—that is the European—culture because we are living in 'its epoch.'[26] More specifically, the discourse of 'third-stage modernists' such as Iqbal and himself is best phrased in terminology inspired by Nietzsche and Bergson.[27]

The actual transposition is a three-stage operation in itself, consisting in an as accurate as possible understanding of the data expressed in the original 'archaic' language, the selection of an appropriate new terminology while accounting for the inevitable cultural connotations influencing this dialectics of communication. Drawing on Oswald Spengler's notion of *Pseudomorphose*, Hanafi called the outcome of this procedure 'pseudo-morphology' but his description appears to reflect what the theorist of translation Even-Zohar refers to as the semi-integration of source languages into target languages.[28]

Although conventionally understood in a negative sense, Hanafi sees a potential for giving pseudo-morphology a positive twist, citing earlier examples from the Islamic heritage such as the work of al-Kindi, al-Farabi, Ibn Sina, and Ibn Rushd, as well as Ibn Taymiyya's critique of formal logic, as earlier constructive implementations.[29] The benefit for the transposed culture consists in opening up 'a multitude of horizons' which can provide new meanings to the original ones, whilst reinscribing the terminology borrowed from the transposing culture with parallel additional meanings. By striving for a homogeneity between two cultures without devaluing or overvaluing one against the other, transposition can thus help reveal a 'unique subjective and intersubjective cultural and intercultural truth.'[30] Terming it an 'interpenetration of cultures,' Chartier relates the importance Hanafi attaches to this aspect of transposition to the influences of Hegel, Husserl, Unamuno, Marcuse and Iqbal.[31]

A detailed look at Hanafi's justification of the thesis's subtitle, '*La Science des Fondements de la Compréhension "Ilm Usūl al-Fiqh,"*' illustrates how transposition is made operational in a concrete sense. The decision to translate '*ilm usūl al-fiqh* as the 'science of the foundations of understanding' is explained by pointing to the architectural associations of the Arabic word *asl* (pl. *usūl*). As something on which a certain order or compilation of knowledge rests, foundation can be understood as giving a reason of being, in the case of *fiqh* this refers to human actions in the form of acts of judgment. The second meaning is that of principle, which Hanafi paraphrases as deductive reasoning.

Finally, it can refer to a source—in the context of Hanafi's project the revealed data providing the analytical material. He also gives three possible translations for *fiqh*: 'anonical methodology,' methodology of jurisprudence, and understanding. Admitting that this last one constitutes a radical innovation, he defends his choice on the grounds that it will prevent Western readers from making too close an association with the legal sciences, which would distract from his objective of establishing a general philosophical as well as a religious methodology.[32] He then closes the circle through a creative correlation of understanding to the three aspects of *asl*:

Understanding in exegesis means to become consciously aware of acts of judgments (1), made through reasoning (2), on the basis of a revealed source of knowledge (3), [...] similar to how these aspects appear in the three different senses of the term 'Asl' as foundation, principle, or as source.[33]

Although designed for completing the Islamic modernist project and reintroducing a human dimension into the study of religion, Hanafi recognised that transposition potentially could have a negative impact on the field of religious studies, by succumbing to a degree of linguistic pedantry or—more seriously—creating an 'illusory humanism' found in those types of rationalism informed by what Sartre called 'bad faith.'[34] As an example of the latter he cited Ali Abd al-Raziq's *Islam wa Usul al-Hukm*, calling it a 'pure and simple importation from a neighbouring culture without any attempt to realise a real pseudo-morphology.'[35] Other shortcomings include the introduction of neologisms, a degree of imprecision, and outside influences. In regard to the latter he adamantly rejected accusations that his work was informed by strong non-Islamic influences, explaining that his transpositions did not so much signify alien influences, as merely reflect their 'linguistic imprints.'[36] In this respect, he regarded his pseudo-morphological approach as reflecting the endogenous intellectual creativity explored by two purveyors of new Muslim intellectualism mentioned in an earlier chapter, Anouar Abdel Malek and Hussein Alatas, and which in one of Hanafi's later writings was explicitly referred to as a project of social dialectics.[37]

Transposition must not only deal with the problem of expression but also meet the challenge of effective communication. Hanafi's treatment of this intersubjective dimension as dialectic process, involving a *conscience donatrice* (the scholar) and *conscience receptive* (the reader), evince an acute awareness of the workings of structural linguistics and semiotics. The communicative process starts with the apprehension of an object of knowledge to which the scholar attached a significance, which in turn leads to the selection of an appropriate term. The reader's point of departure is exactly the opposite; first encountering this term, which is subsequently given meaning before arriving at the thing-in-itself. This Hanafi's description of communicative dialects contains three semiotic elements grounded in Saussure's structural linguistics—a provenance more explicitly acknowledged in a text of Hanafi from 1972 where he uses the notions of term, meaning, and the referenced object.[38]

Reflective analysis

Although in his critique of Islamic modernism he had rejected the intuitionism inherent to the theocentrism of such figures as Maududi and Qutb, Hanafi was convinced this deficiency could be overcome by following Iqbal's lead and applying the 'ensemble of instruments of dissection' from the linguistic-semiotic toolbox of transposition to a 'reflective analysis of everyday experiences.'[39] Inspired by Iqbal's dismissal of the dead metaphysics practised by theologians, and borrowing the shorthand used in the Christian tradition for the various disciplines dealing with the study of religion, Hanafi stated that theology must henceforth be regarded as anthropology, insisting that presenting the 'Science of God' as a 'Science of Man,' or substituting the human for the divine, has tremendous potential for enhancing human understanding of religious phenomena.[40] This radical change of perspective which he later elaborated in an article entitled 'Theologie ou Anthropologie?,' calling it a shift from a vertical to a horizontal orientation, requires an existential methodology grounded in lived human experience rather than a text-based rationalist methodology.[41]

With this decision to trade theology's vertical theocentrism for a horizontal anthropocentric orientation, Hanafi had turned his methodology from a 'top-down' deductive approach into an ascending inductive one. Aside from being a major transformation in intellectual outlook, its analogy to Iqbal's assertion that inductive intellect was born with the emergence of Islam seems to affirm it as a more authentically Islamic method.[42] Moreover, on a generic level it turns the study of religion grounded in everyday experiences into the human science *par excellence*.[43]

Within the framework of his own research these everyday experiences were specifically related to the Islamic tradition. Distinguishing between individual and communal experiences, the former are said to correspond to four of the 'Five Pillars' of Islam, namely: prayer, fasting, almsgiving and pilgrimage, while the latter include ownership, heritage, and marriage.[44] For which of the individual human sciences they form the basis depends on what sort of experiences they are: immediate or perceptive experiences provide the material for jurisprudence, psychology, sociology, and economics; aesthetic experiences lie at the basis of ethics, while the everyday experiences on which Hanafi concentrates constitute the foundation for philosophy or metaphysics.[45] Phrased in existentialist terminology, they constitute the everyday experiences revealing man's primordial relation with the world, in which human reality appears as 'being-in-the-world.' An important consequence of such an understanding is that scholars too can only have recourse to their own experiences as a 'possible source for unveiling truths.'[46]

Conceived as a philosophical investigation, Hanafi implemented his alternative method of analysis in an abstract fashion, but using experiential references that were clearly inspired by Iqbal. As the point of departure for this new methodology, experience is tentatively defined as:

[a]n event not in the sense of its material extensity but rather as psychological intensity. The world is regarded [in terms of] conscious impressions not juxtaposed events. Experience is not some kind of sensibility which determines the relation between an object and the senses but as a concrete situation in everyday life in which consciousness is put to the test.[47]

The extensive aspect of everyday experiences or—put differently—the confrontation of consciousness with a world outside itself, pushed Hanafi towards the notion of 'the other' which, as mentioned in the previous chapter, Husserl had explored in his *Cartesian Meditation V* in order to overcome the problem of solipsism affecting idealist philosophies. To Hanafi, whether referring to the other in an individual, collective, or absolute sense, the notion refers to a field of experience, and can contribute to transcending the limits of experience by counterbalancing the subjectivism of the singular individual experience with inter-subjectivity, whereby the 'identity of several experiences constitutes a degree of human objectivity.'[48] At the same time, Hanafi cautioned against excessive material or formal objectivity because it would result in losing this human dimension: Experiences as impressions on a human consciousness will always remain focused on a certain 'irreducibility, indetermination, and contingent new creation.'[49]

In addition to the intensive and extensive dimensions of experience, Hanafi also introduced a distinction between 'real' experiences, which form the subject matter of thought (*la pensée*), and 'ideal' experiences which are the stuff of revelation.[50] For a general method for the study of religion this has far-reaching consequences. When subscribing to a theocentric perspective on the field of religious studies its metaphysical interests generally extend to speculations about the breaking-in of the transcendent into human existence, but by transforming theology into anthropology and thus turning the study of religion into a human science, the proposed methodology cannot deal with phenomena beyond verifiable human experience. As a reflective analysis of human reality grounded in the experience of being-in-the-world, its basic experiential material is formed by the earlier mentioned revealed data. In the context of religious studies, reflective analysis of everyday experiences means therefore relying on revealed data contained in and transmitted through texts, and relating these to situational human reality.

Although traditional Islamic learning had to some extent recognised this requirement, as demonstrated for example by the inclusion of a subsidiary discipline called *asbab al-nuzul* or 'causes of revelation' in the broader field of Qur'anic exegesis, Hanafi's amplification of the horizontal dimension of lived human experience rather than the transcendent source of revelation privileges the '*appearance* of that reality' over its '*descent* from an outside source.'[51] Clarifying this position is all the more pressing because the Islamic-Arabic idiom contains two different words for revelation: *tanzil* or 'sending down,' which clearly underscores the vertical transcendental vector, and the more immanent term *wahy* or 'inspiration.' Given the objective of the transposition exercise to interpret and not merely translate, it becomes clear why Hanafi prefers appearance (in the sense of revealing or unveiling) over descent.

This reliance on lived experiences for a hermeneutical approach driven by an anthropological turn completes the transformation of Hanafi's approach into an inductive method privileging ascending reality over descending truth.[52] What can be called Hanafi's heresy also shows an affinity with Berger's proposition in his *Heretical Imperative* that 'theological thinking should follow an inductive approach that begins with ordinary human experience.'[53] The latter's own return to Schleiermacher as the father of an inductive method drawing on the 'general human phenomenon of religious experience,' and thus standing at the methodological roots of what came to be known as the phenomenology of religion, bears a strong resemblance to Hanafi's attempt to establish a genuinely Islamic methodology on a similar foundation.[54] Two facets of lived experience are considered particularly relevant for this hermeneutics: the exigencies of an interpreter's own *milieu* and the imperative of internalising the contents of revealed data through life experience, which Hanafi subsequently abstracted into necessity and world horizon—the latter suggesting an amalgamation of Husserl's 'Life-World' and Gadamer's 'fusion of horizons.' According to Hanafi, the interplay between interpretation, necessity and world horizon must be considered as a common feature in all modernisation movements through history.[55]

Returning once again to the Islamic tradition for illustrative material, Hanafi transposed the term 'modernist' for the *mujaddid* said to appear at the beginning of every Islamic century. Just as the Islamic philosophy from al-Kindi onwards are presented as inflections of pseudo-morphology, so too are Ghazali's refutation of Greek-inspired rationalism and Ibn Taymiyya's blanket rejection of all foreign elements, be it theological, philosophical or mystical doctrines as well as 'formal logic including its philosophical, psychological and pragmatic foundations' cast as historical examples of modernising critiques instigated by the demands of the time and informed by the interpreter's intimate familiarity with the doctrines under challenge.[56] As for the representatives of what is more conventionally accepted as Islamic modernism: al-Afghani's call to shake off fatalism, Abduh's institutional reforms, and Iqbal's embrace of 'subjectivity, life, creation,' these too were induced by the need for innovative reinterpretations of the revealed data.[57] By presenting his own project as yet another reworking of the methodological needs of the contemporary world, Hanafi implicitly situated himself in this line of *mujaddidin*.

Historical, eidetic and active consciousness

This reflective analysis of revealed data as the raw material for a philosophical examination of humankind's being-in-the-world starts with the contents of what Hanafi called historical consciousness which are then reinscribed in the eidetic and active consciousness.[58] A core issue with which the historical consciousness grapples is the transmission of lived experiences through these revealed data across time. For example, the discipline of *'ilm usul al-fiqh* conventionally recognises four authoritative modes of transmission: the Qur'an, the Traditions of the Prophet, *ijma'* or 'consensus of the scholars,' and *ijtihad* or 'independent reasoning.' But in order to lift *'ilm usul al-fiqh* from being a juristic tool onto the plane of philosophical thinking, these archaic designations of the four sources of Islamic jurisprudence must be radically rephrased. Hanafi resolves this by transposing them into 'anonymous experience' (*Qur'an*), 'privileged experience' (*Sunna*), 'intersubjective experience' (*ijma'*), and 'individual experience' (*ijtihad*) in their place.[59] Transcending the culturally specific connotations of Islamic dogma, law, and theology, these bold transmutations are reminiscent of Iqbal's rereading of *ijtihad* as the 'principle of movement in the structure of Islam.'[60]

When dealing with revealed data in the form of text, the objective of hermeneutics is not merely a matter of commenting on the language, but of engaging their referential connection with the things-in-themselves.[61] Admitting that subjectivism is the 'dominant characteristic of the adopted method,' Hanafi did not think this would necessarily lead to a relativisation of knowledge, because it remained possible to safeguard at least a degree of objectivity through inter-subjectivity or the cognitive role played by the other.[62] To prevent his own analyses from falling into solipsism, Hanafi invoked the notions of Iqbal's *khudi* or 'ego' and inter-subjectivity. In his reading Iqbal's ego is no other than subjectivity 'as the centre of the world [and] nodal point of inter-subjectivity or community.'[63]

Whereas this link establishes *The Methods of Exegesis* as a continuation of Iqbal's *The Reconstruction* within Islamic modernism, the jargon governing Hanafi's contribution to that project is evidently indebted to phenomenology. The fact that reduction and constitution are singled out as key components of phenomenological investigations points to the undeniable imprint of Ricoeur's observation in his penetrating study of Husserl that 'the constitution is the key to the reduction, and the reduction the key to the thesis of the world.'[64] It also begs the question whether—notwithstanding Hanafi's own immediate acquaintance with Husserl's published oeuvre—its influence is not primarily mediated through Ricoeur's reading.

Reduction or suspension of judgment (*epoché*) must not be confused with 'subtracting something' or a 'mutilation.'[65] Rather, it is a form of modesty demanding the negation of any direct correspondence between real and conscious events, because once a real event has entered consciousness and continues to exist as a conscious form it becomes impossible to know what actually happens. In the context of transforming the study of religion into a rigorous human science, this implies that:

> The reduction of religious matters is constituted by the reduction of the text outside its historical context, that is to say, by setting aside all circumstances in which the text finds itself, or by leaving aside any consideration of the spatio-temporal determinations that relate a text to history.'[66]

As an operation facilitating the shift from historical to eidetic consciousness, reduction can in turn be considered as the key rule of phenomenology, accomplishing the transformation of the actuality of experience, the raw data dealt with by historical consciousness, into the eidetic or ideational realm of the possible. It enables consciousness to shed its original naïveté, called natural attitude by Husserl, allowing it to discover its own capacity of giving sense to what was previously taken as merely given.[67] Thus it can be said that 'reduction removes a limitation and thus frees the whole sweep of consciousness.'[68]

Hanafi's treatment of the eidetic realm is conditioned by the notion that understanding differs from scientific knowledge in the sense that it is: (1) conditioned by the exegete's consciousness, whereas scientific knowledge is impersonal; (2) conjectural and hypothetical, because it is based on the logic of the possible, whereas the logic of necessity governing science is apodictic and categorical, and (3) a foundation for practical science.[69] These qualifications can be traced to the influence of Dilthey's proposition for *Geisteswissenschaften* as a scholarly field distinct from the natural sciences, and are important to take into account for a proper appreciation of what Hanafi means by establishing an exact science for the humanities.[70] Although revealed data contained in historical texts present themselves in consciousness as an *a priori* truth, or what in phenomenological jargon is referred to as eidetic knowledge, they are not to be taken in an apodictic sense because phenomenologically the eidetic as the domain of ideal types deals with the realm of the possible. Consequently, 'reflective analysis of everyday experiences gives a demonstrative proof that is no other than the reality itself tending towards its own truth unveiled in the given revealed datum.'[71]

Giving sense to or creating meaning for these revealed data in the eidetic consciousness is achieved through constitution, the second ground rule of the phenomenological exercise. In Hanafi's formulation:

The Constitution of a religious matter is done by setting up a religious text within consciousness. Constituting a text means describing it as a psychic reality, as the horizons of consciousness or its spontaneous emanations, that is to say, assimilating its content as a human reality.[72]

This kind of set-up or *édification* is therefore not a systematisation, but actually a leaving-behind of any system claiming to be a real image of the outside world. It means 'plunging into the inner core of reality inside an individual consciousness,' which demands a certain spontaneity or *style d'amorçage* that is, although different from both literary and scholarly styles of writing, descriptive and analytical while using common language.[73] Hanafi elaborated in great detail how this has informed the division of the main body of his thesis in which everyday experiences as an expression of the individual consciousness's being-in-the world are constituted under the three aspects of the historical, eidetic, and active consciousness.

To recapitulate: revealed data are received through historically transmitted texts which together constitute a so-called act of reception and are then analysed in the eidetic consciousness through the perspectives of language and causality. Many of the texts from *'ilm usul al-fiqh* contain themselves philological and syntactic studies, but in these cases the linguistic analysis involves an examination of form, origin and function of the language employed in the texts in order to make possible an effective transposition through which the transmitted data can be reread in a contemporary context.[74] Finally, the active consciousness structures an understanding of the world on the basis of this received knowledge. Although this part of active consciousness addresses the important notion of intentionality, in contrast to Ricoeur's analysis of Husserl's phenomenology, it does not feature prominently as one of three core rules governing Hanafi's take on reflective analysis.[75] Instead of Husserl's intentionality, Hanafi introduces extension of the significance of these revealed data into the actual world as the third rule governing his phenomenological methodology.[76]

Structure and creativity in a general Islamic method

In spite of Hanafi's claim that the edification for constituting a reflective analysis must not be taken as systematisation, the main body of the thesis is organised in a highly symmetrical way. Each of the three parts of *The Methods of Exegesis*, dedicated to historical, eidetic, and active consciousness respectively, is again divided in three sections and then subdivided in three chapters.[77] One could charge with Berger that anyone who invents yet another three-fold typology 'should be summarily banned from every decent conversation,' but according to Hanafi this plan imposed itself, because to maintain the integrity of the subject a tri-partite division is rationally the most perfect.[78] To deflect the conflation of edification with systematisation, Hanafi also pointed out that the sequence *The Methods of Exegesis* deviates from the traditional order of interpretative methodologies. Rather than follow the sequence of *praxis*, *historia* and *eidos*, the book starts with a study of historical consciousness, because it is in history that revealed data are first unveiled.[79] After all, Hanafi asks, how can the eidetic or active consciousness be the starting point of a reflective analysis when it is as yet unknown what kind of revealed datum is to be examined or actively realised?

For all intents and purposes, in *The Methods of Exegesis* hermeneutics is presented as a practical 'this-worldly' method.'[80] Surrounding the circle of individual consciousness in which revealed data are first received is the world of others which is in turn encapsulated in the natural world. Manifesting the existentialist streak in Hanafi's phenomenology, these three concentric fields of exploration constitute 'human reality as being-in-the-world' where:

The method of reflective analysis of everyday experiences will find another battlefield. Every transcendent reality becomes immanent in reality. The transcendent going by the name of God becomes immanent in human consciousness. The exterior becomes the interior. The 'descending'—the material fact—rises up to consciousness. Everything becomes human. Man exists the moment he becomes conscious of himself.[81]

This existentialist formulation leads up to the ultimate aim of *The Methods of Exegesis*. Using the revealed data of Islam as primary material for the extrapolation of a general method for the investigation of religious phenomena, Hanafi wants to demonstrate how religion is a truly human science and since he regards, analogous to Husserl, human sciences as methodologies, he concludes that therefore 'religion is essentially a method.'[82] In terms of Berger's sociology of religion, Hanafi provides contemporary Muslims with a plausibility structure that corresponds to the current situation in the Muslim world.[83]

However, his study contains an element that takes the method beyond dry rational interpretation. Hanafi's examination of how revealed data are taken up in historical, eidetic, and active consciousness represents a developmental path which is not merely concerned with an evolution of the soul, but also interested in its real unfolding in the world whereby 'the revealed data become the ideal structure of the world.'[84] His explicit reference to Iqbal's *The Secrets of the Self* is an acknowledgement that his own trajectory draws its inspiration from the poem's description of the three-stage progression of the ego, through obedience to divine law, control of the soul, and divine vice-regency.[85]

While conceived as a contribution to the Islamic modernist project, Hanafi's decision to include both individual and universal intentionality expressed in an alternative three-stage progression traversing 'solipsism, pantheism, and pantheism realising itself through actions of the Self' turns *The Methods of Exegesis* into a phenomenology which can be appropriately called 'transcendental.'[86] This is also supported by Ricoeur, who invoked the 'momentous words countersigned by Husserl' through which the renowned phenomenologist Eugen Fink asserted that on the highest level this implies a third or transcendental ego and therefore a transcendental intentionality of 'true constitution which is productive and creative.'[87]

As something more easily accessible to mysticism or aesthetics than to rational exegesis, subjectivity manifests itself first and foremost in literary works where mysticism and aesthetics can converge.[88] The domain of inter-subjectivity, meanwhile, extending into the world and encompassing an entire culture has the task to transform 'the historical structure of culture into a teleological structure.'[89] This betrays not just the influence of German romanticism, but also of Husserl after his dramatic turnaround in the 1930s, when he 'declared history and teleology as synonymous.'[90] For a Muslim intellectual it also heralds a cultural renaissance turning hermeneutics into a calling rather than a profession, and making the hermeneutician into more than 'an interpreter, a modernist, or thinker: He is essentially a reformer.'[91]

As a creative reworking of a traditional Islamic discipline, Brunschvig described the existentialist phenomenology unfolded in Hanafi's *The Methods of Exegesis* as 'a great adventure [and] total reinterpretation of traditional *usul al-fiqh*.' It seeks not just to revive or modernise some of its concepts in the manner of Abduh or Iqbal but attempts a complete rethinking, turning the book not into yet another legal or sociological study but the work of a well-versed philosopher.[92] In a rare review of *The Methods of Exegesis*, Michel Allard assured 'that nobody with an interest in modern Islam could dispense with reading Hanafi's book.'[93]

Examining Western Phenomenology

While the extensive and detailed discussion of Hanafi's conceptualisation of his phenomenological hermeneutics in *The Methods of Exegesis* is necessary because it is the key that unlocks the rest of his work, the following briefer assessment of *The Exegesis of Phenomenology* confirms Hanafi as representative of the assertive new Muslim intellectuals identified by Charles Adams, who are conversant with the Western academic study of religions and at the same time confident of the potential vibrancy and scholarly rigour of the Islamic heritage.[94]

Even though Islamic culture has to borrow the language of European culture as a more suitable medium for dealing with the exigencies of contemporary times, Hanafi stresses at the same time that the logic derived from *'ilm usul al-fiqh* is superior to that of Europe's dogmatic theology, which tries to pass itself off as revelation. So whereas European philosophical jargon offers a richer language, the schema developed in *The Methods of Exegesis* provides the Muslim world not only with a home-grown general method of philosophical investigation but also with a methodology which, thanks to its inherent coherence, stability and integrity, can find general application beyond the Islamic tradition. In Christian thought hermeneutics is generally regarded as a religious science alongside all the others, instead of being regarded as the principal one which opens up a new form of reflection consisting of a historical critique, linguistic analysis, and practical realisation.[95]

In *The Exegesis of Phenomenology* Hanafi fine-tunes the methodology developed in *The Methods of Exegesis* by contrasting it with an analysis of European philosophy and its attitude towards the phenomenon of revelation, which is allegedly marred by a degree of fragmentation due to the different provenances of the constituent elements of Europe's cultural heritage. The reflection on revealed data received and processed through historical, eidetic, and active consciousness is now applied to the European consciousness by placing it in conversation with European scholars of Bible Criticism and Church history, such as Alfred Loisy, Maurice Blondel, and Rudolf Bultmann. In these interlocutors Hanafi finds useful allies from within the Western tradition to make his case that Judaism and Christian theology have corrupted the revealed data of the Judeo-Christian tradition and chosen to ignore the contributions of Islam.[96]

Where the crisis in Islamic Studies inspired Hanafi to attempt salvaging the Islamic legacy through the adoption of an anthropocentric perspective, in *The Exegesis of Phenomenology* it is the crisis of European consciousness as perceived by Nietzsche, Husserl and Spengler that led him to apply a similar remedy.[97] However, there is an important difference; namely the fact that the expression of the West's historical consciousness has pervaded all other cultures. With Europe at the centre of the world, he identified two 'pathological phenomena': an internal European crisis and 'the Europeanisation' of world outside the West.[98]

The main purpose of analysing these afflictions is to challenge the idea that because of its global influence European culture can claim that the Judeo-Christian tradition is the benchmark against which to measure other religions.[99] Instead European consciousness must be understood as a particular product of its own historical circumstances.[100] Based on the teachings of Guitton, Hanafi identified three discrete moments in the composition of this European consciousness, using his mentor's somewhat idiosyncratic designations. For the revealed data informing its philosophy of existence, Europe relied on the Judeo-Christian legacy, while Graeco-Roman thinking provided it with a philosophy of Enlightenment. It was finally the specific cultural milieu of Europe from which a philosophy of nature arose which enabled the European consciousness to discover its own sources.[101] The impact of these three moments is also reflected in the empiricist, idealist, and existentialist historiographies of Europe's own past.

Hanafi's intention to show how fragmented European culture actually is became clear from his interpretation of certain episodes in European history. Whereas the Protestant Reformation involved a return to the primary sources in order to 'discover the individual consciousness at the heart of the revealed data,' these were then again rejected by Enlightenment thinkers and their 'sole reliance on human reason for the truth.' Finally Europe discovered science, which takes 'reality itself as the first and last guarantee for truth and avoids both abstraction and rational suppositions.'[102] However, because Europe also draws on its Judeo-Christian legacy for its revealed data, it can therefore be considered as a 'centripetal' culture.[103] Transposing 'reform,' 'renaissance,' and 'science' as generic designations for these succesive and singularly European historical events, Hanafi claimed that as a result of Western hegemony during the imperialist age these three notions are now immanently and *a priori* present as pre-given truths in non-European cultures.[104] As a result of Western thought's exclusivist claim to universal validity for what is actually just another particular viewpoint:

...there is a false image of Islam in all segments of European culture. In philosophy it is hardly mentioned as a proper philosophy [...] [n]either Islamology, nor the image of Islam in the comparative history of religions gives a correct image of the finality of its revelation.[105]

Hanafi is not merely contesting Europe's self-assertion as the standard against which other cultures are measured. His reiteration of the counter-claim made in *The Methods of Exegesis* that Islam is capable of furnishing a generally valid and scientifically rigorous method of investigation for religious phenomena, effectively posits Islam as an alternative benchmark. This way Hanafi placed himself in the vanguard of a decolonising world ascertaining its own cultural autonomy and challenging the dominant culture. Even though as a philosopher he is not so much interested in political reflection as in 'inserting thought into history,' he noted that decolonisation and liberation movements in the Third World have 'incited many scholars to reflect not just on the state of affairs in the Third World, but also on the coloniser [...].'[106]

However the European crisis has not yet been fully examined. A thorough analysis is not only still hindered by the myopic views of the thinkers and scholars originating from the affected culture itself, but also by the vehement attacks by non-Westerners on Europe's cultural encroachment on the Third World, which are predominantly of an apologetic and rhetorical nature, because at the time of writing the liberation from Western dominance is still in force.[107] Although less sceptical than Arkoun regarding ideologically motivated responses to Western hegemony and calls for revolutionary action, Hanafi nevertheless recognises that both emic and etic accounts suffer from a comparable lack of critical distance. What is needed is a neutral consciousness, capable of distancing itself from the imprint of the culture under study and of freeing itself from the rhetoricism of its own. According to Hanafi, a non-Western scholar is capable of divesting him or herself from such pre-suppositions through self-education.[108] In other words, a critique of European civilisation requires a scholar placed in an interstitial or liminal position equidistant from the insider and outsider perspectives.

Whilst *The Exegesis of Phenomenology* continues the high apologetics of *The Methods of Exegesis*, the critique of European civilisation creates the additional task of properly assessing religious phenomena in general, including those belonging to Christianity.[109] This has far-reaching consequences: the first study announced the rebirth of the Islam whereas its sequel professes the end of European culture.[110] From a philosophical point of view the mission can actually be phrased less antagonistically, in the sense that a properly understood Islam cannot but reclaim its rightful legacy from European culture, which can be said to have acted as a custodian of the classical Islamic heritage. A substantial part of the preface to *The Exegesis of Phenomenology* is therefore taken up by an explanation of how the two studies not only reinforce each other but are also intertwined on a cultural, academic, and scientific level.[111]

On the level of their academic relation, Hanafi presented *The Methods of Exegesis* and *The Exegesis of Phenomenology* in what could be called his own set of 'theses on Feuerbach,' with the former providing an 'affirmative reality' similar to 'The True or Anthropological Essence of Religion' in *The Essence of Christianity* and the latter counterbalancing it with a 'negative critique' of Europe's dogmatic assertions reminiscent of 'The False or Theological Essence of Religion.'[112] In more ideologically charged language, Hanafi's research also became a 'fight against contrarian truth-claims, historical inauthenticity, the neglect of the humanity, and the disregard of the world.'[113]

Moving towards the substance of *The Exegesis of Phenomenology*, Hanafi proceeded in a similar roundabout manner as Ricoeur's reworking of Western philosophy through a conciliatory engagement with both canonical thinkers and 'hermeneuticians of suspicion.' He defended the approach of his first book as a generally applicable method of interpretation grounded in a progressive critique of Husserl's phenomenological philosophy and its interlocutors. Exploring the phenomenology's specific genealogy he followed in Ricoeur's footsteps by characterising the various interpretations that have been spun off from the 'orthodoxy' of Husserl's founding oeuvre as 'heterodoxies.'[114] As noted earlier, initially Hanafi agreed with Ricoeur that Husserl had conceived of phenomenology as a 'research method rather than a philosophical doctrine.'[115] However towards the end of his review of the secondary literature on Husserl's phenomenology, Hanafi concluded that this corpus constitutes a discipline independent of Husserl's phenomenology and—reversing Ricoeur's qualification of the Husserl's work—he downgraded the bulk of that literature to the level of 'doctrine not method.'[116]

At the core of Hanafi's general criticism of phenomenology is a perceived lack of dynamism, which affected not only Husserl's static theoretical foundations but also the phenomenological ontologies of thinkers like Max Scheler and Georges Gurvitch, Heidegger's existentialism, and even what was considered the cutting-edge of Western thought at the time of Hanafi's writing: the ideas of Sartre, Merleau-Ponty, and Ricoeur.[117] Hanafi contrasted Husserl's theoretical phenomenology with the applied phenomenology that constitutes its multifaceted offspring, noting that the latter had in fact the potential of resolving the problems affecting its parent, because its disposition towards dealing with real rather than imagined objects gave it an orientation towards practical ends, which its theoretical predecessor is decidedly lacking.[118] However, using the writings of Levinas and Ricoeur, and the phenomenology of aesthetics developed by Ricoeur's friend Mikel Dufrenne as examples, it is often difficult to distinguish this so-called applied phenomenology from other human sciences outside the field of philosophy, because its concentration on personal reflections on the experience of everyday life can only be considered philosophical in the most modern sense of the word.[119]

Elaborating on Ricoeur's philosophy of the will, Hanafi saw the former's *The Voluntary and the Involuntary* as a progression from eidetic reduction to a triad of intentionality involving moments of decision, movement, and consent, only to give up this bracketing in the anthropology and hermeneutics developed in *Fallible Man* and *The Symbolism of Evil*. Given these reservations, Hanafi wondered if it was still possible at all to speak of a genuine phenomenological methodology. Lacking the kind of rules found in Husserl's phenomenology, his final verdict on Ricoeur's 'philosophy of the will' had lapsed into psychologism, while his 'Finitude and Culpability' had fallen into formalism and historism.[120]

Leaving the heresies issuing from Husserl's philosophical phenomenology momentarily behind, Hanafi briefly skimmed over philosophy of religion's engagement with the three earlier mentioned dimensions of consciousness, concluding that its treatment lacked both topical and methodological clarity.[121] He then expanded his critique to the adjacent fields of the history of religions, the comparative study of religions, and phenomenology of religions. The fact that all these specialisations originated in Europe, he saw as a real risk of 'taking the schemes of Christian religion as the general criteriology.'[122] Even the phenomenology of religions, in spite of its potential to be developed into a genuine phenomenology, remained stuck at the level of justifying theological approaches, reducing the work of those engaging with it to an art rather than a science.[123] Conseqeuently, when it came to religious studies, 'phenomenology was no more than a term covering a complex assembly of all kinds of philosophical systems and religious sciences.'[124]

Addressing what was at the time one of the most influential studies in the field, Hanafi characterised van der Leeuw's *Religion in Essence and Manifestation* as insufficiently radical, reducing it to just another philosophy of religion, theology, or history. Only the book's epilogue touched briefly on the triple problematic addressed by a phenomenological engagement with interpretation: a critical-historical search for authenticity, a linguistic analysis of the conditions for understanding, and the practical realisation through intentionality and action.[125]

Returning to Transcendental Phenomenology

Because of the 'family resemblance' with his own general Islamic method, Hanafi eventually returned to Husserl.[126] As the culmination of transcendental idealism, phenomenology is to be considered as the method that: (1) points to the way forward for religious studies and, in particular, exegesis; (2) can easily dissect history as the embodiment of the stumbling block that is dogmatic theology; (3) possesses the necessary apparatus for linguistic investigations needed for rigorous interpretation of texts.[127]

As such phenomenology was the terminus of transcendental idealism, which Hanafi considered the most important achievement of Western philosophy. As the third source of European consciousness after the Judeo-Christian and Graeco-Roman legacies, Descartes' work stands at the cradle of modern European thinking, giving rise to two lines of thought, which Hanafi—in a strange and in my view inconsistent reversal of his earlier descriptions—dubbed the 'ascending line of rationalism' and the 'descending line of empiricism,' eventually converging again in Kant's transcendental idealism.[128] He also credited post-Kantian philosophies of Fichte, Hegel, Schelling and Schopenhauer for effecting a 'progress in the teleology of history' and providing a foundation for the later phenomenological approaches.[129] Thus, whereas European consciousness started with the Cartesian *cogito* of early modernity, its point of termination lies in the transcendental *ego* of Husserl's phenomenology.[130]

According to Hanafi, phenomenology must therefore be considered as 'a second renaissance tasked with recapitulating the failures of the first.'[131] Marred by the dualism of empiricism and rationalism, modern thought evinces a gap in European consciousness. It is only at the threshold of the contemporary age that these two lines meet again, and the horizons of transcendental idealism and empirical objectivism merge in the psychologism of transcendental subjectivism, which leads up to 'the way of a transcendental phenomenology marked out by a return to the pregiven life-world.'[132]

In conclusion, says Hanafi, 'only transcendental phenomenology can provide a structured method.'[133] However, in the absence of such a rigorous method any attempt to contribute towards a religious phenomenology is bound to stall at the level of religious philosophy, that is to say a transposition of philosophical systems onto religious phenomena. The only thing that has been achieved so far is an existentialist hermeneutic engagement with human reality which approaches what Hanafi considered a proper phenomenology of exegesis. With a nod to Blondel and Bultmann, he noted that:

Historical consciousness, so often forgotten—is [now] foregrounded, in particular by the method of *Formgeschichte*. The eidetic consciousness follows with an existentialist interpretation using demythologisation. [Also] Active consciousness finds its place—after having been forgotten until now—in the phenomenology of exegesis.[134]

Uniting the approaches of Max Scheler's epistemology and Rudolf Bultmann's demythologisation, the phenomenological method 'has the advantage of taking modern philosophy back into battle against dogmatic theology.'[135] As a comprehensive eidetic approach it comes closest to the reflections on consciousness and reflective analysis of everyday experiences first proposed in *The Methods of Exegesis*. But where Husserl's phenomenology ended with the 'announcement of an imminent crisis in modern times,' *The Methods of Exegesis* comes to the rescue.[136] Hanafi's anticipations of the significance of his investigations were very high:

I announced the beginning of a new consciousness in *The Methods of Exegesis*, and the end of an old consciousness in *The Exegesis of Phenomenology*. But in the privacy of my own mind, it announced the beginning of the East, with Egypt at its centre, and the end of the West.[137]

8

RECONSTRUCTING ISLAM

HERITAGE AND RENEWAL

Intent on expanding the method developed in his doctoral studies into a comprehensive reconstruction of both Islamic and European religious thought, Hanafi referred to his departure from France in 1966 as 'the end of his lesser and the start of his greater Jihad.'[1] But unforeseen and radical political changes hitting the Arab world within a year from his return to Egypt would not only delay the launch of this so-called Heritage and Renewal Project by more than a decade, but also add a more pertinent political charge to his academic work.

Until then the prevailing political orientation among Arab intellectuals had been towards secular ideologies. In post-revolution Egypt, and especially after its triumphant emergence from the Suez Crisis, these found their embodiment in the Nasserist amalgam of domestic national unity (*wataniyya*), Arab solidarity (*qawmiyya*), and economic socialism (*ishtirakiyya*). Reflective of that political climate, Hanafi combined his interest in Islamic thought and affinity with the Muslim Brotherhood with an admiration for Nasser whilst simultaneously retaining his affinity for the Muslim Brotherhood.[2] However the debacle of the Arab-Israeli war of June 1967 had a shattering impact on Arab self-esteem and self-perception. To try and make sense of the disaster, the intelligentsia gave up on 'their "academic" work and turned to the street.'[3] Comparing Egypt's situation to that of Germany after its defeat by Napoleon, for his part, Hanafi saw a need for rebuilding national consciousness along the lines of Fichte.

This increased concern for emancipating his country and a concomitant preoccupation with the developing world-at-large infused Hanafi's writings—like that of many others—with the 'Spirit of Bandung' issuing from the Third-Worldist discourse of the Non-Aligned Movement which had been founded after the Arab-Asia Conference. Although such acute political engagement may seem at odds with Hanafi's earlier more cerebral involvement in finding an endogenous philosophical method, the perceptible return of the 'Islam factor' in both public debate and intellectual discourse throughout the Arab world gave a sudden new relevance to his work as a scholar of religion in what was generally regarded as a secularising world. In this regard he was very much in tune with the recurring interest in the Arab-Islamic civilisational heritage widely noted in post-1967 intellectual histories of the Arab world and which were leading to more 'urgent and poignant' writings on Islamic themes.[4]

Symptomatic of this concern were two high-profile gatherings bringing together a wide array of intellectuals to discuss issues which contained the buzzwords of intellectual discourses throughout the Muslim world for decades to come. At the 1971 Cairo conference on 'Authenticity and Renewal in Contemporary Arab Culture,' the philosopher Shukri Ayyad (1921–1999) had observed that until the 1940s there had actually been no mention of the term *asala* or authenticity in the Arabic critical literature and that it was only introduced in the 1950s to signify an opposition to imitation.[5] Although there was a consensus that any real revivification of Arab civilisation required a creative, historical, and critical comprehension of its heritage, the forum on 'The Crisis of Civilisational Development in the Arab Homeland' held in Kuwait three years later, failed to generate any agreement among the participating thinkers on how to proceed.

According to literary and intellectual historian Issa Boullata, 'there is no doubt that the Kuwait conference was one of the most important cultural events to occur in the Arab world in recent years, if only for the attempt to raise questions,' turning issues of heritage, authenticity and the role of religion in development into a 'hub of much intellectual activity.'[6] With a theoretical and methodological framework for the philosophical study of religion developed in the preceding decade readily at hand, Hanafi's agenda not only defied the assumption of an immediate causal link between the fallout of the war and the return of religion in Arab intellectualism, but suddenly found himself in the vanguard of a rich, varied and growing '*turath* literature.'[7]

From Scholarship to Political Engagement

Hanafi's role as a trailblazer for this alternative Islamic discourse becomes evident from the articles he wrote between 1969 and 1971—prior to the two milestone conferences in Cairo and Kuwait. Later reissued as *Contemporary Issues I & II*, a two-volume collection respectively dealing with Arab-Muslim thought and Western philosophy, they form the hinge between the Sorbonne theses and Hanafi's future Heritage and Renewal Project.[8] Marc Chartier, who attended Hanafi's classes at Cairo University, noted a 'progressive slide from "religious experience" towards "culture"'; expanding what in *The Methods of Exegesis* had been confined to an examination of revealed data into a critique of the Islamic heritage as a whole.[9] Aside from this topical shift, from then on Hanafi has predominantly written in Arabic.

The central thread running through articles such as 'The Mission of Thought' and 'The Role of the Thinker in Developing Countries' is a concern for restoring the integrity of thought in the developing world while reiterating his cautioning against the rhetoricism and dogmatism which tend to mar the writings of independence fighters and other liberation activists. Also the world of Islam had lost its intellectual coherence due to the impact of Western cultural influences. The resulting alienation was affecting Muslims both individually—causing a double or split personality—and on the collective level, leading to dualism in education, culture, and social behaviour.[10] Although he did not interpret it in pathological terms *per se*, in another article, 'Religious Thought and the Doubling of Personality,' he considered this affliction nevertheless symptomatic of the duality that pervades all religious thought.[11] Muslim culture has become so fragmented that the constituent elements of authentic human life—consciousness, self, action and dynamism—have disintegrated, except for a few rare exceptions, such as the work of Iqbal.[12]

The elaborations of this dualism in 'Our Civilisational Position' and 'Our Attitude towards the Western Heritage' are not only firmly integrated into the theoretical framework developed in Paris, but already contain the kernel of the Heritage and Renewal Project.[13] In other essays like 'Authenticity and the Present' and 'Renewal and Stagnation in Contemporary Religious Thought,' Hanafi noted that whereas a single-minded preoccupation with authenticity at the expense of the exigencies of the present will 'derail into blind imitation,' ignoring the past 'results in uprootedness.'[14] In order to revitalise civilisations and their religious traditions, it is imperative to preserve the intimate connection between the past and present. To understand the particular intellectual predicament of the Muslim world, Hanafi suggested its intellectual history can be divided in two distinct periods: one period covering the first seven centuries of the Muslim era and the second from the eighth century until the present. Coincidental with the rebirth of Europe, the decline of Islam set in during this second period. The resultant misconstrued conflation of these two developments has hindered a correct assessment of the relationship between Islamic and European civilisation. In fact, within the framework of a universal history of humankind, it would be more appropriate to consider the European Renaissance as an extension and perfection of Islam's preceding intellectual domination.[15] Challenging Christendom's rejection of Islam as both a continuation and correction of the same revelatory process which had begun with the Old Testament, followed by The Gospel, had already been a key aspect of *The Phenomenology of Exegesis*, Hanafi's contribution to critical Bible studies.

Tracing the genealogy of Islam's intellectual heritage, the first civilisational consciousness emerging out of the proto-Muslims' initial encounter with the raw data of revelation gave rise to traditional Islamic sciences such as *tafsir* and *hadith*. Next, a growing need for knowledge commensurate with the geographical expansion of Islam led to a translation exercise from Greek into Arabic. Initially concentrating on the natural and life sciences, it soon expanded into theoretical disciplines like philosophy and logic. These texts provided the methodological basis for dialectical or discursive theology (*kalam*), proper rational Islamic sciences such as *'ilm usul al-din* or 'the foundations of religious dogma' and *'ilm usul al-fiqh*, as well as purely rational sciences such as philosophy, and even practical Islamic disciplines such as Sufism.[16] A second translation project was initiated in the wake of Napoleon's invasion of Egypt in 1799, enabling the Muslim world to reacquaint itself with Western thinking. Where the earlier translation school had ignored mythology and literature as fields that conflicted with the Islamic worldview, now the realms of 'God, power and sex' were considered taboo.[17]

Indicative of his increasing assertiveness, in a more in-depth examination of these two encounters between Islam and the West, published as 'Our Contemporary Culture between Authenticity and Blind Imitation,' Hanafi no longer spoke of transposing and transposed culture but of 'invading' and 'emerging' cultures.[18] Here Hanafi identified some marked differences between these two moments. Whereas the first translation exercise had at least produced a Spenglerian pseudo-morphology or transposition, no such integration was achieved during the second encounter; resulting in the earlier mentioned alienation from the Islamic heritage.

Hanafi used the doctrine of *tawhid* or 'Unity of God' as an example, because the core theological problem in Islam revolves around what Iqbal had called the 'Oneness of the Divine Self and multiplicity of His Attributes.'[19] Although a sophisticated Muslim modernist like Iqbal was capable of interpreting *tawhid* in terms of revelation as the organising principle of the world or—in an even further abstraction—'transforming ideology into history,' the traditional view of *tawhid* as a theological dogma instead of a science of man still holds sway. This theocentric view also extends to the rest of Islamic learning. In metaphysics man's intellectual faculties are considered dependent on the active intellect, while a rational science like *'ilm usul al-fiqh* 'has remained the captive of jurisprudence, incapable of exceeding its juristic boundaries' and is still not taught as a form of philosophy. Also a practical discipline like Sufism revolves around humankind's anticipation of divine illumination; not even social and other 'real' human sciences have managed to escape from the theological ambit.[20]

To continue the double critique initiated in the Sorbonne theses, Hanafi's new scope of work extended into an examination of the different attitudes displayed by Muslims towards Western civilisation. Distinguishing between complete bedazzlement, a neutral stance and categorical rejection, Hanafi noted that this latter outright dismissal of anything Western on the grounds that it originated from a hegemonic colonising culture was just as essentialist as the first attitude's uncritical embrace, while those remaining neutral are usually only interested in a rather superficial acquaintance with Western philosophies rather than subjecting them to a rigorous examination.[21] Even sophisticated and discerning Muslim intellectuals tended to accept without question those aspects of Western thought that conformed to their own intellectual or psychological outlook. Citing the examples of Taha Husayn's admiration for Cartesian scepticism and Ali Abd al-Raziq's call for the separation of religion and state, such recourse to doctrines arising from the particularities of the European cultural milieu constitute examples of the 'bad faith' described by Sartre and Jankélévitch.[22]

Muslims exhibit the same kind of blind imitation of the West that characterises the attitude towards their own heritage. What is needed instead is an attitude of critical distance and defiance similar to that displayed by critics operating from within the Western civilisation, such as Spinoza, Voltaire, or Feuerbach. Hanafi also pointed to the challenges of rationalist analyses that lose sight of the human dimension by Maurice Blondel, Henri Bergson, and Gabriel Marcel's attack on positivism and empiricism in the name of self.[23] At the same time, he upheld his reservations against certain specific features of Western thought, such as the dualism between spirit and matter or 'schools of personalism' represented by thinkers as different as Kierkegaard, Bergson, Unamuno, Marcel, Jaspers, and Sartre.[24] Therefore Hanafi reiterated the caveat in *The Exegesis of Phenomenology* that a correct assessment of European thought as the product of its own specific circumstances can only be undertaken by someone who looks in from the outside, whose mind does not bear the psychological imprint of Western consciousness, and who can therefore look at it from a truly neutral angle.[25] Only then:

We have the possibility of creating a new science; the study of Western civilisation through a non-Western consciousness. Since we belong to the Third World we could say that we study European consciousness through a Third World consciousness. Just like 'Orientalism'—the study of the Third World by European consciousness—it is possible to establish 'Occidentalism' as the study of European Consciousness by Third World Consciousness. This has been done before by Franz Fanon and other Third World thinkers, but these were all rhetorical political rather than scientific-philosophical endeavours.[26]

Hanafi was of course not the first or only one to make such a suggestion, because at roughly the same time Mukti Ali was proposing the introduction of Western studies in Indonesia. However, by coining the term *istighrab* or 'Occidentalism,' Hanafi had given a name to the critique tentatively unfolded in his *Exegesis of Methodology* and which he would eventually develop into the 'second front' of his Heritage and Renewal Project.

Invoking Husserl's and Lévi-Strauss' apprehension over the increasing influence of technology and growing specialisation in academia to the detriment of generalised and comprehensive philosophical approaches, Hanafi suggests that by developing an endogenous philosophical methodology, the Muslim world could avoid the trial and error of Western thinking and move straight away to the latest achievement in the human sciences: structuralism.[27] It now becomes clear how his writings from around 1970 complement the earlier historical investigations in *The Methods of Exegesis* and *The Exegesis of Phenomenology* with a descriptive analysis of the way Muslims live out their cultures. Borrowing the jargon of structural linguistics and phenomenology, Hanafi explained how instead of a diachronic tracking of its constituent elements he now planned to engage in a synchronic phenomenological study analysing the *eidos* rather than *telos* of Islamic cultures, in particular in those areas still controlled by conservative religious officialdom. According to Hanafi, because Muslims are 'still afraid of addressing religion, considering it as God-given and sacred. It is still not possible to study its doctrines, texts, and history as a human sciences.'[28] Any such attempts led to accusations of heresy or even apostasy.

In the West, however, the perennial questions faced by humankind which previously had been relegated to divine providence or acts of God had now become the subject of critical study and analysis. Thanks to the emergence of the phenomenology of religions and critical Biblical studies among nineteenth-century Protestant and Catholic modernist theologians, the study of religion had been transformed into a human science, just like psychology, linguistics, sociology, economy, history and law. Investigating the links between sacred texts and the formulation of dogma or religious doctrines became a subject of the comparative history of religions. This raises the question of whether psychology could similarly be used to explain sentiments and emotions like fear, faith and God consciousness or whether sociology could contribute to studying the relationship between a religious conception of the world and the practice of rituals. At the same time Hanafi thought it important to remain aware of the typically European characteristics of this scholarship; especially its tendency to equate itself to universal values which poses a threat to the integrity of public and private life in the Third World.[29] As Third World citizens, Muslims fail to recognise that alternative schools of thought and disciplines, such as the Mu'tazila, *kalam* and *'ilm usul al-fiqh*, have originated within the Islamic tradition, providing ample inspiration for an endogenous methodology for studying religions.

The Heritage and Renewal Project

By the time these articles were collected and published, Hanafi had also released the first volume of his Heritage and Renewal Project.

Subtitled *Our Attitude Towards the Old Heritage*, it contains a draft master plan which mirrors the examination of the historical, eidetic and active levels of consciousness in the Muslim world in *The Methods of Exegesis*.[30] However, the definitive scope for the project was not published until 1991, with the release of *An Introduction to the Discipline of Occidentalism: Our Attitude Towards the Western Heritage*. Although this subtitle indicates a continuation of the critique started in *The Exegesis of Phenomenology*, the book also contains the fullest lay-out for the project's three-front campaign: widening the investigations of Muslim attitudes towards the Islamic and Western heritages with an examination of the current situation in the Muslim world in which Hanafi envisioned synthesising the antitheses of the other two critiques into an emancipatory theory of interpretation.[31]

Heritage and Renewal: Our Attitude Towards the Old Heritage

Hanafi insisted that heritage and renewal must be understood in this particular sequential order, because heritage forms the point of departure for a renewal through the reinterpretation of the Islamic tradition according to contemporary demands.[32] Although much of a civilisation's cultural heritage originates in religion, Hanafi nevertheless privileged the former because 'religion is part of heritage and not the other way around, since heritage also contains social, political, cultural and historical elements.'[33] Nor can the contents of a cultural heritage be restricted to what has been officially documented, preserved, and theorised; it must also include those less tangible aspects shaping a culture's mentality and which are often transmitted through more traditional or popular ways, such as the Sufi tradition, axioms, maxims and proverbs in jurisprudence, as well as popular forms of expressing religious sentiments.[34] A similar multiplicity of meanings also applies to the term Islamic, which can either refer to a religious tradition, a civilisation, or even—as had been shown in *The Method of Exegesis*—a philosophical methodology.

In a first exploration of the current status of the issue at hand, Hanafi distinguished two positions towards heritage. One characterised by overconfidence in its self-sufficiency, often associated with a right-wing conservative stance, the other by trust in the adequacy of renewal in the modernist sense with the accompanying debilitating effects of dualism, such as a doubling of personality.[35] Because both are grounded in preconceived ideas on heritage and renewal, such anti-rationalist endogenous and selective exogenous attempts are of limited use.[36] Reminiscent of Madjid's adoption of the dictum 'preserving what is good from the old and adopting what is better from the new,' in *Heritage and Renewal* Hanafi too tried to strike a balance by 'taking from the old what is in accordance with the demands of the present era and measuring the new against the standards of the old.'[37] The novelty of Hanafi's project lies in its theoretical foundation which draws a parallel between the contemporary Muslim world and its historical legacy on the basis of an interpretation of renewal as a re-evaluation of that heritage in the light of the current situation. This way, the descending and ascending methods of analysis, which he had already identified in *The Methods of Exegesis*, will reinforce each other.[38]

In preparing the ground for a further exposition, Hanafi drew on the same stratagem as in his doctoral research. In fact, the *via negativa* used to establish what Heritage and Renewal is *not* and the recapitulation of the crisis in Islamic studies paraphrase in Arabic the relevant sections of *The Methods of Exegesis*.[39] The same is true of renewal: extrapolating from the transposition of the traditional terminology of *'ilm usul al-fiqh*, the wider Islamic heritage must be rephrased in what was now called *mantiq al-tajdid al-lughawi* or a 'logic of linguistic renewal' of the other disciplines of traditional Islamic learning. Taken as a 'field of reflection,' Hanafi said that heritage is open to multiple readings because the text corpora of traditions are in themselves empty of meaning.[40] While these earlier readings were not wrong at the time, clinging to archaic interpretations leads to an anachronistic understanding of the Islamic tradition.

Authenticity can only be retrieved through a reflective analysis on the three levels of consciousness identified in *The Methods of Exegesis*. All the various fields of Islamic intellectual tradition arose under specific circumstances shaping the way in which they were conceived and 'reflecting exactly the kind of problems they were encountering at the time.'[41] By implication, they were not determined for eternity; on the contrary, 'they are relative disciplines which try to give expression to revelation within the confines of the cultural conditions prevailing in the past.'[42] Over time the underlying authentic meaning encapsulated in the Islamic heritage has been lost and Muslims continued to interpret this body of knowledge in the light of those historical circumstances instead of updating it in line with their contemporaneous circumstances.

Hanafi presented three alternative ways for accomplishing such a renewal. In the first instance, he expressed it in conventional phenomenological terms as a reduction or bracketing of all 'civilisational flaws obscuring the first meaning of the text.' The fixation of meaning must be deferred until 'the limits of expression have been transcended' and consciousness can reconstruct the original meaning.[43] This can be done by different means, such as the coining of neologisms through radical transpositions into a terminology derived from European philosophy, applying allegorical or metaphorical readings, and through the retrieval of knowledge expressed in folk wisdom. Shifting from the phenomenological to the existential, new meanings can also be presented as a discovery of different way of being-in-the-world, while according to yet another formulation, consciousness is reconstituted by stripping archaic ways of thinking of their cultural connotations in combination with an analysis of the present situation in order to capture the 'spirit of the time.' By comparing the two against each other, the idealised or eidetic object of the first analysis is then brought in line with the demands of the time established through the second exercise.[44] This third alternative actually forms the objective of the Heritage and Renewal Project, namely a reconstruction of all disciplines of Islamic learning.

These approaches are based on the premise that all Islamic disciplines have emerged from unmediated, philological, intuitive or allegorical readings of revealed texts. By identifying the negative and positive aspects of the fields of traditional Islamic learning, they are then transposed into a language better equipped to deal with contemporary circumstances. The similarity between this exercise and the earlier phenomenological investigations becomes evident from Hanafi's statement that:

The reconstruction of the rational religious sciences is in fact a way to interpret revelation itself by returning to the first origins from which they emerged and [determining] how tradition transformed these into [various] rational sciences, which then become models for the current attempts of turning revelation into an exact science.[45]

Islamic tradition has provided the Muslims with four rational disciplines: foundations of jurisprudence (*usul al-fiqh*), doctrinal foundations (*usul al-din*), philosophy (*hikma*), and Sufism (*tasawwuf*).[46] The 'final objective of "Heritage and Renewal" is to unify all these disciplines into one that is synonymous with civilisation.'[47] To illustrate the feasibility of this ambition Hanafi pointed to such figures as al-Ghazali and Ibn Taymiyya. Rather than considering them in their separate roles as theologian, logician, Sufi, jurist, philosopher and 'foundationalist or *usul* scholar, these respective specialisms should be considered as elements of a consolidated intellectual approach.

Of these four rational Islamic disciplines, *'ilm usul al-fiqh* and Sufism hold the greatest potential for being turned into this exact science because—and here Hanafi reiterated the argument made in *The Methods of Exegesis*—they represent methods not theories, as is the case with the other two disciplines, theology and philosophy.[48] As the principal discipline concerned with meeting the legislative needs of the new Islamic community, *'ilm usul al-fiqh* is a method for studying revelation but with a teleological orientation towards the outward aspects of human reality. This makes it the most important discipline because the current situation in the Muslim world has a more acute need for a descending revelation into the world than in an upward movement towards God.[49] In *Heritage and Renewal* Sufism is added because it is the discipline in which consciousness finds its most articulate practical manifestations. Permeated by psychology, ethics and philosophy, Sufi practices can be considered as the very acts of consciousness.[50] Although also a method, Sufism differs from *'ilm usul al-fiqh* in that its allegorical approach envisages a return to the text as a 'source of serenity.'[51]

On the one hand, the Heritage and Renewal Project can be considered a history of ideas, but by adopting the specific implementation of *ijtihad* as used in jurisprudence, it is also an ideology designed for this desired unification of the Islamic disciplines. By applying *qiyas* or 'reasoning by analogy' on the grounds that it uses from the heritage what serves the common good, *Heritage and Renewal* proceeded along the lines of the same *minhaj fiqhi* or juristic method, which Hanafi had already applied in *The Methods of Exegesis*. Whereas in the latter *'ilm usul al-fiqh* had been raised from a juristic tool to the level of philosophical methodology, in the Heritage and Renewal Project the ways of the *faqih* or jurist were extended to Islamic civilisation as a whole.[52]

Consistent with his constant advocacy of turning theology into an anthropology, Hanafi also wanted to turn the discipline dealing with the core doctrinal foundations of Islam, *'ilm usul al-din*, into a human science. In fact, because its substance deals with the essence of the Islamic faith, early jurists such as Abu Hanifa used to call it 'greater *fiqh.*'[53] This served as a further affirmation for privileging the juristic method as an inventive philosophical methodology, because:

It is the best that Islamic civilisation has brought forth, in the sense that it is an independent discipline using rational scientific language, which expresses man's internal constitution as secular and intentional and his outward aspects as action and behaviour. It has two subsidiary disciplines: 'social *fiqh*' or 'the *fiqh* of being' [...], and *al-fikr al-usuli al-fiqhi* [foundational juristic thought], which tries to extract the civilisational-philosophical phenomena from theology, philosophy and Sufism.[54]

Hanafi went on to argue that by refashioning it into a progressive theology or liberation theology, *'ilm usul al-din* had the potential of being transformed into an up-to-date ideological tool.[55] In the vibrant climate of the Louvain and Temple University campuses in the early seventies, Hanafi had been introduced to Christian liberation theology, studying the writings of Gustavo Gutierrez, Leonardo Boff, Dom Helder Camara, and especially Camillo Torres.[56] Considered from a philosophical-theological perspective, Hanafi's position resonated with Harvey Cox's assessment of liberation theology as 'first and foremost a "theology of praxis" [...] based on the conviction that all human thought is a form of action.'[57] These more radical articulations of Hanafi's politics are also found in a text like 'Théologie ou Anthropologie?,' dating back to 1972 but already containing the key elements of the manifesto-like tract *Leftist Islam*, released a year after the launch of the Heritage and Renewal Project.[58] Together with his interest in the writings of the Ayatollah Khomeini following the developments in Iran after 1979, the theologies of these revolutionary clerics added a more radical flavour to Hanafi's thinking.[59]

Because *Heritage and Renewal* was primarily conceived as a theoretical introduction to the first part of the project, the second and third parts on the Western heritage and the current situation in the Muslim world received only a cursory mention. However, it is important to stress that as a vehicle for the intended unification of the Islamic sciences, Hanafi's Heritage and Renewal Project has two derivative objectives. Hanafi explicitly introduced a strong teleological element into the project, noting that the substance of heritage must be turned into an ideology aiming at the discovery of 'humankind in heritage' by establishing its historicised and existential setting.[60]

A new science: Occidentalism

No publication by Hanafi is surrounded by greater controversy than the first volume of what is referred to as 'the second front' of the Heritage and Renewal Project; the Muslims' attitude towards Western civilisation.[61] Thomas Hildebrandt has made a detailed study of this work and its reception, addressing both positive responses and vehement rejections, some of which culminated in vitriolic *ad hominem* attacks by intellectuals like Tarabishi.[62] Although the substance of this book is only of marginal importance for the present thesis, it situates Occidentalism vis-à-vis Orientalism, which contextualises Hanafi's significance in asserting a place for the contributions by new Muslim intellectuals to Islamic studies. In a recent assessment of the legacy of Edward Said's *Orientalism*, Dan Varisco invoked Hanafi's book as aiming:

To directly oppose and point out the weaknesses of Orientalism through a systematic and discursive othering of European intellectual history. Here is a direct writing back that Said found absent: a seemingly subaltern intellectual on the periphery looks back at the centre that defined the need for peripheral vision. Hanafi mentions Said as one of the individuals who brought attention to Orientalism as an object of study. But he argues that because the Saidians' [sic] reading of the 'West' adopts Western secular humanism by default, it ultimately serves the same role in the modern Arab university as Said attributed to Orientalist texts in the Western academy.[63]

In regard to the Arabic designation for Occidentalism, Varisco has drawn attention to the original meaning of *istighrab* as 'amazement' and 'wonder.'[64] Apart from this aspect of the West (*al-gharb*) as exercising a certain enchantment, even perplexity, it also shares an etymological root with another important notion suffusing Hanafi's analysis of the Muslim attitude towards the Western heritage, namely *ightirab* or 'alienation,' which can lead to a doubling of personality in the individual and cultural dualism on the collective level of civilisation.[65]

Moreover, the concept of Occidentalism also makes discernable the contours of certain unresolved tensions between Hanafi's search for an authentic Islamic method and his simultaneous heuristic reliance on the Western human sciences. For example, it affirms the argument in a recent study on the broader phenomenon of Occidentalism that 'most revolts against Western imperialism [...] have borrowed heavily from Western ideas.' Thus Hanafi's work has become part of an intellectual discourse in which 'Western-style modernity and nativist revolt' are so inextricably enmeshed that 'no Occidentalist [...] can be entirely free of the Occident.'[66] The contention that Occidentalism was actually born in Europe and that its agendas to romantic thinkers like Fichte and Schelling, Slavophiles and Panarabist Ba'thists, problematises Hanafi's quest for a distinctly endogenous intellectual creativity.[67] Then again, Hanafi's affinity with Muhammad Iqbal, identified by Buruma and Margalit as a Muslim who was critical of the West without seeing a need to resort to Occidentalism, offers potential for a degree of rehabilitation.[68]

Thus *Introduction to the Discipline of Occidentalism* stands as a testimony to the agency claimed by subaltern intellectuals in resetting the parameters for the study of their respective cultures—in this case Islam—through a dialectics aiming at a synthesis of the findings of the double critique of their own heritage and that of the Other. In a section dedicated to an examination of the latter, Hanafi took care not to limit it to the 'Western Other,' explaining that:

This is the strife between old and new at the level of civilisation and in the course of history. Every nation is involved in it, and it takes place on the level of the great civilisations. If the West is the I then the East is the Other or—the other way around—if the East is I then the West is the Other. If the Third World is the I, then East and West together are the Other. If the East and the West, that is the developed world in which Socialism and Capitalism compete with each other, is the I, then the Third World as the bloc gravitating around it is the Other. If Japan is the I then the West is the Other as its competitor, or China as its historical 'Other,' or the Soviet Union as the colonising 'Other,' or the coasts of East Asia as its biotopical Other, or the whole world as its source for raw materials and consumer market. [..] If the periphery is the I then the centre is the Other.[69]

Finally, *Introduction to the Discipline of Occidentalism* is important because it contains 'an attempt towards self-criticism.'[70] Having published only the introductory volumes of the first and second parts of the project, as well as a five-volume elaboration of the reconstruction of *'ilm usul al-din* entitled *From Dogma to Revolution*,[71] by 1991 Hanafi realised that the enormity of the Heritage and Renewal Project was too grandiose for any one person to handle and required the input of teams of scholars.[72]

The Enduring Features of Hanafi's Intellectual Hybridity

Although this very partial completion of the Heritage and Renewal Project prevents any conclusive assessment of Hanafi's work as a philosopher and new Muslim intellectual, it is possible to highlight some persistent characteristics featuring in both Hanafi's early phenomeno-logical work and his post-1980 writings on heritage and renewal.

The key aspect under which Hanafi's contributions to Islamic Stud-ies must be considered is the transformation of that field, and by exten-sion the generic study of religions, from a theology to an anthropology. Apart from Hanafi's own emphatic and continuous reiteration of the need for an anthropocentric approach to the study of religion, this preoccupation is also recognised in the secondary literature. My exami-nation has shown that this interest can be traced to Hanafi's formative years and reflect the sustained effect of the teleological élan underlying Romanticism, and more especially 'Fichte's conception of man as demiurge' creating the spatiotemporal manifestations of a transcendent and infinite notion of ego.[73]

Claiming that every anthropomorphism betrays a human exigency, in 'Théologie ou Anthropologie' Hanafi charged that—apart from Mu'tazilism—only European thinkers like Kant, Fichte, and Kierke-gaard pointed a way out of theocentric worldviews.[74] The argument that theology is a false science because it is 'a purely cultural formation [...] not a sacred science, but a purely historical one, subject to the schemata and cultural level of the epoch' sounds very familiar to those acquainted with Foucault's 'discursive formations.'[75] Unfolding his own political 'theology of the left and the right,' Hanafi contrasted the vertical, conservative, right-wing theologies embodied in Roman Catholicism, mysticism and theosophy with the horizontal, progres-sive, leftist theologies that eventually must culminate in anthropology. Scripturalist Protestantism purified from the influences of tradition through the application of historical criticism, especially liberal theol-ogy, offers in this respect the best prospects because 'it is much closer to this highly anticipated anthropology.'[76]

Hanafi characterised *The Methods of Exegesis* as 'a juridical anthro-pology [...] a bold enough model for transforming religion not into theology but anthropology.'[77] Although predominantly concerned with the ideological implications of this transformation, 'Théologie ou Anthropologie' reiterated similar points regarding the role of the Islamic tradition in forging an Islamic equivalent of Feuerbach's anthropology. Hanafi's advocacy of reinterpreting jurisprudence as a field closest to anthropology was motivated by the absence of theologi-cal jargon in its examination of the three great questions of authentic-ity, interpretation and the realisation of the text.

Subscribing to Marx's etymological pun that crossing the 'fiery brook' is a baptism of fire that every philosopher must undergo in order to be able to move from idealism to realism, in an Arabic commentary on Feuerbach's *The Essence of Christianity* Hanafi advocated the more circumventive trajectory of the Young Hegelians, because the Muslim world is in greater need of *tanwir* or 'enlightenment' than *tathwir* or 'revolution.'[78] Although he went along with Feuerbach's diagnosis of alienation and drew similar conclusions: that theology constitutes a false essence of religion, whereas its true essence lies in anthropology, Hanafi added an Islamic dimension. Comparing Feuerbach at one point to the Mu'tazilites, he ended with the ironic observation that if only Feuerbach had studied Islam, he could have saved himself the trouble of writing *The Essence of Christianity*. For Hanafi, modern European philosophy is 'nothing but an attempt to approach the humanism of Islam.' Trading the vertical perspective for a horizontal one, by 'returning from the Kingdom of Heaven to the earthly realm,' Islam had beaten Feuerbach by thirteen centuries.[79] Invoking the Quranic verse: 'This day have I perfected your religion for you,'[80] he identified it as the same kind of convergence as that of the affirmative teleology of Islam and the negative critiques of Christian dogma first introduced in the Sorbonne theses, and offered his essay on Feuerbach as a beginning of Muslim emancipation from their current cultural stagnation.

The earliest critique of Hanafi's anthropology is Michel Allard's review of *The Methods of Exegesis*. Working from Hanafi's presupposition that the Qur'an is not seen from the angle of revealing a transcendent world, but a religious law intended for man, Allard saw the originality of Hanafi's contribution in the exegetical principle that Qur'anic revelation is first and foremost a guide to action and not a source of knowledge. Consequently exegetes should apply an ascending analysis starting from the lived experience of daily life, instead of the conventional descending analysis of the transcendent breaking into the spatio-temporal world.[81] Given Hanafi's claim of being truly innovative Allard expected him to radically bracket dogma and theology, because his position would only be coherent if he could make it plausible that Muslim and general human reality truly converged and that human reason and its limits as formulated in Islam's revealed texts were indeed the true norms of general human reason. However, here he found Hanafi wanting in not rigorously following through with his analyses, so that a potentially interesting approach remained locked in theology.[82]

Hanafi's religious anthropology is closely bound up with linguistic questions, and some of Allard's criticisms carried over to this area. Hanafi characterised anthropology as 'a theology without a traditional vocabulary' and it was the philosopher's task to make that change operational.[83] Allard's appreciation of Hanafi's significance for rethinking the use of language in the study of Islam was evinced by his comment that just from its linguistic plan the revolutionary character of Hanafi's attempt was already clear.[84] However, Hanafi's own imprecision in the use of language marred the efficacy of this transformation, thus threatening the success of the whole undertaking. One fundamental weakness was Hanafi's failure to explain exactly what he understands by 'human,' but the main reason was the ambiguity of *The Methods of Exegesis* which blurred the line between Hanafi's own words and what he had taken from others.[85] Moreover, by transposing the entire terminology into a frame of reference derived from European culture, one would have expected the widest possible use of human categories. Instead, Allard saw Hanafi restricting their validity to the Muslim context only, implying that what is outside Islam is not truly human experience.[86]

Similar reservations were voiced by Paul Nwiya. Noting Hanafi's refusal to use Bultmann's scalpel of demythologisation or apply the *Formgeschichte* of the Gospel with the equal rigour to the Qur'an left everybody guessing as to the extent of the fundamental difference between those holding on to a medieval intellectual mentality and those opting for the more advanced methodologies of the West.[87] Nwiya's charges too left Hanafi open to the accusation of having fallen victim to the same rhetoricism of which he accuses the classical Islamic modernists. Marc Chartier, on the other hand, considered Hanafi's vague language not just as an indication of erudition getting in the way, but also attributed it to the prudence that is required when expressing radically new religious ideas.[88] Egyptian society was and is simply not yet ready for what he has elsewhere called Hasan Hanafi's 'tentative audacity' in regard to religious language and thought.[89]

Since the early 1970s, Hanafi's political ideas had also become a target for fellow philosopher Fouad Zakariyya (b. 1928).[90] A lengthy section in his *Myth and Reality in the Contemporary Islamist Movement* was dedicated to a scathing attack on Hanafi because of his brief flirtation with the ideas of the Iranian and his apparent approval for the actions of the assassins of President Sadat in a series of articles published between in 1981 and 1982.[91] In Zakariyya's view, Islamism is an ideology and politically-motivated discourse that cannot claim to speak on behalf of all Muslims or even be considered truly Islam. Challenging the Islamist advocacy of scripture as good for all times and places as ahistorical, Zakariyya regards Islam as all 'what Muslims have made of it in history.'[92] Interestingly, in defending secularity against Islamists and *turath* thinkers alike, he also employed the 'rhetorism,' just like Hanafi in his critique of Muslim modernist writings on Islam.[93] In Boullata's interpretation, Zakariyya is an exponent of the secular strand of thought opposed to the political agenda of the Islamists and equally critical of the interpretations of the 'heritage advocates' or 'partisans of *turath*,' who from the late 1980s onward found themselves in an increasingly precarious position wedged between Islamists and secularists.

In the intervening decade between the writings of Allard, Nwyia and Chartier, and the publication of Marien van den Boom's study of the humanist dimensions in Hanafi's philosophy, changes in Egyptian society had been for the worst. Recalling his voluntary exile in the United States, the prohibition of lecturing on Islamic philosophy, and his temporary suspension from active duty in 1981, in an interview with van den Boom, Hanafi said that restrictions on openly critical approaches to the study of Islam in the Arab-Islamic world made it impossible to use the methodologies of Western philosophical and religious studies. Consequently, he had to ventilate his 'ideas via a detour, through Spinoza, Feuerbach and Bultmann.'[94] Illustrative of these pressures, by the early 1990s both Hanafi and one of his former students, Nasr Hamid Abu Zayd, had fallen victim to Islamist accusations and vilifications.[95]

Expediency aside, Hanafi's somewhat careless use of language has remained a persisting problem. Olsson criticised his interchangeable and undifferentiated use of terms like 'heritage,' 'religion'—and I would add—'civilisation.'[96] In a similar vein, his more ideologically charged works conflate Egypt, the Arab world, the world of Islam, and even the entire developing or Third World.[97]

These shortcomings notwithstanding, Hanafi retained a vivid interest in exploring the possibilities of applying the advances made in linguistics and semiotics to the study of Islam. Although he has not yet had the chance to elaborate his reconstruction of disciplines like Qur'anic studies in full, in a 1993 essay Hanafi hinted at his ambition to subject the Qur'an to a thematic interpretation using techniques derived from literary criticism grounded in structural linguistics. This method would be founded on the premise that revelations must be taken as revealed data, whereby the revelatory event itself only begins 'after receiving the book, not before.' Consequently, 'the Qur'an is considered as any other text.'[98]

Another feature connected with Hanafi's anthropocentric methodology is humankind's historicity. However, as both the Sorbonne theses and the outlines of the Heritage and Renewal Project show, his philosophical approach is different from that of professional historians. This goes a long way to explain why Mohammed Haddad, a historian trained by Arkoun, takes such a critical view of the intellectual-ideological context of Hanafi's work. Although admitting that *The Methods of Exegesis* is in itself an 'original and remarkable work,' he dismissed it as being too imprisoned in a 1960s outlook.[99] While indeed a product of their time, collectively the Sorbonne theses also represent the most consistent and enduring part of Hanafi's oeuvre. Strongly influenced by the phenomenological approaches prevailing in continental European intellectual circles during the 1950s and 1960s, these writings are 'definitely situated in a general hermeneutical perspective.'[100] However, most problematic to Haddad is Hanafi's idiosyncratic intellectual genealogy. Mystified by the simultaneous reliance on Qutb, Mawdudi, Iqbal, Grunebaum, Massignon and Ricoeur, he questions whether Hanafi's highly personal interpretations can be legitimately presented as a general theory.[101]

Haddad thinks Hanafi's contradictory positions are explained by a blind spot in the latter's historical understanding. More interested in structures than developments, Hanafi regards history not as a formative process creating ideas, but as a carrier or occasion of appearance. Effectively rejecting the notion of historicity, Hanafi still thinks he can safeguard continuity without failing Muslim tradition.[102] The problem with this is, that by divorcing the revealed given data from dogma and history, he has rejected all historical manifestations of religious phenomena. Aside from arousing the ire of the Islamists, as a result of his misunderstanding of the crisis of Orientalism, Hanafi has also alienated the traditionalist and moderate modernist Muslims. His blanket rejection of scientism and rhetoricism made him throw away the baby with the bathwater, while his particular philosophical orientation made him miss the great revolution in French historiography as a result of the impact of the *Annales* School. Although he therefore rejects Hanafi's methodology as a 'new Islamology,' Haddad has recognised his signifi-cance for religious reform and Islamic liberation theology, even specu-lating that the launch of the Heritage and Renewal Project at the beginning of the fifteenth century of the Islamic calendar positioned Hanafi as the potential *mujaddid* or 'renewer' of his age.[103]

In conclusion, transforming the study of religion into an anthropol-ogy or human science has had lasting consequences for Hanafi's herme-neutics. On a level of communication, it has translated into a sustained interest in critically examining the Islamic heritage and re-expressing it in a new language, whereas on the ideological level it forged a human-ist orientation with a teleology directed towards the emancipation of the developing world. But this still leaves the question of how to char-acterise Hanafi as a Muslim intellectual.

Taking into account the amalgam of intellectual influences to which Hasan Hanafi was exposed, we are confronted not so much with a dual personality as with a multiplicity of personalities:

I do not know whether I am a follower of Husserl and Ricoeur, or a born phe-nomenologist, analysing living religions, philosophical and political experi-ences. [Or am I] an old Muslim brother who suffered from Nasser's early persecution in 1954? Maybe I am a mystic describing his psychological states.[104]

Not only does Hanafi self-identify as a phenomenologist in the Sorbonne theses, his language is also cast in the technical and analyti-cal jargon of Husserlian phenomenology, even though he does not give up the possibility of maintaining an existentialist interest in 'lived experience,' which he shares with his mentors Guitton and Ricoeur. In his autobiography Hanafi noted how he favoured the positivist approaches found in Kant and Bergson, while simultaneously drawing on Kierkegaard, Gabriel Marcel and Uthman Amin for the existential perspective.[105] His attempt to combine an existentialist orientation with a rigorously scientific approach to the study of religion, synthesis-ing the reflective analyses of historical and eidetic consciousness into one methodology resembles Husserl's profound revision of transcen-dental idealism after abandoning the *Cartesian Meditation* for an exploration of the Life-World in *The Crisis of the European Sciences*. With the accent no longer placed on the monadic ego but on the 'sur-rounding world in which it is vitally engaged,' phenomenology under-went 'the impressive mutation' which prepared it for the 'astonishing encounter with existential meditation.'[106]

This is what makes Husserl the nodal point in a trajectory along which the ideas informing Hanafi's philosophical outlook travelled, eventually reaching him through the charitable and generous interpretations of his mentor Paul Ricoeur. In order to formulate a philosophical hermeneutics that does 'not cut itself off from those disciplines, which, in their method, turn to interpretation: exegesis, history, and psychoanalysis,' Hanafi appears to follow Ricoeur through the 'narrow gate' of structural-linguistics analysis.[107] In spite of his reservations towards applied phenomenology, the following extensive quote from Walter Lowe's introduction to *Fallible Man* shows the remarkable parallels between Hanafi and Ricoeur:

Ricoeur's second mentor, Edmund Husserl (1859–1938), presents on first impression a marked contrast to Marcel. Whereas Marcel couched his insights in loosely textured, quasi-literary essays, Husserl's work is analytical and highly technical. Whereas Marcel warned against constraining philosophy as a series of problems, Husserl wished to make of philosophy 'a rigorous science' Yet Ricoeur is explicit that *Freedom and Nature* is to be located 'at the meeting point of two demands: those of thought nourished by the mystery of *my* body, and those of thought concerned with the distinctions inherited from Husserlian descriptive method.' If Ricoeur has had any success in bridging the often unreconciled worlds of continental and Anglo-American philosophy, the reason may already be suggested in this early, twofold commitment to existential question and rigorous method.[108]

Replace Iqbal for Marcel, read Islamic and Western heritage for continental and Anglo-American philosophy, and one ends up with the profile of the phenomenological hermeneutician Hanafi.

Throughout his career Hanafi has also positioned himself as a *faqih* or jurist. While working on *The Methods of Exegesis*, he participated in the publication of critical edition of a text on *'ilm usul al-fiqh* by the Mu'tazilite Abu'l-Husayn al-Basri (d. 1085 CE).[109] When developing a new language for re-expressing the archaic terminology of *usul al-fiqh* Brunschvig suggested the transposition procedure which Hanafi eventually adopted. For this reason Hanafi considered his contribution as no less radical than that of the discipline's founder, Imam al-Shafi'i, even presenting *The Methods of Exegesis* as the modern-day equivalent of the latter's *Al-Risala*.[110] Also in the closing words of *An Introduction to the Science of Occidentalism*, Hanafi referred to himself as an 'old *faqih* positioned between two civilisations—representing one, criticising the other, while innovating both.'[111] Finally, when describing his work to Susanne Olsson, he reiterated that he was 'not making theology [...] [but] jurisprudence.'[112]

As my detailed discussions of *The Methods of Exegesis* and *Heritage and Renewal* have shown, because of its scholarly rigour and penetrative approach *'ilm usul al-fiqh* was raised from a typical legal science to the level of a method of philosophical investigation. Thus the tools of the trade of the jurists of the classical period were refashioned into a *'fiqhi* method.' Transforming it further into a general phenomenological hermeneutic by pairing it with the other foundational science of *usul al-din* or 'greater *fiqh*,' and selective borrowings from Western philosophy, Hanafi has produced a 'highly original blend' of *Neo-fiqh*.[113] Hanafi's own interpretation can be found in an article on Ibn Rushd. There he distinguished between 'Ibn Rushd, the jurist' (*al-faqih*) and 'the juristic Ibn Rushd' (*Ibn Rushd faqihan*), whereby the former refers to the practitioner of conventional jurisprudence and the latter to the 'philosophical renewer' engaged in theology, philosophy, medicine and exegesis. The first is the author of *Bidayat al-mujtahid*, the second of *Tahafut al-Tahafut* or *The Refutation of Refutation* and *Fasl al-Maqal* or *The Definitive Statement*.[114] It is also in this sense that Hanafi himself can be regarded as an 'Arab Averroist' or 'Neo-Ibn Rushdian.'[115]

The multilayered autobiographical sketch reflects the various directions from which Hanafi drew inspiration for his general Islamic method and subsequent overly ambitious Heritage and Renewal Project, channelling them into one continuous current of philosophical concerns. The replication of the structure of the phenomenological hermeneutics developed by the young academic philosopher Hasan Hanafi of the 1960s in the revolutionary emancipation project of the organic intellectual of the 1980s suggests a methodological consistency maintained throughout his writings, in spite of any shortcomings in the later ideologically charged elaborations. Consequently, whereas the contours of what Unamuno called the 'wherefore' can already be discerned in the writings from the 1960s, the tensions affecting the 'how' of his methodology remain unresolved.[116]

As a result of the sheer scope of work and the ideological intention underlying his Heritage and Renewal Project, Hanafi's conciliation of the idealist-rationalist *cogito* and the *ego* of existentialist provenance still reflects the utopian teleology of which his virtual interlocutor, Berlin, was so suspicious.[117] He has been unable to respond convincingly to the challenge posed by Berlin's contention that these are not so much methods as incompatible and irreconcilable doctrines.[118] Because of Hanafi's insistence that phenomenology is nevertheless capable of such a synthesis, it is opportune to recall Ricoeur's observation that—to Husserl—the greatness of Descartes lay in having produced 'a philosophy which is at the same time a science and the ground of all sciences within the system of one universal science.'[119]

That is exactly the task Hanafi set for himself. Where Tarabishi resorted to psychoanalysis to describe the project in pathological terms as a case of intellectual megalomania, the Marxist Boullata was not only wary of the scale of the project, but also criticised its failure to account for the material basis of human reality; remaining 'essentially predicated on the prior necessity of spiritual reconstruction'—not an unreasonable conclusion considering Hanafi's self-identification as a mystic.[120] However, Hanafi was also too cerebral and theoretical and because he was unable to make the practical transformations achieved by Nurcholish Madjid, he never gathered the kind of popular following Madjid could command. Moreover, the political intellectual climate in most parts of the Arab world is too restrictive for the emergence of a cultural or civil Islam like in Indonesia. There Hanafi's books feature on the reading lists of the country's network of Islamic universities and institutes of higher education, and a number of them have even been translated into Indonesian.[121]

However, in spite of falling short of his own ambitions and the expectations these had evoked, Hanafi's attempt to reconstruct Islam's intellectual legacy and trying to embed it into the generic field of religious studies remains valuable. As a hermeneutician trying to reconcile the inside view of traditional Islamic learning with the outsider perspective provided by the Western human sciences, he is regarded by some as a cosmopolitan Muslim intellectual, while others consider him a heretic.

'*Oportet haereses esse*'
['We need heretics']

Lucien Febvre, *Combats pour l'Histoire*

'*History and ethnography have often been contrasted on the grounds that the former rests on the critical study of documents by numerous observers, which can therefore be compared and cross-checked, whereas the latter is reduced, by definition, to the observations of a single individual.*'

Claude Lévi-Strauss, *Structural Anthropology*

'*Men resemble their times more than they do their fathers.*'

Arab proverb, quoted in Marc Bloch, *The Historian's Craft*

9

A CULTURAL AND INTELLECTUAL BORDER CROSSER

THE EARLY YEARS OF MOHAMMED ARKOUN

An ethnic Berber from Algeria's Kabylia region, Mohammed Arkoun was initially educated in French in Taourirt-Mimoun and then went to an Arabic secondary school in Oran. This was followed by under-graduate studies in Arabic literature, philosophy, geography and law in Algiers, before moving to France for his postgraduate work at the Sorbonne and a career in academia. Because of this varied cultural and educational exposure, biographer Ursula Günther characterises Arkoun as a 'border crosser' who in spite of this displacement is equally at home in Muslim and European culture. In fact:

[t]his self-chosen 'exile'—which he does not experience as such—enables him to position himself both inside and outside the Islamic cultural zone. Because of this simultaneous engagement and distancing, Arkoun can build bridges and explore new ways, leading out of the immanent limitations and difficulties of the present discourse. As a border crosser he finds himself in a tense relation-ship with both the home and exile culture. Thus he can formulate a double critique of the two societies to which he belongs.[1]

Once he had established himself as a prominent scholar of Islam, positioned in the interstices of cultures and scholarly traditions, Ark-oun described his task as the excavation of 'new fields of research and critical thinking on the stakes not yet perceived, not considered because they are hiding *in-between* the many concepts currently instrumental-ised for ideological polarisation.'[2] While Arkoun's oeuvre is suffused with a 'primacy of method,' at the same time it must be said that his own approach is not very systematic.[3] Although appreciative of the attempts to apply sociological notions in the study of classical Islamic history, Michel Allard—one of the first scholars to take notice of Arkoun—already suggested that a better articulated methodology would make the advocacy of such innovations more convincing.[4]

Acquiring a comprehensive overview of Arkoun's programmatic suggestions is indeed hampered by his tendency to develop one concept out of another, the frequent references to earlier writings, and a habit of completing propositions he has made elsewhere without reiterating the main points.[5] This fragmentation is further aggravated by his preference for the essay and the scholarly article instead of the monograph. It falls thus to the reader to interconnect the resulting multitude of notions and discern the dynamic and coherent new research programme for Islamic studies.[6] Arkoun has high expectations of his audience in another respect as well; assuming that they are already conversant with recent achievements in the humanities and social sciences, or that they at least have the willingness to familiarise themselves on their own accord with these developments. Otherwise, says Arkoun, his 'books would be even more overwhelmingly heavy to handle than they are already.'[7]

Another student of Arkoun's writings—Mohammad El Ayadi—believes that the multifarious ideas employed in the proposed 'renovation of Islamic thinking' require a more explicit clarification of the concepts shaping the Nietzschean vigour of a project bearing an unmistakably personal imprint.[8] In this regard, Arkoun himself noted that his intellectual motivations are not just informed by his academic formation, but also grounded in this existential experience.[9] Students of Arkoun's life before his move to France mention, for example, his disenchantment with the quality of Algeria's pre-independence higher education system. In fact, during his undergraduate years (1949–54) at the University of Algiers, he developed a reputation as something of a rebel by challenging the education authorities up to the ministerial level. He managed to upset the inspector general for Arabic studies to such a degree that it took the intervention of no one less than the famed Islamicist Louis Massignon for Arkoun to be admitted to the Sorbonne for his postgraduate studies.[10]

In a comparative study of the notion of authenticity in the writings of a number of modern and postmodern Muslim thinkers, Robert Lee too characterised Arkoun's propositions for a new approach to the study of Islam as grounded in his 'being in the world,' leading to a 'concrete, lived, felt, particular' conceptualisation of truth claims.[11] Such commentaries and self-reflections appear to affirm Flood's contention in *Beyond Phenomenology* that a scholar's personal biography is relevant for appreciating his or her particular paradigm for studying religions.[12] All the more reason, then, to make a detailed inventory of the various intellectual influences which have not just impacted on Arkoun's reassessment of the Islamic heritage, but also his propositions for a different conceptualisation of the study of Islam as an academic specialisation.

Arabic and Islamic Studies in France

Arriving in Paris on the eve of the Algerian War of Independence, Arkoun found himself in the same tumultuous political and intellectual climate as Hanafi. Unlike Hanafi's identification of his own philosophical preoccupations with the emancipation of the Third World, it appears that amidst the impending end of colonialism and the upcoming Non-Aligned Movement, Arkoun remained very wary of the revolutionaries' embrace of leftist ideologies and their disregard for Algeria's ethnic and religious diversity.[13] In comparison to Arkoun's uncompromising challenge to the blinkers obscuring the views of many proponents of *Tiers Mondisme*, the sceptical attitude of Hanafi towards the polemical rhetoric of authors like Fanon appears thus less critical.[14] Arkoun's uncompromising criticism prefigures his later stance when—as 'a scholar and professor of the History of Islamic Thought'—he felt obliged to translate his objections to the misguided ideological positions of his peers into suggestions for new approaches to what he considers the two major feats of Islamic thinking between the eighth and thirteenth centuries: 'the spectacular success of Greek philosophy and sciences' and 'the expanding horizons of religious reason through dynamic schools of theology and law.'[15]

As an Algerian whose intellectual maturing coincided with his country's struggle for independence, Arkoun says that Massignon's appeal to give one's work a 'personal intonation' inspired him to retain a humanist dimension in his academic labours.[16] This orientation parallels the anthropocentric focus found in the work of the other two new Muslim intellectuals discussed in this study, although Hanafi's use of the tested and already somewhat staid legacy of German phenomenology, Bible criticism and church history, as well as Madjid's reliance on American sociologists of religion appear to follow less radical or adventurous scholarly paths than the ones explored by Arkoun.

The 'new history' of the *Annales* School

After obtaining an *Agrégation* in Arabic Studies in 1956, Mohammed Arkoun took up a dual appointment at a *lycée* and the University of Strasbourg, where he befriended Claude Cahen a Marxist historian of Jewish origin, specialising in the Arab Middle Ages and the Crusades. Cahen introduced Arkoun to the *nouvelle histoire* or 'new history' developed at the same university a quarter of a century earlier by Lucien Febvre and Marc Bloch.[17] Just as these two founders of what came to be known as the *Annales* School remained close after taking up prestigious positions at the Collège de France and the Sorbonne respectively, Arkoun's relationship with Cahen was also sustained after their joint transfer to Paris in 1959, and he credits his mentor with introducing the *Annales* approach to the study of Islamic history. Its challenges to the prevailing 'categorisations, periodisations and problematisations of classical Islamology'—caught in Cahen's slogan *'transgresser, déplacer, dépasser'*—were instrumental in winning over Arkoun to these pioneering approaches to historiography.[18] It would remain a lifelong interest, during which he kept abreast of developments through the three generational shifts which I believe can be discerned in the *Annales* School's own history.

It was thanks to the impact of Durkheim's sociology and the influence of Maurice Halbwachs' work on collective senses of consciousness and memory, that Bloch began imagining a new way of writing history. Dismissing individual historical events as superficial manifestations, he shifted his attention to social facts and collective representations. Febvre's interest in linguistics and psychology meanwhile, led him to interrogate discourses of the past on what he called 'missing words.' In an examination of religion in sixteenth-century France, he was the first to use terms like 'unthinkability'—a reinterpretation of which would later surface in Arkoun's vocabulary.[19] By incorporating such advances in the social sciences, the duo began to conceive of a 'history of mentalities' instead of the conventional focus on politics.[20] Although the time Arkoun became acquainted with their scholarship the *Annales* School had already been transformed from a 'heretical sect' into 'the orthodox church' of French historiography, the adage *Oportet haereses esse* (we need heretics) professed in Febvre's inaugural lecture was still very much applicable to Arkoun's own specialist field.[21]

The impact of the *Annales* School on Arkoun was further compounded by the towering figure of its second generation, Fernand

Braudel. The latter's ten-year teaching experience in Algeria and a stint at the University of São Paolo had broadened his horizons to the extent that it prepared him for a global-historical 'vision of the whole,' in which the Greater Mediterranean featured as a distinct civilisational zone within an even wider geo-historical space which also encompassed its colonial possessions in Africa and on the other side of the Atlantic.[22] Aside from this new spatial awareness, Braudel's other contribution to the rethinking of writing history was his distinction between three different 'speeds' of historical time, translated into a corresponding layered understanding of history: the geographical time of the *longue durée*, the intermediate or social time of *conjonctures*, and short-term individual time reflected in *événements*. Applying these findings in his magisterial *The Mediterranean and the Mediterranean World in the Age of Philip II*, this work would in due course enable Arkoun to better articulate what was already a latent understanding of 'the close (if inverse) relation between African and European history' awakened by his earlier studies of Latin and Roman history.[23]

To this intimidatingly comprehensive scholarly approach, Braudel also added an equally imposing institutional power, aided by 'his remarkable gift for appropriating ideas from other disciplines.'[24] While simultaneously holding a chair at the Collège de France, directing the Centre des Recherches Historiques at the École des Hautes Etudes, and exercising editorial control of the *Annales* journal, he consolidated his influence by grooming the next generation of historians, which included Emmanuel Le Roy Ladurie and Jacques Le Goff, and 'founding another organisation devoted to interdisciplinary research, the Maison des Sciences de l'Homme.'[25] Located in close proximity to the working places of other scholars of the calibre of Claude Lévi-Strauss and Pierre Bourdieu, this created a very fertile intellectual symbiosis, a 'common market' of sorts for the social sciences, but—in Braudel's adamant view—with 'history as the dominant partner.'[26] This 'remarkable amalgam' of developments in the French human sciences formed the surroundings in which Arkoun began his work as a historian of Islam, reflecting his own version of critical history as an all-embracing discipline among the social sciences.[27]

Alongside the influences of Marxism, structural linguistics and anthropology, as well as semiotics and the emergence of a deconstructive discourse criticism, the *Annales* School has become very much part of what, according to Günther, can best be described as the intellectual

Aufbruch of the French political, cultural and academic scene during the 1950s and 1960s.[28] In fact, Arkoun's doctoral studies (1956–68) match almost exactly what O'Brien calls 'the milestone dates in the chronology of dislocation' characterising the 'intellectual upheaval caused by post-war political events.'[29] Aside from the failed anti-Soviet revolution in Hungary and the equally ill-fated Prague Spring, in the case of France this time period is also framed by Algeria's struggle for independence and the student uprising of 1968.

Arkoun as medievalist

The initial encounter with the *Annales* School stimulated Arkoun to pursue a research project governed by its methodologies. When the outbreak of violent hostilities in Algeria frustrated his plans for an ethnography of religious practices in his native Kabylia under the direction of Régis Blachère, Jacques Berque and Gabriel Le Bras, Arkoun decided to shift to a text-based historical topic.[30] At the suggestion of the Islamicist Robert Brunschvig he began working on a study of the intellectual milieu surrounding the tenth- and eleventh-century dynasty of the Buyid (or Buwayhid) viziers. Focusing primarily on the thought of the scholar and writer al-Miskawayh and a number of his interlocutors at the itinerant Buyid courts at Rayy, Isfahan and Baghdad, Arkoun wrote a thesis which earned him the title *Docteur ès lettres*. Its publication in 1970 as *L'humanisme Arabe au 4ᵉ/10ᵉ Siècle: Miskawayh, Philosophe et Historien*, released as part of the prestigious *Études Musulmanes* series edited by the leading historian of philosophy Étienne Gilson and Louis Gardet, a Dominican priest and Islamicist who had studied with Massignon and Maritain, not only established Arkoun's reputation as a medievalist, but also put 'Arab humanism' on the scholarly map.[31]

On first impression this study may seem like a conventional Orientalist study of medieval Islam, but a closer inspection evinces an innovative scholarly approach . The fact that Arkoun concentrates on the writings and ideas of courtiers and men of letters (*udaba*), rather than 'the deeds of great men—captains and kings' already betrays the influence of the *Annales* paradigm: a shift from a narrative of political events towards capturing the mood and outlook of a historical period.[32] Furthermore, his presentation of the figure of Miskawayh is not just embedded in the narrow confines of the Buyid intellectual milieu, but, by a section entitled 'the practice of concrete history,' is fitted into a number of grand rubriques which also bear the unmistakable signature of the *Annales* school: history of events; institutions and political mores; social and economic history; portraits; and isolated notations.[33]

Although explicitly acknowledging the role of scholars like Febvre, Bloch, Braudel, Cahen, and their 'pleiad of great disciples' in turning this new historiography into a success story, Arkoun asserts his own distinctive scholarship and engagement as a Muslim intellectual by also relying on advances made in other human sciences. Profitably drawing on the 'rich debates that were opened up, principally between historians and structuralists,' he thought the historiography of the Muslim world could be enriched by incorporating achievements made in structural linguistics and investing a personal stake through the adoption of 'interiorist and comprehensive method so brilliantly inaugurated by L. Massignon in his study of al-Hallaj.'[34] This 'long detour through a vast field of interdisciplinary investigations' freed Arkoun up to narrow down his own project to a case study of one individual, while at the same time conceiving of it as 'a step towards the understanding of an oeuvre as, at one at the same time, a product of and support for a global socio-cultural reality.'[35]

On the other hand, in a relatively recent meditation he regrets having failed to convince more conservative Islamicists, such as Charles Pellat and Roger Arnaldez, of the value of this alternative method drawing on *nouvelle histoire*, structural linguistics and anthropology, and semiotics. Instead he found himself debating the merits of the *Annales* approach which these 'grand masters' had qualified as one of those 'Parisian fashions,' dismissing it as *'nouvelle imposture.'*[36]

Arkoun and the French Intellectual Scene in the Late Twentieth Century

In spite of such reservations on the part of prominent colleagues Arkoun persevered. Deciding against returning to his homeland he remained in France, embarking on what would become a highly distinguished career as a university professor at the Sorbonne, writer, journal editor, and adviser to various scholarly organisations and international bodies, including UNESCO, the Institute of Ismaili Studies in London and the Aga Khan Foundation. Although he undeniably belongs to the country's intellectual elite, Arkoun's relationships with both the French scholarly establishment and the intelligentsia in the Muslim world have been marked by a degree of unease. Symptomatic of this liminal position is his unwavering commitment to a robust double critique of both the intellectual developments in the Muslim world and existing scholarship in Islamic studies, as well as the careful examination of the human sciences as a whole, and the bold innovations introduced by the pioneering academics who have defined the French contributions to this field during the final decades of the twentieth century, including some on first view perhaps arcane developments in social anthropology.

Roger Bastide's Applied Anthropology

The innovative research programme, which Arkoun began elaborating on the basis of his hands-on work as a medievalist and subsequent inquiry into other scholarly fields, would eventually be presented under the name 'Applied Islamology.' That designation is taken from *Applied Anthropology*, a book written by the French ethnographer and sociologist Roger Bastide.[37] Although this is cursorily acknowledged by Arkoun himself and his biographer Ursula Günther, the connection has never been properly documented.[38] A more detailed examination is important, as it will support another assertion by Günther that Arkoun's 'Applied Islamology' can be regarded as setting an alternative agenda for Islamic studies combining anthropological methods of investigation with a critique of epistemological theory.[39] It will also show the eclecticism that underlies the cosmopolitan attitude of culturally hybrid intellectuals like Arkoun.

Bastide unpacked his 'Applied Anthropology' towards the end of his career in order to formulate a solid social theory for dealing with the phenomenon of acculturation in cultural border situations characterised by hybridisation.[40] It is inspired by his own work on Afro-Brazilian religions and the imaginative approaches developed by local Brazilian social scientists with which he became acquainted during his stay in that country between 1938 and 1954, where he was associated with the newly-founded University of São Paolo. A vibrant academic environment, in the 1930s it had hosted a number of French social scientists, including Claude Lévi-Strauss (whom Bastide succeeded) and Georges Gurvitch, while the presence of Febvre and Braudel brings also the *Annales* School back into the picture.[41]

Brazil provided Bastide not only with the data for his monumental *The African Religions of Brazil: Toward a Sociology of the Interpenetration of Civilizations*, which he published in 1960, the totality of these South American experiences also informed his historical outlook, providing a basis for a theory which would allow him 'to analyze, within a single conceptual framework, individuals, cultures, and social and economic infrastructures, and to clarify the dialectic relationship between the historical transformation of these infrastructures and the religious phenomena in question.'[42] Together with a much earlier study, *The Social Origins of Religion*, written in 1935, *The African Religions of Brazil* and *Applied Anthropology* provide an insight into Bastide's scholarly concerns and help determine how these carried over into Arkoun's Applied Islamology.

Taking 'religion as a central part of mankind's ongoing cultural activity,' Bastide wanted to go beyond to what he called 'the chaos of religious facts,' a position reflecting an appreciation of Durkheim's view of religion as embedded in the totality of social structures—in contrast to the economic reductionism of Marx and to some extent also of Weber.[43] His desire to understand humankind as 'the manipulator of the sacred, and constructor of symbolic worlds,' meanwhile reflects a simultaneous acknowledgement of the contributions made to structural anthropology by Lévi-Strauss.[44] However Bastide was more interested in transformation and change than in constancy and structure, and focused therefore more on such phenomena as acculturation and the interpenetration of civilisations. That is why he also appreciated Comte's views of cultural evolution, the Bergsonian fluid sense of life, and Lévy-Bruhl's sensitivity to the sheer wealth of cultural diversity and the associated questions of understanding and interpreting systems of symbols. These interests directed him further towards the philosophy of Cassirer, the depth-sociology of Gurvitch, and Kardiner's notion of 'basic personality structure,' brought to France by the phenomenologist Mikel Dufrenne.[45]

Understanding acculturation as dialectics between values and social structures, Bastide considered the expression interpenetration of civilisations more accurate than a term like syncretism, which he dismissed as a mere 'mechanical juxtaposition of cultural traits borrowed from two different civilisations.'[46] Accordingly 'in a world where races, ethnic groups, and civilisations mix, the question arises how a more complete theorising of such phenomena can be achieved.'[47] When trying to make sense of a phenomenon like acculturation it is therefore important to find a balance between the cultural concerns of anthropology and sociology's interest in group dynamics and social structures, because 'civilisational clash and interpenetration does not occur in a vacuum but in clearly determined social contexts.'[48] Bastide therefore saw anthropology and sociology as each other's complement, with the concept of collective memory acting as the binding factor, because this 'immediately forces us to take a sociological view of the problem of acculturation.'[49]

The theorising of acculturation is further explored in *Applied Anthropology*, where Bastide contrasts it with the social process of integration. He also takes care to distinguish it from the concept of 'enculturation,' or the transmission of a given culture from one generation to another, which can actually form an obstacle to the acculturation process. Mapping some of the other complexities, he notes that technical and material elements of cultures are more easily transferable than the symbolic elements—such as religious ones. In addition it is important to realise that cultural systems are not always completely coherent and must be considered as dynamic rather than static. Also of interest is Bastide's stress on the 'omnipresent existence of international contradictions,' in which both cohesive centripetal and disintegrating centrifugal forces are at play.[50]

A detour into Lusotropicology

Applied Anthropology had primarily theoretical pretensions and Bastide was the first to admit that the actual practice of applied anthropology was pioneered by Anglo-Saxon social scientists: with the British using their colonial empire as a vast laboratory, while in the United States the internal social problems with first nation and immigrant groups also provided opportunities for experimentation. However, benefitting from his Brazilian experiences, Bastide added the observation that the complexity of the practical issues at hand makes it necessary that such projects are undertaken by multidisciplinary teams, consisting not only of academics but also administrators working in the field of development.[51] This need for interdisciplinary cooperation within an international community of scholars was explicitly taken on board by Arkoun.[52]

The theoretical principles underlying Bastide's applied anthropology were first articulated within the framework of an idiosyncratic scholarly specialism, known as 'Lusotropicology' developed by the ethnologist and sociologist Gilberto de Mello Freyre.[53] He popularised his ideas through a colourful trilogy portraying plantation life around the 'big houses' in his native north-eastern Brazil greatly admired by Fernand Braudel as an image of a microcosm and metaphor for the region's social and cultural hybridity. These writings established Freyre as an exponent of Brazil's Modernist Movement, which was not just transforming the art world, but the intellectual scene in its wider sense.[54]

Although Freyre presented his exploration of 'the bio-social and cultural relations of man with the tropics' and of foreigners—in his case the Portuguese—with the indigenous populations of their colonies under the neologism 'tropicology,' he was actually not claiming to be doing anything new.[55] In fact he traces the first centres of lusotropical knowledge to the sixteenth-century Portuguese university at Coimbra and colonial outposts like Goa and Recife, *The Lusiads* of Camões and Mendes Pinto's *Peregrineção* as its first exponents.[56] Emerging in a climate which Panikkar referred to as Portugal's 'renascence of philosophy,' these writings were based on the authors' experiential knowledge rather than metaphysically-founded epistemologies, and Freyre had therefore no hesitation to see in Camões a forerunner of the American pragmatist philosopher Dewey.[57]

Even more pertinent in the context of the present attempt to sketch the connections between Arkoun, Bastide and Freyre, is the latter's assertion that this 'pragmatic increase of the value of existence' resulted from the contacts between Christians, Jews and Muslims in the Iberian Peninsula before the Age of Discovery. In his assessment Arab-Islamic knowledge was not so much a matter of theoretical acquisition as the outcome of human intercourse.[58] Hailed as a 'new scientific humanism' by Bastide and Gurvitch, Freyre attributed this favourable response from the Europeans to a reorientation in European social thought, which had started the early twentieth century.[59] Following in the tracks of what Freyre calls 'Hispanic Science' this change of direction in the human sciences is reflected in the works of Croce, Bergson and Weber, which he regards as being imbued with a personal quality found in Nietzsche and Freud but lacking in Durkheim.[60]

In one of the chapters in *Applied Anthropology*, entitled 'Defence and Illustration of Marginality,' Bastide ties his excursion into to his earlier work on the marginalisation of those affected by psychopathological conditions, underscoring the important role played by 'cultural marginals as leaders of the acculturative gambit.'[61] Invoking the findings of North-American scholars that 'simultaneous integration into two cultures, far from being considered as marginality, is seen by sociologists as a normal evolution and a progression by progressive internalisation of the values, ideas and norms seen as superior,' this also affirms the contention made throughout this book that because they *are* cultural hybrids and intellectual border crossers, new Muslim intellectuals such as Arkoun hold great potential for revitalising scholarly fields such as the study of Islam.[62]

Aside from its mediation through Bastide, the affinities between Lusoptropicology and Arkoun's Applied Islamology can also be approached through Bourdieu's *Le Sens Pratique*. In this study conducted in Arkoun's native Kabylia, Bourdieu too 'emphasised the experiential character and the practical, empirical, unwritten scope of the "values," norms, and "symbolic capital" which underlie and regulate the status of each member of the group.' In Arkoun's view, this 'practical sense' provides a suitable cognitive framework for examining the dynamics between the group, the status of the person, and mediating role of cultural phenomena like beliefs, collective rituals, myths, proverbs, and the grander schemes of religion, doctrines, law, arts and literature. Arkoun considers Bourdieu's privileging of the group at the expense of personal autonomy a particularly useful tool in studying those societies, including Islamic ones, which have remained 'more closely attached to the oral than to the written tradition.'[63]

The emergence of historical anthropology

In addition to his interest in the advances made in the social sciences, Arkoun also kept abreast of the considerable transformations affecting the *Annales* School, which, if not leading to an intellectual fragmentation, at the very least were making it more polycentric than before.[64] On the one hand, its economic and cultural history writing witnessed a comprehensive 'quantitative revolution' advocated by the likes of Labrousse and Chaunu, while on the other there occurred a distinct reaction against such determinist approaches, evident in attempts to revive the narrative and a return to the histories of mentalities. After decades of marginalisation under the oppressive influence of the Braudelian focus on socio-economic history, the late 1970s witnessed an 'anthropological turn' towards the study of culture and symbolism.

In contrast with earlier generations who would 'raid' the discipline of anthropology every so often for new concepts, the new breed of *Annales* historians represented by Le Goff and Duby had the more serious intention of developing a hybrid discipline called *ethnohistoire* or 'historical anthropology.'[65]

As a pioneering interdisciplinary recipe combining 'Braudelian *structures*, Labroussian *conjuncture*, and the new historical demography' employed by other *Annales* historians, it stimulated studies on topics such as health, sexuality, the experience of childhood, death, sacred places, as well as mundane aspects of material culture, like food and dress.[66] Inspired by Mauss and Malinowski, as well as contemporary scholars like Turner, Bourdieu, and De Certeau, the third *Annales* generation began producing so-called 'microhistories.'[67]

In studies like *Time, Work, and Culture in the Middle Ages* and *The Medieval Imagination*, Le Goff amplifies the connection between social and intellectual change, inviting a different way of looking at the Middle Ages and making a case for accounting for the way mental structures and habits of thought are mediated through an intellectual apparatus distinctive for this particular period in history. As a social and economic historian trained in the tradition of Bloch, Duby was particularly interested in 'the history of ideologies, cultural reproduction, and the social imagination.'[68] This new approach, which he refers to as the 'anthropology of the past' or 'archaeology of the daily life,' had a profound influence on Arkoun. Especially the notion of the imaginary—or *l'imaginaire*—introduced by Althusser, but given wider currency by the sociologist and philosopher Cornelius Castoriadis, frequently recurs in Arkoun's writings, whereby he explicitly acknowledges his indebtedness to Castoriadis, Le Goff and Duby.[69]

Also incorporated into the revised history of mentalities under the *Annales* paradigm is a heightened awareness that ideology 'is not a passive reflection of society, but a plan for acting upon it.'[70] This realisation coincides with another generational shift in the *Annales* School and reflects the impact of postmodernist theories issuing from structural linguistics and anthropology on the writings of scholars such as Roger Chartier, Pierre Nora and Jacques Revel.[71] Grounded in the earlier mentioned notion of 'the imaginary,' their cultural histories are marked by 'a return to the ideas of Maurice Halbwachs on the social framework of memory' and informed by the philosophy of Foucault.[72] What their predecessors had still regarded as objective structures were now said to be culturally constituted or constructed, turning society itself into a collective representation. Economic and social relations do not determine cultural ones, but are themselves 'fields of cultural practice and cultural production.'[73]

The influences of the 'prophets of extremity'[74]

It is important to note that there has also been an inverse effect of the *Annales* School on Foucault, whose archaeology or genealogy bears 'at the very least a family resemblance to the history of mentalities.'[75] Although he was a quintessential outsider, Foucault's own historical investigations invite further comparisons with the *Annales* School. His erasure of the subject links up with the displacement of the history of events and its dismissal of the significance of individual historical actors in the *Annales* paradigm. Whilst his favouring of interplays, correlations, dominances, ruptures, and new forms rather than structures may have led him to produce a general history rather than a total history, the breadth and ambition of his undertaking was nevertheless acknowledged by Braudel.[76] Leaving no place for human agency in this space of dispersal, Foucault recognised power as the organising principle regulated by discursive formations, and what interested him were the rules governing these discourses. When investigating power relations, Foucault did not look for causalities in the form of evolution or recurrences. Instead his genealogical method seems to follow in the footsteps of Bloch, tracing 'beginnings, *not* origins.'[77]

In spite of differences in elaboration, this points up another resemblance with the *Annales* School. As Patricia O'Brien argues: having 'refashioned historical understanding through practice rather than theory,' Foucault's writings on history represent a method, not a theory, thus paralleling the claim of the *Annales* paradigm that 'a theory of social change is not necessary for a consistent methodology.'[78] Although Arkoun's humanism puts him at odds with Foucault's dispersal of man, the latter's interrogation of power relations and 'methodological centrality of discourse' in history is highly relevant for Arkoun's own methodology.[79]

Besides shaping Arkoun's work indirectly under the *Annales* paradigm, these more 'recent trends in French academic thought' have also left a more immediate imprint on Arkoun.[80] Well aware of the controversies raised by the writings of his fellow Algerian, Jacques Derrida,

Arkoun is adamant that the latter's introduction of the notion of logo-centrism into the postmodern intellectual vocabulary is important to the field of Islamic studies, in spite of the fact that 'not one historian of Islamic philosophy and theology paid any attention to the ensuing debate.' Even though Arkoun has no intention of entering the fracas surrounding the concept's philosophical merits, he considers it methodologically relevant. Without taking sides, he thinks it is 'important to show that the impact of logocentrism on Islamic thought is as strong, although less durable, as it was on European medieval thought.'[81] To demonstrate this point, he used the concept in an article on al-'Amiri, one of the members of the circle of Buyid courtiers he had studied in his dissertation.[82]

Connecting the dots: The influence of Paul Ricoeur

To understand Arkoun's simultaneous reliance on the historiography of the *Annales* School and structuralist and poststructuralist theories, it is instructive to consider the American anthropologist Marshall Sahlins' *Historical Metaphors and Mythical Realities*, in which he explores the interfaces between structural anthropology and the *Annales* School. By relating Braudel's *longue durée* and *histoire événementielle* to Lévi-Strauss's 'order of structure' and 'order of events,' Sahlins developed a 'structural historical anthropology.'[83] In this reading, structure 'refers to the cultural categories, conceived—Saussure-like—as a conceptual grid,' creating an operational field for the interface of the two core themes of the book: cultural reproduction and transformation. Whereas reproduction manages the dialectic of history as culturally ordered and cultural schemes as historically ordered, transformation describes how the innovation of cultural schemes is accomplished through 'the actual practices of historical actors.'[84]

As an example of the 'blurring of genres' which accompanies such a paradigmatic shift from structural to historical anthropology, Aletta Biersack credits Sahlins with performing 'the same intellectual feat that the philosopher Paul Ricoeur accomplishes in his essay on language, "Structure, Word, Event," which openly takes on the challenge of reconciling structuralism with hermeneutics.'[85] The invocation of Ricoeur raises an important point because, whereas the anthropological model reigned supreme among the *Annales* historians of the 1980s, I suggest that their use of terms like 'appropriation' and 'transformation' point directly towards Ricoeur's *Hermeneutics and the Human Sciences*. Moreover, Arkoun's use of the work of the structural linguist Emile Benveniste in defining his own alternative programme for Islamic Studies shows, to my mind, an immediate affinity with Ricoeur's use of the Danish structuralist Louis Hjelmslev in articulating his hermeneutics.

The interconnections between Arkoun, the *Annales* School and Ricoeur do not end here. Braudel's distinction between geographical, social, and individual time has in turn been very relevant for the subsequent development of Ricoeur's philosophy of time. However, the latter's criticism of Braudel's depreciation of events and human history, as well as the challenge of his thoughtful meditations in both *Time and Narrative* and *La Mémoire, l'Histoire, l'Oubli* to the alleged reductionism of the quantitative methodologies favoured by Braudel actually prepared the ground for Ricoeur's ingenious salvation of narrativity.[86] In fact, Ricoeur singled out Duby and Le Goff's 'historical anthropology of the pre-industrial West' as the prime source for his restoration of the narrative through the concept of emplotment.[87] Aside from a concern with the relation between time and narrative, the revised histories of mentalities resulting from 'joining history together with disciplines for which time is not a major category' enabled Ricoeur to establish what Arkoun explores through the notions of 'logocentrism,' 'exhaustive tradition,' and 'the unthought': namely that ordinary people, often denied the right to speak by dominant forms of discourse, regain their voice through these alternative histories.[88]

In a final analysis, the *Annales* School's advocacy of bringing together a variety of disciplines, such as economics, demography, and models of structuralist analysis developed by Lévi-Strauss was driven by a desire for creating new ways of writing history. Arkoun too can be considered an exponent of the *Annales* School, regarded by Ricoeur as subscribing to a 'strict adherence to the profession of the historian' and concerned with providing a 'methodology for those actually in the field.'[89] However, at the same time, Ricoeur's customary detours along the hermeneutical spectrum of *Annales* scholarship in order to reconcile the School's uncompromising adherence to the 'historian's craft'[90] with more speculative approaches to the objectives of historiography, is reflected in Arkoun's ability to remain attentive to French overtures to the philosophy of history represented by Raymond Aron.[91] This, in turn, makes it also possible to discern parallels between Mohammed Arkoun's primacy of method and Hasan Hanafi's preoccupation with finding a genuine Islamic methodology for philosophical investigation.

10

APPLIED ISLAMOLOGY

Arkoun introduced the term Applied Islamology for the first time in *Essais sur la Pensée Islamique*.[1] Framed by an epistemological reflection on Muslim and Western scholarship on Islam, while functioning as an ancillary to the earlier identified personal and humanist concerns which permeate his oeuvre; it seeks to articulate a critical examination of what is alternatively referred to as Islamic thought or Islamic reason. As described in the preceding chapter, mapping the genesis of this innovative research programme is complicated by the fact that Arkoun tends to continuously revise, delete, replace parts of his earlier writings or add and return to previous work. While it gives the project fluidity, it poses a challenge when trying to obtain an accurate and comprehensive overview of its purview.

It is therefore not entirely surprising that, in the preface to the second edition of *L'Humanisme Arabe* published twelve years after its first release, Arkoun registers his disappointment over the fact that neither his interpretation of Arab-Islamic Humanism nor his 'methodological overtures and problematics' had received the anticipated response.[2] I therefore surmise that the frustration born from this experience was an important motivation for his attempt to relaunch Applied Islamology as a distinct alternative research agenda, as becomes clear from the inclusion of an article published in 1976 under the title 'Pour une Islamologie Appliquée' as the opening chapter in what is regarded as his most significant essay collection: *Pour une Critique de la Raison Islamique*.[3] Together with 'Towards a Renewal of Arabic Studies' and 'the tasks of the Muslim Intellectual,' this text sets the agenda for a new approach to the academic study of Islam involving specialists from both the Muslim world and the West.[4]

Whereas the alternative ways of engaging with the Islamic heritage by other innovative Muslim intellectuals still bear the recognisable contours of the various disciplines of traditional Islamic learning, Arkoun's programme is presented under rubrics of his own design, using often idiosyncratic jargon which forces him to constantly clarify his terminology.[5] In spite of the negative reactions from fellow scholars, like *Annales* historian Marc Bloch, Arkoun insisted that such nomenclature is a necessary evil if one wants to 'transgress received knowledge.'[6] Arkoun also consistently argues that Islamicists must avail themselves of the achievements in other fields of the human sciences, especially those more advanced in critical self-examination of the assumed progress made by Western rationalist thought since the seventeenth century.[7]

Arkoun's Double Critique of Western and Muslim Scholarship in Islam

Arkoun's early work in medieval Islamic history and Arab humanism was already shaped by his dissatisfaction with the way Islam is studied both in the Muslim world and in the West.[8] After an initial stocktaking of the field in a caveat included the published version of his doctoral thesis, his Applied Islamology research agenda was grounded in a double critique against both the tradition of Muslim intellectualism and Western Orientalist scholarship, with which Arkoun continued to engage throughout his career.

Considering ideology critique as one of Applied Islamology's major objectives, he set out to historicise contemporary Muslim discourse in order to unveil the ideological prejudices which underlie the dogmatic definitions used in the existing Islamic literature and which obscure, or even hinder, a comprehensive rereading of what he calls the exhaustive Muslim tradition.[9] With a slight adaptation of the Foucauldian term 'historico-transcendental thematic,' Arkoun also challenges the 'mytho-historico-transcendental thematic' dominating the approaches of Western scholarship to the study of Islam, leaving only differences of accentuation between Muslim and Western experts.[10] In both instances Arkoun discerns the same naïvety in regard to 'concepts such as origin, genesis, evolution, development, tradition, influence, mentality, unity and universality of signification and so forth.'[11]

In the beginning Arkoun was primarily concerned with the Arab world. Both his thesis and the article 'Towards a Renewal of Arabic Studies' show that in the 1960s and 1970s, Arkoun tended to use 'Arab' and 'Islamic' interchangeably.[12] However, when—coincidental with the shift in the political domain from secular ideologies towards 'religious mythology'—references to the Muslim *umma* began to 'substitute the imagery of the Arab Nation,' Arkoun not only adjusted his terminology, but also recognised the need for a clearer circumscription of the two domains.[13] From then on, he defined 'Arabic Thought' as any writing or expression in the Arabic language regardless of the author's ethnic or religious origins, sex, or philosophical views, distinguishing it from the much broader field of 'Islamic Thought,' which involves all Muslims in their linguistic, cultural and historical diversity. But because the connection between Arab culture and Islam is both close and deep, Arkoun recognised that non-Arab Muslims participate to a considerable extent in 'Arab heritage.'[14]

The double critique of both Muslim and Western scholarship on Islam was first spelled out in an edited volume, entitled *Essais sur la Pensée Islamique*, where Arkoun also presents Applied Islamology as a remedy for the shortcomings they share, namely an emphasis on philological studies rather than critical epistemological interrogation. Reiterating a point he had already made in his doctoral thesis, according to Arkoun's diagnosis:

The real problem that classical Islamology poses is its solidarity with the postulates of what we have elsewhere defined as the *cultural configuration of the Classical Age* [...]. It is time to move beyond morality and ideology-enwrapped conveniences in order to develop a contrasting critical epistemological reflection on two systems: the classical Arab-Islamic system and the Western system.[15]

On a later occasion, Arkoun rephrased his criticism in terms borrowed from Derrida's deconstructionist jargon and the semiotics of Roland Barthes, suggesting classical Islamology forms part of the Western logosphere: 'a linguistic mental space shared by all those who use the same language with which to articulate [what] is claimed as a unifying *Weltanschauung*, while classical Islam had constituted a logosphere of its own.' Consequently, both discourses diminish the 'intellectual horizons of reason' because they narrow down its critical functions, thereby contributing to the expansion of the realm of what Arkoun refers to as 'the unthinkable.'[16]

When discussing the state of affairs in Islamic Studies in the French academe, Arkoun seems to follow in the footsteps of Ricoeur, entering the field of hermeneutics through the 'narrow gate' of structuralism.[17] Arkoun's statement that '[a]ccurate description must precede interpretation; but interpretation cannot be attempted today without a rigorous analysis, using linguistics, semiotic, historical, and anthropological tools' appears to this author as an attempt to emulate Ricoeur's generous or charitable interpretations.[18]

Critique of Western scholarship on Islam

Arkoun's main problem with the preoccupation in classical Islamology with philology and *Formgeschichte* is that it leaves fundamental philosophical issues unaddressed. As a result, 'the essential question about truth, for religious reasoning as well as for the most critical philosophical kind, is totally absent' from its academic purview.[19] The most important task of scholars, according to Arkoun, is 'to problematise all systems that claim to produce meaning.'[20] In the case of Islamic studies that means the specialism must be raised to the same level of fertile criticism as has been witnessed in European scholarship in other fields since the seventeenth century.

Classical Islamology should free itself from the narrow outlook it shares with traditional Islamic learning. Instead of 'limiting itself to the curiosities of the task of a philological restoration of the text,' it should draw on linguistics and social sciences, which contextualise philology within a 'structure of personal relationships.'[21] According to Arkoun this criticism applies not only to the impressive body of scholarship left behind by the giants from the past, such as Goldziher, Nöldeke, Andreae, Bell, and Paret. To his regret it still applies to acknowledged present-day experts such as Andrew Rippin, Gerald Hawting, Stefan Wild, and the late John Wansbrough, whose 'research does not seem to have broadened its horizons or inquiries.'[22] At the same time it is important to note that Arkoun did appreciate the considerable achievements of the orientalists, making it clear that 'the philological rigour, which is one of classical Islamology's traits, remains indispensible' and acknowledging his own indebtedness to the data it provides.[23]

In an outright challenge to claims for a *status aparte* for Islamic studies, Arkoun points out that, as text, the Qur'an is 'only one among a number of objects of study that have the same level of complexity and the same abundance of meanings,' whether one looks at the foundational text of Judaism, Christianity, Buddhism or Hinduism. He pushes the issue even further by asking why religious text corpora should be treated as any different from the Platonic and Aristotelian legacy, or even 'the corpus of the French Revolution or that of the October Revolution of 1917.'[24] Expanding from the study of scriptures to the wider field of religious studies, he brings the history of religions into the discussion as well. Calling it 'a rather marginal discipline,' because its scope of work 'spills over into many other disciplines,' Arkoun has a point when he charges that this specialism too still tends to ignore the oral legacy of the general population, even though 'they are the most directly concerned audience for this research and form by far the largest and most convinced corpus of consumers of systems of belief and non-belief.'[25]

The ensuing frustration of any comprehensive approach in the study of religious phenomena in Islamic contexts is further aggravated by the growing interest in 'the political concerns associated with militant forms of Islam' and a commensurate decline of attention to 'the study of Islam as a religion.'[26] So when a more 'pragmatic Islamology,' driven by a younger generation of Islamicists with backgrounds in social sciences rather than philology, succeeded in marginalising classical Islamology during the 1980s and 1990s, Arkoun decided he must include their approach in his critique as well.[27]

Reared on a diet from the *nouvelle cuisine* of the *Annales* paradigm, it was Bloch's *The Historian's Craft* that inspired Arkoun to introduce an alternative to this pragmatic Islamology, insisting 'on the need to practise a progressive-regressive method, combining the long-term perspective with the short-term perspective' in order to counteract this new kind of research into the socio-political issues of the Muslim world solely through the short-term perspective of the 'history of events.'[28] Apart from his own contributions to counteract these tendencies, Arkoun remarks that he has also 'pointed systematically to the pioneering Western researchers in the field of Qur'anic studies and Islamic thought in general, to a point where I have been accused by Muslim colleagues of ignoring or excluding Muslim contributions to the field.'[29]

Such challenges are also linked to Arkoun's objection to criticising classical Islamology on purely ideological grounds, as the Saidian anti-Orientalism camp has done.[30] Throughout his career he has consistently refused to use the term Orientalism, suggesting instead the use of the term 'Western scholarship on "Islam" and "Muslim" societies.'[31] At the same time Arkoun is not deaf to some of the arguments made by the critics of the tradition of Western scholarship on non-Western cultures. For example, he agrees with Said and Foucault regarding the importance of power relations in scholarship. Ironically, it is now the power of anti-Orientalist polemics itself which leads to a deplorable occurrence of self-censorship on the part of certain Western Orientalists.[32] According to Arkoun, the hostility of the anti-Orientalists' camp towards Western scholarship of Islam is still caught up in 'the revolt against colonialism, making an objective exchange almost impossible.'[33] It is this view that informs to a large extent his criticism of Muslim intellectualism.

Critique of Muslim intellectualism

On the grounds of the last observation, I am sceptical of Ursula Günther's claim that Arkoun's criticisms towards Western Islamicists are 'sharper and more incisively formulated than his critique of Muslim thought.'[34] On the contrary, his uncompromising challenges of Muslim intellectualism form part of his overall concern with Islamic reason in both the past and in the present. Arkoun has made a concerted effort to expose the biases, blind spots and weaknesses that have obscured and hindered Islamic thinking since the classical era. As for contemporary Muslim discourses on Islam, he directs his comments to three types of intellectuals: Western-educated scholars, the *'ulama* establishment, and those scholars who still abide by the methodological and theoretical tradition of the *'ulama*, accepting their 'episteme and theological aprioris.'[35]

A common point of criticism that is applicable to all three groups is their inability to transcend the limitations set by what Arkoun calls Islam's 'myth of origins.'[36] This closed system, aptly captured in the verbal metaphor of *tanzil* (the sending down of the revelation) imposes a 'vertical view of man onto all creatures, history, the terrestrial world, and the universe.'[37] It also enforces a fixed research perspective focusing on 'textual sources, scholasticism, and orthodoxy,' turning the higher education curricula in the Muslim world into a atrophied and compartimentalised system with no place for philosophy in the departments of theology and Arabic literature, while the philosophers ignore literary studies.[38] Thus the logocentrist approach continues not only to influence the *'ulama* and those relying on similar theoretical models, but, because it also informs classical Islamology, it has even impacted via this detour on Western-educated Arab-Muslim intellectuals with an interest in that academic field, in particular those associated with the Arab Renaissance or *Nahda*.[39]

Like Hanafi, Arkoun singles out Taha Husayn and Ali Abd al-Raziq as examples of the intellectual naïveté plaguing this strand of thought, which mirrored the triumph of positivism and capitalism in the West, but failed to appreciate how the seventeenth-century crisis in European consciousness had also led to critical examinations of rational thought, at the very moment when Islamic civilisation collapsed, returning to the archaism of illiterate societies and retaining only a scholastic reproduction of its earlier learning.[40] Aside from these inadequate attempts to integrate Western thought, in Arkoun's analysis the overall reaction of the Muslim intelligentsia against 'historicist-philological positivism' was no different from that of many 'Christians during the modernist crisis of the nineteenth century.'[41]

Although it would have been conceivable that Muslim intellectualism opened itself up to modern historical criticism during the post-war struggles for independence struggles, things soon ground to a halt. Arkoun identifies two reasons for that. First, what had started as a fight for political liberation inspired by nationalist ideas was soon accompanied by an ideological shift towards Marxism. Many achievements of the liberal age were brushed aside as products of bourgeois culture and replaced by what he refers to as 'the paradigm of "engaged literature and thought" imported by Marxist-Communist "intellectuals."'[42] This view is very much shaped by developments in his native Algeria. As mentioned in an earlier chapter, on various occasions Arkoun showed himself critical of the *Tiers Mondisme* emanating from the 1955 Asia-Africa conference in Bandung, which was also espoused by the FNL leadership, but did not tolerate any plurality of views:

The spirit of Bandung was a significant reference point for all those who embraced the socialist model of economic and political action as a way of quick deliverance from historical backwardness. The great majority of leading intellectuals, scholars and artists supported the socialist revolution with their works, teaching, military rhetoric and their strong desire to reach high positions as political decision-makers. Historians, sociologists and political scientists have not yet assessed the negative intellectual and cultural consequences of this massive adhesion to a dogmatic, totalitarian ideology [...] That is why

I have chosen to concentrate on this neglected aspect of the history of thought in contemporary Islamic contexts.[43]

It is at this point that Arkoun parts ways with other contemporary Muslim intellectuals, including Hanafi who embedded his 'Heritage and Renewal' agenda wholeheartedly in the Third Worldist project. The rift widens further when Arkoun accuses them of remaining susceptible to the ideological manipulation of discourses. Thus, as the political course altered in the late 1970s as a result of the apparent failure of imported secular ideologies to live up to their expectations, and an Islamic resurgence began to dominate the public sphere, the same intellectuals embraced this new discourse with a similar uncritical enthusiasm.[44] For example, many Muslim, but also non-Muslim, intellectuals—including Hanafi and Foucault—had welcomed the Iranian revolution and the so-called fundamentalist movements surfacing in its wake as an exponent of third world intellectual assertiveness and emancipation.

Arkoun, on the contrary, remained very critical of the Islamic paradigm that was replacing the Marxist-inspired ideologies. His scepticism was not confined to the short-term political realm, but extends to its epistemological flaws as well—not surprising for a scholar interested in more long-range histories of mentalities. He disqualifies the apologetic discourse of, for example, the Muslim Brotherhood as 'totally anachronistic, remote from any concept of the historicity of meaning.'[45] On similar grounds he also challenged the writings on Islamic studies by Muslim intellectuals with applied sciences backgrounds, such as Shahrur and Bennabi. More recently he has taken on the proponents of the 'Islamisation of knowledge,' who claim that the Qur'an presages modern scientific knowledge.[46]

Against the background of this debate on knowledge and power, Arkoun is highly sceptical of authoritative claims to interpreting Islamic culture and thought by many of his fellow intellectuals on grounds of their supposedly greater epistemological engagement in comparison to Western specialists.[47] Not afraid of naming names, aside from Hasan Hanafi, Arkoun also includes Hichem Djaït, Muhammad Abid al-Jabiri, Abdallah Laroui, Mohamed Talbi, and Fouad Zakariyya among those 'Muslim scholars who add their own political or religious gloss on the shortcomings of erudite Western descriptive scholarship.'[48]

Arkoun's attitude towards these figures is therefore much more critical than Ursula Günther leads us to believe and also calls into question the validity of her decision to categorise Arkoun as one of them.[49] In this regard, I am more inclined to agree with Armando Salvatore's qualification of Arkoun as 'the most interesting example of a contemporary Muslim intellectual' who, in the wake of the post-1967 tendencies towards the re-essentialisiation of Islam, opts instead for distanciation and focuses on the methodological requirements for salvaging the 'transcultural dynamics between civilisations.'[50] It were these kind of considerations which lie at the root of the alternative research agenda proposed under the name Applied Islamology.

The Programme of Applied Islamology

At its initial introduction, Arkoun defined one of the main tasks for a future Applied Islamology as the exploration, mapping and critical examination of Islam's so-called 'exhaustive tradition.'[51] Taking into account the influence of the *Annales* paradigm on Arkoun's ideas on historiography, this term can be understood as a 'totalised history of mentalities' for the Muslim world.[52] An early example of such an attempt on Arkoun's part is found in the essay 'Islam versus Development,' where he surveys the philosophical implications of critical issues with which present-day Muslims are confronted, such as development, liberation, the relationship between tradition, culture, and economics, in order to separate the 'false' questions from the 'essential' ones.[53] In another instance, he invokes the seminal work done by Massignon and Corbin to stress the importance of including the Shi'ite tradition within the purview of Applied Islamology.[54]

Arkoun explains how compiling an inventory of this exhaustive tradition in effect means taking 'recourse to a *via negativa*,' because it implies excavating what Islamic thought has until now either ignored, neglected, failed to subject to critical interrogation, or rejected out of hand as being part of the civilisational heritage of the Muslim world.[55] It is in this context that the twin terms *impensé* and *impensable*—'the unthought' and 'the unthinkable'—are introduced as articulations of a key characteristic of the logospheres of various cultures.[56] Calling them Arkoun's 'central *Terminus Technicus*,' Günther stresses the point—also noted by Arkoun himself—that the Unthought/Unthinkable must be regarded as a historical rather than a philosophical category.[57] In every culture an intricate interplay of political and social pressures determines:

What [...] a tradition of thought allow[s] us to think in a particular period of its evolution [...] A number of ideas, values, explanations, horizons of meaning, artistic creations, initiatives, institutions and ways of life are thereby discarded, rejected, ignored or doomed to failure by the long-term historical evolution called tradition or 'living tradition' according to dogmatic theological definitions. Voices are silenced, creative talents are neglected, marginalised or obliged to reproduce orthodox frameworks of expression, established forms of aesthetics, [...]. The unthought is made up of the accumulated issues declared unthinkable in a given logosphere.[58]

Grounded in a reinterpretation of Febvre's earlier noted 'unthinkability,' Arkoun's pairing of the Unthinkable/Unthought permeates his methodology. Its significance for his interest in modes of thinking is further reflected in the titles of publications such as *Rethinking Islam Today* (1987), *Rethinking Islam: Common questions, Uncommon Answers* (1994), and *The Unthought in Contemporary Islamic Thought* (2002).

In order to open up the discursive realm closed off by a culture's governing logocentrism, Arkoun initially formulated a fourteen-point agenda, leapfrogging through the key 'cognitive fields and moments' of Islamic intellectual history. The inception of the Qur'an and embryonic Muslim community or what he calls the 'Medina experience'; the role of the Companions and the early Sunni Caliphate and Shi'i Imamate in transforming a living tradition into a traditionalisation of the *Sunna*; the emergence of academic disciplines in Islamic learning (foundational sciences, the synthesising of Hellenist *falsafa* and Eastern *hikma* into a philosophical tradition accommodating both reason (*logos*) and poetry (myth), the functioning of reason in the rational sciences, and—in combination with the imaginary—in historiography, geography, poetry, and oral literatures); as well as the transition from the 'practical sense' embodied in scholastic knowledge and empirical know-how into positivist reason flourishing in the early modernist experience of *Nahda*, followed by the revolutionary episode with its new social imaginaries, until the final confrontation with the 'metamorphosis of meaning' at the end of the twentieth century.[59] In this final stage, Arkoun anticipates opening up the demanding horizon of a 'plurality of meanings' in which the epistemological questioning will reach its most radical limit.[60]

Such an ambitious exercise requires an 'appropriation of new instruments of analysis, theorising and understanding,' and the collective efforts of international teams of academic specialists.[61] For the next twenty years, Arkoun would busy himself fine-tuning this comprehensive agenda, eventually reformulating it into a series of what he calls abstract heuristic 'topoi' or 'lieux de connaissance' modelled into six epistemological 'triangles' of key notions through which the itinerary of his critique of Islamic reason can be plotted.[62]

The point of departure is constituted by two anthropological triangles grouping together 'Violence, Sacred, Truth' and 'Revelation, History, Truth,' the latter of which can be joined to a cognitive triangle of 'Language, History, and Thought.'[63] The other four are a theological-philosophical triangle examining the medieval disputes over 'Faith, Reason, Truth'; a hermeneutical triangle designed to liberate the metaphysical definition of 'Time, Narrative, and Ultimate Truth' and open up a hermeneutical circle—clearly inspired by Ricoeur—which examines the dialectics of understanding to believe and believing to understand.[64] Finally, there are the empirical triangle of 'Mind, Society and Power,' examining the historical functioning of the 'three D's in Arabic'—Dīn, Dunya, Dawla—and a philosophical-anthropological triangle represented by 'Rationality, Irrationality, Imaginary' dealing with the 'social institution of mind' and the 'imaginary institution of society.'[65] Opening up a wide spectrum of historical, anthropological and linguistic dimensions the intellectual itinerary comes back full circle to the two anthropological triangles from which it started.

The coverage of such a vast epistemological field must be matched with an equally broad heuristic apparatus. As part of it, Arkoun conceived another set of terms: 'Qur'anic Fact' versus 'Islamic Fact,' which are not intended to cast doubt on the historic veracity of revelation or degrade the Islamic tradition, but introduced only for the purpose of 'epistemological distanciation.'[66] First mentioned in La Pensée Arabe, Arkoun's use of this binary can be considered conventional to the extent that 'the Qur'an is the obligatory point of departure for any critical re-examination of the Arab-Islamic past.'[67] The dialectic between the two 'facts' is later described as presupposing:

The identification of the 'Qur'ānic fact' as a historical, linguistic, discursive stage different from the subsequent stage called Islamic fact with all the political, theological, juridical, mystical, literary and historiographical expansions, elaborations and doctrinal disputes. The distinction does not mean an endorsement of the theological status of the Qur'an as the Revelation remaining above human history; both the Qur'ānic and Islamic fact should be examined as components of concrete history [...].[68]

Also elsewhere Arkoun points out how readers often mistake the Qur'anic Fact for a 'fideistic view to preserve the dogma of the divine authenticity.' In his view, however, it must be understood as a concrete 'historical manifestation, at a time and in precise [sic] socio-cultural milieu, of an oral discourse which accompanied, for a period of twenty years, the concrete historical action of a social actor called Muhammad ibn 'Abd Allah.'[69]

If the heuristic proposition of revelation as a social, linguistic and literary construct is accepted, then it follows that any theological judgments must be suspended and that the occurrence of revelation can be subjected to a phenomenological approach.[70] Arkoun assures that such suspension still respects the 'basic theological propositions shared by all Muslims.'[71] For example, while recognising the distinction between the Qur'an as *Umm al-Kitab*, or 'Heavenly Book,' and *Mushaf*, that is the physical copy of the Qur'an text as historically revealed in human language, Arkoun suggests that:

This *Mushaf* [...] would be more aptly named the Official Closed Corpus which the interpreting community has accepted and will continue to accept for the foreseeable future as a *tanzīl*, a revealed given (*donné révélé*) that abolishes through interpretation and in experience, i.e. in the course of history, the status of the corpus as analysed by historians.[72]

In order to excavate the deeper epistemological levels, Arkoun suggests that, to understand the Qur'an as revelation, it is imperative to displace the theological perspective by the introduction of the procedures and rules used in discourse analysis. Since the 1970s, Arkoun has used the structural linguistics developed by Benveniste to articulate the interpersonal dimensions of revelation.[73] The first extensive exploration of the potential of structural linguistics and semiotics can be found in his landmark contribution to Qur'anic studies, published under the title *Lectures du Coran*.[74] In a much later study, Arkoun presents his Qur'anic discourse analysis as an examination of metaphoric organisation; semiotic structure; and intertextuality, adding that the 'epistemological failure' of classical Islamology to take such tools into account is evident in the writings from Nöldeke to Wansbrough.[75] On the other hand, Arkoun's advocacy of Greimas' groundbreaking work in the semiotic study of myth is accompanied by the caveat that he is not using its abstract and highly technical vocabulary just 'for the sake of complexity or "Parisian Mode" [sic] as many Anglo-Saxon scholars use to say ironically, but in order to perform a specific intellectual task.'[76]

The decision to explore this discursive alternative enables Arkoun to rephrase the description of the previous quote in the following contrasting terms:

This annunciation [revelation] can be called prophetic discourse and establishes an arena of communication between three grammatical persons, a *speaker* who articulates the discourse contained in the Heavenly Book; a first *addressee* who transmits the message of the enunciation as an event of faith; and a second *addressee*, *al-nās* (the people).[77]

The Ricoeurian catholicity of Arkoun's approach is reflected by the continuing influence of the *Annales* paradigm even in his discourse analysis, as becomes evident from his characterisation of intertextuality as 'the horizontal historical reading of the Qur'ānic discourse in the perspective of the very *longue durée* (to use the famous conceptualisaton of F. Braudel) including not only the Old Testament and the Gospel [...] but also the collective religious and cultural memories of the ancient Near East.'[78] To break down the dogmatic restrictions of the theologies developed in Judaism, Christianity and Islam, Arkoun suggests substituting his concept of 'societies of the Book-book' for that of the 'peoples of the Book' (the *ahl al-Kitāb* of the Qur'an), because it presents a framework of greater sociological, linguistic and cultural intelligibility.[79] The hyphenation 'Book-book' is employed as a device to underscore the inseparability of the theological concept of the heavenly Book as Holy Scripture, and the cultural, historical and anthropological concept of book as an artefact facilitating the transformation of orality and illiteracy into literacy and written culture. Arkoun argues that the detour through the social sciences implied in this new concept of 'societies of the Book-book' increases its cognitive fecundity to the extent that it can 'restore the complexity of the linguistic, sociological, political and cultural dimensions' and thus historicise anew what was dehistoricised by the sublimation of 'book' into Scripture.[80]

As far as other alternative approaches to the study of Qur'an are concerned, Arkoun has expressed more than once his regret over the absence of an equivalent to Northrop Frye's *The Great Code* in Qur'anic studies.[81] However, he does acknowledge that importance of Sayyid Qutb's interventions in raising a theoretic debate on the use of literary criticism in the analysis of the Qur'an and cites Issa Boullata's

Literary Structures of Religious Meaning in the Qur'ān as an example of how scientific curiosity has been extended to dimensions of revelation which had so far been avoided or ignored.[82] Further proof of his own constant efforts to stay abreast of developments in other adjacent fields are the references to the Sufi poet and theosophist Muhyi al-Din Ibn al-'Arabi (1165–1240) and studies of the latter's monumental oeuvre by, for example, Henri Corbin because of their significance for the metaphoric values of the Qur'anic language and the role of the imaginary.[83]

In order to re-establish the connections between poetry and philosophy, two fields which, in the Islamic intellectual tradition had withdrawn behind watertight separators, the same methods of discourse analysis must also be applied to the other constituent elements of the Closed Official Corpus or Islamic logosphere, namely the body or Qur'an commentaries (tafsir), the *hadith* collections containing the 'Traditions of the Prophet' and key source for his biography (sira), as well as mystical texts. Its sophisticated use of the advances made in the study of language will make it possible to rediscover the homologue functions of both poetry and philosophy as both try to transfigure reality through linguistic means, using particular lexicons, forms of rhetoric, and styles.[84]

Arkoun expands the exhaustive tradition, through which the Qur'anic Fact had become part of the Islamic Fact, beyond the Official Closed Corpus into a much broader domain encompassing a rich tradition of the 'oral populist delivery of a simplified orthodox creed,' supporting the 'beliefs, customs and cultural mores of many ethno-linguistic groups' living in Central and Southeast Asia, India, China, Central Asia, and parts of North Africa, who 'do not even have access to the Arabic original of the Qur'an.'[85] Aside from the simplified theologies associated with oral traditions since the tenth century, a survey of exhaustive tradition must also account for its modern-day equivalent in the form of populist religious expressions spread through the mass media.[86] Another contemporary phenomenon that needs to be included in the category of Islamic Fact is the new fault line introduced by secularism and modern reasoning, dividing 'those who accept the spiritual content and function of Revelation and those who reject it as "scientifically" or empirically obsolete.'[87]

Within the framework of a phenomenological analysis these last three aspects of the exhaustive tradition can be captured in the earlier mentioned anthropological and philosophical triangles of 'Violence,

Sacred, Truth' and 'Rationality, Irrationality, and Imaginary.' The last one can be considered particularly relevant in the quest for 'Revelation, History, Truth' as a kind of overarching historical anthropology of the Islamic fact as a living tradition.[88] As the middle term in this last triangle, history points towards a perpetual dialectics governing the relation between revelation and truth. In this regard it is also important to note the distinction which Arkoun makes between historicity and historicism. As an adherent of the *Annales* paradigm he subscribed to the former as an 'expanding practice of critical history as an all-embracing discipline among the social sciences.'[89] He also recognised its significance for the philosophical inquiries undertaken by figures like Vico, Herder, Dilthey, Heidegger, Sartre, Aron, and Ricoeur, which then gave rise to:

two different scientific practices, namely positivist historicism and the radical historicity of the human mind itself that is inseparable from its socio-historical institution. Historicism has imposed and still imposes its view that only events, facts and individuals whose real existence is evidenced in authentic documents, can be accepted as the subject of real history; thus excluding all the collective beliefs and representations which activate the collective imaginary and are determinant forces sustaining the historical dynamic.[90]

The approach proposed by Arkoun is clearly situated within that practice of radical historicity, which appreciates 'the anthropological status of the imagination as a creative faculty in all artistic beliefs and political visions' but which is ignored or misunderstood by the proponents of the positivist posture of reasoning represented by historicism for whom only documentary evidence constitutes real history. It has also been rendered as anathema by the logocentric historicism represented by the Official Close Corpus upheld by the various Islamic orthodoxies—Sunni, Shi'i as well as Khariji. In fact, radical historicity is considered blasphemous by 'all those Muslims who cannot grasp the idea that historicity is not just an intellectual game invented by Westerners for Westerners, but concerns the human condition since the emergence of man on this earth.'[91] It must therefore be regarded as the contemporary Unthought for the present-day Muslim world, equivalent to the earlier philosophical explorations by the rationalist theologians of the Mu'tazila School, Ibn Sina and Ibn Rushd.

Arkoun is not blind to the mismatch between the initial contingency of the Qur'anic fact and the 'inexhaustible dynamism of the mythical-historical consciousness that draws nourishment from it.'[92] For that

reason the educational function of semiotic analysis must be comple-
mented by the hermeneutical triangle of 'Time, Narratives and Absolute Truth' which articulate how believers have translated the temporal
mode of Qur'anic time into existential time and engendered the conflation of religious, worldly, and political processes captured in Arabic as
Din, Dunya wa Dawla. That is why only a radical deconstruction of
power relations through the anthropological triangle of 'Violence,
Sacred, and Truth' can disentangle the constant competition for control of the religious function between state authorities and militants
striving for their version of an Islamic political regime. This kind of
deconstructive analysis is a suitable instrument for distinguishing
between meaning and significance—a crucial difference of which non-
practitioners of discourse analysis are scarcely aware.

In Arkoun's view that is a consequence of the present-day education
system, in particularly the French one, where a combative secularism
keeps one of the vital 'human channels for the production of meaning'
completely out of the public realm, leaving all religious affairs exclusively to the pertaining religious institutions and thus preventing the
development of any form of critical investigation of religious phenomena.[93] However, at the same time the system confers upon its religiously
illiterate citizens the right to express their uninformed opinion on these
issues leading to a kind of 'semantic disorder' which has also had an
impact on the academic fields under discussion. To underline this last
point, Arkoun recalls his own experiences as an academic. Whether
lecturing to Muslim or Western audiences, he had to 'respond to all
types and levels of objection, rejection, confusing mixtures of subjective beliefs, ideological representations and irrational statements presented as undisputable ascertained knowledge.'[94]

If anything, such incidents bring another epistemological conflict to
the surface. Uncomfortable with the uncertainties and subversions of
the reflective hermeneutics generated by discourse analysis, the believer
demands the certainty of a *Heilsgeschichte* affirming the 'true' meaning
of the text. While claiming to promote the dignity of the individual, this
form of arbitrary and simplistic exegesis has become a powerful tool in
the hands of militants throughout the Third World, who can thus 'sac-
ralise, ritualise, and ideologise collective representations, political institutions and social, moral and legal orders.'[95] It is at this point that
Arkoun's triangle of 'Violence, Sacred, Truth' fuses with both the
empirical triangle of 'Mind, Society, Power' and the philosophical-anthropological triangle connecting 'Rationality, Irrationality, Imaginary.'

In order to reconcile the existential concern for the meaning of life with the plurality of meanings flowing from a heuristic apparatus such as the one employed by Arkoun, there is a need for transcending Islam's truth claims within Muslim societies and towards other religious traditions as they all tend to remain locked in the Bermuda triangle of 'Violence, Sacred, Truth.' The research strategy which can accommodate an explanatory theory expansive enough for religious phenomena in general must therefore reach beyond the relatively narrow confines of Applied Islamology and extend the critique of Islamic reason to not just religious reason, but onto a meta-plane of reason in a generic sense. However, that theoretical model is embedded in wider intellectual questions, which have occupied Arkoun throughout his scholarly career and must be presented in the context of the core ideas shaping those concerns.

11

RETHINKING ISLAM

FROM ISLAMIC HUMANISM TO EMERGING REASON

We have seen that with *L'Humanisme Arabe*, Arkoun had established his scholarly credentials as an Islamicist and how his challenges of existing Muslim and non-Muslim scholarship in Islam provided the impetus for his Applied Islamology project, which was first introduced in *Pour une Critique de la Raison Islamique*. Together these two publications lay out the abiding themes of his oeuvre: Humanism and Islamic reason. A further survey of his bibliography shows namely that this first interest recurs at frequent intervals in his writings, and in a 1993 conference address he even explicitly recounted that humanism had been his 'field of research and thinking for at least twenty years.'[1] As for the second theme, he singled out Miskawayh's treatise on ethics as the 'privileged domain for investigating responses to the question of the rapport between Islamic and Greek thinking,' a relationship which remained central to his critique of Islamic reason.[2] An annotated translation of this text even accompanied his principal doctoral thesis and thus constitutes the starting point of Arkoun's lifelong preoccupation with the epistemological questions in the study of religion.[3]

Humanism and Personalism

This sustained concern for humanism is not only responsible for the unmistakable anthropocentric focus of Arkoun's research approach, but also indicative of his abiding interest in the notion of the 'person.'

To explore the latter he used Kardiner's concept of 'Basic Personality Structure,' which was introduced into French intellectual discourse through Dufrenne's *La Personnalité de Base: Un Concept Sociologique* (1953). Dufrenne's general observation that, by the 1950's, Kardiner's work on social psychology had become part and parcel of North American cultural anthropology would strike a chord with historians working within the *Annales* paradigm who regard this after all as a 'neighbour discipline.'[4] However, a closer inspection of Kardiner's 'The Concept of Basic Personality Structure as an Operational Tool in the Social Sciences' will show why the notion itself holds an appeal for *Annales* School historians.

In this condensed survey, Kardiner begins with the observation that human adaptation to the environment can be viewed in various ways: the morphological terms of biology's interest in long-term phases of human adjustment; the engagement in the behavioural sciences with the concept of culture and institution; and psychological investigations of adaptive processes which cover short spans of time.[5] It is easy to see how congenial this point of departure is to the concepts of geographical, social, and individual time introduced into French historiography by Braudel, as noted in an earlier chapter. Kardiner's empiricism merges psychological and anthropological techniques, combining the lessons learned from psychoanalysis with the conception of 'cultures as functional wholes and the study of primitive societies as entities and the notion of Basic Personality Structure functioning as the integrative factor which accomplishes what in learning theory is known as the "acculturation" of the young generation into becoming adult members of society.'[6] Drawing on data from different cultures, Kardiner was interested in mapping how this 'deeper fabric of their personalities was moulded on similar lines.'[7]

For his own research Arkoun has relied primarily on Dufrenne's assessment of the relevance of Kardiner's theory for sociological and historical studies, namely the dialectical function of Basic Personality Structure as the 'middle term between the primary institutions by which it is determined and the secondary institutions it determines.'[8] Arkoun first used it in *L'Humanisme Arabe* to test its fecundity as a method by writing a very specific intellectual biography of Miskawayh:

Not as the ritual examination of exterior facts, but—quite the contrary—by focusing on its non-written and unsaid core, on all these 'primary institutions' (myths, rites, beliefs, traditions, etc.), which condition the awakening of a perception, how a judgment is made, or a calling is affirmed, in a more decisive and durable way than if one were simply studying it under the name intellectual formation.[9]

With this approach he anticipated discovering the social-psychological function of Miskawayh's oeuvre in 'the elaboration, diffusion and conservation of a humanism that is characteristic of an entire civilisation.'[10] Such an understanding of the intellectual output in a historical era as both the product of and support for a socio-cultural reality dovetails with Dufrenne's explanation of primary institutions as having not so much historical, sociological, or morphological primacy in a given culture, but rather as being the taking-off point for the individual. They define the social milieu into which the individual is conditioned and, through what Dufrenne calls their 'biographical and chronological signification,' they determine his personality.[11]

However, in good Braudelian fashion, Arkoun was not going to rely on this one tool. From structural linguistics he appropriated the recognition that in writing a history of ideas one must also account for the synchrony and diachrony which 'convey the two interconnected sides of every reality.'[12] However, in *L'Humanisme Arabe* he nevertheless gives more weight to the synchronic dimension, because he was less interested in the Platonic, Aristotelian or Neo-Platonic provenances of the ideas employed by Miskawayh than in the dynamics and logical structures which allowed him to describe 'a shared imaginary landscape.' This he considered the 'more urgent and important task for the historian of ideas' and he expected Islamicists to acquire an active familiarity with the latest developments in the humanities and social sciences.[13]

A few years later Arkoun again tested the relevance of Kardiner and Linton's theories in Islamic contexts by using them in a study of Ghazali.[14] Only this time, he transformed it into a 'pluridisciplinary approach,' combining Basic Personality Structure with another notion which until then had been all but ignored by Islamicists: 'mythical consciousness,' citing not only the work of Eliade and Barthes, but also making references to Bloch, Gurvitch, and Durand.[15] In 1989, in an essay entitled 'Actualité de la Personne dans la Pensée Islamique,' Basic Personality Structure featured again as part of the heuristic apparatus taken from a variety of disciplines which he had developed for the Applied Islamology Project.[16] This time it was applied to a comprehensive study of political leaders in the contemporary Muslim world, including Bourguiba, Hasan II, Boumedienne, Nasser, Gaddafi, and

Saddam Hussein, as well as so-called 'contra-leaders,' such as Sayyid Qutb, Sadat assassin Abd al-Salam Faraj, and representatives of the 'in-between' world of intellectuals.[17] This essay also includes references to the Christian thought of Ivan Gobry, Nicolai Berdyaev's personalism, and the sociological work of Mauss and Bourdieu, while Arkoun's plea for a multilayered examination of 'the status of the person in the Islamic domain' through a combination of ethnographic, anthropological and sociological approaches also evinces the continuing influence of Roger Bastide even in these more topical studies.[18]

The most recent publication demonstrating Arkoun's persisting concern for retaining a humanist perspective is *Humanisme et Islam: Combats et Propositions* (2005). Presented as a testimony to his intellectual itinerary from the publication of *L'Humanisme Arabe* onwards, it integrates his exposure to a wide variety of teachings between 1945 and 2004. The sequence of the book's chapters also bears witness to the various scholarly tools which Arkoun fashioned into an 'intellectual dynamics' reflective of the three operative terms derived from the way his mentor Claude Cahen practised his metier as a historian: *transgresser, déplacer, dépasser*.[19] The collection contains an essay on ethics looking at the notion of happiness and the quest for salvation throughout Islamic history, before moving on to Arkoun's work as a critic, featuring essays on the study of Islamic history and law, the role of the intellectual, and a reflection on Islamic thought, before closing with a brief autobiographical portrait in which he reiterates the importance of addressing both the written and non-written legacies of the Muslim peoples.

From Religious Reason to Emerging Reason

Arkoun's preoccupation with critiquing 'thought' and 'reason' can not only be deduced from the titles of his essay collections and individual articles, but has also been explicitly articulated in an explanation of how he sees his writings about the intellectual history of the Muslim world differ from others in that:

...[it] proposes a way of thinking, rather than essays in traditional scholarship based on primary sources. Not that I do not use such sources extensively, but my interpretation of them is informed by a strategy which differs from that usually employed for the purpose of providing a descriptive, narrative, factual and cumulative presentation of what they contain. [...] This cognitive strategy has never been used before in interpreting the types of discourse produced by Muslims to express their Islam, or in approaching them as a subject of study alongside the Western literature on Islam and Muslim societies.[20]

Establishing this association between 'critique' and 'reason' has invited speculations about the influence of Kant, but which Arkoun emphatically denies.[21] Aside from this personal assertion, any 'plagiarism of Kant' can effectively be disproved by accounting for the provenance of his heuristic apparatus.[22] Arkoun's critique of Islamic reason does neither contain an argument of causality nor share the metaphysical foundations of Kant's philosophy, but is—on the contrary—much closer to Bloch and Foucault's challenge of the quest for origins.[23] Another contrast with Kant, who situates reason, judgment and religion within the confines of individual consciousness, is that Arkoun agrees with Bastide's view of religion as embedded in the totality of social structures, while his radical historicity privileges the collective notion of memory. On both accounts Arkoun's approach must therefore also be set apart from Hanafi's, who does draw on Kantian thought for his interrogations of historical, eidetic and active consciousness.

It makes more sense to consider Arkoun's project as a genealogy or archaeology in the line of Derrida's 'archive' and Foucault's excavation of 'pre-existing discursive fields.'[24] Evidence for his affinity with these postmodernist critical discourses can be obtained from the statement by Arkoun that:

My point is about the epistemic and epistemological barrier that has always separated 'Orientalist' scholarship from the innovative, creative standpoints of reason emerging in the scholarship applied to European cultures and societies since the late sixties.[25]

However, at the same time it is important to stress that, in spite of sharing their interest in deconstructing logospheres and investigating the power relations dominating discursive formations, Arkoun does not want to be called a postmodernist. The reason for this is not simply his disagreement with the way Foucault has rendered human agency ineffective, but even more so because he regards postmodernism as very much part of the Western logosphere, which he wants to include in his critique.[26] Instead he has suggested at one point that the line of thought he represents should be called 'meta-modern reason.'[27] That is also the reason why I think that Robert Lee's assessment of Arkoun as venturing 'to the very edge of postmodernism' only to return into modernist fold because of 'his embrace of truth' is wrong.[28]

Arkoun also objects to comparing Muslim figures such as al-Ghazali to Descartes or Pascal and Ibn Khaldun to Montesquieu, because that would 'endow Islamic reason with some usurped status.'[29] Without resorting to apologetics for a specifically Islamic form of reason in the vein of Ibn Taymiyya's *Refutation of the Logicians*—or his own contemporary Hasan Hanafi for that matter—Arkoun admits that it is indeed possible to identify 'a foundational method that built solidly on the rich literature of the *Usul al-fiqh*.'[30] The fact that he mentions Ibn Taymiyya's rejection of systems of thought that are 'alien' to Islam and his acceptance of *usul al-fiqh* as a form of 'procedural reason' shows Arkoun has consulted a similar archive as Hanafi, but he subjects it to a more rigorous investigation than the latter.[31] Arkoun's interest is directed towards the epistemologies of the formative period of Islamic learning and aims at defining the historical situation in which such knowledge arose. Within the early framework of Applied Islamology this was explored in an examination of al-Shafi'i's *Al-Risala* and its interlocutors, using both the tools of classical Islamology and Bourdieu's *Le Sens Pratique*, while in 'Profil de la Conscience Islamique,' he places the contemporary Muslim thinker Anwar al-Jundi in conversation with Ghazali and Ibn Rushd in order to illustrate how persistent the constraints imposed by the logocentrism of the Islamic tradition can be.[32]

However, by the late 1990s a shift became discernable in the focus of Arkoun's critique of reason as he moved from the historical anthropological approach of the Applied Islamology programme towards what he calls 'historical epistemology,' through which he seeks to articulate his cognitive concerns regarding the generic study of religion in more explicit terms than before.[33]

There are two reasons for this change in emphasis. First of all, the emergence of pragmatic Islamology with its predominant interest in contemporary socio-political issues promoting a narrative history of events. Applied Islamology was not unappreciative of this concern for short-term data, but, consistent with the *Annales* paradigm from which it drew its inspiration, Arkoun's alternative research programme viewed them 'from the dual perspective of the *"longue durée"* explored by historians, and of the contemporary social inquiry that impinges on the future.'[34] However, what he saw as pragmatic Islamology's relapse into the superficiality associated with the tendency of the political to 'narrow the field of knowledge and interpretation to what the most visible, influential and outspoken actors say and decide,' made Arkoun aware that he was not achieving his goal of improving the epistemological rigour in Islamic studies.[35] That realisation became even more acute after 9/11, when the threat of a complete breakdown of communications between cultures in an increasingly interconnected world under the influence of an unprecedented process of globalisation forced him to radicalise his position even further.[36] This new urgency is also noticeable in the changing format of his essays, which now begin to 'combine a critical review of modern studies devoted to the early and contemporary periods of what is generally called "Islam," with the systematic deconstruction of the original texts used in these studies as sources of genuine information.'[37] More than anything else it is this development which characterises Arkoun as a critic and not a caretaker or informant only providing data on a particular religious tradition for further examination.[38]

The other reason for stressing this need for epistemological rigour was Arkoun's growing dissatisfaction with the lack of critical thinking about religion in interreligious dialogues or interfaith forums. As early as 1978, in an article entitled 'Propositions pour un autre Pensée Religieuse'—written in 1978 in response to the World Conferences of Religions for Peace (WCRP) in Kyoto 1970 and Louvain 1974, and in anticipation of the 1979 session in New York—he had already pleaded for a different way of engaging with religion, not from the perspective of this or that religious tradition, 'but from a perspective of solidarity among peoples.'[39] According to Arkoun, there was still an epistemological separation between, on the one hand, various forms of theological thinking, which remain apologetic in nature and defensive of distinctive religious orthodoxies and communities, and, on the other hand, the scholarly research conducted in university circles which focuses more on generic questions affecting all religions.

Based on his own decades-long involvement in these inter-religious dialogues, he had to conclude that in spite of the efforts of the WCPR, the World Council of Churches, and the Vatican's Secretariat for Non-Christian Religions little was achieved in terms of a more critical engagement with the study of religion. This disappointment parallels his growing frustration with classical Islamology, where 'methodological conservatism and indifference of scholarship to radicalising a critical anthropology of the cultures of the world' had incited Arkoun to formulate Applied Islamology as a distinct new research agenda in the first place.[40]

COSMOPOLITANS AND HERETICS

Not surprisingly, in order to articulate this further fine-tuning of his work on Islamic reason and religious thought Arkoun saw a need to introduce another term to his ever-expanding glossary, 'emerging' or 'emergent' reason.[41] Carrying this expansion of the scope of his research into the next millennium, the term became capitalised and was provided even with an abbreviation: 'Emerging Reason (E.R.).'[42] The advocacy of Emerging Reason is thus grounded in a decades-long trajectory, partly paralleling the development of Applied Islamology but nevertheless running on a separate track en route to a comprehensive understanding of the religious phenomenon in general. Whereas Hanafi drew on the Islamic heritage for affirmation and on the Christian tradition to demonstrate where it fell short of a general method for the study of religion, Arkoun's Emerging Reason wants to subject any type of reason or any conceivable line of thought to the same rigorous critical examination. Although initially introduced as an alternative 'third posture' of thinking, it is more accurate to consider Emerging Reason as a fourth strand—in addition to the existing forms of religious, philosophical and scientific-teletechnological reason.[43] This last term was not of Arkoun's own invention, but taken from Derrida's vocabulary as found in the essay 'Faith and Knowledge: The Two Sources of "Religion" at the Limits of Reason Alone.'[44]

The conceptualisation of Emerging Reason was inspired by a book called *L'Institution sociale de l'Esprit* (1999), written by the Belgian philosopher of law Jean de Munck. As a legal scholar he proposes substituting substantive religious reason and instrumental or tele-techno-scientific reason with a procedural pragmatic reason. Reluctant to be confined by the juridical connotations of procedural reason, Arkoun persists in his preference for using the term Emerging Reason, because it 'goes beyond the punctual, particular methodological improvements actualised in some fields of research, or in some disciplines applied to the study of different aspects of Islam and other non-Western cultures.'[45] A further reason for not wanting to adopt this procedural-legal approach is that within the Islamic tradition the foundational sciences of *usul al fiqh* and *usul al-din*, notwithstanding their 'scientific' pretensions, are still bound up in the same attitudes of religious reason as the Christian and Jewish traditions of thought, even though the latter two have 'been challenged, shaken, politically marginalised and intellectually disqualified by the reasoning of Enlightenment.'[46]

Recently, however, religious reason has actually been 'reactivated by the monopoly of legal violence acquired by the modern state,' and even more so when this domain became a bone of contention between the political establishment and religiously-inspired opposition groups of fundamentalist persuasion.[47] But even when this is left aside, Arkoun remains dissatisfied with both Enlightenment and postmodern reason, because so far they have been unable to propose real alternatives to 'the principles, categories, definitions, and forms of reasoning inherited from theological reason, on the one side, and enlightened, scientific reason on the other.'[48] Even the 'undeniable advances in cultural anthropology' have failed in calling into question the assumed universality of Western reason and in 'introducing a more humanist rationality into the perception of non-Western cultures.'[49]

Consequently, there are as yet no alternative imaginaries capable of competing beyond merely 'procedural modifications within the Western enclosure.' Arkoun alleges that, notwithstanding the efforts of prominent interventionists such as Nietzsche, Heidegger, Habermas, Gadamer, Rawls, and Taylor, the 'dominant cognitive postures of classical modernity and postmodernity' are not just locked away in their own versions of the Unthought, but have also consistently failed to integrate 'trajectories of reason historically linked to non-"Western" contexts for the production of meaning.'[50]

Being a part of instrumental tele-techno-scientific reason, both classical and pragmatic Islamology never reached the 'threshold of intelligibility' that would allow them to contribute to a comprehensive critique of reason by presenting data from the epistemological routes travelled within the Islamic civilisation. Pointing back to his personal experiences as an Algerian Berber, Arkoun also warns against the pitfalls of a supposedly emancipating Third Worldism. Although he is not 'saying that the struggles of dominated peoples should be abandoned or ignored,' he encourages those involved to be ambitious and 'aim at horizons of meaning, shown henceforth by Emerging Reason.'[51] Whilst this subversion of the various strands of Western thought is more radical than Hanafi's, from a formal point of view Arkoun too is waging a three-front campaign similar to the Heritage and Renewal Project, because:

Emerging Reason has the responsibility for managing the violence inherent in the structures of truth promoted and defended by the three historically present postures of reason: the (theologico-ethico-juridical) religious posture, the sci-

219

entific teletechnological posture that manages globalisation, and the philo-sophical posture still in the grip of the modernity of classical age.[52]

When setting some markers for what is in effect a cognitive strategy for the study of religious phenomena, the influence of Bastide's Dur-kheimian *Applied Anthropology* and the recognition of religion as a 'product of the interplay between the political, cultural and economic,' cause Arkoun to regard religion as both a 'simple social fact' and an 'ideological factor.'[53]

In a field of competing ideologised forms of religious reason it must then also be admitted that—historically—Islamic reason has been in constant confrontation with European reason, which became increas-ingly hegemonic in character. The epistemological-ideological condi-tioning of the relationship between the Muslim world and Christendom explains why Arkoun has 'always denounced the unequal situations which have condemned the Islamo-Christian dialogue from the outset to stay imprisoned in the polemical framework of the old heresio-graphic literature.'[54] The blame for this rests certainly not solely with the West, because while Christian thinkers faced up to the major intel-lectual shifts affecting Europe, their Muslim counterparts tended to stand aloof. In a later instance Arkoun even claims that Islam's seces-sion from the 'monotheistic religious phenomenon' had already occurred very soon after its emergence, when it insisted on establishing its auton-omy in relation to Judaism and Christianity. One of the gravest conse-quences of this attitude is that Islam does not even recognise itself as 'an integral part of this very archaic and yet very persistent archive.'[55]

To break this impasse Arkoun envisages that the expanded research agenda of the Emerging Reason Project can help end Islam's exile from the critical debates on (post)modernity and enable it to re-insert itself into a '*comparative history of theologies* of the three religions closest to each other by virtue of their linguistic, cultural and symbolic refer-ences.'[56] Its success depends on the acknowledgement of intersubjective communication as a mutual recognition of cultures and an agenda grounded in a heuristic definition of the religious phenomenon as embedded in an exhaustive tradition, or as he formulates it, know 'the entirety of distinctive characteristics that make it possible to identify the *specificity of the religious authority* in relation to the political, cultural, judicial, ethical, aesthetic, and economic authorities.'[57] Clearly inspired by the *Annales* paradigm, the danger of such a comprehensive defini-tion that leaves out so little is that, as Traian Stoianovich observed, it loses its specificity, thus blunting its analytical incisiveness.[58]

In a move that is again reminiscent of the catholicity marking Ricoeur's philosophical method, Arkoun attempts to make his definition operative by placing religion in a spacious hermeneutical circle which can accommodate the premise of religion as a social fact, his interest in the critique of discursive productions, and his humanist concerns. For this purpose he borrows another 'hazardous' definition of the religious, coined by Daniele Hervieu-Léger, which imagines it as the outcome of the social realisation of a belief tradition in a community. At the same time, the humanist in Arkoun stresses that this sociological manifestation of 'the dialectic between reason and imagination, rational and imaginary' is not the whole picture, because in the end 'the religious is the domain of totalisation of reality insofar as it is always mediatised [sic] by the perception, reception, and verbalisation of human beings for human beings.'[59]

Arkoun insists that theology must start questioning the use of findings in the social sciences and to criticise its own inherited constructs, for example, by analysing the prophetic function in the same way as anthropologists have deciphered the emergence of heroic figures in social groups. Believers may object that this removes religious truth from the equation and 'distorts the balance of the sacred and the profane,' but if one is willing to suspend theological definitions then 'one can easily recognise in the prophetic function several components of the historico-psychological-sociological mechanisms leading to the emergence of heroes.'[60] To a scholar working in the *Annales* tradition, the resilience of great men and heroes in the face of modernity and the survival of what in an earlier chapter were referred to as the 'societies of the Book-book' with their supposedly outdated beliefs, value systems and world vision pose some very interesting questions.

The archaeological strategy proposed under the aegis of Emerging Reason continues to reflect a similar cognitive order as the Applied Islamology Project: It commences (1) with an inventory of languages of religion, proceeds (2) with an investigation of religious truth and Official Closed Corpuses, reintroduces (3) the empirical triangle of religion, politics and society, and then expands (4) into the human experience of the divine, ending on a Ricoeurian note with (5) 'hope' as the force of upheaval and historic deployment of humanity. In regard to this last point Arkoun states that:

The concept of hope subsumes at one and the same time the totality of visions attaching to religions under the name of eschatological hope and the new programs offered by the so-called secular ideologies to the contemporary imagination in the context of civil religions.[61]

Aside from its resonance with Ricoeur's philosophical engagement, using a concept such as hope also demonstrates that Arkoun's critique of reason through discourse analysis does not have to lead to the scepsis or nihilism so frequently found in works written in a postmodernist vein. The proposed heuristic devices serve only as a 'methodological strategy intended to liberate the human mind from the increasingly alienating pressures of mythologies, fictions and illusions.'[62] In fact, in Arkoun's case it remains closely tied to the humanist interests and concerns which colour his work as well. As noted in the outline of the Emerging Reason strategy, Arkoun's critique of various strands of reason is executed in the light of 'the unanimously accepted idea that they involve cultural productions of *humankind by humankind for humankind on humankind.*'[63] The significance of Emerging Reason is succinctly wrapped up in the English-language coda 'The Answers of Applied Islamology,' which not only evinces the close relationship between these two research agendas, but in which Arkoun also testifies that all his work is done in the service of salvaging humankind's dignity 'from a century characterised by the scandalous defeat of humanist thought,' during which the 'disposable thought' represented by the tele-techno-scientific reason reigns supreme.[64] Just as with his qualification of Arkoun as a postmodernist thinker, Lee's verdict that he has gone to the 'brink of nihilism' fails to give sufficient weight to these humanist concerns and to the influence of a thinker like Ricoeur.[65]

In Search of New Scholars and Audiences

Like Applied Islamology, the Emerging Reason Project also requires the involvement of international teams of experts from disciplines across the spectrum of the human sciences.[66] In fact, given the project's even broader scope and the greater epistemological pertinence of this exercise, what is required is an 'intellectual and scientific vigilance one associates with the most exacting of philosophers.' Arkoun describes the intellectuals who match this profile as *chercheur-penseurs* or 'scholar-thinkers.'[67] As examples of the sort of work he expects to be produced within the context of this more comprehensive critique, Arkoun invokes *La Théologie en Postmodernité*, written by the Swiss theologians Pierre Gisel and Patrick Evrard, and Paul Ricoeur's *La*

Mémoire, l'Histoire, l'Oubli.[68] The latter in particular is hailed as a 'deeply perceptive and innovative work reflect[ing] the growing dimension of intelligibility offered by Emerging Reason.'[69] Arkoun's appreciation of Ricoeur also extends to his philosophy in general which aims at 'putting together again, re-articulating, and re-appropriating domains of reflexive thought and knowledge accumulated by the social sciences such as history, sociology, linguistics and anthropology.'[70]

On the other hand, Gisel and Ricoeur's narrow self-definitions as philosopher and theologian respectively are not conducive to transcending the compartmentalisation in academic specialisation. Even 'a thinker like Paul Ricoeur, a man of uncommon intellectual generosity and spiritual richness, confine[s himself] to the example of Western Christianity.'[71] To a degree this can be explained by the fact that Ricoeur works in the geo-historical and geocultural space of the West, which also happens to be the place with the largest concentration of scholar-thinkers, the most advanced scientific and cultural resources, and the democratic values needed to create the political and intellectual climate required for the kind of critical examinations envisaged for the Emerging Reason. As a promising attempt to close the gap between theology and philosophy, Arkoun cites Jean-Yves Lacoste's *Le Dictionnaire de Théologie*. In this book Lacoste maps the diverse trajectories of Judaic, Christian and Islamic religious thought. In regard to the latter, Arkoun adds the observation that this should not be confined to *kalam*, but must encompass other disciplines, 'especially exegesis, the sources of religion and the sources of law [...], historiography and even *adab* in its specific dimension during the classic period.'[72] He suggests appropriating Lacoste's approach to rewrite the history of thought within the context of restoring the Mediterranean space as a distinct geo-historical concept along Braudelian lines.

In his exploration of the sometimes awkward relations between the different academic specialisations dealing with the study of religion, Arkoun presents Michel Meslin's *L'Expérience Humain du Divin* as an example of how theology and religious studies can be brought closer together. However, although appreciative of its comprehensive endeavour to 'problematise the permanent elements common to all human experience of the divine,' Arkoun believes that the book's value is undermined by its failure to account for the 'theoretical revisions concerning the secularisation of modern societies.'[73] His awareness of the urgency of this pressing question has already become clear from his earlier noted apprehension regarding the neglect of critical introductions to the religious roots of the world civilisations in the contemporary education system.

In 'Social Science as Challenge of Islam,' Arkoun expresses his worries over the fact that present-day social sciences barely concern themselves with the scientific and philosophical relevance of redefining the religious phenomenon of developments in the Muslim world and deplores the lack of interaction between history, political science, ethnography, anthropology, and sociology in regard to defining a theoretical framework for the study of Islam.[74] Arkoun blames the Third Worldist discourse and its preoccupation with contingent political stakes for the feeble attempts towards analysing and interpreting generically used terms such as Islam, the West, modernity, secularisation, fundamentalism, or civil society. According to him, 'the philosophical expression is dramatically absent in all social science research that claims to deal with what they call Islam.' Instead social scientists content themselves with token invocations of Durkheim, Weber, Lévi-Strauss, Geertz and Bourdieu or obligatory references to Abdel Malek's article on Orientalism which, even though it has had a level of exposure comparable to Huntington's Clash of Civilisations, Arkoun dismisses as 'quickly written and altogether tame.'[75]

At the Muslim end of this spectrum it is even more difficult to find exponents matching the profile of the scholar-thinker. Arkoun's criticism of scholars with whom he is often grouped together has already been noted in an earlier chapter. In a more recent update he has repeated his observation that:

Modernising intellectuals such as Ridhwan al-Sayyid, Mohamed Talbi, Hichem Djaït, M. Abed al-Jabri, Abdallah Laroui touch upon questions treated within the enclosure [of logocentrism], but without going so far as to include the dogmatic kernel of faith as the cognitive regulator of revelation, the mythical-historical structure of the discourse of belief, the prophetic discourse within the limitations of linguistic, semiotic, historical and anthropological analysis, the basic import of anthropological triangles such as 'Violence, Sacred, Truth'; 'Language, History, Thought'; 'Revelation, History, Truth,' 'Religion, Society, Politics.'[76]

He adds that the younger Muslim intelligentsia—often holding academic positions in Europe or North America, or at least trained there for teaching in their countries of origin—perpetuate the illusory continuity of nineteenth-century Muslim Reformism, locked up in a discourse of 'unthinkables, unthoughts, and institutionalised ignorance.'[77]

Inversely, because Arkoun's own insistence on remaining alert to the epistemological questions affecting a field like Islamic studies drove him towards a heuristic apparatus of Western provenance, suggesting that other Muslim scholars too start exploring these innovative but often controversial methodologies, he has also provoked reactions from the fellow Muslim intellectuals he challenged. On occasion this has led to personal attacks, such as the one by the otherwise tolerant Mohamed Talbi in *Jeune Afrique* which so dumbfounded Arkoun that he could not resist quoting it at length in one of his own publications.[78]

When not contending with outright rejection, Arkoun has also had to cope with a considerable degree of disregard for his innovations of rethinking the field of Islamic Studies. The approaches developed in his case studies of medieval intellectual history in the 1960s and 1970s have had little imitation. In the 1980s, Applied Islamology too was either ignored or given a hostile reception, and, so far, the Emerging Reason agenda has met with the same fate. And yet Arkoun has insisted that: 'I am not complaining about the lack of interest in my contributions to scholarship. I know that my way of sharing the concerns of scholarship is different from the merely descriptive, narrative, informative style of scholarship.'[79] However, when assessing the impact of critical scholarship on the interfaith dialogues going since the Second Vatican Council, he showed himself rather bitter:

I've participated in so many of them, and I can tell you that they're absolutely nothing. It's gossip. There's no intellectual input in it. There is no respect for scholarship in it. A huge scholarship has already been produced devoted to the question of faith and reason. All this is put aside and we ignore it. We just congratulate one another, saying, 'I respect your faith, and you respect mine.' This is nonsense.[80]

In conclusion then, like Hanafi, Arkoun never developed the kind of following that can be considered as a distinct 'school.' Even among his own graduate students he has had to notice a reluctance to adopt his radical methodologies in their own work: for Muslims they were too dangerous, while the non-Muslim students found his heuristics too demanding for a thesis.[81] Searching for alternative audiences, Arkoun began—like Hanafi—to address a broader public, relying on the international lecture circuit to spread his message:

Fortunately, I have been comforted and always encouraged by the reactions of thousands of listeners of all ages, ethno-cultural backgrounds and nationalities from around the world. It is with those publics that I was able to test the validity of the methodological and strategic choices of applied Islamology. I no longer count those students of mine at La Sorbonne or those listeners at the odd conference who, years later, let me know their satisfaction with those moments when they were in a position to decipher Muslim discourses with the framework and thinking tools specific to applied Islamology. I gauge each time how much those publics are deprived, not only of basic information about Islam and the societies where the Islamic fact is at work, but even more so of the thinking tools that would allow them to feel intellectually and civically engaged in the unequal struggles between traditional religious cultures and the so-called modern cultures equipped to *judge* the ones preceding them.[82]

It appears that Arkoun has found a particularly receptive audience in Indonesia. Not only has he travelled there for speaking engagements, but—as noted earlier—his writings also feature on the reading lists of the curricula taught at the country's state Islamic universities, while several of his books have been translated into Indonesian.[83] Moreover, no less than three monograph-size studies dedicated to Arkoun have appeared in Indonesian as well.[84] This interest extends also beyond the country's system of Islamic higher education. Young intellectuals graduating from these institutions—often associated with the plethora of think tanks and NGOs linked with organisations such as the *Muhammadiyah* and NU, or issuing more spontaneously from either Postra or JIL circles—continue to engage with Arkoun's ideas, exploring the possibilities of applying his findings in their own writings.[85]

'Realistic Cosmopolitanism cannot remain content with demarcating itself from the totalitarian features of universalism. It also needs universalism if it is to avoid falling into the opposite trap of postmodern particularism.'

Ulrich Beck, *Cosmopolitan Vision*

'People are different, the cosmopolitan knows, and there is much to learn from our differences. Because there are so many human possibilities worth exploring, we neither expect nor desire that every person or every society should converge on a single model of life.'

Kwame Anthony Appiah, *Cosmopolitanism: Ethics in a World of Strangers*

'Nations and religions greatly impoverish themselves when they repress and dismiss dissenting voices.'

Anouar Majid, *A Call for Heresy*

'For premodern man, heresy is a possibility—usually a rather remote one; for modern man, heresy typically becomes a necessity.'

Peter L. Berger, *The Heretical Imperative*

12

NEW MUSLIM INTELLECTUALS

COSMOPOLITAN AND HERETICAL

The welcoming reception of Arkoun and Hanafi's ideas in Indonesia, reflected by invitations for speaking engagements, the production of translations of their writings into Indonesian, and contributions by Indonesian scholars to the secondary literature on these two thinkers, is indicative of the country's higher degree of openness to intellectual debates on religion in comparison to other parts of the Muslim world and shows the importance of approaching the intellectual history of the contemporary Muslim world from a global perspective. However it also invites a caveat on the ambit of these intellectuals themselves. Notwithstanding his Third-Worldist pretensions, Hanafi's efforts towards the intellectual emancipation of the Muslim world concentrate primarily on the Arabic-speaking world and his home country of Egypt in particular. Notwithstanding his reliance on Braudel's notion of an Atlantic-Mediterranean geo-historical space and his borrowings from Bastide's Lusotropicology, Arkoun's purview of the Maghrebian and Mediterranean configurations are significantly narrower than Hodgson's advocacy of a global history of the Islamicate regions undergirding the cosmopolitan Islam to which Madjid subscribes. The global span of this new Muslim intellectual discourse also calls into question how useful academic configurations such as area studies programmes are for the study of contemporary Islam. Where Middle Eastern studies have claimed Islam as their province, a field such as Southeast Asian studies has allowed this important aspect of that region's culture to slip away from its domain.

Clearly there are differences between the ideas of Madjid, Hanafi and Arkoun. Teasing out the different epistemological and methodological concerns of these Muslim Islamicists, my examination has demonstrated that, even without fully subscribing to McCutcheon's methodological reductionism or agnosticism, the respective approaches of Madjid, Hanafi, and Arkoun can be related to the increasing critical distance reflected in the taxonomy distinguishing between theological, phenomenological and critical-anthropological approaches to the study of religious phenomena.

As a national Muslim student leader with connections in both the traditionalist and modernist Muslim communities, Nurcholish Madjid started his career firmly on the inside of engaged Islamic discourse. Committed to revamping the intellectual rigour of Indonesian Muslim thought rather than striving for political success, his provocative slogan 'Islam, Yes; Islamic Party, No!' diverted much of the attention away from his subtle engagement with epistemological, sociological, and theological questions, such as the place of rational thought in Islamic learning and the importance of reconciling the need for secularisation and desacralisation with the spiritual needs of Muslims in contemporary society.

The academic work of the 'theologian' Nurcholish Madjid's work may not have the methodological astuteness and depth of Hanafi or Arkoun, but he has proved to be a bold proponent of innovative thought, a perceptive contrapuntal reader of received scholarship, and competent historian of Islam with strong analytical skills. An enterprising individual working on the crossroads of academia, civil society and politics, his ability to translate academic achievements into concrete actions by creating new platforms and fora for intellectual re-engagement with the Islamic heritage or taking part in initiatives deployed by others, make him not only the most successful of the three in gaining public exposure for his own ideas, but also a key figure in shaping an intellectual climate and academic environment in Indonesia conducive to the ideas of other innovators, such as Hanafi and Arkoun. Throughout his career Madjid remained what McCutcheon calls a caretaker of a religious tradition, helping turn Indonesia into one of the most promising venues were these alternative approaches to Islamic Studies can root.

Although not addressing the concrete questions regarding the exact nature of personal beliefs or piety in the same way as Nurcholish Madjid, the 'humanist phenomenologist' Hasan Hanafi makes no secret of the ideological motivations behind his contribution to the Islamic modernism project by trying to finalise the reconstruction of Islamic religious thinking first started by Muhammad Iqbal. Whereas his driven commitment towards emancipating Muslims may have affected the academic rigour of his later elaborations of the Heritage and Renewal Project, he has made an effort to remain true to the methodological underpinnings developed in his earlier phenomenological investigations.

This search for a fundamental philosophical method of investigation imposes a level of abstraction which makes it difficult to discern how such an approach may actually be employed in Islamic studies. However, by testing it in transforming the discipline of *usul al-fiqh* into a general philosophical method and in assessing the achievements of Bible exegesis in the Christian tradition, Hanafi has demonstrated its potential for practical application. Such philosophical interrogations of this kind are a solitary cerebral exercise, so it is not entirely strange that Hanafi's decision to continue the expansion of his project to the full field of traditional Islamic learning as a solo project ended in an unintended sacrifice of profundity for comprehensiveness. By the time he presented the massive introduction to the second part of his tripartite Heritage and Renewal Project, Hanafi was forced to acknowledge that the scope of this undertaking requires a collective scholarly input. However, such criticism should not diminish the appreciation for Hanafi's dogged pursuit of disciplined phenomenological research and safeguarding consistency in his approach.

The 'anthropologist of credibility' Mohammed Arkoun was even more acutely aware of the need for international scholarly teamwork and academic interdisciplinarity than his Indonesian and Egyptian peers. Perhaps at a certain degree to the detriment of his own engagement in substantive work, he seems to have resigned himself to the constant advocacy and persistent reiteration of the outlines for a new comprehensive research agenda required for creating the paradigm shift that is needed to implement his proposed Applied Islamology. At the same time, his earlier hands-on research on the intellectual history of the medieval Muslim world and incidental work in Qur'anic studies have established his credentials as a first-rate historical anthropologist of Islam and a pioneer in applying linguistic theories and semiotics in Islamic studies.

To my mind, this is where the validity of McCutcheon's taxonomy and my agreement with his methodological reductionism ends. The writings of Madjid, Hanafi and Arkoun also confirm Mark Taylor's challenge of McCutcheon's dichotomy between theological and anthropological-historical approaches to the study of religion as too simplistic. Taylor's identification of an 'interplay between order/disorder, location/dislocation, structuring/destructuring, and figuring/disfiguring,' which can only take place 'along the margins of established disciplines and at the boundaries of cultures and traditions' is more congenial to the cosmopolitan attitudes informing the ways in which Madjid, Hanafi and Arkoun operate.[1] If anything, it shows also how innovative their pioneering efforts from the 1960s actually were.

Moreover, instead of relegating scholarly writings to mere discursive formations and rhetoric, I have tried to retain a phenomenological approach of sorts, in the sense that I work from the premise that intellectuals like Hanafi, Arkoun and Madjid deserve the courtesy of assuming that they intended to say something substantial about the meaning and significance of the Islamic tradition for its adherents. Here the notions of 'travelling theories' and 'travel of ideas' are helpful tools in assessing the interfaces between various strands of thought and the ways in which religious phenomena acquire their meaning and significance.

In the case of Madjid, these consist in the debates on the modernisation-secularisation thesis, Fazlur Rahman's propositions for restructuring the study of Islam and his expectations of the renewal of Indonesian Islamic thought, the revisionist history of Islam advocated by Hodgson, and the indigenisation of the Islamic legacy in Indonesia (*keindonesiaan, pribumisasi*). Hanafi's reconstruction of the Islamic *turath* is grafted on an analysis inspired by Husserlian phenomenology, a critique of Western religious thought emerging from Higher Bible criticism, French Catholic modernism, and the teleology underlying German Romanticism, which forms an important ingredient in his commitment to the emancipation of the Third World. Simultaneously attaining the greatest critical distance from the subject matter, while remaining in close proximity to the French intelligentsia, Arkoun's eclectic borrowings from *Annales* historiography, structural linguistics and its anthropological counterpart, semiotics and applied anthropology are used for an incisive critique of all forms of reason and an attempt to restore the Unthought and Unthinkable of religious traditions to its rightful place.

Aside from grasping the complexity of Islamic studies as a social formation, the notion of travelling theory also highlights the retained or reclaimed agency by subalterns and exponents of deviant or heretical discourses, or what in regard to the study of Islam can also be referred to as enlightened or affirmative Orientalism, and more recently Post-Orientalism.[2] It also points a way out of the dilemma of how to reconcile the new Muslim intellectuals' challenge of the dominant Orientalist approach with their decision to oppose it by utilising alternative discourses of Western provenance. Moreover travelling theories change during their journey because the relationship between their origin and destination is dialectical, creating in effect the Third Space where 'the whole body of resistant hybridisation comes into being in the form of fragile syncreticism, contrapuntal recombinations and acculturation.'[3]

In the wider context of contemporary intellectual history, the liminal space occupied by Madjid, Hanafi, and Arkoun is found in what Anouar Majid calls the 'zones of intelligence' inhabited by those committed to 'unstructured monastic nomadism.'[4] Instilled with a little dose of postmodernism, their heresies open up new perspectives on the study of Islam. The ambiguity brought about by their cultural hybridity defies easy categorisation, an 'occupational hazard' for these new Muslim intellectuals working in the borderlands between cultures and academic milieus. But cultural hybridity might not necessarily be such a bad thing, because its inherent plurality of identities can perhaps avoid the trap of what the French-Lebanese writer Amin Maalouf refers to as one-dimensional 'murderous identities.'[5]

Even though Madjid, Hanafi and Arkoun have been in conversation with different elements of Western scholarship in the humanities and social sciences for fleshing out their respective epistemological and methodological approaches there are a number of common points.

First of all, all three advocate a multilayered understanding of the relationships between authenticity, tradition and modernity. While interested in different aspects of these notions and interpreting them in their own particular ways, they recognised the complex interplay that is at work between the tenets of the Islamic faith, the culturally specific ways in which these have historically unfolded in the various Islamicate traditions, and the efforts to reform and renew Islamic learning in accordance with the demands of different contemporary Muslim societies. In contrast with the signature slogan 'back to the Qur'an and the Sunna' which invites a literalist interpretation of the Islamic Scripture and the practices of the *Salaf* generations, Madjid, Hanafi and Arkoun suggest a comprehensive engagement with the cumulative Islamic heritage or *turath*. Their approaches draw on the accumulated and exhaustive traditions of scholarship, account for practices of disenfranchised and marginalised Muslim communities, and apply a sophisticated methodological apparatus borrowed from a variety of scholarly fields and disciplines developed in the Western academe.

Next, they share a concern for the place of reason in Islam. There is an affinity between the case made by Madjid that rationalisation is not the same as Westernisation and Arkoun's meta-critique of the various strands of reason, while the former's insistence that rational thought is compatible with the message of Islam and that restoring it to its rightful place as a prerequisite for the modernisation or renewal of the vigour of the Muslim *Umma* is also very similar to Hanafi's mission of reconstructing the various disciplines of traditional Islamic learning in order to equip Muslims with the intellectual means to face the contemporary world. A further parallel exists between Hanafi's transformation of religious sciences from a vertical theology into a horizontal anthropology and Madjid's identification of separate epistemes for the two respective domains of human life; a rational epistemology governing the horizontal axis of relations among humans in their this-worldly existence and the spiritual attainments through which humankind's vertical relationship with the transcendent is understood.

This points to a third similarity: the anthropocentric focus of the oeuvres of Madjid, Hanafi and Arkoun is informed by commonly held humanist concerns, which have an important consequence for their characterisation as new Muslim intellectuals. If it is accepted, as Mishra and Hodge argue, that postmodernists have made 'humanism, with its essentialism and mistaken historical verities' the object of their critique, then the three scholars who have been discussed here are no postmodernists.[6] Neither can they be accused of complicit postcolonialism which is allegedly the prevailing form of postcolonialism as a result of 'an increasing alliance with the postmodern at the level of theory,' and its increasing predominance in the political realm.[7] Read together with the other two commonalities—their sophisticated understanding of Islamic heritage and the workings of reason—Madjid, Hanafi and Arkoun represent an oppositional postcolonialism that exercises its agency through endogenous intellectual creativity grounded in the acceptance of cultural hybridity rather than a misleading essentialist or unsubstantiated purist understanding of authenticity.

As for politics, I believe it is fair to state that Madjid, Hanafi and Arkoun oppose the conflation of religion and state. As Salvatore has argued, during the 1950s and 1960s, Islamists were largely absent from Arab-Islamic discourse. Consequently, thinkers like Arkoun and Hanafi spent their formative years in an environment dominated by secular political discourses, but not entirely devoid of a broader intellectual interest in exploring the cultural-religious heritage of the Arab-Islamic world. This supports the argument I have made for a careful qualification of the return of religion in Muslim public life. While it may be true that, since the 1970s, there has been a resurgence in Islamist politics, it is important to recognise the continuity in the intellectual interest in the role of religion in shaping Muslim societies. In this regard, the new Muslim intellectuals even seem to have been ahead of leading Western sociologists advocating what the latter refer to as desecularisation, detraditionalisation, or Second Modernity.[8]

The new Muslim intellectualism that has been investigated here has found a more positive response in Indonesia than anywhere else in the Muslim world. Although there may not yet be a great deal of interest elsewhere in the ideas propounded by thinkers from the eastern fringe in the rest of Muslim world, there certainly are indications of an increasing assertiveness on the part of Southeast Asia's Muslim intellectuals and a growing awareness elsewhere of the significance of what is transpiring in Indonesia, raising interesting questions concerning the validity of the centre-periphery polarity and inviting speculations on the future of this relationship.

The current Secretary General of ASEAN and former foreign minister of Thailand, Surin Pitsuwan, observed in a *Newsweek* interview, in 2002, that 'for all Islam's history, Southeast Asia was considered a backwater. But the flows of globalisation now need to be reversed. Islam must learn not from the center but rather the periphery.'[9] Two years later, the Malaysian Arts, Culture and Heritage Minister Datu Seri Rais Yatim came out against the 'Arabisation' of Malay culture, encouraging his countrymen to 'challenge those who condemn deep-rooted practices of the Malay community as unIslamic [sic].'[10] Shabbir Akhtar, a Muslim philosopher with teaching experience in Malaysia, also noted that the closed linkage between Islam and Arab culture needs to be ruptured, adding that Indonesia as the core Muslim nation on the Far Eastern frontier is leading the charge against 'Arabolatry.'[11]

Since then, developments in Southeast Asia have even caught the imagination of the political establishment in Washington, where Missouri Senator Christopher Bond published a book entitled *The Next Frontier: Southeast Asia and the Road to Global Peace with Islam*.[12] The current Obama administration has also not stayed behind, with the president dispatching Secretary of State Hillary Clinton to Jakarta for her first major international mission. In his latest book on the role of Islam in Indonesia, Nasir Tamara cites her as saying that, 'if you want to know if Islam, democracy, modernity and women's rights can coexist, go to Indonesia.'[13] Meanwhile, the main protagonist of Tamara's book, President Susilo Bambang Yudhoyono, confidently positioned his country as a bridge between the Muslim World, Asia and the West in a speech delivered at the London School of Economics in the fringes of the G20 summit in April 2009.[14]

Unfortunately in the last few decades the intellectual climate in many parts of the Muslim world, and Indonesia is no exception, has witnessed a growing internal antagonism between various Muslim groups. Prior to the fall of the Soeharto regime, a commentator like Robert Hefner showed himself carefully optimistic regarding the prospects of Islamic renewal efforts driven by leading spokespersons of civil pluralism like Nurcholish Madjid. Hefner anticipated Indonesia providing an alternative ideology, not just for the hard version of secularisation, but also for those reactionary Muslim movements associated with terror and violence.[15] However he also made a reservation regarding the fact that the New Order Regime left unresolved 'the difficult question of which variant of Islam is to guide the Muslim community into the next phase of Indonesia's national development.'[16] Indicative of the precarious position of new Muslim intellectuals, even in Indonesia, was the condemnation of Nurcholish Madjid's views in a *fatwa* issued by the *Majelis Ulama Indonesia* (MUI) or 'Council of Indonesian Islamic Scholars,' in 2005, whereas a few years earlier, there had been widespread public calls for him to stand as a candidate in the country's presidential elections.[17]

Madjid's 'smuggling method' for introducing new ideas resembles Hanafi's detours via Spinoza, Lessing, Sartre, Feuerbach and Bultmann. However this tactic, reminiscent of what Leo Strauss discussed in *The Persecution and the Art of Writing* could not always save Hanafi.[18] After clashing with the al-Azhar establishment in 1997, a few years later an Islamist website declared Hanafi a 'Freethinker of the Religious Left.'[19] Arkoun's stoic focus on identifying and testing complicated theories and methodologies developed in the Western human sciences, together with his firm entrenchment in the French academe, have generally kept him out of the firing lines in which Hanafi and Madjid would occasionally find themselves. However, his outspoken criticisms of the ideological overtones in the work of his Muslim colleagues has led some to speculate on Arkoun's commitment to the 'Muslim cause' and question his faith.[20]

As exponents of the first generation of Muslim intellectuals coming of age in postcolonial times, Madjid, Hanafi, and Arkoun have mediated a cosmopolitan Islam—the contours of which could already be discerned in the work of earlier South Asian thinkers and scholars such as Iqbal and Fazlur Rahman, as well as Indonesians like Mukti Ali and Harun Nasution. This torch is now passed on to younger generations belonging to Indonesia's Liberal Islamic Network (JIL) and the hybrid new intellectualism of the NU referred to as Post-Traditionalism, as well as the Muslim diasporas in Europe and North America. But that is another story.

NOTES

PREFACE

1. Gulf News, 1 October 2006.
2. Gillespie (2007); Ichwan (2005). Indicative of this changing atmosphere is the appointment of Saudi-trained Muslim officials as Minister of Religious Affairs, after a string of moderate and even liberal incumbents, who had often been educated at Western universities: Said Agil Husin Al Munawar (2001–4) has studied in Makkah and served with the MUI (1990–8), while Maftuh Basyuni (2004–9) is a graduate from Al-Madinah University and former diplomat serving further stints in Saudi Arabia.
3. Jeune Afrique 2122, 7 September 2001.
4. Taji-Farouki 2004: 10.

1. INTRODUCTION: WRITING AN INTELLECTUAL HISTORY
OF THE CONTEMPORARY MUSLIM WORLD

1. The following is by no means an exhaustive list of works discussing this phenomenon under a variety of designations: Abaza (2002); Abdullah (1996); Abu-Rabi' (1996), (2004); Abu Zayd (2004); Bagader (1994); Benzine (2005); Boullata (1990); Effendy (2003); Feener (2007); Kamrava (2006); Mandaville (2001); Meeker (1991); Martin (2001); Saleh (2001); Taji-Farouki (2004); Taji-Farouki and Nafi (2004); Vogt et al. (2008); Woodward (1996); Yavuz (2003). Although these works deal primarily with representatives from the Sunni tradition, the literature on contemporary Shi'ism also refers to 'new religious intellectuals,' cf. Dabashi (2004); Ghamarzi-Tabrizi (2008).
2. Cf. Bhabha (1994).
3. Abu-Rabi' 2004: 160.
4. Boullata 1990: 25.
5. This has led to designations such as 'Arab Averroists of the Twentieth Century' (cf. von Kügelgen 1996) and the less elegant 'neo-Ibn Rushdians' (van Bruinessen, personal communication, 19 January 2004).

6. Salvatore 1997: 165.
7. A recent attempt towards such a reassessment from a global perspective is found in 'An Uncertain Trajectory: Islam's Contemporary Globalization 1971–1979,' Ayesha Jalal's contribution to *The Shock of the Global: The 1970s in Perspective* (Jalal 2010).
8. Cf. for example, Binder's *Islamic Liberalism* (1988), Lee's *Overcoming Tradition and Modernity* (1997); and Salvatore's *Islam and the Political Discourse of Modernity* (1997), as well as *Intellectual Origins of the Islamic Resurgence in the Modern Arab World* and *Contemporary Arab Thought: Studies in Post-1967 Arab Intellectual History* by the Islamicist Ibrahim M. Abu-Rabi'.
9. Salvatore 1997: xviii.
10. Cf. video recording of 'Critical Issues in the debate on Islam,' Library of Congress, 27 June 2001. http://www.loc.gov/locvideo/mslm/mslmintl/. Downloaded 25 March 2008.
11. In spite of the titles suggesting a broad engagement, the early mentioned landmark study by Binder (1988) and Salvatore's prize-winning book focus almost exclusively on Arab intellectuals. Even Mandaville's *Transnational Muslim Politics* (2001) and Armajani's *Dynamic Islam: Liberal Muslim Perspectives in a Transnational Age* (2004) deal primarily with the Arabic-speaking world or Arab intellectuals residing in the West. Only a handful of anthologies, edited volumes, and comparative studies give a more comprehensive coverage of contemporary Muslim intellectualism, but such collections do not present a coherent narrative. Cf. Esposito and Voll (2001); Kamrava (2006); Kurzman (1998); Taji-Farouki and Nafi (2004); Vogt et al (2008).
12. Cf. also Binder 1976: 2ff. and Feener 2007: 264–5.
13. Burke 1979: 242. Hodgson reserved the designations 'Islam' and 'Islamic' for the 'properly religious' in order to distinguish it not only from 'Islam-dom' as a geographical domain and the *oikoumene* of 'complex of social relations,' but also from the aggregate of 'Islamicate' cultures centred on lettered traditions in Arabic, Persian, Turkish, Malay and other languages (Hodgson 1974 i: 58–9). For critiques of Hodgson, cf. the reviews of Bulliet (1978) and Wansbrough (1977).
14. Madjid 2003b: 3.
15. Hefner 1997a: 8.
16. Johns 1984: 116.
17. Federspiel 2002: 327.
18. For a more recent contribution to the study of this particular intellectual milieu, cf. Lukens-Bull 2005.
19. Roff 1985: 7. *Abangan* refers to a syncretised form of religion, incorporating Islamic, Buddhist, Hindu and animist elements, practised by nominal Muslims in rural Java; *Priyayi* are the cultural customs and traditions associated with Javanese court culture; *Santri* is used for pious, mostly urban, Muslims seeking to adhere to the ritual and legal requirements also

observed elsewhere in the Muslim world (Fealy and Hooker 2006: xxxiii-li).

20. Cf. also Binder 1988: 101; Varisco 2005: 32.
21. Woodward 1989: 3.
22. Cf. also the further fine-tuning of this research in the more recent work by Andrew Beatty (1999, 2009), Timothy Daniels (2009), and Patrick Guinness (2009).
23. Hefner 1997a: 10. At the same time, he seems sympathetic to Geertz's defence that by the time Hefner himself and his peers began publishing their findings Indonesia was already in the grip of an Islamic revival, making them more consciously aware of the place of Islam in Indonesian culture (Hefner 1985: 15). Also Woodward admits that the Islamic revival of the late 1970s and 1980s 'caused western scholars to take Islam more seriously' (Woodward 1996: 15).
24. Bowen 1995: 81–2.
25. Bowen 1995: 73.
26. In a lecture entitled 'The Localization of "The Malays": Comments from a New Book,' SOAS Centre for South East Asian Studies, London, 11 June 2009.
27. Smith 1957: 295.
28. Fazlur Rahman 1982: 125.
29. Bakri and Mudhofir 2004: 92.
30. Mandaville 2001: xii.
31. Eickelman and Anderson 1997: 43.
32. McCutcheon 2003: xvi.
33. Ayoob 2008: 40.
34. Feener 2007: 273.
35. Taji-Farouki 2004: 3.
36. Adams 2001: viii-ix.
37. Matthes 2005: 23.
38. Berger 1980: 127; Cox 1984: 176.
39. Martin 1969: 62; Cox 1984: 176.
40. Bruce 2001: 88.
41. Berger 1970: 188.
42. Cf. Fazlur Rahman 1979: 315–30; Kamrava 2006: 1–20; Ramadan 2005: 23–30; Saeed 2007: 395–404; Shepard 2004: 61–103.
43. Burke 2009: 1–2.
44. Burke 2009: 34.
45. Ayoob 2008: 39.
46. Bagader 1999: 119–20.
47. Salvatore 1997: 24, cf. also *turathiyun judud* or 'new partisans of the heritage' (Flores 1988).
48. The substantial contribution of such publications is often debatable. For example, the editors of *Orientalism, Islam and Islamists* insist that, even after the 'devastating critique' of Said's 'splendid study,' further research is

needed and that their book 'is another contribution to the growing literature performing the post-mortem of Orientalism,' which to my mind is
effectively an admission of flogging a dead horse, cf. Hussain et al. 1984: 1.

49. Hentsch 1992: 75.
50. Rodinson 1987: 44.
51. Rodinson 1987: 52.
52. Sen 2005: 140–53.
53. Binder 1988: 97ff.
54. Cf. also Irwin 2006: 251.
55. Turner 1994: 53.
56. Waugh 1978: 192.
57. Burke 1979: 243–4; Turner 1994: 54–66.
58. Hourani 1978: 55.
59. Burke 1979: 252.
60. Binder 1988: 117.
61. Binder 1988: 115.
62. King 1999: 84–5.
63. Binder 1988: 120–1.
64. King 1999: 84–5.
65. King 1999: 86. Cf. also Clifford 1988: 261; Fox 1992: 152.
66. King 1999: 86.
67. Alatas 1981.
68. Abdulghani (1964), cf. also Boullata 1990: 87ff. For more recent updates:
    cf. Berger (2004), Cho and Chen, Hadiz (2004); Malley (1996).
69. 'L'Orientalisme en Crise' (1963). It is ironic that two Christian Arabs felt
    compelled to challenge Western representations of the Muslim world.
70. Abaza 2002: 124.
71. Gupta 1992: 64–6.
72. Preston 1997: 323.
73. McCutcheon 1997: 89.
74. Albinus 2006: 524.
75. McCutcheon 2003: 147–8.
76. McCutcheon 2001.
77. McCutcheon 2003: 186. The term is borrowed from Michel de Certeau.
78. Cf. Roberts 2009; Taylor 2009.
79. McCutcheon 2003: 147.
80. McCutcheon 2003: 163, n. 2.
81. Majid 2007: 14.
82. McCutcheon 2003: 148.
83. McCutcheon 2003: 147.
84. McCutcheon 2003: 153.
85. The most detailed examination is found in the MA thesis written by
    Budhy Munawar-Rachman (1998), for many years the managing director
    of the Paramadina Foundation and one of Madjid's closest associates.
    Written at the *Sekolah Tinggi Filsafat Driyarkara*, an institution for higher

education run by Jesuits and Franciscans, this theological examination of Madjid's neomodernist hermeneutics addresses his philosophical arguments for religious experience, for Islam as a source for self-realisation, and for how Islam can meet the challenges of modernity. Budhy Munawar-Rachman also edited a four-volume encyclopaedia on Madjid's oeuvre (Munawar-Rachman 2006a).

86. An Indonesian translation of Barton's thesis was published by the Paramadina Foundation as: *Gagasan Islam Liberal: Telaah terhadap Tulisan-tulisan Nurcholish Madjid, Djohan Effendi, Ahmad Wahib dan Abdurrahman Wahid, 1968–80* [Liberal Islamic Thought: A Study of the Writings of Nurcholish Madjid, Djohan Effendi, Ahmad Wahid and Abdurrahman Wahid]. For the present research I have had access to author's updated manuscript of the forthcoming English publication (Barton 1999).

87. The title he has given to his overarching and comprehensive analysis of both Muslim and Western civilization, cf. 'Master Plan for the "Heritage and Renewal Project"' (Hanafi 1980: 203ff.).

88. Cf. Esposito and Voll 2001: 74–5; Haddad 1998: 50–6.

89. Apart from two much briefer studies of specific publications by Hanafi, cf. Shimogaki (1988), Hildebrand (1998). As far as material in Arabic is concerned, I have seen the festschrift edited by Atiyah (1997), and I am aware of studies by Barbari (1998) and Hattar (1986), and a number of unpublished PhD and MA theses (Abd al-Rahman 1992, Ahmad 1995, Jam'a n.d.), but I have not been in a position to consult them.

90. Lee 1997: 146.

91. Cf. Günther 2004a: 13.This somewhat inelegant translation is taken from Thériault and Peter 2006. The closest French equivalent would probably be *frontalier*: 'the grim Swiss word for those who, materially and psychologically, dwell near or astride borders' (George Steiner quoted in: Cronin 2000: 44).

92. Both Hanafi and Arkoun use the French term 'islamologie'—also commonly used in Scandinavian languages and Dutch—to refer to the study of Islam as a field of scholarly inquiry (cf. the German equivalent *Islamwissenschaft*).

93. Haleber and Koningsveld have published a study in Dutch under the title *De Wereld van Mohammed Arkoun* (1991).

94. 'Tradition, Modernity and Metamodernism: Discussing the Thought of Mohammed Arkoun' (1996).

95. *Nalar Islam dan Nalar Modern: Berbagai Tantangan dan Jalan Baru* (1994); *Berbagai Pembacaan Quran* (1997).

96. 'Mohammed Arkoun on Modern Islam' (1998).

97. 'Societies of the Book' and Interreligious Dialogue: A Study of the Thought of Mohammed Arkoun' (2001).

2. REFASHIONING THE STUDY OF ISLAM
AND THE MUSLIM WORLD

1. McCutcheon 2003: 141.
2. Cf. McCutcheon 1999: 6; McCutcheon 2003: 153.
3. Albinus 2006: 524.
4. Flood 1999: 9.
5. Flood 1999: 40.
6. Also referred to as history of religions and comparative religion.
7. Cf. Richard Palmer's *Hermeneutics: Interpretation Theory: Interpretation Theory in Schleiermacher, Dilthey, Heidegger, and Gadamer* (1969) and Peter Berger's *The Heretical Imperative* (1980). Illustrative of Husserl's central importance is his influence on other important twentieth-century philosophers as diverse as Fink, Levinas, Sartre, Merleau-Ponty, Adorno, and Habermas, cf. Russell 2006: 198.
8. Waardenburg 1969: 315–30.
9. Flood 1999: 16.
10. Bijlefeld 1972: 4. As incumbent of the Islamic Studies chair, Bijlefeld was the successor of Duncan Black MacDonald (1863–1943).
11. Richard Martin 2001: 5.
12. Richard Martin 2001: 10–1.
13. Adams 1967: 187–8.
14. Cf. Waardenburg 1995: 419.
15. Cf. Waardenburg 1995: 439ff. One of Hanafi's former students, Nasr Hamid Abu Zayd has gone furthest in this regard. Waardenburg's proposition to regard Islam as a 'religion of protest,' in the sense that the prophetic word introduces revolutionary changes to existing worldviews, also resonates with the motivating forces behind Hanafi and Arkoun's scholarly innovations (Waardenburg 1995: 426–7).
16. Gadamer 2004: 325.
17. Gadamer 2004: 306. For a discussion of the Betti-Gadamer debate, cf. Palmer 1969: 46–65. Cf. also the more recent contributions by Thomas Seebohm (1986, 2004).
18. The translators of *Truth and Method* note that Ricoeur has translated it as 'consciousness open to the effects of history' (Gadamer 2004: xv). In fact, Ricoeur offered two: (1) 'consciousness exposed to the effects of history'; (2) 'consciousness of historical efficacy' (Ricoeur 1981: 70).
19. Gadamer 2004: 267ff.
20. King 1999: 72–3.
21. Flood 1999: 85.
22. Flood 1999: 47 (original emphasis).
23. Cf. McCutcheon 2003: 6–8.
24. Flood 1999: 14.
25. Flood 1999: 9.
26. King 1999: 73.

27. Flood 1999: 144ff.; King 1999: 49.
28. Flood 1999: 68.
29. King 1999: 53.
30. Flood 1999: 86.
31. Ricoeur 1981: 131.
32. Ricoeur 1984: x; Flood 1999: 63
33. Reagan 1996: 74; Wallace 1995: 1.
34. Ricoeur 1966: 341.
35. Johnson 1981: 15.
36. Ricoeur 1981: 160.
37. Ricoeur 1981: 164.
38. Flood 1999: 85. The quote is from Gadamer 2004: 295.
39. Burke 2009: 2.
40. Mishra and Hodge 1991: 404–5.
41. Mishra and Hodge 1991: 411.
42. Hall 1996: 243.
43. Hall 1996: 242.
44. Hall 1996: 253.
45. Hall 1996: 254–5.
46. Hall 1996: 247.
47. Mishra and Hodge 1991: 409.
48. Hall 1996: 254; Mishra and Hodge 1991: 411.
49. Wolf 2000: 129.
50. Wolf 2000: 133.
51. Hall 1996: 251.
52. Wolf 2000: 134.
53. Wolf 2000: 135.
54. King 1999: 86.
55. King 1999: 92–3, 106–7, 148–9.
56. That this is feasible is corroborated by another theorist's observation that 'the Islamic world is the most familiar example of a whole range of debates and projects that have little to do with boundaries,' turning it into one of 'the crucibles of the postnational political order' (Appadurai 1996: 22).
57. Mandaville 2001: 132.
58. Said 1984: 227.
59. Mandaville 2001: 86.
60. Mandaville 2001: 94.
61. Mandaville 2001: 105.
62. Appadurai 1996: 11; Nederveen Pieterse 1995: 46.
63. Nederveen Pieterse 1995: 53.
64. Nederveen Pieterse 1995: 45; Robertson (1995).
65. Beck (2002).
66. Beck 2004: 438.
67. Hollinger 2002: 227.

68. Cf. Beck (1998) and (1999).

69. Hollinger 2002: 228; Tomlinson 2002: 244; Vertovec and Cohen 2002: 4–5.

70. Knecht and Feuchter 2008: 11. Cf. Abegebriel (2007); Masaeli (2008); Wahid (2007a), Wahid (2007b); Masaeli (2008); Yilmaz (2008).

71. Vertovec and Cohen 2002: 13.

72. Hannerz 1990: 239.

73. Chan 2002: 194.

74. Chan 2002: 207; Hannerz 1990: 238; Tomlinson 2002: 252.

75. Werbner 1997: 21.

76. Papastergiadis 1997: 274, 279.

77. Clifford 1997: 276.

78. Werbner 1997: 4–5, 11–12.

79. Werbner 1997: 5.

80. Albinus 2006: 524.

81. Matthes 2005: 25–7.

82. Appadurai 1996: 7.

83. Berger 2001: 191. Cf. also Bruce 2001: 88; Luckmann 2001: 19; Turner 1998: 156.

84. Berger 1967: 46–7.

85. Berger 1970: ix. Cf. also Berger et al. (1974) *The Homeless Mind*.

86. David Martin 2001: 15.

87. Bernice Martin 2001: 155ff.

88. David Martin 2001: 15.

89. Berger 1980: 27.

90. Berger 1980: 127. Cf. also Dorrien 2001: 35.

91. Berger 1980: 139.

92. Berger 1980: 154.

93. Berger 1999: 10–1.

94. Berger 1970: 86.

95. David Martin 2005: 138.

96. Heelas 1996: 2.

97. Heelas' mentor Ninian Smart puts its differently, suggesting instead that 'rather we are busy as ever retraditionalizing.' Like any other period in time, this is an era of 'the invention and reinvention of traditions not of detraditionalization' (Smart 1998: 86–7).

98. Heelas 1996: 9.

99. Heelas 1998: 3.

100. Heelas 1998: 7.

101. Hefner 1998: 151.

3. FROM *WUNDERKIND* TO *ENFANT TERRIBLE*: THE EARLY CAREER OF NURCHOLISH MADJID

1. Robinson 2001: 203–4.

2. Laffan 2003: 33.

3. Cf. Alatas (1997); De Jonge and Kaptein (2002); Freitag and Clarence-Smith (1997); Mandal (1994); Mobini-Kesheh (1999); Osman (2006).

4. Laffan 2003: 36.

5. Cf. Laffan 2003: 103–14.

6. Lafan 2003: 131. Cf. also Azra 1994: 94–8; Roff 1970: 73–8.

7. Laffan 2003: 143, 149, 172; Matheson and Hooker (1988); Mobini-Keshe (1996); Proudfoot (1993).

8. Laffan 2003: 171–3. Cf. also Abdullah (1972).

9. Laffan 2003: 233.

10. Federspiel 2006: 38–9. Cf. also Alatas 2005: 162–3.

11. Federspiel 2006: 29.

12. Laffan 2003: 179.

13. Cf. Abu Shouk (2002), Blum-Wahn (1997).

14. Laffan 2003: 226; Federspiel 2006: 33–4.

15. Steenbrink 1996: 156.

16. Two extensive discussions of Natsir's career in English are: Burns (1981) and Ihza (1995).

17. Woodcroft-Lee 1984: 78. Cf. also Adnan 1990: 450–1; Ihza 1995: 135.

18. Federspiel 2006: 43.

19. Boland 1971: 77–81; Saleh 2001: 121–35.

20. Saleh 2001: 105ff.

21. Boland 1971: 44.

22. Boland 1971: 9–10.

23. Woodcroft-Lee 1984: 79.

24. Boland 1971: 25–7.

25. Boland 1971: 54.

26. Boland 1971: 38.

27. Boland 1971: 108.

28. Saeed 1999: 182–3.

29. Meuleman 2002: 284.

30. Kull 2005: 47. Cf. Fathimah 1999: 9–14; Barton 2002: 67–72, 120–1.

31. For the difference between *pesantren* and *madrasa*, cf. Steenbrink (1974).

32. Barton 2002: 12; Fathimah 1999: 17.

33. He was called an '*anak Masyumi kesasar*' or 'stray member of Masyumi' (Bakri and Mudhofir 2004: 75).

34. Stauth 2002: 59. For a portrayal of Taman Siswa, cf. Dewantara (1967).

35. Barton 2002: 122; Fathimah 1999: 18.

36. Castles 1966: 31.

37. Bakri and Mudhofir 2004: 76.

38. Fathimah 1999: 21. Steenbrink compared it to a Jesuit college (Steenbrink 1993: 28). In Boland's critical view 'modern' referred to the school's facilities and curriculum structure, but not the administration's religious outlook, which he considered traditionalist (Boland 1971: 117).

39. Bakri and Mudhofir 2004: 75.
40. Madjid 1979: 153.
41. Hassan 1980: 97; Rahardjo 2002: 306.
42. Boland 2001: 85. For discussions of these rebellions, cf. van Dijk (1981), Hiroko (1975) and Dengel (1986).
43. Boland 1971: 94.
44. Ihza 1995: 127–8.
45. Madjid 1979: 148
46. Rahardjo 2002: 308.
47. Cf. Adnan 1990: 458; Barton 1999: 53; Effendy 2003: 73; Fathimah 1999: 29–30; Hassan 1980: 118; Hefner 2000: 117.
48. Rahardjo 2002: 298.
49. Its key architect was General Ali Murtopo of the Special Intelligence Bureau (OPSUS) assisted by a special 'think tank,' the Center for Strategic and International Studies (Hefner 1997b: 78–9; cf. also Adnan 1990: 454, 459).
50. Cf. Ihza 1995: 129.
51. Hefner 1997b: 78–9, 86–7.
52. Abdullah 1996: 49.
53. Hefner 1997b: 79; Saleh 2001: 240. In a detailed study Federspiel estimates this cohort at between 100–200 individuals, seventeen of whom he assesses as influential and representative. His survey also includes Madjid as the only IAIN academic (Federspiel 1992: 5).
54. Nurcholish Madjid traced the roots of this 'generation gap' back to the time of HMI's foundation in 1947, which had taken place against the will of the Masyumi leaders, having pinned their hopes on another student organisation: the 'Indonesian Young Muslims' Movement' (*Gerakan Pemuda Islam Indonesia*, GPII) (Madjid 1979: 146).
55. Fathimah 1999: 31–3.
56. Cf. Effendy 2003: 72–4; Hassan 1980: 109; Liddle 1997: 11; Steenbrink 1993: 30.
57. Barton 1999: 72.
58. Madjid 1979: 49.
59. Barton 2002: 123.
60. Madjid 1979: 150.
61. Madjid 1987: 181–90.
62. Madjid 1970: 6, 19.
63. Madjid 1987: 175.
64. Effendy 2003: 71. Liddle says Madjid learned the term 'secularisation' from Bellah (Liddle 1997: 11). Even though also Madjid refers to Bellah in a later publication, Steenbrink credits Harvey Cox as the original source because he is already mentioned in the 1968 essay (Madjid 2005a: xxviii; Steenbrink 1993: 30).
65. Hassan 1980: 122; 139.
66. Hefner 1997b: 86; Jabali and Subhan 2007: 54.

67. Kull 2005: 106.
68. Madjid 1979: 145.
69. Madjid 1970: 2.
70. Madjid 1970: 9–10.
71. *Pembaruan* is the new spelling.
72. Madjid 1979: 30.
73. Madjid 1970: 4.
74. Hefner 1998: 159.
75. Madjid 1987: 255.
76. Madjid 1987: 256.
77. Madjid 1987: 245–8.
78. Madjid 1972: 40–2.
79. Madjid 1972: 38.
80. Madjid 1987: 242–3.
81. Rahardjo 1987: 22.
82. Berger 1961: 177.
83. This is Madjid's preferred translation, inspired by the writings of Muhammad Asad (Mulyadi 2001: 16–7).
84. Hakim 2006: 12.
85. Madjid 1970: 8; 1987: 242.
86. Madjid 1987: 246–8.
87. Cf. Hassan 1980: 114; Madjid 1987: 182–3, 264–5.
88. Barton 1999: 72.
89. Madjid 1987: 257–8. The version in question is XLV: 24: 'they say, "There is only our life in this world: we die, we live, nothing but time destroys us." They have no knowledge of this; they only follow guesswork. Their only argument,' (Abdel Haleem 2004: 325).
90. Madjid 1987: 160.
91. Madjid 1979: 152.
92. Bellah 1976: 147.
93. Bellah 1976: 151.
94. Bellah 196: 152–4.
95. Bellah 1976: 165.
96. Bakri and Mudhofir 2004: 103ff.; 136; Rahardjo 1987: 22–6.
97. On the relation between New Order's development policies and Dependency Theory, cf. Effendy 2003: 86.
98. Moreover, Berger himself observed during a visit to Indonesia that translations of his books are indeed popular among Muslim intellectuals because of their non-reductionist sociological approach (Berger 2001: 197).
99. Cf. Berger 1967: 83–6; Madjid 1987: 182–3.
100. Berger 1967: 86.
101. Madjid 1987: 185–6.
102. Dorrien 2001: 29.
103. Inspired by Sartre's '*La Mauvaise Foi*' (Berger 1961: 89).

104. Berger 1961: 150.
105. Berger 1961: 177.
106. Berger 1967: 11–7.
107. Berger 1980: 76ff.
108. Steenbrink dismisses the dissertation as a disappointing compilation of texts on Javanese mysticism (personal communication, 14 March 2007).
109. Azra 1994: 84–104.
110. Hassan 1980: 130.
111. Hassan 1980: 122–3.
112. Hassan 1980: 124.
113. *Al-Qur'an: 'Arabiyyun Lughatan wa'Alamiyyun Ma'nan.'* Steenbrink translates it as 'The Qur'an, Arabic in its Wording, Universal in its Meaning' (1993: 31), Johns and Saeed suggest 'The Qur'an, Arabic in Language, Universal in Significance' (Johns and Saeed 2004: 73). Barton's 'The Qur'an viewed as an Arabic book and its relationship to its Human Environment' is evidently based on the Indonesian *'Al-Qur'an sebagai Buku Berbahasa Arab dan Hubungnya dengan Kemanusiaan Kandungnya'* (Barton 1999: 67).
114. Nadroh 1999: 24.
115. Steenbrink 1996: 156.
116. Munhanif 1996: 85–91. There is some doubt whether Mukti Ali was indeed awarded a doctorate in Pakistan, given the fact that he obtained 'only' an MA at McGill (personal communication from Karel Steenbrink, 14 March 2007).
117. Jabali and Jamhari 2002: 20–2.
118. Munhanif 1996: 93.
119. Munhanif 1996: 97, 99. Cf. also Boland 1971: 205–11; Steenbrink 1999: 284–5.
120. Boland 1971: 208.
121. Munhanif 1996: 100.
122. Effendy 2003: 70.
123. Steenbrink 1999: 285.
124. Munhanif 1996: 106–7.
125. Cf. Barton 2002: 106; Effendy 2003: 89–90.
126. Barton 2002: 102. Cf. also Baso (2006); Rumadi (2008); Salim and Ridwan (1999).
127. Cf. Muzani 1994: 93–9: Martin and Woodward 1997: 161–3.
128. Published in Indonesian under the more provocative title *Muhammad Abduh dan Teologi Rasional Mu'tazilah* (1987).
129. Cf. his *Teologi Islam Rasional: Apresiasi Terhadap Wacana dan Praksis* (Nasution 2001).
130. Cf. Muzani 1994: 101–4.
131. Saeed 1999: 187.
132. Muzani 1994: 123.

133. Meuleman 2002: 285–6.
134. Saeed 1999: 185.
135. Martin and Woodward 1997: 159.
136. Azra 1994: 114; Muzani 1994: 105–112.
137. Saleh 2001: 201–2.
138. Federspiel 2006: 66.
139. Barton 1995b: 15–6.
140. Hassan 1980: 97.

4. ENGAGING WITH ISLAMIC TRADITION

1. Barton 1997: 332–3.
2. Fathimah 1999: 38.
3. For a detailed account of this episode in Fazlur Rahman's career, cf. Hewer (1998).
4. Armajani 1999: 283–9; Benzine 2004: 124–8; Saeed 2004: 38–9.
5. Fazlur Rahman 1979: 323.
6. Cf. Fazlur Rahman 1979: 316; 1982: 85.
7. Fazlur Rahman 1979: 321.
8. Fazlur Rahman 1979: 322–8.
9. Izutsu (1964) and (1966). Cf. also Partin (1970).
10. For concise analyses of this rereading of the Qur'an, cf. Benzine (2004) and Saeed (2004).
11. Fazlur Rahman 1982: 1–3.
12. Fazlur Rahman 1982: 37.
13. Fazlur Rahman 1982: 141.
14. Fazlur Rahman 1982: 5–7.
15. Fazlur Rahman 1982: 145–51.
16. Fazlur Rahman 1982: 153.
17. Fazlur Rahman 1982: 156.
18. Fazlur Rahman 1982: 157–9.
19. Cf. Palmer 1969: 46–64.
20. Fazlur Rahman 1982: 9.
21. Fazlur Rahman 1982: 10–11.
22. Rahardjo 2002: 304.
23. Hefner 2000: 115; Liddle 1997: 13. While working on his dissertation, Nurcholish Madjid also completed a translation of selected texts by authors of the classical Islamic tradition (Madjid 1984a).
24. Hodgson 1974: i 38.
25. Cf. Hodgson 1974: i 50–1. Cf. also Burke 1979: 251.
26. Turner 1994: 64.
27. Hourani 1978: 55.
28. Turner 1994: 61.
29. Hodgson 1974: ii 470; Madjid 1984b: 58.
30. Fazlur Rahman 1979: 318.

31. Madjid 1984b: ii.
32. Madjid 1984b: iii.
33. Madjid 1984b: 18–9.
34. Madjid 1984b: 23.
35. Madjid 1984b: 42, 181ff.
36. Madjid 1984b: 222.
37. Madjid 1984b: 41.
38. Madjid 1984b: 29–31.
39. Madjid 1984b: 41–3.
40. Madjid 1984b: 81.
41. Madjid 1984b: 77ff.
42. Madjid 1984b: 56.
43. Characterised as 'fiqhism' (Madjid 1987: 255–6).
44. Madjid 1984b: 53.
45. Madjid 1984b: 50–2.
46. Madjid 1984b: 240.
47. Cf. Kull 2005: 101.
48. Fathimah 1999: 39.
49. Liddle 1997: 13.
50. The only exception is 'Methodology and Orientation of the Future Study of Islam,' (Madjid 2000: 1–27).
51. Madjid 2003b: 3–18.
52. Madjid 2003b: 3.
53. Madjid 2005a: 358–70.
54. Madjid 2003b: 4–6.
55. Hefner 1997a: 8.
56. Saleh 2001: 259.
57. Madjid 2003b: 5.
58. Madjid 2003b: 6. Cf. also 'Islam and Local Culture: The Issue of Reciprocal Acculturation' (Madjid 2005a: 542ff.).
59. Hodgson 1974: ii, p. 551, n. 2.
60. Madjid 2003b: 75. He made an explicit exception for Steenbrink, cf. Madjid 2003b: 76–7.
61. With the caveat that this affected primarily the relationship with Western Christianity, because the Eastern traditions managed to keep their 'original Semitic cultural roots intact' and maintain 'smooth relations' with their Muslim neighbours (Madjid 2003b: 68–9).
62. Madjid 2003b: 159–60.
63. Madjid 1987: 190.
64. Madjid 2003b: 67, 73. Huub de Jonge has shows this is too negative an interpretation of the Snouck Hurgronje's attitude towards Muslims, cf. de Jonge 2002: 219ff.
65. Madjid 2003a: 44.
66. Madjid 2003b: 4, 10–11.
67. Madjid 2003b: 160.

68. Madjid 2003b: 17.
69. Madjid 2003b: 13.
70. Madjid 2003b: 16.
71. Madjid 2003b: 145.
72. Cf. the political biography by Ali Rahnema (2000).
73. Jahanbegloo 2004: xv. For a detailed study of both historical and contemporary Persian and Shi'ite influence cf. Yusuf (ed.) (2004) and Marcinkowski (2006) respectively.
74. Madjid 2003b: 211.
75. Cf. Behnam 2004: 5–6, Gheissari 1998: 74ff.; Lotfalian 2004: 20–1.
76. Madjid 2003b: 212.
77. Madjid 2003b: 213.
78. Madjid 2003b: 146.
79. Madjid 2003b: 217.
80. Madjid 2003b: 214.
81. Madjid 1997: 67–8.
82. Hodgson 1974: iii, 186 and Hodgson 1974: i, 52–3.
83. Madjid 1997: 87–8.
84. Madjid 1997: 76.
85. Munawar-Rachman 1998: 151, n. 56. Cf. also Madjid 2003a: 118ff., and Nugroho (2006).
86. Madjid 2003b: 215.
87. Madjid 2003b: 216.
88. Madjid 2003b: 216, original emphasis.
89. Madjid 2003b: 217.
90. Madjid 2003b: 144.
91. Cf. Eisenstadt (1972).
92. Madjid 2005a: 556, n. 16.
93. Ali and Effendy 1986: 167.
94. Ali and Effendy 1986: 169.
95. Ali and Effendy 1986: 175.
96. Cf. Ali and Effendy 1986: 176–7.
97. Madjid 2005a: 554. Cf. Gadamer 2004: 278ff.
98. Brown 1999: 3.
99. Madjid 2003b: 217.
100. Madjid 2003a: 33, 35; 2003b: 107; 2005a: 554.
101. Ali and Effendy 1986: 170.
102. Palmer 1969: 59.
103. Fathimah 1999: 46–7, Kull 2005: 77.
104. Cf. Saleh: 2001: 252; Liddle 1996: 324.
105. Madjid 2005a: lii-liv.
106. Cf. Madjid 2005a: 130–58.
107. Cf. also Madjid 2003b: 221–30.
108. An image taken from Sura 3:103. Cf. Madjid 2005a: 130; Madjid 2005a: xiii-xv.

109. Madjid 2005a: 425–48, for the English translation: cf. Madjid 2003b: 113–29.
110. Madjid 2003b: 124. Cf. Smith 1964: 75.
111. Madjid 2003b: 115, 122–3.
112. Madjid 2003a: 36.
113. Madjid 2005a; 157–200; English translation: Madjid 2003b: 130–55.
114. Madjid 2003b: 130.
115. Madjid 2003b: 132–3.
116. Madjid 2003b: 135–7.
117. Madjid 2003b: 146.
118. Wahyudi 2002: 256.
119. Madjid 2003a: 61.
120. Johns and Saeed 2004: 78.
121. Madjid 2005a: 300.
122. Cf. also Madjid's inaugural lecture on occasion of his appointment to full professor, entitled 'Man's Vicegerency and the Reformation of the World,' in which he 'tried to systematize the concept of an Islamic anthropology' (Zamharir 2004: 103).
123. Madjid 2005a: 302–4.
124. Stevens and Schmidgall-Tellings 2004: 651.
125. Cf. McCutcheon (2001).
126. Madjid 2005a: 362.
127. Steenbrink 1993: 31.
128. Madjid 2003b: 172.

5. REACTUALISING ISLAM: UNIVERSAL DOCTRINE
AND CULTURAL COSMOPOLITANISM

1. Hefner 1997b: 86.
2. Munawar Sjadzali (1925–2004) studied in Exeter and at Georgetown University, where he obtained an MA in political philosophy with a thesis on Muslim political parties in Indonesia (Effendy 1995: 120, n. 42). Together with Rasjidi, Mukti Ali, and Nasution, he belonged to the first batch of Indonesian students to obtain advanced degrees in Islamic Studies from Western universities (Ali and Effendy 1986: 168, n. 3).
3. Hefner 1997b: 90–2.
4. Or 'reaktualisasi' in Indonesian, cf. Effendy 1995: 102; Sjadzali (1991).
5. Effendy 1995: 110–1.
6. Hefner 1997b: 86–9; Vatikiotis 1994: 127.
7. Jabali and Jamhari 2002: viii. Both Hefner and Kull have drawn attention to the DDII's hostility towards the reform of the IAINs and the policy of sending students to Western universities (Hefner 2000: 109–10; Kull 2005: 71–2). While students continued to travel to North America, Europe, and Australia for advanced studies, a 1996 Memorandum of Understanding with Saudi Arabia and the opening of branches of al-Azhar University on

IAIN campuses are evidently intended to placate these critics. However, given the decline of al-Azhar's reputation in the Egyptian setting, the government also explored alternatives in India, Iran, and Malaysia (cf. Meuleman 2002).

8. Taken from the Arabic *Madhhab*, it has the conscious connotation of an Islamic school of thought.

9. The other ones are: Bahtiar Effendy, Badri Jatim, Hadimulyo, Irchamni Sulailman, Ali Munhanif, Ahsan Ali Fauzi, Ahmad Thaha, Nanang Tahqiq, Saiful Muzani, Muhamad Wahyuni Nafis, Nasrulah Ali Fauzi, Jamal D. Rahman (Kull 2005: 210–2).

10. Cone 2002: 54.

11. Abdullah 1996: 53–63.

12. Vatikiotis 1994: 135–6.

13. Hefner 1997b: 89; 2000: 122; Steenbrink 1993: 29.

14. Azra 2002: 36.

15. Meuleman (2002).

16. Hefner 1992b: 92. cf. also Adnan 1990: 459; Muzani 1996: 123; Saleh 2001: 246–7.

17. Hefner 1997b: 93. The organisation itself gives two explanations for this name: presenting it as contractions of the Sanskrit expression *parama*, meaning 'giving priority' and *din*, the Arabic word for religion, or the Spanish *para* or 'pro' and *madina*, the Arabic word for 'city' or 'place of civilisation or polity,' cf. http://www.paramadina.or.id/tentang-kami [Last accessed 7 April 2010].

18. Kull 2005: 264.

19. Hefner 2000: 119ff. The essays in *Islam: Doctrine and Civilisation* have their origins in presentations to the KKA (Madjid 2005a: viii).

20. Preston 1997: 323.

21. Cf. Hefner 2000: 125; Kull 2005: 76, 193.

22. Metcalf 2007: 145.

23. Steenbrink 1993: 33.

24. Stevens and Schmidgall-Tellings 2004: 337. Cf. Fachry Ali's comments in Kull 2005: 212, and also Nafis and Rifki (2005).

25. Steenbrink 1993: 33.

26. Madjid 2003b: 84–5.

27. Madjid 2003b: 87.

28. Madjid 2003b: 108.

29. Anwar 2006: 63–4.

30. Madjid 2003b: 90.

31. Madjid 2003b: 90–2.

32. Madjid 2003b: 99. Cf. also Steenbrink 1993: 35–6.

33. Madjid 2003b: 101.

34. Hakim 2006: 16.

35. Kull 2005: 276.

36. Madjid 2003b: 103.

37. Madjid 2003b: 106–7.
38. Kull 2005: 276
39. Madjid 2003b: 77. Cf. also Fathimah 1999: 104; Hidayat and Nafis 2003; Kull 2005: 157.
40. Madjid 2005a: 254–8.
41. Madjid 2002: 188. Cf. also Madjid: 1997: 123–32.
42. Kull 2005: 261.
43. Steenbrink 1993: 41.
44. Rahardjo 2002: 299–304; Feener 2007: 274. Cf. also Ihza 1995: 132–7.
45. Bakri and Mudhofir 2004: 77–8.
46. Kull 2005: 217.
47. Barton 1991: 82–5.
48. Barton 1997: 328.
49. Barton 1991: 69, n.2.
50. Fazlur Rahman 1982: 85.
51. Kull 2005: 64.
52. Johns and Saeed 2004: 76–7.
53. Rahardjo 2002: 306.
54. Munawar-Rachman 1998: 4.
55. Fathimah 1999: 102–5.
56. Waugh 1999: 31.
57. Waugh 1999: 34.
58. Saeed 2004: 39.
59. Kull 2005: 67.
60. Fazlur Rahman 1982: 126–9.
61. Barton 1991: 78–9.
62. Rasjidi (1972); Anshari (1973); Hassan (1980).
63. Cf. Giddens 1971: ix.
64. Kull 2005: 221.
65. Madjid 2005a: 235ff.
66. Kull 2005: 221–2.
67. Vatikiotis 1996: 156.
68. Kull 2005: 74, cf. also Ruthven 1989.
69. Ali and Effendy 1986: 170.
70. Ali and Effendy 1986: 171.
71. Cf. Ali and Effendy 1986: 186.
72. Ali and Effendy 1986: 187.
73. Ahmad Baso claims a distinction must be made between NU Muda and Postra (Baso 2006: 165–6).
74. For example the Lakpesdam (http://www.lakpesdam.or.id) and the Wahid Institute (http://www.wahidinstitute.org/) and gusdur.net (http://www.gusdur.net).
75. Cf. Bruinessen (2007) and Howell (2007).
76. Kull 2005: 223. Cf. Abshar-Abdalla 2006: 143–61.

77. Baso (2005), (2006); El-Dardiry (2005); Ghazali (2005); Harjanto (2003); Nurdin (2005); Rumadi (2008); Salim and Ridwan (1999).
78. Abdul Hadi 2006: 98.
79. Bakri and Mudhofir 2004: 77.
80. Bakri and Mudhofir 2004: 81.
81. Rahardjo 2002: 305.

6. THE TRANSFORMATION OF A MUSLIM MODERNIST: THE EARLY YEARS OF HASAN HANAFI

1. Cf. Akhavi 1997: 378; Hildebrand 1998; 35–6; Kügelgen 1994: 209, 215; Salvatore 1997: 232, 245; Riexinger 2007: 77ff.
2. Cf. Boom 1984: 210. My position is supported by Esposito & Voll 2001: 79; von Kügelgen 1994: 206–9; Salvatore 1997: 233.
3. Boullata 1995:98; Esposito and Voll 2001: 77; Salvatore 1997: 232. Olsson even suggests Hanafi writes on three different levels addressing the general public, the intellectual middle class and an academic elite respectively (Olsson 2004: 19).
4. Hanafi 2000 i: 531–4.
5. Cf. Allard (1969); Boom (1984); Chartier (1972), (1973); Esposito & Voll (2001); Nwiya (1971); Wahyudi (2002).
6. *Les Méthodes d'Exégèse: Essai sur la Science des Fondements de la Compréhension "Ilm Usul al-Fiqh'* (Hanafi 1965) . When writing in English, Hanafi translates the French *exégèse* as 'hermeneutics.' In view of the complexities associated with terms like 'exegesis,' 'hermeneutics,' 'interpretation,' and 'understanding,' I have decided to opt for the closest possible etymological equivalent.
7. *L'Exégèse de la Phénoménologie: l'État Actuelle de la Méthode Phénoménologique et Son Application au Phénomène Religieux* (Hanafi 1980a). *La phénoménologie de l'Exégèse: Essai d'une Herméneutique Existentielle à Partir du Nouveau Testament* (Hanafi 1988a).
8. *Al-Turath wa'l-Tajdid: Mawqifuna min al-Turath al-Qadim* (Hanafi 1980b).
9. The characterisation 'prophetic' is derived from van den Boom's article 'The Thinker as Prophet' cf. Boom (1992).
10. Cf. Hanafi 1989 vi: 207ff.
11. Hanafi 1989 vi: 221–2.
12. Hanafi 1989 vi: 229.
13. Hanafi 1989 vi: 227.
14. Hanafi 1989 vi: 223, 226.
15. Calvert 2000: 90.
16. Shepard 1996: xxx.
17. Calvert 2000: 91.
18. Ruthven 2002: 83.
19. Carré 2004: 7.

20. Moussalli 1992: 35.
21. Moussalli 1992: 97; Shepard 1996: xxiv. Cf. also Judy (2004).
22. Moussalli 1992: 127.
23. For a detailed discussion cf. Khatab (2002).
24. Carré 2004: 8; Bergesen 2008: 5.
25. Salvatore 1997: 190–1.
26. Hanafi 1989 v: 170, 182, 187. Cf. also Leonard Binder's 'Tasawwur: An Aesthetic Theory of the Qur'an' and 'Qutb's Theory of the Aesthetic' (Binder 1988: 188–94). Ibrahim Abu-Rabi', who questions the 'disjointed and mechanical treatment' of Qutb's intellectual, singling out Hanafi's dichotomy of an 'early/mature Qutb' for his explicit criticism, had to admit that in the multifaceted dimensions of Qutb's thought one can delineate distinct literary, social and religious critiques (Abu-Rabi' 1996: 139).
27. Hanafi 1989 vi: 226–7.
28. Hanafi 1989 vi: 208, n. 1.
29. Hanafi 1989 vi: 226–7, 238–9, 244 n.10.
30. Hanafi 1989 vi: 228–9.
31. Hanafi 1989 vi: 222.
32. Lee 1997: 57–8; Masud 2005: 376–7.
33. McDonough 1970: 16.
34. Hamilton Gibb called him 'the most interesting figure in the whole modern Islamic community, but also intellectually the most elusive' (Gibb 1947: 59).
35. Lee 1997: 79.
36. Lee 1997: 59. Cf. also the chapter 'Selfhood's Aesthetic' in Javed Majeed's *Muhammad Iqbal: Islam, Aesthetics and Postcolonialism* (2009).
37. Lee 1997: 58.
38. Lee 1997: 62.
39. Moussalli 1992: 103–5. Another indication of this rift was Qutb's growing reliance on other South Asian Muslim thinkers, such as Abul Ala Maududi and Abul Hasan Nadwi, cf. Binder 1988: 172; Zollner 2007: 415.
40. The same year in which his Bengali counterpart Rabindranath Tagore presented a series of lectures at Manchester College in Oxford, which were published as *The Religion of Man* (1931).
41. McDonough 1970: 17; Gibb 1947: 81.
42. Fazlur Rahman 1982: 132–3.
43. Fazlur Rahman 1984: 160.
44. Lee 1997: 61. For Bakhtin, cf. Mihailovic (1997).
45. Majeed 2009: 96.
46. Cf. also Majeed 2009: 95, 144.
47. Hanafi 1989 vi: 223.
48. He adds that he did not venture into Anglo-Saxon philosophy, a strand of thought which, he says, has still not affected his philosophical sensibilities (Hanafi 1989 vi: 232).

49. Berlin 1991: 195.
50. Hanafi 1989 vi: 233.
51. Hanafi 1987: 35.
52. Hanafi 1989 vi: 211.
53. Towards the end of his academic career, Hanafi published a study in Arabic on Fichte with exactly that title (Hanafi 2003).
54. Berlin 1991: 58.
55. Most likely a reference to Hendrik Gillot (1836–1916), a Dutch Protestant theologian and pastor, ministering for many years in St. Petersburg, where he also acted as mentor to Lou Andreas-Salomé (1861–1937), the Russian philosopher and psychoanalyst who befriended Wagner, Nietzsche, Freud and Rilke.
56. Hanafi 1989 vi: 238.
57. Berlin 1991: 197, and also 35ff. For 'grammar of resistance,' cf. Ramin Jahanbegloo in an interview with Danny Postel: http://www.logosjournal. com/issue_5.2/jahanbegloo_interview.htm. [Last accessed, 5 June 2008].
58. Hanafi 1989 vi: 138.
59. Hanafi 2001 i: 532. More recently, Pallesen has argued that Spinoza and Kierkegaard were also instrumental to Ricoeur's hermeneutics of religion (Pallesen 2008: 46, 48 50, 53).
60. 'Lorsque je cherche le visage de l'étudiant qui m'a le plus appris, je trouve à la Sorbonne, dans les années soixante, un musulman nommé Hanafi' (Guitton 1988: 106).
61. Hanafi 1989 vi: 235.
62. Hanafi 1989 vi: 236.
63. Guitton 1988: 107.
64. Hanafi 1989 vi: 235.
65. Guitton 1988: 108.
66. Guitton 1988: 106.
67. Hanafi 1989 vi: 236.
68. Hanafi 1989 vi: 240.
69. Hanafi 1989 vi: 243.
70. Haddad 1998: 63.
71. He had obtained all available published material in German from the Netherlands (Hanafi 1989 vi: 239). At the time only a fraction of Husserl's work had become public, with 30,000 handwritten pages deposited in the Husserl Archives at Louvain awaiting editing, cf. Ricoeur 1999: 13.
72. Hanafi 1989 vi: 239–40.
73. Husserl 1970: 23. Cf. also Ricoeur 1999: 162–4; Russell 2006: 184–6.
74. Hanafi 2001 i: 488. In Arabic he uses the generic term 'ilm (plural: 'ulum) where this distinction disappears as it can refer to both 'science' and 'discipline.'
75. Hanafi 1989 vi: 241–3.
76. Hanafi 1989 vi: 241.

77. Ricoeur acquired this experience during his internment in a German prison camp during the Second World War, where he began translating Husserl's work together with fellow prisoner and philosopher Mikel Dufrenne, cf. Reagan 1996: 9–10.
78. Iqbal 1974: 54.
79. Robinson 2004: 53.
80. Iqbal 1974: 198.
81. Hanafi 1989 vi: 241–2.
82. Ricoeur 1999: 42.
83. Hanafi 1989 vi: 228.
84. Cf. Ricoeur's observation that 'the greatness of Descartes, according to Husserl, lies in his having produced the project of a philosophy which is at the same time a science and the ground of all sciences within the system of one universal science' (Ricoeur 1999: 83).
85. Hanafi 1989 vi: 232.
86. Ricoeur 1999: 35.
87. Ricoeur 1999: 45.
88. Ricoeur 1999: 205.
89. Hanafi 1965: lxxxvii; Hanafi 1980b: 75ff.
90. Hanafi 1965: 51.
91. Hanafi 1989 vi: 242.
92. Hanafi 1989 vi: 231.
93. Lee 1997: 66.
94. Hanafi 2000 i: 519.
95. Hanafi 1965: vi-ix.
96. Hanafi 1965: ix n. 4.
97. Hanafi 1965: xi; Hanafi 1989 vi: 230.
98. Hanafi 1989 vi: 240.
99. Hanafi 1965: xi. For a discussion of hermeneutics as a general discipline, cf. Palmer 1969: 69, 94–7; Berger 1980: 127.
100. Gadamer 2004: 3; xxxiii.
101. Cf. respectively Gadamer 2004: 278; 301; 237–8, 305.
102. Gadamer 2004: 309.
103. Cf. Seebohm (1986).
104. Hanafi 1980b: 77–119.
105. Hanafi 1965: lxxii-lxxviii, lxxxiii-lxxxvi.
106. Hanafi 1965: cxl.
107. Hanafi 1965: lxxxvii, cxxxix-xl. Rendered as 'rhétorisme' in French. Acknowledging the non-existence of this noun, Hanafi felt obliged to create this neologism from the French adjective 'rhétorique.'
108. Hanafi 1965: cxlvi-cxlvii.
109. Hanafi 1965: cxl.
110. Hanafi 1965: lxxxvii, cf. Waardenburg 1969: 315–30.
111. Hanafi 1965: cxli.

112. Since the publication of Karl Popper's The Poverty of Historicism (1957), the confusion between 'historism' and 'historicism' has increased, in particular because of the persistent tendency in English to conflate the two (cf. Dussen 1986: 104ff).
113. Hanafi 1965: cliv-cxlix.
114. Cf. also Hanafi 1991: 636ff.
115. Hanafi 1965: clix, cf. also Hanafi 1980a: 16. For detailed elaborations of the notions of centripetal and centrifugal, cf. Hanafi 1991: 609ff.; and Hildebrand 1998: 25–6.
116. Berlin 1990: 12.
117. Hanafi notes that his later engagement in the 'reflective analysis of everyday experiences' actually falls in this analytical method (Hanafi 1965: cliv).
118. Hanafi 1965: cxlix.
119. Hanafi 1965: cxlix.
120. Hanafi 1965: clxiii.
121. Hanafi 1965: clxii.
122. The other three can each be subdivided into three manifestations: phraseology, encyclopaedic ampflication, causalisation (tautology); praise, comparison, polemics (apologetics); poetry, prose, discourse (rhetoric), cf. Hanafi 1965: clxvi-clxxv.
123. Hanafi 1965: clxxvi.
124. Hanafi 1965: clxxvii.

7. THE SEARCH FOR METHOD

1. Hanafi 1965: xii.
2. Hanafi 1965: vi, xii, cf. also Hanafi 1989 vi: 231.
3. Hanafi 1965: xvi-xix.
4. Hanafi 1965: xciv.
5. Iqbal 2002: 304.
6. Hanafi 1965: xxv.
7. Cf. Hanafi 2000 ii: 207.
8. Hanafi 1965: xxx, n. 1.
9. This particular distinction between 'interpretation' and interprétisation reminds one of the terminology developed by Ricoeur for translating phenomenological and hermeneutical texts from the German: compréhension [Verständnis, understanding] explication [Erklärung, explanation] explicitation [Auslegung, explication] interprétation [Deutung, interpretation] (Ricoeur 1981: 28).
10. Hanafi 1965: xxxii, xlviii-xlix.
11. Hanafi 1965: xxxii.
12. Hanafi 1965: xxxii, xlix.
13. Hanafi 1965: xlvii; Ricoeur 1999: 4.

14. Hanafi 1965: xxi.
15. Feuerbach 1989: xvi.
16. Hanafi 1965: xxix-xxx.
17. Hanafi 1965: liii.
18. Hanafi 1965: xlvii-lxvii.
19. Hanafi 1965: cxcii.
20. Cf. Akhavi 1997: 393.
21. Cf. Hanafi 1965: 458.
22. Hanafi 1965: lxxxvii.
23. Hanafi 1965: lxxxiii.
24. Hanafi 1965: cxxi. For an analysis of Hanafi's transpositions using the idiom and concepts developed in Translation Studies, cf. Kersten (2007).
25. Hanafi 1965: lxxxv. For Jakobson's views, cf. Bassnett 2002: 23 and Steiner 1992: 274–5.
26. Hanafi 1965: cvi-xcvii.
27. Hanafi 1965: xciv n. 5.
28. Hanafi 1965: cix. Cf. Spengler 1980: 784; Even-Zohar (1990).
29. Hanafi 1965: cx.
30. Hanafi 1965: cix.
31. Chartier 1973: 610.
32. Hanafi 1965: xxxvi.
33. Hanafi 1965: xxxix.
34. Hanafi 1965: cxii-cxiii. On bad faith, cf. also Berger 1961: 186ff.
35. Hanafi 1965: cxiii, n. 1.
36. Hanafi 1965: cxv-cxvi.
37. Hanafi 2000 1: 538.
38. Cf. Hanafi 1972: 258.
39. Hanafi 1965: xxv-xxvi. Cf. the chapter on knowledge and experience in *The Reconstruction* (Iqbal: 1974: 1–27).
40. Iqbal 1974: 97; Hanafi 1965: lxviii.
41. Hanafi 1965: xxii. Cf. also Hanafi (1972); Boom 1984: 89ff.
42. Iqbal 1974: 126.
43. Hanafi 1965: cclxx. Cf. also Boom 1984: 97.
44. Hanafi 1965: ccxli-ccliii.
45. Hanafi 1965: clxxxvii.
46. Hanafi 1965: clxxxiv.
47. Hanafi 1965: clxxxi. There is a parallel with Iqbal's depiction of the Infinite, the nature of which 'consists *in intensity and not extensity*; and the moment we fix our gaze on intensity, we begin to see that the finite ego must be distinct, though not isolated, from the Infinite. Extensively regarded I am absorbed by the spatio-temporal order to which I belong. Intensively regarded I consider the same spatio-temporal order as a confronting "other" wholly alien to me. I am distinct from and yet intimately related to that on which I depend for my life and sustenance' (Iqbal 1974:

118). Cf. also Chapter 2 of *The Reconstuction*, 'The Philosophical Test of the Revelations of Religious Experience' (Iqbal 1974: 28–61).

48. Hanafi 1965: clxxxix.
49. Hanafi 1965: clxxxviii.
50. Hanafi 1965: clxxxi.
51. Hanafi 1965: cxci. Cf. also Hanafi 1981b: 55–6.
52. Hanafi 1965: cxcii.
53. Berger 1980: ix.
54. Berger 1980: 68–9.
55. Hanafi 1965: cxciii-cxciv.
56. Hanafi 1965: cxcv.
57. Hanafi 1965: cxcvi.
58. Hanafi 1965: cxcvii. The Arabic equivalents to which these transpositions respectively correspond are: *rawi*, *mufassir*, and *mukallaf* or *mujtahid* (Hanafi 1965: 552).
59. Hanafi 1965: 63ff.
60. Iqbal 1974: 148.
61. Hanafi 1965: cciii-ccviii.
62. Hanafi 1965: ccix.
63. Hanafi 1965: ccx n.1.Cf. Iqbal 1974: 95–123.
64. Ricoeur 1999: 19.
65. Ricoeur 1999: 17.
66. Hanafi 1965: ccxii.
67. Ricoeur 1999: 147.
68. Ricoeur 1999: 18.
69. Hanafi 1965: xl.
70. Cf. George Steiner's observation that 'the application of the concept of exact science to the study of language is an idealized simile. This is not a negative judgement. It is only an attempt to state the criteria of exactitude' (Steiner 1992: 119).
71. Hanafi 1965: ccx.
72. Hanafi 1965: ccxviii-ccxix.
73. Hanafi 1965: ccxxi-iii Also Ricoeur has stressed that constitution is not the same as construction or creation, but 'rather the unfolding of the intendings of consciousness which are merged together in the natural, unreflective, naïve grasp of a thing' (Ricoeur 1999: 9).
74. Hanafi 1965: ccxxvii-ccxxviii, 165ff.
75. Cf. Ricoeur 1999: 20.
76. Hanafi 1965: ccxxxii.
77. Hanafi 1965: ccxxviii ff. Except for the part on active consciousness, in which the three sections consist of two chapters each, 'due to "dyadic" division of actions according to position and intention, whereby another dyadic division can be made between universal and individual intentions' (Hanafi 1965: ccxxvii-ccxxviii).
78. Berger 1980: 60.

79. Hanafi 1965: 15.
80. Hanafi 1965: cclx.
81. Hanafi 1965: cclxii.
82. Hanafi 1965: cclxx.
83. Berger 1967: 45ff.
84. Hanafi 1965: cclxxiii.
85. Cf. Lee 1997: 65.
86. Hanafi 1965: cclxxiii.
87. Ricoeur 1999: 27.
88. Hanafi 1965: cclxxi-clxxii.
89. Hanafi 1965: cclxxiii.
90. Ricoeur 1999: 151.
91. Hanafi 1965: cclxxv.
92. Hanafi 1965: i.
93. Allard 1969: 83.
94. Adams (1967), (2001).
95. Cf. Hanafi 1980a: 16–57.
96. Hanafi 1980a: 27–9, 43.
97. Hanafi 1980a: 3–5.
98. Hanafi 1980a: 6. Cf. Madjid's reference to Jalal Al-e Ahmad's *gharbzadegi* or 'westoxification.'
99. Hanafi 1980a: 43.
100. Hanafi 1980a 4–5.
101. Hanafi 1980a: 15–6, and 274ff.
102. Hanafi 1980a: 12, 44–7.
103. Hanafi 1980a: 16.
104. Hanafi 1980a: 12.
105. Hanafi 1980a: 46.
106. Hanafi 1980a: 6.
107. He gives Franz Fanon's *The Wretched of the Earth* as an example (Hanafi 1980a: 7 n. 13).
108. Hanafi 1980a: 8–9.
109. Hanafi 1980a: 24ff.
110. Hanafi 1980a: 6, n. 12. Cf. also Hanafi 1980b: 212; and Hanafi 1989 vi: 232, 246.
111. Hanafi 1980a: 16–62.
112. Hanafi 1980a: 47. Cf. Feuerbach 1989: xvi; 33ff; 185ff., cf. also Hanafi 1979: 53.
113. Hanafi 1980a: 48.
114. Hanafi 1980a: 69.
115. Ricoeur 1999: 71.
116. Hanafi 1980a: 209.
117. Hanafi 1980a: 74–97; 162ff.
118. Hanafi 1980a: 74–97; 162ff.
119. Hanafi 1980a: 164.

120. Hanafi 1980a: 175.
121. Hanafi 1980a: 470ff.
122. Hanafi 1980a: 534–5.
123. Hanafi 1980a: 554.
124. Hanafi 1980a: 558.
125. Hanafi 1980a: 571.
126. Hanafi 1980a: 231ff. The expression is from Clarke and Byrne (1993: 7), Hanafi speaks of *voisinage* (57), and *parenté* (63).
127. Hanafi 1980a: 63.
128. Hanafi 1980a: 305, 310, 322.
129. Hanafi 1980a: 332.
130. Hanafi 1980a: 292.
131. Hanafi 1980a: 341.
132. Hanafi 1980a: 342.
133. Hanafi 1980a: 577.
134. Hanafi 1980a: 582.
135. Hanafi 1980a: 593.
136. Hanafi 1980a: 347.
137. Hanafi 1989 vi: 246.

8. RECONSTRUCTING ISLAM: HERITAGE AND RENEWAL

1. Hanafi 1989 vi: 246.
2. Haddad 1998: 51–3. A more recent study of the influence of Nasserism on Hanafi is Riexinger (2007).
3. Hanafi 1981b: 7.
4. Boullata 1990: 2.
5. Boullata 1990: 14.
6. Boullata 1990: 25.
7. Binder 1988: 298.
8. The first volume consists primarily of brief journalistic articles, the second of much longer entries on Spinoza, Voltaire, Kant, Hegel, Weber, Husserl, Unamuno, Jaspers and Marcuse.
9. Chartier 1973: 611.
10. Hanafi 1981b: 19, 50, 62.
11. Hanafi 1981b: 119–34.
12. Hanafi 1981b: 62.
13. Cf. also Chartier 1973: 615.
14. Hanafi 1981b: 50.
15. A point to which he would constantly return, cf. Hanafi 1980b: 210; 1987: 33; 1991:188ff, 204ff.
16. Hanafi 1981b: 56–7.
17. Hanafi 1981b: 57.
18. Hanafi 1981b: 61–2.

19. Iqbal 1974: 62.
20. Hanafi 1981b: 57.
21. Hanafi 1981b: 62–4.
22. Hanafi 1981b: 64–5, 69, 131–3. Cf. Also Hanafi 1965: cxiii.
23. Hanafi 1981b: 64–7.
24. Hanafi 1981b; 73–5.
25. Cf. Hanafi 1965: 8–9, 15 and 274ff.
26. Hanafi 1981b: 76.
27. Hanafi 1981b: 68.
28. Hanafi 1981b: 69.
29. Hanafi 1981b: 73–5.
30. Hanafi 1980b: 203ff.
31. Hanafi 1991: 9–15, Hanafi 1980b: 214ff.
32. Hanafi 1980b: 9. Olsson regards such authentication of the Islamic tradi-
    tion as a functionalist approach a reason enough to foreground renewal
    by reversing the two notions in the title of her study (Olsson 2004).
    Akhavi calls Hanafi's approach 'instrumentalist' (Akhavi 1997: 388).
33. Hanafi 1980b: 21.
34. Hanafi 1980b: 10–15. cf. also Hanafi 1981b: 120–8.
35. Hanafi 1980b: 26.
36. Hanafi 1980b: 31–3.
37. Hanafi 1980b: 31. *Al-Akhdh min al-qadim ma yutaffiqu ma'a al-'asr,
    wa'irja' al-jadid li-maqayis al-qadim.*
38. Hanafi 180b: 34.
39. Hanafi 1980b: 37–116.
40. Hanafi 1980b: 152; Hanafi 2000 ii: 21.
41. Hanafi 1980b: 157.
42. Hanafi 1980b: 158.
43. Hanafi 1980b: 165–6.
44. Hanafi 1980b: 166–8.
45. Hanafi 1980b: 173.
46. Hanafi 1980b: 188.
47. Hanafi 1980b: 199.
48. Hanafi 1980b: 186.
49. Hanafi 1980b: 196.
50. Hanafi 1980b: 155.
51. Hanafi 1980b: 186.
52. Hanafi 1980b: 201.
53. Hanafi 1980b: 205.
54. Hanafi 1980b: 206.
55. Hanafi 1980b: 205. Elsewhere he also called it a theology of the hand, cf.
    Hanafi 1977: 123–75.
56. Hanafi 1989 vi: 256–8. An extensive discussion of Torres is found in:
    Hanafi 1981b: 297–333.
57. Cox 1984: 136.

58. Hanafi (1981a). For a detailed analysis of this work, cf. Shimogaki (1988).
59. Cf. also Flores 1988: 27; Goddard 1996: 143.
60. Hanafi 1980b: 208.
61. Hanafi 1991: 15
62. Hildebrand (1998). For his challenging 'Diagnosis: The doubling of the intellect in the writings of Hasan Hanafi,' Tarabishi relied to a great extent on psychoanalysis (Tarabishi 1991: 105–271).
63. Varisco 2007: 152–3.
64. Varisco 2007: 265.
65. Hanafi 1991: 25.
66. Buruma and Margalit 2004: 143–4.
67. Buruma and Margalit 2004: 89–90, 145–6. Buruma and Margalit underwrite Berlin's view of Romanticism as part of a Counter-Enlightenment triggered by hurt national pride (Buruma and Margalit 2004: 77–9). Given his earlier reference to Fichte and the restoration of national confidence, Hanafi would probably not disagree.
68. Buruma and Margalit 2004: 123.
69. Hanafi 1991: 695–6. The title of the chapter was later used for a *Festschrift* dedicated to Hanafi, cf. Atiyah (1997).
70. Hanafi 1991: 778ff.
71. Hanafi (1988b).
72. Hanafi 1991: 791. Since then two further multi-volume studies have been released: *From Transmission to Innovation: Reconstruction Attempt of the Philosophical Sciences* (2002) and *From Text to Reality: Reconstruction Attempt of the Foundations of Jurisprudence* (2005).
73. Berlin 1991: 42, 190.
74. Hanafi 1972: 240–1.
75. Hanafi 1972: 235.
76. Hanafi 1972: 256.
77. Hanafi 1972: 246.
78. Hanafi 1979: 83.
79. Hanafi 1979: 53.
80. Surah 5:3.
81. Allard 1969: 91.
82. Allard 1969: 94–7.
83. Hanafi 1972: 238.
84. Allard 1969: 89.
85. Allard 1969: 93.
86. Allard 1969: 95.
87. Nwyia 1971: 96.
88. Chartier 1973: 607.
89. Chartier 1972: 1.
90. Chartier 1973: 617–8.
91. Zakariyya 2005: 65–103.

92. Boullata 1990: 154–5.
93. Zakariyya 2005: 23.
94. Boom 1984: 90.
95. Cf. Navarro (2006); Olsson (2008).
96. Olsson 2004: 199.
97. Cf. Hanafi 1980b: 21, 51ff; 1981b: 11ff; 1989 vi: 252ff. Cf. also Olsson 2004: 93–5; Riexinger 2007: 63ff.
98. Hanafi 2000i: 495.
99. Haddad 1998: 53.
100. Haddad 1998: 52.
101. Haddad 1998: 54.
102. Haddad 1998: 56.
103. Haddad 1998: 68–9.
104. Hasan Hanafi, e-mail communication, 16 June 2008.
105. Hanafi 1989 vi: 209 n. 2.
106. Ricoeur 1999: 12.
107. Ricoeur 2004: 15.
108. Ricoeur 1986: xiii.
109. Hanafi 1980 vi: 231–2; cf. also Basri (1964).
110. Hanafi 1965: xc.
111. Hanafi 1991: 791.
112. Olsson 2004: 60, n. 36.
113. Salvatore 1995: 206. For Wael Hallaq this was reason enough not to include Hanafi's contributions in his seminal study of the history of *fiqh* (Hallaq 1995: 213 n.8).
114. Hanafi 1996a: 116.
115. von Kügelgen 1996; van Bruinessen, personal communication, 19 January 2004.
116. Unamuno 1954: 37.
117. Berlin 1991: 44, 187–99.
118. Berlin 1991: 45–6.
119. Ricoeur 1999: 83.
120. Boullata 1990: 45.
121. Hasan Hanafi (1998) *Kiri Islam: Antara modernisme dan postmodernisme*, Jakarta: Lkis; Ibid. (2000) *Turas dan Tajdid: Sikap Kita terhadap Turas Klasik*. Yogyakarta: Titian Ilahi Press and Pesantren Rasca Sarjana Bismillah Press; Ibid (2000) *Oksidentalisme: Sikap Kita terhadap Tradisi Barat*. Jakarta: Paramadina; Ibid (2002) *Tafsir Fenomenologi: Kondisi Aktual Metode Fenomenologi dan Penerapannya pada Fenomena-fenomena Keagamaan*. Translated by Yudian Wahyudi. Yogyakarta: Pesantren Pasca Sarjana Bismillah Press; Ibid (2002) *Sendi-sendi Hermeneutika: Membumikan Tafsir Revolusioner*. Translated by Yudian Wahyudi. Yogyakarta: Titian Ilahi Press and Pesantren Pasca Sarjana Bismillah Press; Ibid (2003) *Dari Akida ke Revolusi: Sikap Kita terhadap Tradisi Lama*. Jakarta: Paramadina; Ibid (2003) *Oposisi Pasca Tradisi:*

Yogyakarta: Syarikat Indonesia; Ibid (1992) *Islamologi 2: Dari Rasion-alisme ke Empirisme* Yogyakarta: LKis; Hanafi, Hasan, Nurcholish Madjid et al (2007) *Islam dan Humanisme: Aktualisasi Humanisme Islam di Tengah Krisis Humanisme.* Universal. Semarang and Yogya-karta: IAIN Walisongo with Pustaka Pelajar.

9. A CULTURAL AND INTELLECTUAL BORDER CROSSER: THE EARLY YEARS OF MOHAMMED ARKOUN

1. Günther 2004a: 13.
2. Arkoun 2002: 125.
3. Salvatore 1997: 249.
4. Allard 1971: 118.
5. In one of his most recent publications, Arkoun provides a list of key con-cepts in chronological order and also refers the reader to the more detailed index of *The Unthought in Contemporary Islamic Thought* (2002) (Ark-oun 2007: 32). He also notes his intention to develop a technical diction-ary of his own terminology (Arkoun 2007: 37, n, 8).
6. Günther 2004b: 126; Benzine 2004: 95.
7. Arkoun 2007: 36, n.1.
8. Ayadi 1993: 45.
9. Arkoun 1987: 1. Cf. also 'I have explained in my various writings how my Algerian origins, and my involvement in contemporary Algerian history since the 1950s [...] imposed on me, as a scholar and professor of Islamic Thought, the obligation to rethink and rewrite this entire history within the dialectic of the thinkable/unthinkable, thought/unthought' (Arkoun 2002: 13).
10. Benzine 2004: 92–3; Günther 2004a: 26.
11. Lee 1997: 145.
12. Flood 1999: 38.
13. Arkoun 1998b: 125, 142–3.
14. Arkoun 2002: 15.
15. Arkoun 2002: 13. Cf. also Allard 1971: 118–9.
16. Arkoun 2005: 7.
17. Arkoun 2005: 78ff. The movement took its name from the journal founded by Febvre and Bloch in 1929, *Annales d'histoire économique et sociale.* The term *nouvelle histoire* was introduced by Fernand Braudel, but became more popular after the publication of Jacques Le Goff's 1978 book of the same title.
18. Arkoun 1997: 39–40; 2002: 132–3; 2005: 77ff.
19. In his study *The Problem of Unbelief in the Sixteenth Century* (1942), Febvre argued that Rabelais could not be associated with atheism, for want of appropriate linguistic and conceptual tools at the time (Clark 1990: 181).
20. Burke 1990: 9–30.

21. Burke 1990: 31.

22. Burke 1990: 32–3.

23. Burke 1990: 41.

24. Burke 1990: 49.

25. Cf. Hunt 1989: 2–3.

26. Clark 1990: 181; Burke 1990: 43–4.

27. Arkoun 2002: 89. Although elsewhere he mentions anthropology as the key discipline (Arkoun 2002: 34).

28. Günther 2004a: 27. Cf. also Benzine 2004: 94.

29. O'Brien 1989: 43.

30. This was apparently such a disappointment to Berque that he ignored Arkoun's work ever since (Günther 2004a: 32).

31. Günther 2004a: 33.

32. Burke 1990: 6.

33. Arkoun 1982a: 387.

34. Arkoun 1982a: 11–2.

35. Arkoun 1982a: 13.

36. Arkoun 2005: 83.

37. The original French version appeared in 1971, the English translation followed in 1973.

38. Arkoun 1973: 9; Günther 2004a: 123.

39. Günther 2004a: 107.

40. Bastide 1973: 1–13.

41. Cf. Richard Price's Foreword (Bastide 1978: vii).

42. Bastide 1978: x.

43. Bastide 1978: 3–6.

44. Bastide 1978: ix; 6, cf. also Bastide 1973: 166; 1978: 9.

45. Bastide 1973: 1–8, 118; 1978: ix, 1–8; Ibid 2003: viii-ix, xxviii-xxix, 78, 157–61, 167.

46. Bastide 1978: x.

47. Bastide 1978: 12.

48. Bastide 1978: 383.

49. Bastide 1978: 386.

50. Bastide 1973: 41–50.

51. Bastide 1973: 21–2.

52. Arkoun 1984a: 19.

53. The most extensive study of Freyre and his work in English is *Gilberto Freyre: Social Theory in the Tropics* by Peter Burke and Maria Lucia G. Pallares-Burke.

54. Published in English as *The Masters and the Slaves* (1946, org. 1931), *The Mansions and the Shanties* (1963, org. 1936) and *Order and Progress* (1970, org. 1959) . Burke 1990: 101. Cf. also Nist (1967) and Cleary (1999).

55. Freyre 1961a: 9–10. Bastide spells it 'Luso-Tropocology,' but I prefer to follow Freyre's 'Lusotropicology,' cf. Bastide 1973: 87–9. In contemporary

publications on Brazilian Studies one finds now also the term 'tropicalism' (For this last information I thank Abdool Karim Vakil of the Department for Portuguese and Brazilian Studies at King's College London).

56. Freyre 1961b: 111–28; 129–38.
57. Freyre 1961b: 24–6.
58. Freyre 1961b: 37–8, 42.
59. Freyre 1961a: 103.
60. Freyre 1961b: 10.
61. Bastide 1973: 94.
62. Bastide 1973: 96.
63. Arkoun 2002: 215.
64. Burke 1990: 65.
65. Burke 1990: 79–80.
66. Burke 1990: 59.
67. Burke 1990: 80–3.
68. Burke 1990: 72.
69. Arkoun 2002: 274, cf. also Burke 1990: 113. In 1974, Arkoun had cooperated with Le Goff in organising a conference and subsequently editing its proceedings into a joint publication, cf. Arkoun and Le Goff (1978). Six years later he contributed to a special issue of the *Annales* journal on Islam, cf. Valensi (1980).
70. Burke 1990: 73.
71. Hunt 1989: 7.
72. For the influence of Halbwachs on the *Annales* School cf. Ricoeur 2000: 146–51; 231ff.
73. Burke 1990: 84–5; Hunt 1989: 7.
74. Cf. Allan Megill (1987) *Prophets of Extremity: Nietzsche, Heidegger. Foucault, Derrida.*
75. Burke 1990: 102.
76. O'Brien 1989: 33–4.
77. O'Brien 1989: 37; cf. 'The Idol of Origins' (Bloch 2004: 24ff.).
78. O'Brien 1989: 46 and 38 respectively.
79. Cf. O' Brien 1989: 36; for Foucault's 'disperal of man,' cf. Binder 1988: 109ff.
80. Binder 1988: 161–2.
81. Arkoun 2002: 31–2.
82. 'Logocentrisme et Vérité Religieuse dans La Pensée Islamique: D'après al-I'lām bi-manāqib al-Islām d'al-Āmirī,' *Studia Islamica* 35 (1971) pp. 5–51.
83. Biersack 1989: 84. Here Biersack also draws attention to Braudel's tribute to Lévi-Strauss' structuralism, by renaming 'geohistory' as 'structural history.'
84. Biersack 1989: 86.
85. Cf. Biersack 1989: 91. For 'blurred genres,' cf. also Geertz 2000: 19ff.
86. Ricoeur 1984: 101–4.

87. Ricoeur 1984: 106–9; cf. also Burke 1990: 76 and 85.
88. Ricoeur 1984: 110.
89. Ricoeur 1984: 95.
90. Cf. Bloch (2004).
91. Arkoun 2002: 89.

10. APPLIED ISLAMOLOGY

1. Arkoun 1973: 8.
2. Arkoun 1982a: 10.
3. Arkoun 1984a: 43–64.
4. Cf. 'Pour un Renouveau des Etudes Arabes' appeared in 1972 in *Cahiers de Tunis* 10:77–78, pp. 231–40 (Arkoun 1972), while 'Les tâches de l'intellectuel musulman. Intellectuels et militants dans le mond islamique au VIIe-XXe' was first published in 1988 in *Cahiers de la Méditerranée* 37, pp. 1–34. It was later reprinted in *Penser l'Islam aujourd'hui* (1993). An extended version entitled 'Statut et tâches de l'intellectuel encontextes islamiques' was included in *Humanisme et Islam* (Arkoun 2005: 131–86).
5. Arkoun 2002: 11–23. Indicative of Arkoun's awareness of this additional barrier, is the inclusion of a chronological overview of the introduction of key terms in one of his latest publications, cf. Arkoun 2007: 32.
6. Arkoun 2007: 32. Cf. Bloch 2004: 129ff.
7. Arkoun 1984a: 57ff.
8. Arkoun 1984a: 7ff.; 1997: 33ff.; 2002: 66ff. 2005: 131ff.
9. Arkoun 1973: 9–10.
10. Arkoun 2002: 117, n. 12.
11. Arkoun 1982a: 9–10.
12. Cf. also the comment of Allard on *Arab Humanism*, which in his view would be more accurately defined as '*humanisme arabo-musulman*,' cf. Allard 1971: 125. Kraemer takes a different position. Qualifying '*humanisme musulman*' as an ambivalent expression, he says that 'the question is about humanism *within* Islamic civilization' (Kraemer 1984: 147). Elsewhere he has nevertheless acknowledged that his own 'notion of humanism is closest to the view of M. Arkoun,' cf. Kraemer 1992: xxv.
13. Arkoun 1984b: 262.
14. Arkoun 1985: 156.
15. Arkoun 1973: 9.
16. Arkoun 2002: 12. 'Logosphere' was first used in *La Pensée Arabe*, cf. Arkoun 1975: 51ff.
17. Ricoeur 2004: 15.
18. Arkoun 1997: 43.
19. Arkoun 2002: 41.
20. Arkoun 2002: 36.

21. Arkoun 2002: 45–6.
22. Arkoun 2002: 53.
23. Arkoun 1973: 8. Cf. also Arkoun 1984a: 60–1; 1997: 42; 2002: 46.
24. Arkoun 2002: 47.
25. Arkoun 2002: 44.
26. Arkoun 1997: 40.
27. 'Pragmatic Islamology' must not be confused with Leonard Binder's 'Pragmatic Orientalism,' cf. Binder 1988: 107ff.
28. Arkoun 2002: 10. Cf. also Bloch 2004: 29ff.
29. Arkoun 2002: 51.
30. Arkoun 1984a: 48; 1997: 33. Cf. also Ayadi 1993: 46; Boullata 1990: 79; Lee 1997: 160.
31. Arkoun 2002: 35.
32. Arkoun 2002: 46–7.
33. Günther 2004a: 111.
34. Günther 2004a: 114.
35. Günther 2004a: 109.
36. Arkoun 2002: 51.
37. Arkoun 1984a: 194. Cf. also Arkoun 2002: 85.
38. Günther 2004a: 110; Arkoun 1984a: 9.
39. Arkoun 1973: 8.
40. Arkoun 1984a: 27–8. Cf. also Arkoun 2002: 88; Binder 1988: 161–9.
41. Arkoun 2002: 43.
42. Arkoun 2002: 88.
43. Arkoun 2002: 15. For a discussion of Algeria's place in the discourse on Third Worldism, cf. Robert Malley (1996).
44. Arkoun 2002: 43, 88.
45. Arkoun 2002: 69.
46. Arkoun 2007: 37, n. 9. For an extensive discussion of this phenomenon, cf. Leif Stenberg's *The Islamization of Science: Four Muslim Positions Developing an Islamic Modernity* (1996).
47. Arkoun 1997: 42–3.
48. Arkoun 2002: 132.
49. Günther 2004a: 44.
50. Salvatore 1997: 252.
51. Arkoun 1973: 10.
52. Cf. Ayadi 1993: 48.
53. Arkoun 1973: 297ff.
54. Arkoun 1984a: 129–53.
55. Arkoun 1984a: 35.
56. Günther has called it Arkoun's *Terminus Technicus*,
57. Günther 2004a: 177, n. 34; Günther 2004a: 96; Arkoun 1987: 13.
58. Arkoun 2002: 11–2.
59. Arkoun 1984a: 11–2.
60. Günther 2004a: 69.

61. Arkoun 1984a: 19. Cf. also Arkoun 1984a: 48, 53; 1995: 332–40; 1997: 33; 2000: 134–5.

62. Arkoun 2002: 87.

63. This last triangle can be traced back to the essay 'Comment Étudier la Pensée Islamique?,' the introduction to *Pour Une Critique de la Raison Islamique*, preceding the article in which the Applied Islamology agenda was outlined, cf. Arkoun 1984a: 21.

64. Cf. Ricoeur 2004: 294. Arkoun had already relied on this triangle in his *Lectures du Coran* (1982b: 49).

65. Arkoun 2002: 87–91.

66. Ayadi 1993: 60.

67. Arkoun 1975: 117.

68. Arkoun 2002: 262.

69. Arkoun 2000: 213.

70. Arkoun 2002: 70–3.

71. Arkoun 2002: 71.

72. Arkoun 2002: 57.

73. Arkoun 1975: 11.

74. Arkoun 1982b: xxv-xxvii, 5–13. It also contains references to the writings of Khalaf Allah, Izutsu, Eliade, Ricoeur (p. 5) and the challenges of 'traditional exegesis' by the hermeneuticians of suspicion: Nietzsche, Marx and Freud (p. 14).

75. Arkoun 2002: 80. Cf. also his analysis of Surah 9, cf. Arkoun 2002: 96–110.

76. Arkoun 2002: 82.

77. Arkoun 2002: 45.

78. Arkoun 2002: 84.

79. Its central importance to Arkoun's nomenclature is evident from the three essays he has published on this theme: Arkoun 1988a; 1988b; and 2002: 111–25.

80. Arkoun 2002: 114–5.

81. Arkoun 2001a: 425; 2002: 58, 80.

82. Arkoun 2002: 58, 85.

83. Arkoun 2002: 81, 274.

84. Arkoun 1984a: 12–25.

85. Arkoun 2002: 70–1. Arkoun was himself initiated into Islam through the Berber oral tradition, cf. Arkoun 2002: 71 n. 1. Apart from this biographical aspect, in regard to the importance of oral traditions, he has elsewhere also referred to to the work of the ethnologist Georges Balandier on African cultures, cf. Arkoun, 1984a: 15.

86. Arkoun notes that the opposition between the masses ('*awamm*) and the elite (*khawass*) has been an 'axis in the Arab-Islamic view of the social and historical space' since the Middle Ages, cf. Arkoun 1984a: 23; Arkoun 2002: 44. The privileging of access to knowledge was already an issue

in the debate between Ibn Rushd and Ghazali, cf. Colville 1999: xxii, 76ff.

87. Arkoun 2002: 71.
88. Arkoun 2002: 86–8.
89. Arkoun 2002: 89.
90. Arkoun 2002: 89–90.
91. Arkoun 2002: 89.
92. Arkoun 2002: 91.
93. Arkoun 2002: 96.
94. Arkoun 2002: 93.
95. Arkoun 2002: 93.

11. RETHINKING ISLAM: FROM ISLAMIC HUMANISM TO EMERGING REASON

1. Arkoun 2001b: 13. Cf. also 'Peut-on Parler d'Humanisme en Contexte Islamique?' (Arkoun 1999) and 'Rétour à la Question de l'Humanisme dans les Contextes Islamiques' (Arkoun 2005: 15–51).
2. Arkoun 1982a: 11.
3. Mohammed Arkoun (1969) *Traité d'Ethique: Traduction Française avec notes du Tahdhīb al-akhlāq de Miskawayh.* Damascus: French Institute.
4. Burke 1990: 80.
5. Kardiner 1945: 107–8.
6. Kardiner 1945: 108–9.
7. Kardiner 1945: 116. His data came from five societies: Marquesas, Tanala, Comanche, Alor, and Plainville, later augmented with material from Sikh culture and the Ojibwa, Kardiner 1945: 110–7. Cf. also Dufrenne 1953: 157.
8. Dufrenne 1953: 281ff.
9. Arkoun 1982a: 13–4.
10. Arkoun 1982a: 14.
11. Dufrenne 1953: 288.
12. Arkoun 1982a: 14–5.
13. Arkoun 1982a: 15.
14. Arkoun 2002: 86.
15. Arkoun 1973: 241ff.
16. Arkoun 1989: 4.
17. The most extensive application of personality structure in the Arab-Islamic context is Hichem Djait's *La Personnalité et le Devenir Arabo-Islamiques* (1974). Cf. also Abu-Rabi' 1996: 34–5.
18. Arkoun 1989: 4–6.
19. Arkoun 2005: 14.
20. Arkoun 2002: 9–10.
21. Günther 2004a: 17, n. 16; 77.

22. Arkoun 2007: 35.
23. Bloch 2004: 24–5.
24. Arkoun 2007: 21.
25. Arkoun 2002: 32.
26. Arkoun 2002: 26.
27. Arkoun 1995/6: 10. Cf. also Günther 2004a: 77, 91, and 105 (fig. 4).
28. Lee 1997: 147.
29. Arkoun 2007: 35.
30. Arkoun 2007: 34.
31. For this designation 'procedural,' cf. Arkoun 2002: 23 and 'Pour une Critique de la Raison Juridique' (Arkoun 2005: 187–243).
32. Arkoun 1984a: 65–99 and 101–27.
33. Arkoun 2002: 10 and 215ff.
34. Arkoun 2007: 25.
35. Arkoun 2007: 29.
36. Arkoun addressed the growing importance of globalisation in 'Present-Day Islam Between its Tradition and Globalization' (Arkoun 2000: 178–221). The impact of 9/11 is discussed in *De Manhattan à Bagdad: au-delà du Bien et du Mal* (2003). Indicative of this radicalisation is the publication of a second edition of *The Unthought in Contemporary Islamic Thought* under a new title: *Islam: To Reform or to Subvert?* (2006).
37. Arkoun 2002: 9. Examples are 'A Critical Introduction to Qur'ānic Studies' (Arkoun 2002: 37–65), 'Pour une Critique de la Raison Juridique' and 'Pour une Histoire Réflexive de la Pensée Islamique' (Arkoun 2005: 187–243; 245–92).
38. Cf. McCutcheon 2003: 147, 150–1.
39. Arkoun 1978: 198.
40. Arkoun 1998b: 125.
41. Arkoun 1998b 124; cf. also Arfaoui 1999.
42. Arkoun 2002: 23.
43. Arkoun 1998b: 124–5.
44. Published in: Derrida and Vattimo (1998) *Religion: Cultural Memory in the Present*, pp. 1–78; reprinted in: Derrida (2002) *Acts of Religion*, pp. 40–101.
45. Arkoun 2002: 23.
46. Arkoun 2002: 27.
47. Arkoun 1998b: 124.
48. Arkoun 2002: 27.
49. Arkoun 2002: 18. This in spite of efforts by such scholars as Mead, Malinowski, Geertz and Lévi-Strauss, who 'preferred to open the cognitive horizons of the Western mentality to other cultures and mentalities,' (Arkoun 2002: 36).
50. Arkoun 2002: 19
51. Arkoun 1998b: 125.
52. Arkoun 1998b: 125.

53. Arkoun 1998b: 129.
54. Arkoun 1998b: 130.
55. Arkoun 2007: 22.
56. Arkoun 1998b: 131.
57. Arkoun 1998b: 140.
58. Cf. Hunt 1980: 3.
59. Arkoun 1998b: 144.
60. Arkoun 2002: 116–7.
61. Arkoun 1998b: 148.
62. Arkoun 2002: 123.
63. Arkoun 1998b: 144.
64. Arkoun: 2007: 29.
65. Lee 1997: 156.
66. Arkoun 1998b: 144.
67. Arkoun 1998b: 131. The Arabic equivalent is *'alim mujtahid*, cf. Haleber and Van Koningsveld 1991: 291.
68. Arkoun 1998b: 130–1; Arkoun 2002: 27–8.
69. Arkoun 2002: 28.
70. Arkoun 2002: 130.
71. Arkoun 1998b: 140.
72. Arkoun 2002: 137–8.
73. Arkoun 1998b: 141. Arkoun refers to the work of Bellah and Hervieu-Léger as important revisionist of the secularization thesis.
74. Arkoun 1998c.
75. Arkoun 1998c: 200–1.
76. Arkoun 2005: 152.
77. Arkoun 2005: 145–6.
78. Arkoun 2002: 52–3, n. 1.
79. Arkoun 2002: 32.
80. Interview with John L. Allen (2008), for the *National Catholic Reporter*. 18 May. Posted at http://ncrcafe.org/node/1841. [Last accessed, 23 July 2008].
81. Arkoun 2002: 89.
82. Arkoun 2007: 34.
83. Putro 1998: 6; Saeed 1999: 185. Aside from *Nalar Islam dan Nalar Modern: Berbagai Tantangan dan Jalan Baru* and *Berbagai Pembacaan Quran*, there is a 2005 translation of some of Arkoun's writings on interfaith dialogue, published as *Islam Kontemporer: Menuju Dialog Antar Agama*. Yogyakarta: Pustaka Pelajar.
84. Meuleman (1996), Putro (1998), Ruslani (2000). Cf. the reviews in the introduction.
85. Cf. Baso (2005) and (2006); a search of the website of the Liberal Islam Network (JIL) produces a return of over four dozen articles: http://islamlib.com/id/arsip/. [Last accessed 18 June 2009].

12. NEW MUSLIM INTELLECTUALS: COSMOPOLITAN AND HERETICAL

1. Taylor 2009: 110, 114.
2. Dabashi (2009).
3. Wolf 2000: 135.
4. Majid 2007: 176.
5. Cf. his book *Identités meurtrières* (1996), translated as *In the Name of Identity: Violence and the Need to Belong* (2000).
6. Mishra and Hodge 1991: 405.
7. Mishra and Hodge 1991: 413.
8. Berger (1999), Heelas (1996), Beck (2004).
9. Zakaria (2002).
10. Wong (2004).
11. Akhtar 2008: 164.
12. Bond and Simmons (2009).
13. Tamara 2009: xii.
14. http://www.lse.ac.uk/collections/LSEPublicLecturesAndEvents/pdf/20090331_BambangYudhoyono.pdf
15. Metcalf 2007: 145.
16. Hefner 1998: 160.
17. Kull 2005: 196–7. For in depth discussions cf. Gillespie (2007), Ichwan (2005).
18. In this book Spinoza is presented as resorting to exactly the same stratagem of writing between the lines (Strauss 1988: 142–201).
19. Abu Qatada al-Falastini (2005), 'Hasan Hanafi: Zandaqa al-yasār al-dīnī,' *Minbar al-Tawhīd wa'l-Jihād*, http://www.tawhed.ws/r?i=1834. [Last accessed 10 October 2005].
20. Cf., Mohammed Talbi in *Jeune Afrique* 2122, 7 September 2001.

BIBLIOGRAPHY

Abaza, Mona (2002), *Debates on Islam and Knowledge in Malaysia and Egypt: Shifting Worlds*, London: RoutledgeCurzon.

Abd al-Rahman, Khayra bint Muhammad (1992), 'Minhaj qira'a al-turath lada Hasan Hanafi,' unpublished MA Thesis, Nouakchott.

Abdel Haleem, Muhammad A.S. (2004), *The Quran: A New Translation*, Oxford: Oxford University Press.

Abdel-Malek, Anouar (1963), 'L'orientalisme en Crise,' *Diogène* 44, pp. 109–42.

Abdel-Malek, A., A.A. Belal, and H. Hanafi (eds) (1972), *Renaissance du monde arabe*, Algiers: J. Duculot.

Abdel Malek, Anouar and Amar Nath Pandeya (1981), *Intellectual Creativity in Endogenous Culture*, Tokyo: United Nations University.

Abdulghani, R. (1964), *Bandung Spirit: Moving on the Tide of History*, Jakarta: Prapantja.

Abdul Hadi W.M. (2006), 'Islam di Indonesia dan Transformasi Budaya,' in Abdul Halim (2006), pp. 93–109.

Abdul Halim (ed.) (2006), *Menembus Batas Tradisi: Menuju Masa Depan yang Membebaskan: Refleksi atas Pemikiran Nurcholish Madjid*, Jakarta: Universitas Paramadina and Kompas.

Abdullah, Taufik (1972), 'Modernization in the Minangkabau World: West Sumatra in the Early Decades of the Twentieth Century,' in Holt et al. (1972), pp. 179–245.

Abdullah, Taufik (1986), 'The Pesantren in historical perpective,' in Abdullah and Siddique (1986), pp. 80–107.

Abdullah, Taufik (1996), 'The Formation of a New Paradigm? A Sketch on Contemporary Islamic Discourse,' in Woodward (1996), pp. 47–88.

Abdullah, Taufik and Sharon Siddique (eds) (1986), *Islam and Society in Southeast Asia*, Singapore: ISEAS.

Abegebriel, A.M. (2007), 'Mazhab Islam Kosmopolitan Gus Dur,' in Wahid (2007), pp. v-xxxiv.

BIBLIOGRAPHY

Abou Shouk, Ahmed Ibrahim (2002), 'An Arabic manuscript on the Life and Career of Ahmad Muhammad Sūrkatī,' in de Jonge en Kaptein (1997), pp. 203–18.

Abshar-Abdalla, Ulil (2006), 'Apa Setelah Nurcholish Madjid?,' in Abdul Halim (2006), pp. 143–61.

Abu-Rabi', Ibrahim M. (1996), *Intellectual Origins of Islamic Resurgence in the Modern Arab World*, Albany: State University of New York Press.

Abu-Rabi', Ibrahim M. (2004), *Contemporary Arab Thought: Studies in Post-1967 Arab Intellectual History*, London/Sterling (Va): Pluto Press.

Abu-Rabi', M. Ibrahim (ed.) (2006), *The Blackwell Companion to Contemporary Islamic Thought*, Oxford: Blackwell Publishing.

Abu Zayd, Nasr Hamid (2004), *Rethinking the Quran; Towards a Humanistic Hermeneutics*, Utrecht: Humanistics University Press.

Adams, Charles J. (1967), 'The History of Religions and the Study of Islam,' in Kitagawa and Eliade (1967), pp. 177–93.

Adams, Charles J. (2001), 'Foreword,' in Martin (2001), pp. vii-ix.

Adnan, Zifirdaus (1990), 'Islamic Religion: Yes, Islamic (Political) Ideology: No! Islam and the State in Indonesia,' in Budiman (1990), pp. 441–77.

Ahmad, Sidi bin Sayyid (1995), 'Al-Turath wa'l-Gharb fi Fikr Hasan Hanafi,' unpublished MA Thesis, Nouakchott.

Ahmed, Akbar S. and Hastings, Donnan (eds) (1994), *Islam, Globalization and Postmodernity*, London: Routledge.

Akhavi, Shahrough (1997), 'The Dialectic in Contemporary Egyptian Social Thought: The Scripturalist and Modernist Discourses of Sayyid Qutb and Hasan Hanafi,' *International Journal Of Middle East Studies*, 29, pp. 377–401.

Akhtar, Shabbir (2008), *The Quran and the Secular Mind: A Philosophy of Islam*, London: Routledge.

Alatas, Syed Farid (1997), 'Hadramaut and the Hadrami Diaspora: Problems in Theoretical History,' in Freitag and Clarence-Smith (1997), pp. 19–34.

Alatas, Syed Farid (2005), 'Alatas and Shari'ati on Socialism: Autonomous Social Science and Occidentalism,' in Hassan (2005), pp. 161–79.

Alatas, Syed Hussein (1981), 'Social Aspects of Endogenous Intellectual Creativity: The Problem of Obstacles—Guidelines for Research,' in Abdel Malek and Pandeya (1981), pp. 462–70.

Albinus, Lars (2006), Review of: *The Discipline of Religion: Structure, Meaning, Rhetoric*, by Russell T. McCutcheon, *Journal of the American Academy of Religion*, 74:2, pp. 524–8.

Ali, Fachry and Bahtiar Effendy (1986), *Merambah Jalan Baru Islam: Rekonstruksi Pemikiran Islam Indonesia Masa Orde Baru*, Bandung: Mizan.

Allard, Michel (1969), 'Un Essai d'Anthropologie Musulmane,' *Travaux et Jours* 32 pp. 83–97.

Allard, Michel (1971), 'Humanisme Arabo-Musulman,' *Travaux et Jours* 40, pp. 115–27.

BIBLIOGRAPHY

Allen, John L. (2008), 'Seeking Dialogue with "Islam of the People,"' *National Catholic Reporter*, 7(37) (23 May).

Anshari, Endang Saifuddin (1973), *Kritik Atas Faham dan Gerakan 'Pembaharuan' Drs. Nurcholish Madjid*, Bandung: Bulan Sabit.

Appadurai, Arjun (1996), *Modernity at Large: Cultural Dimensions of Globalization*, Minneapolis: University of Minnesota Press.

Arazi, Albert, Joseph Sadan, David J. Wasserstein (eds) (1999), *Compilation and Creation in Adab and Lugha: Studies in Memory of Naphtali Kinberg (1948–1997)*, *(Israel Oriental Studies* XIX).

Arfaoui, Hasan (1999), 'Raison Émergente et Modernités dans le Contexte arabo-Musulman, Entretien avec Mohamed Arkoun,' *Le Monde Arabe dans le Recherche Scientifique* 10/11, pp. 97–112.

Arkoun, Mohammed (1972), 'Pour un renouveau des études arabes en France,' *Cahiers de Tunisie* 10, pp. 231–40.

Arkoun, Mohammed (1973), *Essais sur la Pensée Islamique*, Paris: Maisonneuve & Larose.

Arkoun, Mohammed (1975), *La Pensée Arabe* Paris: Presses Universitaires de France.

Arkoun, Mohammed (1978), 'Propositions pour une Autre Pensée Religieuse,' *Islamochristiana* 4, pp. 197–206.

Arkoun, Mohammed (1982a), *L'humanisme Arabe au 4ᵉ/10ᵉ siècle: Miskawayh, Philosophe et Historien*, 2nd Edition, Paris: J. Vrin [1970].

Arkoun, Mohammed (1982b), *Lectures du Coran*, Paris: Maisonneuve & Larose.

Arkoun, Mohammed (1984a), *Pour une Critique de la Raison Islamique*, Paris: Maisonneuve & Larose.

Arkoun, Mohammed (1984b), 'La Place et des Fonctions de l'Histoire dans la Culture Arabe,' *Histoire et diversité des cultures. Études preparées pour l'UNESCO*, pp. 259–83.

Arkoun, Mohammed (1985), 'Al-Turath: Muhtawahu wa-Huwiyatuhu wa-Ijābatuhu wa Salbiyatuh,' in Yasin (1985), pp. 155–67.

Arkoun, Mohammed (1987), *Rethinking Islam Today*, Washington DC: Georgetown University, Center For Contemporary Arab Studies.

Arkoun, Mohammed (1988a), *The concept of Revelation: From Ahl al-Kitāb to the Societies of the Book-book*, Claremont: Claremont Graduate School.

Arkoun, Mohammed (1988b), 'The Notion of Revelation: From Ahl al-Kitāb to the Societies of the Book,' *Die Welt des Islams* 28: 1/4, pp. 62–89.

Arkoun, Mohammed (1989), 'Actualité de la Personne dans la Pensée Islamique,' *Die Welt des Islams* 29:1/4, pp. 1–29.

Arkoun, Mohammed (1995),'Islamic Studies: Methodologies,' *The Oxford Encyclopedia of the Modern Islamic World*, vol. 2, pp. 332–40.

Arkoun, Mohammed (1995/6), 'Clarifier le Passé pour Construire le Future,' *Confluence Méditerranée*, 16, digital version at, http://www.ccefr.org/upload/45113e5aecb96.pdf [Last accessed 18 July 2008].

Arkoun, Mohammed (1997), 'The Study of Islam in French Scholarship,' in Nanji (1997), pp. 33–44.

Arkoun, Mohammed (1998a), 'Islam, Europe, the West: Meanings-at-Stake and the Will-to-Power,' in Cooper et al. (1998), pp. 172–89.

Arkoun, Mohammed (1998b), 'From Inter-Religious Dialogue to the Recognition of the Religious Phenomenon,' *Diogenes*, 182:46/2, pp. 123–151.

Arkoun, Mohammed (1998c), 'Social Science as Challenge to Islam: Introductory Reflections,' in Stauth (1998), pp. 197–220.

Arkoun, Mohammed (1999), 'Peut-on parler d'humanisme en contexte islamique?,' in Arazi et al. (1999), pp. 11–22.

Arkoun, Mohammed (2000), 'Present-Day Islam Between its Tradition and Globalization,' in Daftari (2000), pp. 179–221.

Arkoun, Mohammed (2001a), 'Contemporary Critical Practices and the Qur'ān,' in *Encyclopaedia of the Qur'ān*, Leiden: Brill, vol. 1 (A-D), pp. 412–31.

Arkoun, Mohammed (2001b), 'From Islamic Humanism to the Ideology of Liberation,' In: Elders (2001), pp. 13–21.

Arkoun, Mohammed (2002), *The Unthought in Contemporary Islamic Thought*, London: Saqi Books.

Arkoun, Mohammed (2005), *Humanisme et Islam: Combats et Propositions*, Paris: Librairie Philosophique Vrin.

Arkoun, Mohammed (2006), *Islam: To Reform or to Subvert?*, London: Saqi Books.

Arkoun, Mohammed (2007), 'The Answers of Applied Islamology,' *Theory, Culture & Society* 24:2, pp. 21–38.

Arkoun, Mohammed and Jacques Le Goff (1978), *L'Étrange et le Merveilleux dans l'Islam Medieval*, Paris: Actes du Collogue tenu au Collège de France à Paris, en mars 1974, Association pour l'avancement des Études Islamiques, Centre de Littérature et Linguistiques Arabes du CNRS.

Arkoun, Mohammed and Joseph Maïla (2003), *De Manhattan à Bagdad: Au-delà du Bien et du Mal*, Paris: Desclée de Brouwer.

Armajani, Jon Mehrdad, (1999), 'Islamic thought in the West: Sacred texts, Islamic History, and Visions of Islam in a Transnational Age (Fatima Mernissi, Leila Ahmed, Fazlur Rahman, Mohammed Arkoun),' PhD Thesis, Santa Barbara: University of California.

Armajani, Jon Mehrdad, (2004), *Dynamic Islam: Liberal Muslim Perspectives in a Transnational Age*, Dallas: University Press of America.

Atiyah, Ahmad Abd al-Halim (ed.) (1997), *Jadal al-Ana wa'l-Akhar: Qira'at Naqdiyah fi Fikr Hasan Hanaf fi 'Id Miladihi al-Sittan*, Cairo: Madbouli.

Ayadi, Mohammed El-, (1993), 'Mohammed Arkoun ou l'ambition d'une modernité intellectuelle,' in Collectif (1993), pp. 43–71.

Ayoob, Mohammed (2008), *The Many Faces of Political Islam: Religion and Politics in the Muslim World*, Ann Arbor: University of Michigan Press.

Azra, Azyumardi (1994), 'Guarding the Faith of the *Ummah*: The Religio-Intellectual Journey of Mohammad Rasjidi,' *Studia Islamika* 1(2), pp. 87–119.

Azra, Azyumardi (2002), 'Globalization of Indonesian Muslim Discourse: Contemporary Religio-Intellectual Connections between Indonesia and the Middle East,' in Meuleman (2002), pp. 31–50.

Azra, Azyumardi (2004), *The Origins of Islamic Reformism in Southeast Asia: Networks of Malay-Indonesian and Middle Eastern 'Ulamā in the Seventeenth and Eighteenth Centuries*, Honolulu: University of Hawai'i Press and Allen & Unwin.

Azra, Azyumardi, Dina Afrianti and Robert Hefner (2007), 'Pesantren and Madrasa: Muslim Schools and National Ideals in Indonesia,' in Hefner and Zaman (2007), pp. 172–98.

Bachtiar, Harsja W. (1973), 'The Religion of Java: A Commentary,' *Bhratara: Indonesian Journal of Cultural Studies* 5(1), pp. 85–118.

Bagader, Abubaker A. (1994), 'Contemporary Islamic Movements in the Arab World,' in Ahmed and Donnan (1994), pp. 114–26.

Bagir, Haidar (ed.) (2002), *Manusia Modern Mendamba Allah: Renungan Tasawuf Positif*, Jakarta: Imam.

Bakri, Syamsul and Mudhofir (2004), *Jombang Kairo, Jombang Chicago: Sintesis Pemikiran Gus Dur dan Cak Nur dalam Pembaruan Islam di Indonesia*, Solo: Tiga Serangkai.

Barbari, Ahmad Muhammad Salim, al- (1998), *Ihkaliyat al-Turath fi 'l-Fikr al-'Arabi al-Mu'asir: Dirasa Muqarina bayna Hasan Hanafi wa Muhammad 'Abid al-Jabiri*, Cairo: Dar al-Hadara.

Barton, Gregory (1991), 'The International Context of the Emergence of Islamic Neo Modernism in Indonesia,' in Ricklefs (1991), pp. 72–86.

Barton, Gregory (1995a), 'The Emergence of Neo-Modernism; a, Progressive, Liberal, Movement of Islamic Thought in Indonesia: A Textual Study Examining the Writings of Nurcholish Madjid, Djohan Effendi, Ahmad Wahib and Abdurrahman Wahid 1968–1980.' PhD Thesis. Monash University.

Barton, Gregory (1995b), 'Neo-Modernism: A Vital Synthesis of Traditionalist and Modernist Islamic Thought in Indonesia,' *Studia Islamika* 2(3), pp. 1–75.

Barton, Gregory (1997), 'Indonesia's Nurcholish Madjid and Abdurrahman Wahid as Intellectual *Ulama*: The Meeting of Islamic Traditionalism and Modernism in Neo-Modernist Thought,' *Islam and Christian-Muslim Relations* 8(3), pp. 323–50.

Barton, Greg (1999), 'Islamic Liberalism in Indonesia,' unpublished manuscript.

Barton, Greg (2002), *Abdurrahman Wahid: Muslim Democrat, Indonesian President*. Honolulu: University of Hawai'i Press.

Baso, Ahmad (2005), *Islam Pascakolonial: Perselingkuhan Agama, Kolonialisme, dan Liberalisme*, Bandung: Mizan.

Baso, Ahmad (2006), *NU Studies: Pergolakan Pemikiran antara Fundamentalisme Islam dan Fundamentalisme Neo-Liberal*, Jakarta: Penerbit Erlangga.

Basrī, Abū al-Husayn al- (1964), *Kitāb al-Mu'tamad fi Usūl al-Fiqh*. Critical edition. Edited by Dr. Muhammad Hamīdullah, Dr. Muhammad Bekir, Hasan Hanafi. Damascus: Institut Français de Damas.

Bassnett, Susan (2002), *Translation Studies*, London: Routledge.

Bassnett and André Lefevere (1998), *Constructing Cultures: Essays on Literary Translation*, Clevedon: Multilingual Matters.

Bastide, Roger (1973), *Applied Anthropology*, London: Croom Helm [French original: 1971].

Bastide, Roger (1978), *The African Religions of Brazil: Toward a Sociology of the Interpenetration of Civilizations*, Baltimore: Johns Hopkins University Press [French original: 1960].

Bastide, Roger (2003), *The Social Origins of Religion*, Minneapolis: University of Minnesota Press, [French original: 1935].

Beatty, Andrew (1999), *Varieties of Javanese Religion: An Anthropological Account*, Cambridge: Cambridge University Press.

Beatty, Andrew (2009), *A Shadow Falls in the Heart of Java*, London: Faber & Faber.

Beck, Ulrich (2000), 'The Cosmopolitan Perspective: Sociology of the Second Age of Modernity,' *British Journal of Sociology* 51(1), pp. 79–105.

Beck, Ulrich (2004), 'The Truth of Others: A Cosmopolitan Approach,' *Common Knowledge* 10:3, pp. 430–40.

Beck, Ulrich (2006), *The Cosmopolitan Vision*, Translated by Ciaran Cronin. Cambridge: Polity Press.

Behnam, Jamshid (2004), 'Iranian Society, Modernity and Globalization,' in Jahanbegloo (2004), pp. 3–14.

Bellah, Robert (1976), *Beyond Belief: Essays on religion in a post-traditional world*, New York: Harper and Row, [1970].

Benda, Harry (1958), *The Crescent and the Rising Sun*, The Hague: W. van Hoeve.

Benzine, Rachid (2004), *Les Nouveaux Penseurs de l'Islam*, Paris: Albin Michel.

Berger, Mark T. (2004), 'After the Third World? History, Destiny and Fate of the Third Worldism,' *Third World Quarterly* 25:1, pp. 9–39.

Berger, Peter L. (1961), *The Precarious Vision: A Sociologist Looks a Social Fictions and the Christian Faith*, Garden City (NY): Doubleday.

Berger, Peter L. (1967), *The Sacred Canopy: Elements of a Sociological Theory of Religions*, Garden City (NY): Doubleday.

Berger, Peter L. (1970), *A Rumour of Angels: Modern Society and the Rediscovery of the Supernatural*, Garden City (NY): Doubleday.

Berger, Peter L. (1980), *The Heretical Imperative: Contemporary Possibilities of Religious Affirmation*, London: Collins.

Berger, Peter L. (1999), *The Desecularization of the World: Resurgent Religion and World Politics*, Grand Rapids: Willem. B. Eerdmans Publishing Co.

Berger, Peter L. (2001), 'Postscript,' in Woodhead et al. (1991), pp. 189–98.

Berger, Peter L., Brigitte Berger and Hansfried Kellner (1974), *The Homeless Mind*, Harmondsworth: Penguin Books.

Berger, Peter, Grace Davie and Effie Fokas (2008), *Religious America, Secular Europe? A Theme and Variations*, Aldershot: Ashgate.

Bergesen, Albert J. (ed.) (2008), *The Sayyid Qutb Reader: Selected Writings on Politics, Religion, and Society*, London: Routledge.

Berlin, Isaiah (1991), *The Crooked Timber of Humanity: Chapters in the History of Ideas*. Edited by Henry Hardy, London: Fontana Press.

Bhabha, Homi K. (1994), *The Location of Culture*, London: Routledge.

Biersack, Aletta (1989), 'Local Knowledge, Local History: Geertz and Beyond,' in Hunt (1989), pp. 72–96.

Bijlefeld, Willem A. (1972), 'Islamic Studies within the Perspective of the History of Religions,' *The Muslim World* 62(1), pp. 1–11.

Binder, Leonard (1988), *Islamic Liberalism: A Critique of Development Ideologies*, Chicago: Chicago University Press.

Bloch, Marc (2004), *The Historian's Craft*, Translated by Peter Putnam and with an introduction by Peter Burke, Manchester: Manchester University Press [1949].

Blum-Wahn, J. (1997) 'Al-Manar and Ahmad Soorkattie,' in Riddell and Street (1997), pp. 295–208.

Bock, Heike, Jörg Feuchter, Michi Knecht (eds) (2008), *Religion and its Other: Secular and Sacral Concepts and Practices in Integration*, Frankfurt: Campus Verlag.

Boland, Bernard Johan (1971), *The Struggle of Islam in Modern Indonesia*, The Hague: N.V. Nederlandsche Boek- en Steendrukkerij.

Bond, Christopher S. and Lewis M. Simmons (2009), *The Next Frontier: Southeast Asia and the Road to Global Peace with Islam*, Hoboken: John Wiley.

Boom, M. van den (1984), 'Bevrijding van de Mens in Islamitisch Perspektief: M.A. Lahbabi en H. Hanafi, Filosofen uit de Arabisch-Islamitische wereld' [Liberation of Man in an Islamic Perspective: M.A. Lahbabi and H. Hanafi, Philosophers from the Arab-Islamic world], PhD Thesis, Amsterdam: Free University of Amsterdam.

Boom, M. van den (1992), 'De Denker als Profeet: Hasan Hanafi' [The Thinker as Prophet: Hasan Hanafi], in Peters and Meijer (1992), pp. 17–34.

Boom, M. van den (1993), 'From Dogma to Revolution: An Interpretation of H. Hanafi's *Min al-'Aqîda ilâ al-Thawra* (5 Vols. Cairo 1984–1985),' Hong Kong: *Congress paper 34th International Congress Asian and North African Studies*.

Boullata, Issa J. (1990), *Trends and Issues in Contemporary Arab Thought*, Albany: State University of New York Press.

Bowen, John (1995), 'Western Studies of Southeast Asian Islam,' *Studia Islamika* 2(3), pp. 69–85.

Brown, Daniel (1999), *Rethinking Tradition in Modern Islamic Thought*, Cambridge: Cambridge University Press.

Bruce, Steve (2001), 'The Curious Case of the Unnecessary Recantation: Berger and Secularization,' in Woodhead et al. (2001), pp. 87–100.

Bruinessen, Martin van (2006), 'Divergent Paths from Gontor: Muslim Educational Reform and the Travails of Pluralism in Indonesia,' in Bakker and Aritonang (206), pp. 192–202.

Bruinessen, Martin van (2007), 'Saints, Politicians and Sufi Bureaucrats: Mysticism and Politics in Indonesia's New Order,' in Bruinessen and Howell (2007), pp. 92–112.

Bruinessen, Martin van and Julia Day Howell (eds) (2007), *Sufism and the 'Modern' in Islam*, London: I.B. Tauris.

Brunschvig, Robert (1961), 'La Situation de l'Islamologie,' *Correspondance d'Orient. No 5. Colloque sur la sociologie musulmane*, Bruxelles: Centre pour l'Étude des problèmes du monde musulman contemporain, pp. 11–14.

Bulliet, Richard W. (1978), Review of: *The Venture of Islam* by Marshall Hodgson, *Journal of the American Oriental Society* 98(2), pp. 157–8.

Burke, III, Edmund (1979), 'Islamic History as World History: Marshall Hodgson's "The Venture of Islam,"' *International Journal of Middle East Studies* 10, pp. 241–64.

Burke, Peter (1990), *The French Historical Revolution: The* Annales *School 1929–89*, Cambridge: Polity Press in association with Basil Blackwell.

Burke, Peter (2009), *Cultural Hybridity*, Cambridge: Polity Press.

Burke, Peter and Maria Lucia G. Pallares-Burke (2008), *Gilberto Freyre: Social Theory in the Tropics*, Oxford: Peter Lang.

Burns, Peter (1981), *Revelation and Revolution: Natsir and the Panca Sila*, Townsville: James Cook University of North Queenslands.

Buruma, Ian and Avishai Margalit (2004), *Occidentalism: A Short History of Anti-Westernism*, London: Atlantic Books.

Calvert, John (2000), '"The World is an Undutiful Boy!" Sayyid Qutb's American Experience,' *Islam and Christian-Muslim Relations* 11(1), pp 87–103.

Carré, Olivier (2004), *Mysticism and Politics: A Critical Reading of* Fī Zilāl al-Qur'ān *by Sayyid Qutb (1906–1966)*, Translated from the French by Carol Artigues and revised by W. Shepard, Leiden: E.J. Brill.

Castles, Lance (1966), 'Notes on the Islamic School at Gontor,' *Indonesia* 1, pp. 30–45.

Chan, K.B. (2002), 'Both Sides, Now: Culture Contact, Hybridization, and Cosmopolitanism,' in Vertovec and Cohen (2002), pp. 191–208.

Chartier, Marc (1972), 'La pensée religieuse à la recherché d'un nouveau langage: l'audacieuse tentative du philosophe Egyptian Hassan Hanafi,' *Comprendre* 5(3), pp. 1–15.

Chartier, Marc (1973), 'La rencontre Orient-Occident dans la pensée de trois philosophes égyptiens contemporains: Hasan Hanafi, Fu'ād Zakariyyā, Zakī Nagīb Mahmūd,' *Oriente Moderno* 53(7–9), pp. 603–42.

Cho, Hee-Yeon and Kuan-Hsing Chen (2005), 'Editorial Introduction Bandung/Third Worldism,' *Inter-Asia Cultural Studies* 6(4), pp. 474–5.

Clark, Stuart (1990), 'The *Annales* Historians,' in Skinner (1990), pp. 177–98.

Clarke, J.J. (1999), *Oriental Enlightenment: The Encounter Between Asian and Western Thought*, London: Routledge.

Clarke, Peter and Peter Byrne (1993), *Religion Defined and Explained*, London: Macmillan.

Cleary, David (1999), *Race, nationalism and social theory in Brazil: Rethinking Gilberto Freyre*, Cambridge (Mass): David Rockefeller Center for Latin American Studies, Harvard University.

Clifford, James (1997), *Routes: Travel and Translation in the Late Twentieth Century*, Cambridge (Mass.): Harvard University Press.

Collectif (1993), *Penseurs Maghrébins Contemporains*, Casablanca: Éditions Eddif.

Collective (1987), *Al-Falsafa fi al-Watan al-'Arabi al-Mu'asir*, Beirut: Markaz Dirasat al-Wahda al-'Arabiya.

Colville, Jim (1999), *Two Andalusian philosophers*, London: Kegal Paul.

Cone, Malcolm (2002), 'Neo-Modern Islam in Suharto's Indonesia,' *New Zealand Journal of Asian Studies* 4(2), pp. 52–67.

Cox, Harvey (1965), *The Secular City*, London: Macmillan.

Cox, Harvey (1984), *Religion in the Secular City*, New York: Simon & Schuster.

Cronin, Michael (2000), 'History, Translation, Postcolonialism,' in Simon and St Pierre (2000), pp. 22–52.

Dabashi, Hamid (2004), *Iran: A People Interrupted*, London: The New Press.

Dabashi, Hamid (2009), *Post-Orientalism: Knowledge and Power in a Time of Terror*, Piscataway (NJ): Transaction Publishers.

Daftari, Farhat (ed.) (2000), *Intellectual Traditions in Islam*, London: I.B. Tauris.

Daniels, Timothy (2009), *Islamic Spectrum in Java*, Farnham and Burlington (VT): Ashgate.

Dardiry, Ramy el- (2005), 'Islam Encountering Enlightenment: Clash or Symbiosis? A Comparative Analysis of the Dutch and Indonesian Discourse on Liberal Islam,' Course report, Enschede: University of Twente.

Dengel, Holk H. (1986), *Darul-Islam: Kartosuwirjo's Kampf um einen Islamischen Staat in Indonesien*, Wiesbaden: Franz Steiner Verlag.

Derrida, Jacques (2002), *Acts of Religion*, Edited and with an introduction by Gil Anidjar, London: Routledge.

Derrida, Jacques and Gianni Vattimo (1998), *Religion: Cultural Memory in the Present*, Translated by David Webb, Stanford: Stanford University Press [1996].

Dewantara, Ki Hadjar (1967), 'Some Aspects of National Education and the Taman Siswa Institute of Jogjakarta,' *Indonesia* 4, pp. 150–68.

Dijk, Cornelis van (1981), *Rebellion under the banner of Islam: The Darul Islam in Indonesia*, The Hague: Martinus Nijhoff.

Djait, Hichem (1974), *La Personnalité et le Devenir Arabo-Islamiques*, Paris: Seuil.

Dorrien, Gary (2001), 'Berger: Theology and sociology,' in Woodhead et al. (2001), pp. 26–39.

Dufrenne, Mikel (1973), *The Phenomenology of Aesthetic Experience*. Evanston: Northwestern University Press [1953].

Dufrenne, Mikel (1953), *La Personnalité de Base: Un Concept Sociologique*. Paris: Presses Universitaires de France.

Dussen, W.J. van der (1986), *Filosofie van de Geschiedenis: Een Inleiding*. Muiderberg: Coutinho.

Effendy, Bahtiar (1995), 'Islam and the State in Indonesia: Munawir Sjadzali and the Development of a New Theological Underpinning of Political Islam,' *Studia Islamika* 2(2), pp. 97–121.

Effendy, Bahtiar (2003), *Islam and the State in Indonesia*, Singapore: Institute for South East Asian Studies.

Eickelman, Dale F. and Jon W. Anderson (1997), 'Print, Islam, and the Prospects for Civic Pluralism: New Religious Writings and Their Audiences,' *Journal of Islamic Studies* 8:(1), pp. 43–62.

Eisenstadt, Samuel (1972), 'Intellectuals and Tradition,' *Daedalus* 101, pp. 1–19.

Elders, Fons (ed.) (2001), *Forum 2001 Symposium: Humanism towards the Third Millennium*, Amsterdam and Brussels: VUB Press.

Esposito, John K. and John O. Voll (2001), *Makers of Contemporary Islam*, Oxford: Oxford University Press.

Even-Zohar, Itamar (1990), 'Polysystem Studies,' *Poetics Today: International for the Theory and Analysis of Literature and Communication* 11(1), pp. 1–268.

Fathimah, Siti (1999), 'Modernism and the Contextualization of Islamic Doctrines: The Reform of Indonesian Islam Proposed by Nurcholish Madjid,' unpublished MA Thesis, Montreal: Institute of Islamic Studies, McGill University.

Fazlur Rahman (1979), 'Islam: Challenges and Opportunities,' in Welch and Cachia (1979), pp. 315–30.

Fazlur Rahman (1980), *Major Themes of the Qur'ān*, Minneapolis and Chicago: Bibliotheca Islamica.

Fazlur Rahman (1982), *Islam and Modernity: Transformation of an Intellectual Tradition*, Chicago: University of Chicago Press.

Fealy, Greg and Virginia Hooker (2006), *Voices of Islam in Southeast Asia: A Contemporary Sourcebook*, Singapore: ISEAS Publications.

Featherstone, Mike, Scott Lash and Roland Robertson (eds) (1995), *Global Modernities*, London: Sage.

Federspiel, Howard (1992), *Muslim Intellectuals and National Development in Indonesia*, Commack (NY): Nova Science Publications.

Federspiel, Howard (2002), 'Contemporary South-East Asian Muslim intellectuals: An examination of the Sources of their Concepts and Intellectual Constructs,' in Meuleman (2002), pp. 327–50.

Federspiel, Howard (2006), *Indonesian Muslim Intellectuals of the 20th Century*, Singapore: ISEAS.

Feener, R. Michael (2007), 'Cross-Cultural Contexts of Modern Muslim Intellectualism,' *Die Welt des Islams* 47(3–4), pp. 264–82.

Feith, Herbert (1962), *The Decline of Constitutional Democracy in Indonesia*, Ithaca: Cornell University Press.

Ferguson, Niall, Cahrles S. Maier, Erez Manela, Daniel J. Sargent (eds) (2010), *The Shock of the Global: The 1970s in Perspective*, Cambridge (Mass): The Belknap Press of Harvard University Press.

Feuerbach, Ludwig (1989), *The Essence of Christianity*, 2nd edition, Translated by George Eliot, New York: Prometheus Books [1854].

Flood, Gavin (1999), *Beyond Phenomenology: Rethinking the Study of Religion*, London: Cassell.

Flores, Alexander (1988), 'Egypt: A New Secularism?,' *Middle East Report*, July-August 1988, pp. 27–30.

Freitag, Ulrike and William Clarence-Smith (eds) (1997), *Hadhrami Traders, Scholars and Statesmen in the Indian Ocean, 1750s-1960s*, Leiden, New York and Cologne: E.J. Brill.

Freyre, Gilberto (1961a), *Portuguese Integration in the Tropics: Notes Concerning a Possible Lusotropicology Which Would Specialize in the Systematic Study of the Ecological-Social Process of the Integration in Tropical Environments of Portuguese, Descendants of Portuguese and Continuators of Portuguese*, Lisbon: Realização Grafica da Tipografia Silvas.

Freyre, Gilberto (1961b), *The Portuguese and the Tropics: Suggestions Inspired by the Portuguese Methods of Integrating Autocthonous People and Cultures Differing from the European in a New, or Luso-Tropical Complex of Civilisations*, International Congress of the History of Discoveries, Lisbon: Executive Committee for the Commemoration of the Vth centenary of the death of Prince Henry the Navigator.

Gadamer, Hans-Georg (2004), *Truth and Method*, 2nd Revised Edition, Translation revised by Joel Weinsheimer and Donald G. Marshall, London: Continuum [Translation 1975, 1960].

Geertz, Clifford (1960), *The Religion of Java*, Glencoe (Ill): The Free Press of Glencoe.

Geertz, Clifford (1968), *Islam Observed: Religious Development in Morocco and Indonesia*, Chicago: University of Chicago Press.

Geertz, Clifford (2000), *Local Knowledge: Further Essays in Interpretative Anthropology*, 3rd Edition, N.P.: Basic Books.

Ghamari-Tabrizi, Behrooz (2008), *Islam and Dissent in Postrevolutionary Iran: Abdolkarim Soroush, Religious Politics and Democratic Reform*, London: I.B. Tauris.

Ghazali, Abd Moqsith (ed.) (2005), *Ijtihad Islam Liberal: Upaya Merumuskan Keberagamaan yang Dinamis*, Jakarta: Jaringan Islam Liberal.

Gheissari, Ali (1998), *Iranian Intellectuals in the 20th Century*, Austin: University of Texas Press.

Gibb, Hamilton A.R. (1947), *Modern Trends in Islam*, Chicago: University of Chicago Press.

Giddens, Anthony (1971), *Capitalism and Modern Social Theory*, Cambridge: Cambridge University Press.

Gillespie, Pierre (2007), 'Current Issues in Indonesian Islam: Analysing the Council of Indonesian Ulama Fatwa no. 7 Opposing Liberalism, Pluralism and Secularism,' *Journal of Islamic Studies* 18(2), pp. 202–40.

Gisel, Pierre and Patrick Evrard (1996), *La Théologie en Postmodernité. Actes du 3e Cycle de Théologie Systématique des Facultés de Théologie de Suisse Romande*, Geneva: Labor et Fides.

Goddard, Hugh (1996), *Muslim Perceptions of Christianity*, London: Grey Seal.

Goff, Jacques Le (1980), *Time, Work and Culture in the Middle Ages*, Translated by Arthur Goldhammer, Chicago and London: University of Chicago Press [1977].

Goff, Jacques Le (1988), *The Medieval Imagination*, Translated by Arthur Goldhammer, Chicago and London: University of Chicago Press [1985].

Goff, Jacques Le (1992), *History and Memory*, Translated by Steven Randall and Elizabeth Claman, New York: Columbia University Press [1977].

Goff, Jacques Le, with Rogier Chartier and Jacques Revel (1978), *La Nouvelle Histoire*, Paris: Retz.

Guinness, Patrick (2009), *Kampung, Islam and the State in Urban Java*, Singapore: National University of Singapore Press in association with the Asian Studies Association of Australia.

Guitton, Jean (1963), *Le Christ Écartelé: Crises et Conciles dans l'Église*, Paris: Perrin Evreux.

Guitton, Jean (1988), *Un Siècle, une Vie*, Paris: Éditions Robert Laffont.

Günther, Ursula (2004a), *Mohammed Arkoun: Ein moderner Kritiker der islamischen Vernunft*, Würzburg: Ergon Verlag.

Günther, Ursula (2004b), 'Mohammed Arkoun: towards a radical rethinking of Islamic thought,' in: Taji-Farouki (2004), pp. 125–68.

Gupta, Akhil (1992), 'The Song of the Nonaligned World: Transnational Identities and the Reinscription of Space in Late Capitalism,' *Cultural Anthropology* 7(1), pp. 63–79.

Haddad, Mohamed (1998), 'Pour Comprendre Hasan Hanafi,' *Institut des Belles Lettres Arabes* 61, pp. 49–69.

Hakim, Abdul 'Dukkun' (2006), 'Islam, Inklusivisme, dan Kosmopolitanisme,' in Abdul Halim (2006), pp. 3–22.

Haleber, Ron and Pieter Sjoerd van Koningsveld (1991), *Islam en Humanisme: De Wereld van Arkoun*, Amsterdam: VU Uitgeverij.

Hall, Stuart (1996), 'When was "The Post-Colonial"? Thinking at the Limit,' in Chambers and Curti (1996), pp. 242–60.

Hallaq, Wael (1993), *Ibn Taymiyya against the Greek Logicians*, Oxford: Oxford University Press.

Hallaq, Wael (1995), *Law and Legal Theory in Classical and Medieval Islam*, Aldershot: Variorum.

Hanafi, Hasan (1965), *Les Méthodes d'Exégèse: Essai sur la Science des Fondements de la Compréhension "'Ilm Usul al-Fiqh"*, Cairo: Conseil Supérieur des Arts, des Lettres et des Sciences Socials.

Hanafi, Hasan (1972), 'Theologie ou Anthropologie?,' in A. Abdel-Malek, A.A. Belal, H. Hanafi (1972), pp. 233–64.

Hanafi, Hasan (1977), *Religious Dialogue and Revolution: Essays on Judaism, Christianity and Islam*, Cairo: Anglo-Egyptian Bookshop.

Hanafi, Hasan (1979), Al-Ightirab al-Dini 'inda Feuerbach,'*'Alam al-Fikr* 1, pp. 41–68.

Hanafi, Hasan (1980a), *L'Exégèse de la Phénoménologie: l'État Actuelle de la Méthode Phénoménologique et son Application au Phénomène Religieux*, Cairo: Dar al-Fikr al-Arabi [1966].

Hanafi, Hasan (1980b), *Al-Turath wa'l-Tajdid: Mawqifuna min al-Turath al-Qadim*, Cairo: al-Markaz al-'Arabi li'l-Bahth wa'l-Nashr.

Hanafi, Hasan (1981a), *Al-Yasar al-Islami: Kitabat fi al-Nahda al-Islamiyya*, Cairo: Self-published.

Hanafi, Hasan (1981b), *Qadaya Mu'asira 1: Fi Fikrina al-Mu'asir*, Beirut: Dar al-Tanwir [1976].

Hanafi, Hasan (1982a), *Qadaya Mu'asira 2: Fi al-Fikr al-Gharbi al-Mu'asir*, Beirut: Dar al-Tanwir [1977].

Hanafi, Hasan (1982b), *Dirasat Islamiyya*, Beirut: Dar al-Tanwir.

Hanafi, Hasan (1987), 'Mawqifuna al-Hadari,' in Collective (1987), pp. 13–42 [1986].

Hanafi, Hasan (1988a), *La Phénoménologie de l'Exégèse: Essai d'une Herméneutique Existentielle à Partir du Nouveau Testament*, Cairo: Anglo-Egyptian Bookshop.

Hanafi, Hasan (1988b), *Min al-'Aqida ila 'l-Thawra*, 5 vols, Cairo: Madbouli.

Hanafi, Hasan (1989), *Al-Din wa'l-Thawra fi Misr 1952–1981*, 6 Vols, Cairo: Madbouli.

Hanafi, Hasan (1991), *Muqaddima fi 'Ilm al-Istighrab*, Cairo: Al-Dar al-Fanniyya li'l-Nashr wa'l-Tawzi'.

Hanafi, Hasan (1996a), 'Ibn Rushd Faqihan,' *Alif: Journal of Comparative Politics* 16, pp. 116–45.

Hanafi, Hasan (1996b), 'Method and Thematic Interpretation of the Qur'an,' in Wild (1996), pp. 195–211.

Hanafi, Hasan (2000), *Islam in the Modern World*, 2 Vols, Cairo: Dar al-Kebaa [1995].

Hanafi, Hasan (2002), *Min al-Naql ila 'l-Ibda': Muhawala I'ada Bina' 'Ulum al-Hikma*, Cairo: Dar al-Kebaa.

Hanafi, Hasan (2003), *Fichte: Faylusuf al-Muqawamah* [Fichte: Philosopher of Resistance], Cairo: Egyptian Philosophical Association.

Hanafi, Hasan (2005), *Min al-Nass ila 'l-Waqi'a: Muhawala I'ada Bina' 'Ilm Usul al-Fiqh*, Cairo: Markaz al-Kitab li'l-Nashr.

Hannerz, Ulf (1990), 'Cosmopolitans and Locals in World Culture,' *Theory, Culture & Society* 7, pp. 237–51.

Harjanto, Nicolaus Teguh Budi (2003), 'Islam and Liberalism in Contemporary Indonesia: The Political Ideas of *Jaringan Islam Liberal* (The Liberal Islam Network),' Unpublished MA dissertation, Athens (OH): The College of Arts and Sciences of Ohio University.

Hassan, Muhammad Kamal (1980), *Muslim Intellectual Responses to 'New Order' in Indonesia*, Kuala Lumpur: Dewan Bahasa dan Pustaka.

Hassan, Muhammad Kamal (1987), 'The Response of Muslim Youth Organizations to Political Change: HMI in Indonesia and ABIM in Malaysia,' in Roff (1987), pp. 180–96.

Hassan, Riaz (2005), *The Local and the Global: Social Transformation in Southeast Asia: Essays in Honour of Professor Syed Hussein Alatas*, Leiden: Brill.

Hattar, Nahid (1986), Al-Turath, al-Gharb, al-Thawra: Bahth hawl al-Asala wa'l-Mu'asira fi Fikr Hasan Hanafi. Amman: Shuqayr w al-Ukasha li Tiba'a wa a'-Nashr wa 'l-Tawzi'.

Heelas, Paul (1996), 'Introduction: Detraditionalization and its Rivals,' in Heelas et al. (1996), pp. 1–20.

Heelas, Paul (1998), 'Introduction: on differentiation and dedifferentiation,' in Heelas et al. (1998), pp. 1–18.

Heelas, Paul, Scott Lash and Paul Morris (eds) (1996), *Detraditionalization: Critical Reflections on Authority and Identity*, Oxford: Blackwell Publishers.

Heelas, Paul, David Martin and Paul Morris (eds) (1998), *Religion, Modernity and Postmodernity*, Oxford: Blackwell Publishers.

Hefner, Robert W. (1985), *Hindu Javanese: Tengger tradition and Islam*, Princeton: Princeton University Press.

Hefner, Robert W. (1997a), 'Introduction: Islam in an Era of Nation States: Politics and Religious Renewal in Muslim Southeast Asia,' in Hefner and Horvatich (1997) pp. 3–40.

Hefner, Robert W. (1997b), 'Islamization and Democratization in Indonesia,' in Hefner and Horvatich (1997), pp. 75–127.

Hefner, Robert W. (1998), 'Secularization and citizenship in Muslim Indonesia,' in Heelas et al. (1998), pp. 147–68.

Hefner, Robert W. (2000), *Civil Islam: Muslims and Democratization in Indonesia*, Princeton: Princeton University Press.

Hefner, Robert W. and Patricia Horvatich (eds) (1997), *Islam in an Era of Nation-States: Political and Religious Renewal in Muslim Southeast Asia*, Honolulu: University of Hawai'i Press.

Hefner, Robert W. and Muhammad Qasim Zaman (eds) (2007), *Schooling Islam: The Culture and Politics of Modern Muslim Education*, Princeton: Princeton University Press.

Hentsch, Thierry (1992), *Imagining the Middle* East, Translated by Fred Reed, Montreal: Black Rose Books.

Hewer, Christopher T.R. (1998), 'Fazlur Rahman: A Reinterpretation of Islam in the Twentieth Century,' Unpublished PhD Thesis, Birmingham: University of Birmingham.

Hidayat, Komaruddin and Muhamad Wahyudi Nafis (2003), *Agama Masa Depan: Perspektif Filsafat Perennial*, Jakarta: Gramedia Pustaka Utama.

Hildebrand, Thomas (1998), *Emanzipation oder Isolation vom westlichen Lehrer? Die Debatte um Hasan Hanafi's Einführung in die Wissenschaft der Okzidentalistik*, Berlin: Klaus Schwarz Verlag.

Hiroko Horikoshi (1975), 'The Dar-ul-Islam Movement in West-Java, 1948–62: An Experience in the Historical Process,' *Indonesia* 20, pp. 58–86.

Hodgson, Marshall G.S. (1974), *The Venture of Islam: Conscience and History in a World Civilization*, 3 Volumes, Chicago: The University of Chicago Press.

Holt, P.M., Ann K.S. Lambton, Bernard Lewis (eds) (1970), *The Cambridge History of Islam. Volume 2. The Further Islamic Lands, Society and Civilization*, Cambridge: Cambridge University Press.

Hourani, Albert (1978), Review of: *The Venture of Islam* by Marshall Hodgson, *Journal of Near Eastern Studies* 37(1), pp. 53–62.

Howell, Julia Day (2007), 'Modernity and Islamic Spirituality in Indonesia's New Sufi Networks,' in Bruinessen and Howell (2007), pp. 217–40.

Hunt, Lynn (ed.) (1989), *The New Cultural History*, Berkeley, Los Angeles: University of California Press.

Hussain, Asaf, Robert Olson and Jamil Qureshi (eds) (1984), *Orientalism, Islam, and Islamists*, Brattleboro (VT): Amana Books.

Husaini, Adian (2005), *Nurcholish Madjid. Kontroversi Kematian dan Pemikiranya*, Jakarta: Khairul Bayan.

Husserl, Edmund (1970), *The Crisis of European Sciences and Transcendental Philosophy: An Introduction to Phenomenological Philosophy*, Translated and with an introduction by David Carr, Evanston: Northwestern University Press [1954].

Ichwan, Moch. Nur (2005), '"Ulamā," State and Politics: Majelis Ulama Indonesia After Suharto,' *Islamic Law and Society* 12(1), pp. 45–72.

Ihza, Yusril (1995), 'Combining Activism and Intellectualism: The Biography of Mohammad Natsir (1908–1993),' *Studia Islamika* 2(1), pp. 111–47.

Iqbal, Muhammad (1974), *The Reconstruction of Religious Thought in Islam*, New Delhi: Kitab Bhavan [1930].

Iqbal, Muhamad (1978), *The Secrets of the Self: A Philosophical Poem*, Translated by R.A. Nicholson, New Delhi: Arnold-Heinemann.

Iqbal, Muhammad (2002), 'Islam as a Moral and Political Ideal,' in Kurzman (2002), pp. 304–13.

Irwin, Robert (2006), *Dangerous Knowledge: Orientalism and its Discontents*, New York: Overlook Press.

Israeli, R. and A.H. Johns (eds) (1984), *Islam in Asia: Volume II Southeast and East Asia*, Boulder: Westview Press.

Izutsu, Toshihiko (1964), *God and Man in the Koran: Semantics of the Koranic Weltanschauung*, Tokyo: Keio Institute of Cultural and Linguistic Studies.

Izutsu, Toshihiko (1966) *Ethico-Religious concepts of the Qur'an*, Montreal: McGill University Press.

Jabali, Fuad and Arief Subhan (2007), 'A New form of Contemporary Islam in Indonesia,' in Sukma and Joewono (2007), pp. 54–78.

Jabali, Fuad and Jamhari (2002), *IAIN & Modernisasi Islam di Indonesia*, Jakarta: Logos Wacana Ilmu.

Jahanbegloo, Ramin (Ed.) (2004), *Iran between Tradition and Modernity*, Oxford: Lexington Books.

Jalal, Ayesha (2010), 'An Uncertain Trajectory: Islam's Contemporary Globalization 1971–1979,' in Ferguson et al. (2010), pp. 319–36.

Jam'a, Muhammad (n.d), 'Ishkaliyyat al-tajdid bayna Hasan Hanafi wa 'Abd Allah al-'Arwi,' PhD Thesis, Beirut: University of Lebanon.

Johns, A.H. (1984), 'Islam and the Malay World: An Exploratory Survey with Some Reference to Quranic Exegesis,' in Israeli and Johns (1984), pp. 115–61.

Johns, Anthony H. and Abdullah Saeed (2004), 'Nurcholish Madjid and the Interpretation of the Qur'an: Religious Pluralism and Tolerance,' in Taji-Farouki (2004a), pp. 67–96.

Johnson, John B. (1981), 'Editor's Introduction,' in Ricoeur (1981), pp. 3–26.

Jonge, Huub de (2002), 'Contradictory and against the Grain: Snouck Hurgronje on the Hadramis in the Dutch East Indies (1889–1936),' in de Jonge and Kaptein (2002), pp. 219–234.

Jonge, Huub de and Nico Kaptein (eds) (2002), *Transcending Borders: Arabs, Politics, Trade and Islam in Southeast Asia*, Leiden: KITLV Press.

Judy, Ronald A.T. (2004), 'Sayyid Qutb's *Fiqh al-Waqi'i*, or New Realist Science,' *Boundary* 2 31(2), pp. 113–48.

Judy, Ronald A.T. (2004), 'Sayyid Qutb's *Fiqh al-Waqi'i*, or New Realist Science,' *Boundary* (3)2, pp. 113–48.

Kamrava, Mehran (2006), *The New Voices of Islam: Rethinking Politics and Modernity. A Reader*, Berkeley; University of California Press.

Kardiner, Avram (1945), 'The Concept of Basic Personality Structure as an Operational Tool in the Social Sciences,' in Linton (1945) pp. 107–22.

Kersten, Carool (2007), 'Bold Transmutations: Rereading Hasan Hanafi's Early Writings on *Fiqh*,' *Journal of Comparative Islamic Studies* 3(1), pp. 22–38.

Khatab, Sayed (2002), '*Hakimiyyah* and *Jahiliyya* in the Thought of Sayyid Qutb,' *Middle Eastern Studies* 38(2), pp. 145–70.

Khuri, Richard K. (1994), 'A Critique of Hasan Hanafi Concerning his Reflections on the Scarcity of Freedom in the Arab-Muslim world,' in Mardin (1884), pp. 86–115.

King, Richard (1999), *Orientalism and Religion: Postcolonial Theory, India and 'The Mystic East,'* London: Routledge.

Knecht, Michi and Jörg Feuchter (2008), 'Introduction: Reconfiguring Religion and its Other,' in Bock et al. (eds), pp. 9–20.

Kockelmans, Joseph J. (ed.) (1967), *Phenomenology: The Philosophy of Edmund Husserl and Its Interpretation*, Garden City (NY): Doubleday & Company.

Kraemer, Joel L. (1984), 'Humanism in the Renaissance of Islam: A Preliminary Study,' *Journal of the American Oriental Society* 104, pp. 135–65.

Kraemer, Joel L. (1992), *Humanism in the Renaissance of Islam: The Cultural Revival during the Buyid Age.* 2nd edition, Leiden: Brill.

Kügelgen, Anke von (1994), *Averroës und die arabische Moderne: Ansätze zu eigene Neubegründing des Rationalismus im Islam*, Leiden: E.J. Brill.

Kügelgen, Anke von (1996), 'A Call for Rationalism: "Arab Averroists" in the Twentieth Century,' *Alif: Journal of Comparative Poetics* 16, pp. 97–132.

Kull, Ann (2005), *Piety and Politics: Nurcholish Madjid and His Interpretation of Islam in Modern Indonesia*, Lund: Department of History and Anthropology of Religions, Lund University.

Kurzman, Charles (ed.) (1998), *Liberal Islam: A Sourcebook*, Oxford: Oxford University Press.

Kurzman, Charles (ed.) (2002), *Modernist Islam 1840–1940: A Sourcebook*, Oxford: Oxford University Press.

LaCoque, André and Paul Ricoeur (1998), *Thinking Biblically: Exegetical and Hermeneutical Studies*, Translated by David Pellauer, Chicago: University of Chicago Press.

Laffan, Michael Francis (2003), *Islamic Nationhood and Colonial Indonesia: The Umma below the Winds*, London: RoutledgeCurzon.

Lee, Robert D. (1997), *Overcoming Tradition and Modernity: The Search for Islamic Authenticity*, Boulder: Westview Press.

Leeuw, Gerardus van der (1986), *Religion in Essence and Manifestation*, Translated by J.E. Turner with appendices incorporating the additions of the second German edition by Hans H. Penner, Princeton: Princeton University Press [1938].

Lévi-Strauss, Claude (1968), *Structural Anthropology I*, Translated from the French by Claire Jacobson and Brooke Grundfest Schoepf, London: Allen Lane and the Penguin Press, [1963; org. French 1958].

Liddle, R. William (1996), '*Media Dakwa* Scripturalism: One Form of Islamic Political Thought and Action in New Order Indonesia,' in Woodward (1996), pp. 323–56.

Liddle, R. William (1997), 'Improvising Political Cultural Change: Three Indonesian Cases,' in Schiller & Schiller (1997): 1–53.

Linton, Ralph (ed.) (1945), *The Science of Man in the World Crisis*, New York: Columbia University Press.

Lombard, Denys (1990), *Le Carrefour Javanais: Essay d'Histoire Globale*, 3 Volumes, Paris: Éditions de l'École des Hautes Études en Sciences Sociales.

Lotfalian, Mazyar (2004), 'Keywords in Islamic Critiques of Technoscience: Iranian Postrevolutionary Interpretations,' in Jahanbegloo (2004), pp. 15–24.

Luckmann, Thomas (2001), 'Berger and his collaborator(s),' in Woodhead et al. (2001), pp. 17–25.

Lukens-Bull, Ronald (2005), *A Peaceful Jihad: Negotiating Identity and Modernity in Muslim Java*, New York: Palgrave Macmillan.

Maalouf, Amin (2000), *In the Name of Identity: Violence and the Need to Belong*, Translated from the French by Barbara Bray, New York: Arcade Books.

Madjid, Nurcholish (1970), *Pembaharuan Pemikiran Islam*, Jakarta: Islamic Research Centre.

Madjid, Nurcholish (1972), 'Sekali Lagi Tentang Sekularisasi,' in Rasjidi (1972), pp. 31–42.

Madjid, Nurcholish (1979), 'The Issue of Modernization Among Muslims in Indonesia: From a Participant's Point of View,' in Davis (1979), pp. 143–55.

Madjid, Nurcholish (1984a), *Khazanah Intelektual Islam*, Jakarta: Bulan Bintang.

Madjid, Nurcholish (1984b), 'Ibn Taymiyya on Kalâm and Falsafa (A Problem of Reason and Revelation in Islam),' PhD Thesis, Chicago: University of Chicago.

Madjid, Nurcholish (1987), *Islam Kemodernan dan Keindonesiaan*, Bandung: Mizan.

Madjid, Nurcholish (1994), 'Islamic Roots of Modern Pluralism, *Indonesian Experiences*,' *Studia Islamika* 1(1), pp. 55–77.

Madjid, Nurcholish (1997), *Tradisi Islam: Peran dan Fungsinya dalam Pembangunan di Indonesia*, Ed. Kasnanto, Jakarta: Paramadina.

Madjid, Nurcholish (2000), 'Metodologi dan Orientasi Study Islam Masa Depan,' *Jauhar: Jurnal Pemikiran Islam Kontekstual* 1(1), pp. 1–27.

Madjid, Nurcholish (2002), 'Tasawuf dan Kekuasan Politik,' in Bagir (2002), pp. 181–8.

Madjid, Nurcholish (2003a), *Islam Agama Kemanusiaan: Membangung tradisi dan Visi Baru Islam Indonesia*, Ed. Muhammad Wahyuni Nafis, Jakarta: Paramadina, [1995].

Madjid, Nurcholish (2003b), *The True Face of Islam-Essays on Islam and Modernity in Indonesia*, Rudy Harisyah Alam and Ihsan Ali-Fauzi (eds), Voice Centre, Ciputat, Indonesia.

Madjid, Nurcholish (2005a), *Islam Doktrin dan Peradaban: Sebuah Telaah Kritik tentang Masalah Keimanan, Kemanusiaan, dan Kemodernan*, Jakarta: Paramadina [1992].

Madjid, Nurcholish (2005b), 'Interpreting the Qur'anic Principle of Religious Pluralism,' in Saeed (2005), pp. 209–25.

Madjid, Nurcholish (2005d), 'Islam Sebagai Agama Hibrida,' in Ghazali (2005), pp. 61–64.

Madjid, Nurcholish (2007), *Islam Universal*, Yogyakarta: Pustaka Pelajar, 2007.

Majeed, Javed (2009), *Muhammad Iqbal: Islam, Aesthetics and Postcolonialism*, London: Routledge.

Majid, Anouar (2007), *A Call of Heresy: Why Dissent is Vital for Islam and America*, Minneapolis: University of Minnesota Press.

Malley, Robert (1996), *The Call from Algeria: Third Worldism, Revolution and the Turn to Islam*, Berkeley: University of California Press.

Mandal, Sumit Kumar (1994), 'Finding Their Place: A History of Arabs on Java under Dutch Rule, 1800–1924,' PhD Thesis, New York: Columbia University.

Mandaville, Peter (2001), *Transnational Muslim Politics: Reimagining the Umma*, London: Routledge.

Marcinkowski, Christoph (2006), 'Facets of Shi'ite Islam in Southeast Asia: Thailand and Indonesia,' *Working Paper No. 120*, Singapore: Nanyang Technological University, Institute for Defence and Strategic Studies.

Martin, Bernice (2001), 'Berger's Anthropological Anthropology,' in Woodhead et al. (2001), pp. 154–88.

Martin, David (1969), *The Religious and the Secular: Studies in Secularization*, London: Routledge and Kegan Paul.

Martin, David (2001), 'Berger: An Appreciation,' in Woodhead et al. (2001), pp. 11–6.

Martin, David (2005), *On Secularization: Towards a revised general theory*, Aldershot: Ashgate Publishing Co.

Martin, Richard C. (1977), Review of *The Venture of Islam* by Marshall Hodgson, *Journal of the American Academy of Religion* 45(1), p. 104.

Martin, Richard C. (ed.) (2001), *Approaches to Islam in Religious Studies*, Oxford: OneWorld [1985].

Martin, Richard C. and Mark R. Woodward, with Dwi S. Atmaja (1997), *Defenders of Reason in Islam: Mu'tazilism from Medieval School to Modern Symbol*, Oxford: Oneworld.

Masud, Muhammad Khalid (2005), 'The Construction and Deconstruction as an Ideology in Contemporary Muslim Thought,' *Asian Journal of Social Sciences* 33(3), pp. 363–83.

Matheson, Virginia and M.B. Hooker (1988), 'Jawi Literature in Patani: The Maintenance of an Islamic Tradition,' *Journal of the Malay Branch of the Royal Asiatic Society* 61(1), pp. 1–86.

Matthes, Joachim (2005), 'Is Secularisation a Global Process? An Exercise in Conceptual History,' in Hassan (2005), pp. 19–29.

McCutcheon, Russell T. (1997), *The Manufacturing of Religion: The Discourse of Sui Generis Religion and the Politics of Nostalgia*, London: Oxford University Press.

McCutcheon, Russell T. (1999), *The Insider/Outsider Problem in the Study of Religion: A Reader*, New York: Cassell.

McCutcheon, Russell T. (2001), *Critics not Caretakers: Redescribing the Public Study of Religion*, Albany: State University of New York Press.

McCutcheon, Russell T. (2003), *The Discipline of Religion: Structure, Meaning, Rhetoric*, London: Routledge.

McDonough, Sheila (1970), *The Authority of the Past: A Study of Three Muslim Modernists*. AAR Studies in Religion 1. Chambersburg (Pa.): American Academy of Religion.

Meeker, Michael E. (1991), 'The New Muslim Intellectuals in the Republic of Turkey,' in Tapper (1991), pp. 189–219.

Metcalf, Barbara (2007), 'Islam in Contemporary Southeast Asia: History, Community, Morality,' in Rippin (2007), pp. 137–47.

Meuleman, Johan (1996), *Tradisi, Kemodernan dan Metamodernisme. Memperbincangkan Pemikiran Mohammed Arkoun*, Yogyakarta: LKiS.

Meuleman, Johan (ed.) (2002), *Islam in the Era of Globalization: Muslim Attitudes towards Modernity and Identity*, London: Routledge.

Mihailovic, Alexandar (1997), *Corporeal Words: Mikhail Bakhtin's Theology of Discourse*, Evanston: Northwestern University Press.

Mishra, Vijay and Bob Hodge (2006), 'What is post(-)colonialism?,' *Textual Practice* 5(3), pp. 399–414.

Mobini-Kesheh, Natalie (1996), 'The Arab Periodicals of the Netherlands East Indies, 1914–1942,' *Bijdragen Koninklijk Instituut voor Taal-, Land-, en Volkenkunde* 152-II, pp. 236–56.

Mobini-Kesheh, Natalie (1999), *The Hadrami Awakening: Community and Identity in the Netherlands East Indies, 1900–1942*, Ithaca: Southeast Asian Program Publications (SEAP).

Moussalli, Ahmad S. (1992), *Radical Islamic Fundamentalism: The Ideological and Political Discourse of Sayyid Qutb*, Beirut: American University of Beirut.

Mulyadi, Sukidi (2001), *Teologi Inklusif Cak Nur*, Jakarta: Kompas.

Munawar-Rachman, Budhy (1998), 'Pemikiran Keislaman Nurcholish Madjid: Sebagai Hasil Dari Hermeneutika Neo-Modernisme,' MA Thesis in Philosophy, Jakarta: Sekolah Tinggi Filsafat Driyarkara.

Munawar-Rachman, Budhy (ed.) (2006), *Ensiklopedi Nurcholish Madjid: Pemikiran Islam di Kanvas Peradaban*, Jakarta: Paramadina & Mizan.

Munhanif, Ali (1996), 'Islam and the Struggle for Religious Pluralism in Indonesia: A Political Reading of the Religious Thought of Mukti Ali,' *Studia Islamika* 3:1, pp. 79–126.

Muzani, Saiful (1994), 'Mu'tazilah Theology and the Modernization of the Indonesian Muslim Community: An Intellectual Portrait of Harun Nasution,' *Studia Islamika* 1(1), pp. 91–131.

Nadroh, Siti (1999), *Wacana Keagamaan & Politik Nurcholish Madjid*, Jakarta: RajaGrafindo Persada.

Nafis, Muhamad Wahyuni and Achmad Rifki (2005), *Kesaksiaan Intelektual. Mengiringi Kepergian Sang Guru Bangsa*, Jakarta: Paramadina.

Nakamura, Mitsuo, Sharon Siddique and Omar Farouk Bajunid (eds) (1999), *Islam and Civil Society*, Singapore: ISEAS.

Nanji, Azim (ed.) (1997), *Mapping Islamic Studies: Genealogy, Continuity and Change*, Berlin: Mouton de Gruyter.

Nasution, Harun (1987), *Muhammad Abduh dan Teologi Rasional Mu'tazilah*, Jakarta: Universitas Indonesia Press.

Nasution, Harun (2001), *Teologi Islam Rasional: Apresiasi Terhadap Wacana dan Praksis*, Abdul Halim (ed.), Jakarta: Ciputat Press.

Navarro, Alain (2006), 'Egypt Professor Compares Koran to Supermarket,' http://www.dailystaregypt.com/article.aspx?ArticleID=3234 [Last accessed 26 May 2008].

Nederveen Pieterse, Jan (1995), 'Globalizaton as Hybridization,' in Feather-stone et al. (1995), pp. 45–68.

Nist, John (1967), *The Modernist Movement in Brazil: A Literary Study*, Austin: University of Texas Press.

Noer, Deliar (1973), *The Modernist Muslim Movement in Indonesia 1900–42*, Singapore: Oxford University Press.

Nugroho, Alois Agus (2006), 'Postmodernisme, Toleransi Multikultursal, dan Solidaritas Ekologis,' in Abdul Halim (2006), pp. 272–84.

Nurdin, Ahmad Ali (2005), 'Islam and State: A Study of the Liberal Islamic Network in Indonesia 1990–2004,' *New Zealand Journal of Asian Studies* 7(2), pp. 20–39.

Nwyia, Paul (1971), 'L'Islam Face à la Crise du Language Moderne,' *Travaux et Jours* 38, pp. 81–101.

O'Brien, Patricia (1989), 'Michel Foucault's History of Culture,' in Hunt (1989), pp. 25–46.

Olsson, Susanne (2004), *Renewal and Heritage: The Quest for Authenticity in Hasan Hanafi's Islamic Ideology*, Uppsala: Uppsala University.

Olsson, Susanne (2008), 'Apostasy in Egypt: Contemporary Cases of *Hisbah*,' *The Muslim World* 98(1), pp. 95–115.

Osman, Mohammad Redzuan (2006), 'The Importance of Arab Migration and its Importance in the Historical Development of Late Nineteenth and Early Twentieth Century Malaya,' Paper presented at the *15th World History Annual Conference*. Long Beach (CA). Downloaded from: http://eprints. um.edu.my/77/1/The_Arabs_Migration_and_Its_Importance_in_the_His-torical_Development_of_the_Late_Nineteenth_and_E.pdf, [Last accessed 2 April 2010].

Pallesen, Carsten (2008), 'Philosophy of reflection and biblical revelation in Paul Ricoeur,' *Studia Theologica: Nordic Journal of Theology*, 62, pp. 44–62.

Palmer, Richard E. (1969), *Hermeneutics: Interpretation Theory in Schleier-macher, Dilthey, Heidegger, and Gadamer*, Evanston: Northwestern University Press.

Papastergiadis, N. (1997), 'Tracing Hybridity in Theory, in P. Werbner and T. Modood' (eds), pp. 257–81.

Peters, Rudolph en Roel Meijer (eds) (1992), *Inspiratie en Kritiek: Moslimse Intellectuelen over de Islam*, Muiderberg: Coutinho.

Preston, Peter Wallace (1997), *Development Theory*, Cambridge (Mass.): Blackwell Publishers.

Progressive Islam August 1954-December 1955), 2 Vols. Microfilm R0010084 BP1 P1. Library, National University of Singapore.

Proudfoot, Ian (1993), *Early Malay Printed Books: A provisional account of materials published in the Singapore-Malaysia area up to 1920, noting holdings in major public collections*. Kuala Lumpur: Academy of Malay Studies and Library of the University of Malaya.

Putro, Suadi (1998), *Mohammed Arkoun Tentang Islam & Modernitas*, Jakarta: Paramadina.

Rahardjo, M. Dawam (1987), 'Islam dan Modernisasi: Catatan atas Paham Sekularisasi Nurcholish Madjid,' in Madjid (1987), pp. 11–31.

Rahardjo, M. Dawam (2002), *Islam dan Transformasi Budaya*, Yogyakarta: Dana Bhakti Prima Yasa.

Rahnema, Ali (2000), *An Islamic Utopian: A Political Biography of Ali Shari'ati*, London: I.B. Tauris.

Ramadan, Tariq (2005), *Western Muslims and the Future of Islam*, Oxford: Oxford University Press.

Rasjidi, Muhammad (1972), *Koreksi Terhadap Drs. Nurcholish Madjid Tentang Sekularisasi*, Jakarta: Bulan Bintang.

Rasjidi, Muhammad (1977), *Documents pour servir à l'histoire de l'Islam à Java*, Paris: École Française d'Extrême-Orient.

Reagan, Charles (1996), *Paul Ricoeur: His Life and His Work*, Chicago: The University of Chicago Press.

Ricklefs, Merle C. (1991), *Islam in the Indonesian Social Context*, Clayton: Centre of Southeast Asian Studies Monash University.

Ricoeur, Paul (1966), *Freedom and Nature: The Voluntary and the Involuntary*. Translated by Erazim V. Koháč, Evanston: Northwestern University Press [1950].

Ricoeur, Paul (1981), *Hermeneutics and the Human Sciences: Essays on Language, Action and Interpretation*, Edited and translated by John B. Thompson, Cambridge: Cambridge University Press.

Ricoeur, Paul (1984), *Time and Narrative*, Volume 1, Translated by Kathleen McLaughlin and David Pellauer, Chicago: University of Chicago Press.

Ricoeur, Paul (1986), *Fallible Man*. Translated by Charles A. Kelbley, introduction by Walter J. Low, New York: Fordham University Press [Translation 1965, 1960].

Ricoeur, Paul (1995), *Figuring the Sacred: Religion, Narrative, and Imagination*, Translated by David Pellauer and edited by Mark I. Wallace, Minneapolis: Fortress Press.

Ricoeur, Paul (1999), *Husserl: An Analysis of His Phenomenology*, Evanston: Northwestern University Press [1967].

Ricoeur, Paul (2000), *La Mémoire, l'Histoire, l'Oubli*, Paris: Seuil.

Ricoeur, Paul (2004), *The Conflict of Interpretations: Essays in Hermeneutics I*. Edited by Don Ihde, London: Continuum [Translation 1974, 1969].

Rida, Muhammad Rashid (2002), 'Renewal, Renewing, Renewers,' in Kurzman (2002), pp. 77–85.

Riddell, Peter G. (1990), *Transferring a Tradition: 'Abd al-Ra'ūf Al-Singkilī Rendering into Malay of the Jalālayn Commentary*, Berkeley: Center for South and Southeast Asian Studies, University of California at Berkeley.

Riddell, Peter G. (2001), *Islam and the Malay-Indonesian World. Transmission and Responses*, Hawai'i: University of Hawai'i Press.

Riddell, Peter G. & Tony Street (eds) (1997), *Islam; Essays on Scripture, Thought and Society. Festschrift in Honour of Anthony H. Johns*, Leiden: Brill.

Riexinger, Martin (2007), 'Nasserism Revitalized: A Critical Reading of Hasan Hanafi's Project "The Islamic Left" and "Occidentalism" (and their Uncritical Reading)' *Die Welt des Islams*, 47(1), pp. 63–118.

Rippin, Andrew (1981), Review of *Major Themes in the Qur'an* by Fazlur, *Bulletin of the School of Oriental and African Studies*, 44(2), pp. 360–3.

Rippin, Andrew (ed.) (2007), *Defining Islam: A Reader*, London and Oakville: Equinox.

Roberts, Tylor (2009), 'All Work and No Play: Chaos, Incongruity and *Différance* in the Study of Religion,' *Journal of the American Academy of Religion*, 77:1, pp. 81–104.

Robertson, Roland (1995), 'Glocalization: Time-Space and Homogeneity-Heterogeneity,' in Featherstone et al. (1995), pp. 25–44.

Robinson, Francis (2001), *The 'Ulama of Farangi Mahall and Islamic Culture in South Asia*, London: Hurst.

Robinson, Francis (2004), 'Other-Worldy and This-Worldy Islam and the Islamic Revival,' *Journal of the Royal Asiatic Society*, Series 3, 14(1), pp. 47–58.

Rodinson, Maxime (1987), *Europe and the Mystique of Islam*. Translated by Roger Veinus. London: I.B. Tauris [1980].

Roff, William R. (1964), 'The Malayo-Muslim World of Singapore at the Close of the Nineteenth Century,' *Journal of Asian Studies* 24(1), pp. 75–90.

Roff, William R (1970), 'Indonesian and Malay Students in Cairo in the 1920s,' *Indonesia*, 9, pp. 73–87.

Roff, William R. (1985), 'Islam Obscured? Some Reflections on Studies of Islam and Society in Southeast Asia,' *Archipel*, 29(1), pp. 7–34.

Roff, William R. (1987), 'Islamic Movements: One or Many?,' in Roff (ed.), pp. 31–52.

Roff, William R. (ed.) (1987), *Islam and the Political Economy of Meaning: Comparative Studies of Muslim Discourse*, Berkeley: University of California Press.

Rumadi (2008), *Post Tradisionalisme Islam: Wacana Intelektualisme dalam Komunitas NU*, Cirebon: Fahmina Institute.

Ruslani (2000), *Masyarakat Kitab dan Dialog Antarama: Studi atas Pemikiran Mohammed Arkoun* Yogyakarta: Bentang, 2000.

Russell, Matheson (2006), *Husserl: A guide for the Perplexed*, London: Continuum.

Ruthven, Malise (1989), *The Divine Supermarket: Shopping for God in America*, London: Vintage Books.

Ruthven, Malise (2002), *A Fury for God: The Islamist Attack on America*, London: Granta Books.

Saeed, Abdullah (1997), 'Ijtihad and Innovation in Neo-Modernist Islamic Thought in Indonesia,' *Islam and Christian-Muslim Relations*, 8(3), pp. 279–95.

Saeed, Abdullah (1999), 'Towards Religious Tolerance Through Reform in Islamic Education: The Case of the State Institute of Islamic Studies in Indonesia,' *Indonesia and the Malay World*, 27(79), pp. 177–91.

Saeed, Abdullah (2004), 'Fazlur Rahman: A Framework for Interpreting the Ethico-Legal Content of the Qur'an,' in Taji-Farouki (ed.), pp. 37–66.

Saeed, Abdullah (ed.) (2005), *Approaches to the Qur'ān in Contemporary Indonesia*, London: Oxford University Press and the Institute for Ismaili Studies.

Saeed, Abdullah (2007), 'Trends in Contemporary Islam: a Preliminary Attempt at a Classification,' *Muslim World* 97(3), pp. 395–404.

Sahlins, Marshall (2000), *Historical Metaphors and Mythical Realities: Structure in the Early History of the Sandwich Islands Kingdom*, Ann Arbor: University of Michigan Press [1983].

Said, Edward (1981), *Covering Islam: How the Media and Experts Determine How We See The Rest of the World*, London and Henley: Routledge and Kegan Paul.

Said, Edward (1984), *The Text, the World, and the Critic*, London: Faber & Faber.

Said, Edward (1995), *Orientalism*, 3rd edition, London: Penguin Books [1978].

Sajoo, Armyn B. (ed.) (2002), *Civil Society in the Muslim World: Contemporary Perspectives*, London: I.B. Tauris.

Saleh, Fauzan (2001), *Modern Trends in Islamic Theological Discourse in 20th Century Indonesia: A Critical Survey*, Leiden, Boston, and Cologne: Brill.

Salim, Harus and Muhammad Ridwan (eds) (1999), *Kultur Hibrida: Anak Muda NU di Jalur Kultural*, Yogyakarta: LKiS.

Salvatore, Armando (1995), 'The Rational Authentication of Turath in Contemporary Arab Thought: Muhammad 'Abid al-Jabiri and Hasan Hanafi,' *Muslim World* 85(3–4), pp. 191–214.

Salvatore, Armando (1997), *Islam and the Political Discourse of Modernity*, Reading: Ithaca Press.

Schiller, Jim and Barbara Martin-Schiller (eds) (1997), *Imagining Indonesia: Cultural Politics and Political Culture*, Athens: Ohio University Center for International Studies.

Seebohm, Thomas (1986), 'Facts. Words and What Jurisprudence can Teach Hermeneutics,' *Research in Phenomenology*, vol. 16(1), pp. 25–40.

Seebohm, Thomas W. (2004), *Hermeneutics: Method and Methodology*, Dordrecht: Kluwer Academic Publishers.

Sen, Amartya (2005), *The Argumentative Indian: Writings on Indian Culture, History and Identity*. London: Penguin Books.

Shepard, William (1996), *Sayyid Qutb and Islamic Activism: A Translation and Critical Analysis of Social Justice in Islam*, Leiden: E.J. Brill.

Shepard, William (2004), 'The Diversity of Islamic Thought: Towards a Typology,' in Taji-Farouki and Nafi (2004), pp. 61–103.

Shimogaki, Kazuo (1988), *Between Modernity and Post-Modernity: The Islamic Left and Dr. Hasan Hanafi's Thought: A Critical Reading*, Tokyo: The Institute of Middle Eastern Studies, International University of Japan.

Simon, Sherry and Paul St Pierre (eds) (2000), *Changing the Terms: Translating in the Postcolonial Era*, Ottowa: University of Ottowa Press.

Sjadzali, Munawir (1991), *Islam and Governmental System*, Jakarta: INIS.

Skinner, Quentin (1990), *The Return of Grand Theory in the Human Sciences*, Cambridge: Cambridge University Press [1985].

Smart, Ninian (1998), 'Tradition, retrospective perception, nationalism and modernism,' in Heelas et al. (1998), pp. 79–87.

Smith, Jonathan Z. (1982), *Imagining Religion: From Babylon to Jonestown*, Chicago: University of Chicago Press.

Smith, Jonathan Z. (2004), *Relating Religions: Essays in the Study of Religion*, Chicago: University of Chicago Press.

Smith, Wilfred Cantwell (1957), *Islam in Modern History*, Princeton: Princeton University Press.

Smith, Wilfred Cantwell (1964), *The Meaning and End of Religion*, New York: Mentor Books.

Speelman, Gé (ed.) (1993), *Muslims and Christians in Europe. Breaking New Grounds. Essays in Honour of Jan Slomp*, Kampen: Kok.

Spengler, Oswald (1980), *Der Untergang des Abendlandes: Umrisse einer Morphologie der Weltgeschichte*, Munchen: C.H. Beck [1923].

Stauth, Georg (2002), *Politics and Cultures of Islamization in Southeast Asia: Indonesia and Malaysia in the Nineteen-Nineties*, Bielefeld: Transcript Verlag.

Steenbrink, Karel (1974), *Pesantren, Madrasah, Sekolah: Recente Ontwikkelingen in Indonesisch Islamonderricht*, Meppel: Krispo Repro.

Steenbrink, Karel (1993), 'Nurcholish Madjid and Inclusive Islamic Faith in Indonesia,' in Speelman (1993), pp. 28–43.

Steenbrink, Karel (1996), 'Recapturing the Past: Historical Studies by IAIN-Staff,' in Woodward (1996), pp. 155–92.

Steenbrink, Karel (1999), 'The Pancasila Ideology and an Indonesian Muslim Theology of Religions,' in Waardenburg (1999), pp. 180–96.

Steiner, George (1992), *After Babel: Aspects of Language and Translation*, 2nd Edition, Oxford: Oxford University Press [1975].

Stenberg, Leif (1996), *The Islamization of Science: Four Muslim Positions Developing an Islamic Modernity*, Lund: University of Lund.

Stevens, Alan M. and A. Ed. Schmidgall-Tellings (eds) (2004), *A Comprehensive Indonesian-English Dictionary*, Athens (OH): Ohio University Press.

Strauss, Leo (1988), *Persecution and the Art of Writing*, Chicago: The University of Chicago Press [1952].

Taji-Farouki, Suha, (ed.) (2004), *Modern Intellectuals and the Qur'an*, London: Oxford University Press in association with the Institute for Ismaili Studies.

Taji-Farouki, Suha and Basheer M. Nafi (eds) (2004), *Islamic Thought in the Twentieth Century*, London: I.B. Tauris.

Tamara, Nasir (2009), *Indonesia Rising: Islam, Democracy and the Rise of Indonesia as a Major Power*, Singapore: Select Publishing.

Tarabishi, Jurji (1991), *Al-Muthaqqafun al-'Arab wa'l-Turath: Aal-Tahlil al-Nafsi li-'Isab Jama'i*, London: Riyadh al-Rayyes.

Taylor, Mark C. (2009), 'Refiguring Religion,' *Journal of the American Academy of Religion* 77(1), pp. 105–19.

Thériault, Barbara and Frank Peter (2006), 'Islam and the "Carriers" of European National Identities,' *ISIM Newsletter* 17, p. 62.

Turner, Bryan S. (1976), Review of: *The Venture of Islam* by Marshall Hodgson, *Contemporary Sociology* 5(2), pp. 192–3.

Turner, Bryan S. (1994), *Orientalism, Postmodernism and Globalism*, London: Routledge.

Turner, Bryan S. (1998), *Weber and Islam: A Critical Study*, London: Routledge and Kegan Paul [1974].

Unamuno, Miguel (1954), *The Tragic Sense of Being*, London: Dover Publications.

Valensi. Lucette (ed.) (1980), 'Recherches sur l'Islam, histoire et anthropologie,' *Annales, Economies, Societies, Civilisations* 35:3–4.

Varisco, Daniel Martin (2005), *Islam Obscured. The Rhetoric of Anthropological Representation*, New York: Palgrave and MacMillan.

Varisco, Daniel Martin (2007), *Reading Orientalism: Said and the Unsaid*, Seattle: The University of Washington Press.

Vatikiotis, Michael R.J. (1994), *Indonesian Politics under Suharto: Order, Development and Pressure for Change*, London: Routledge.

Vatikiotis, Michael R.J. (1996), *Political Change in Southeast Asia: Trimming the Banyan Tree*, London: Routledge.

Vertovec, Steven and Robin Cohen (eds) (2002), *Cosmopolitanism: Theory, Context and Practice*, Oxford: Oxford University Press.

Vogt, Kari, Lena Larsen and Christian Moe (eds) (2008), *New Directions in Islamic Thought: Exploring Reform and Muslim Tradition*, London: I.B. Tauris.

Waardenburg, Jean-Jacques (1969), *L'Islam dans le Miroir de L'Occident*, The Hague and Paris: Mouton [1962].

Waardenburg, Jacques (ed.) (1995), *Scholarly Approaches to Religion, Interreligious Perceptions, and Islam*, Bern: Peter Lang.

Jacques Waardenburg (ed.) (1999), *Muslim Perceptions of Other Religions: A Historical Survey*, Oxford: Oxford University Press.

Wahid, Abdurrahman (2007a), *Islam Kosmopolitan: Nilai-nilai Indonesia & Transformasi Kebudayaan*, Jakarta: The Wahid Institute.

Wahid, Abdurrahman (2007b), Prolog: Universalisme Islam dan Kosmopolitanisme Peradaban Islam, in Madjid (2007) pp. 1–11.

Wahyudi, Yudian (2002), 'The Call: "Back to the Qur'an and the Sunna": A Comparative Study of the Resources of Hasan Hanafi, Muhammad 'Abid al-Jabiri, and Nurcholish Madjid,' PhD Thesis, Montreal: McGill University.

Wahyudi, Yudian (2003), 'Arab Responses to Hasan Hanafi's *Muqaddima fi'Ilm al-Istighrāb'*, *Muslim World* 93(2), pp. 233–48.

Wahyudi, Yudian (2006), 'Hasan Hanafi on Salafism and Secularism,' in Abu-Rabi' (2006), pp. 256–70.

Wallace, Mark I. (1995), 'Introduction,' in Ricoeur (1995), pp. 1–32.

Wansbrough, John (1977), Review of *The Venture of Islam* by Marshall Hodgson, *Bulletin of the School of Oriental and African Studies*, 40(1), pp. 169–70.

Wansbrough, John (1984), '*Lectures du Coran* by Mohammed Arkoun,' *Bulletin of the School of Oriental and African Studies, University of London* 47(2), p. 413.

Waugh, Earle H. (1978), 'An Evasive Vision: The Venture of Islam,' *History of Religions* 18(2), pp. 192–7.

Waugh, Earle H. (1999), 'The Legacies of Fazlur Rahman for Islam in American [sic],' *American Journal of Islamic Social Sciences* 16(3), pp. 27–44.

Welch, Alford and Pierre Cachia (eds) (1979), *Islam: Past Influence and Present Challenge*, Festschrift in honour of William Montgomery Watt, Edinburgh: Edinburgh University Press.

Werbner, Pnina (ed.) (2008), *Anthropology and the New Cosmopolitanism: Rooted, Feminist and Vernacular Perspectives*, New York: Berg.

Werbner, Pnina and Tariq Modood (eds) (1997), *Debating Cultural Hybridity: Multi-cultural Identities and the Politics of Anti-Racism*, London: Zed Books.

Wild, Stefan (ed.) (1996), *The Qur'an as Text*, Leiden: Brill.

Wolf, Michaela (2000), 'The *Third Space* in Postcolonial Representation,' in Simon and St. Pierre (2000), pp. 127–45.

Wong, J.H.L. (2004), 'Stop "Arabising" Malay Culture,' Rais Yatim, *The Star*, 17 April, (Electronic version), retrieved 3 August 2009 from, http://thestar.com.my/news/story.asp?file=/2004/4/17/nation/7779945&sec=nation

Woodcroft-Lee, Patricia (1984), 'From Morocco to Merauke. Some Observations on the Shifting Pattern and the World Islamic Community, as Revealed in the Writings of Muslim Intellectuals in Indonesia,' in Israeli and Johns (1984), pp. 67–114.

Woodhead, Linda with Paul Heelas and David Martin (eds) (2001), *Peter Berger and the Study of Religion*, London: Routledge.

Woodward, Mark R. (1989), *Islam in Java: Normative Piety and Mysticism in the Sultanate of Yogyakarta*, Tucson: University of Arizona Press.

Woodward, Mark R. (ed.) (1996), *Toward a New Paradigm: Recent Developments in Indonesian Islamic Thought*, Tempe: Arizona State University Program for Southeast Asian Studies.

Yavuz, M. Hakan (2003), *Islamic Political Identity in Turkey*, Oxford: Oxford University Press.

Yusuf, Imtiyaz (ed.) (2004), *Measuring the Effect of Iranian Mysticism on Southeast Asia*, Bangkok: Cultural Centre of the Embassy of the Islamic Republic of Iran.

Zakaria, Fareed (2002), 'Look East for the Answer,' *Newsweek*, 4 November Issue.

Zakariyya. Fouad (2005), *Myth and Reality in the Contemporary Islamist Movement*, Translated and with an introduction by Ibrahim M. Abu-Rabi', London: Pluto Press.

Zamharir, Muhammad Hari (2004), *Agama dan Negara: Analisis Kritik Pemikiran Politik Nurcholish Madjid*, Jakarta: Murai Kencana.

INDEX

307

ily of, 51–2; founded Paramadina Foundation (1986), 91; head of Union of Southeast Asian Islamic Students (1967–9), 54; image of, 50; influence of, 45; *Islam: Doctrine and Civilisation: A Critical Analysis of the Problem of Faith, Humanity and Modernity* (1992), 84–5, 87, 92; *Islam: A Religion for Mankind*, 86; 'Islam in Indonesia: A Move from the Periphery to the Center', 77; *Islamic Tradition: Its Role and Function in the Development of Indonesia*, 81; 'Islamic Universalism and Islamic cultural Cosmopolitanism', 85, 229; methodology of, 100; MUI issued *fatwa* against (2005), xiii; *Nilai-Nilai Dasar Perjuangan* ('Basic Values for Struggle'), 55; president of HMI (1967–71), xiii-xiv, 53–4; reformism of, 24; role in Renewal of Islamic Thought movement, 19–20, 73, 89, 96, 99; scholarship of, 18–19, 232; 'The Necessity of Renewing Islamic Thought and the Problem of the Integration of the Ummat' (1970), 56; 'The Qur'an, Arabic in Language, Universal in Meaning' (1968), 63

Mahfouz, Naguib: stabbing of (1994), xiii; writings of, 4

Maison des Sciences de l'Homme

Majelis Ulama Indonesia (Indonesian Council of Ulama):

Makdisi, George: research of, 74–5

Makkah: 46; publishing houses in, 47

Malaysia: 91, 235

Malinowski, Bronislaw: 189

Mandeville, Peter: 36; view of Third Space, 36; writings of, 9

Mannheim, Karl: cultural analysis work of, 39

Mansoer, Mas: member of Muhammadiyah, 49; philosophical views of, 49

Marcel, Gabriel: 170–1; criticism of positivism and empiricism in name of self, 156

Marcuse, Herbert: influence of, 131

Maritain, Jacques: 12

Martin, David: *A General Theory of Secularisation* (1978), 40; *On Secularisation* (2005), 40; sociological studies of, 12

Martin, Richard: 29

Marx, Karl: 99, 166; economic reductionism of, 185; *The German Ideology* (1846), 114; writings of, 12

Marxism: 199; adherents of, 173, 180, 199; influence of, 16, 181

Masjumi: 55

Massignon, Louis: 11, 178–9, 183, 201; influence of, 169; mentor of Hasan Hanafi Hasanayn, 120; teaching career of, 62

Masyumi (Masjumi): dissolved by Soekarno, 53

al-Maududi, Abu'l-Ala: influence of, 169; leader of *Jamaat-e-Islami*, 70

Mauss, Marcel: sociological works of, 214

Mazhab Ciputat: members of, 91

McCutcheon, Russell: 19, 25, 87, 102; criticisms of, 28, 232; critique of Chicago School's *sui generis* approach to religion, 27, 31–2; methodological reductionism of, 230; taxonomy of, 231; *The Discipline of Religion* (2003), 17, 27; *The Manufacturing of Religion* (1997), 17; theories of, 17–18, 31–2, 38–9

McGill University: 66, 90, 97; faculty of, 84, 97–8; Institute of Islamic Studies (IIS), 9, 62;